Pro Scalable .NET 2.0 Application Designs

Joachim Rossberg
Rickard Redler

Apress®

Pro Scalable .NET 2.0 Application Designs

Copyright © 2006 by Joachim Rossberg and Rickard Redler

ISBN: 1-4302-1160-1

Lead Editor: Ewan Buckingham
Technical Reviewer: Jason Lefebvre
Editorial Board: Steve Anglin, Dan Appleman, Ewan Buckingham, Gary Cornell, Tony Davis, Jason Gilmore, Jonathan Hassell, Chris Mills, Dominic Shakeshaft, Jim Sumser
Project Manager: Beckie Stones
Copy Edit Manager: Nicole LeClerc
Copy Editor: Julie M. Smith
Assistant Production Director: Kari Brooks-Copony
Production Editor: Lori Bring
Compositor and Artist: Kinetic Publishing Services, LLC
Proofreader: Linda Seifert
Indexer: Broccoli Information Management
Interior Designer: Van Winkle Design Group
Cover Designer: Kurt Krames
Manufacturing Director: Tom Debolski

For information on translations, please contact Apress directly at 2560 Ninth Street, Suite 219, Berkeley, CA 94710. Phone 510-549-5930, fax 510-549-5939, e-mail info@apress.com, or visit http://www.apress.com.

The source code for this book is available to readers at http://www.apress.com in the Source Code section.

To Karin
Opus, you will always be with me in my heart
Gaston, this one is for you as well
—Joachim Rossberg

To Jenny & Leah
—Rickard Redler

Contents at a Glance

Contents

Foreword

There's no doubt in my mind that the two authors of this book, Joachim Rossberg and Rickard Redler, share a wealth of knowledge about the options Microsoft offers enterprises willing to create applications on the .NET platform. In this book, they share that wealth of knowledge with the rest of us.

The greatest value from this book probably comes from the higher priorities given to the breadth than to the depth of the book's different subjects. Its perspective is that of the strategic architect rather than that of the programmer. This is also the expressed purpose of its authors; in the book's introduction, they clearly state that the book is focused on design rather than diving deep into specifics.

True to this statement, the content of the book spans a wide collection of subjects, including technologies as disparate as content management, Unified Modeling Language (UML), Object Role Modeling (ORM), Windows Operating System versions, Network Load Balancing (NLB), Microsoft Cluster Service (MSCS), Internet Information Services (IIS), and SQL Server.

Having said that, I must also mention that some of the book's chapters do in fact include surprising levels of detail. This is especially true in Chapter 4, which covers architecture, scalability, availability, and the security of the Windows Server family, and in Chapter 7, which is about Internet Information Services.

In their discussion of the enterprise application architecture in Chapter 5, the authors show that they are with the times; one of their sources of inspiration for this chapter is Microsoft's reference architecture for applications and services, which was published in December 2002. This chapter presents a condensed overview of the design patterns first presented by Eric Gamma et al., otherwise known as the Gang of Four. It also contains an overview of the typical application layers that together form an enterprise application, and some useful coding conventions. Mainly, though, the chapter gives an overview of the different technologies that Microsoft has made available to an architect designing such an application, and the pros and cons of each of these technologies. It's worth noticing that even a subject such as content management gets fair coverage in this chapter.

It goes without saying that web services have a prominent place in the book, having its own chapter (Chapter 6). This is one of the most information-filled chapters, including several code examples. It covers not only basic XML web services, but also SOAP extensions and some of the Web Services Enhancements that are being standardized.

Scalability and performance are all-pervading themes throughout the book. Each time the authors present a product or a technology, they also include a section about how it can affect the performance and scalability of the application being architected. The book is full of recommendations on which powerful hardware to use under different circumstances and how best to configure your system. For example, Chapter 7 gives advice on which performance counters to monitor on your Web server and which kinds of values you should expect and strive for.

This book should be especially valuable for those architects, designers, and developers who are new to enterprise development in Microsoft environments; this includes both those used to designing and building smaller-sized applications for Microsoft Windows and those used to designing and building enterprise-class applications in other environments such as J2EE. It should also be a fine book for university classes, because it gives students such a good overview of the technologies many of them will live with once they're out of the university. Joachim and Rickard have all the reason in the world to be proud of what they have achieved with this book.

Sten Sundblad

Microsoft MSDN Regional Director (RD)

About the Authors

JOACHIM ROSSBERG was born in 1967, the year of the Summer of Love. He grew up in the southeast part of Sweden just outside the small town of Kalmar.

After school he worked for ten years as an assistant air traffic controller in Halmstad on the Swedish west coast. There he also met his wife, Karin. The urge to learn more grew stronger, and after some years he started studying psychology. This led to studies at the University of Gothenburg, where he finished his bachelor's degree in psychology in 1998. During this time, his interest in computers began, and he switched to studying informatics instead.

After graduating from university in 1998, he began working in the IT business as a consultant at one of the world's six largest IT consultancies. After some years there, rewarding him with great experiences, he decided to try a smaller company, and is now employed at Know IT Consulting in Gothenburg. Joachim has during these years been working as a system developer, system designer, project manager, and infrastructure designer. Nowadays he mainly focuses on project management, but still keeps his technical interest alive. He has also, along with Rickard, been a driver for the Microsoft competence network at Cap Gemini Ernst & Young. Although he is Microsoft focused—as evidenced by his MCSE, MCSA, MCSD, and MCDBA certifications—he also works with other techniques and vendors.

Joachim has also had a company on the side called O.R. Education and Development. This company offered trainings, conferences, and courses in computer-related areas. Nowadays these are performed under the flag of Know IT Consulting.

Joachim and Karin live in Gothenburg with their two cats. In his spare time, he likes to read (anything non-technical), listen to music, and watch movies (he used to work at two cinemas in Kalmar in his youth). He also spends a lot of time at the gym, running, or inline skating.

RICKARD REDLER was born in 1973 in town of Örebro located in the middle of Sweden. Early in his life, Rickard discovered the abstract world of computers when the Sinclair machine and the Commodore 20/64 were born. From that time on, computers were a part of his life.

During his studies at the University of Örebro, he found that the courses at the university didn't give him the practical experience necessary to be a good programmer. He therefore decided to run his own company to get real-life experience—and also to make some money. Although his company did quite well, in 1997 Rickard decided to become an employee of Cap Gemini Ernst & Young in Örebro. Early on, Rickard was involved in the competence network at Cap Gemini Ernst & Young, and when he and his wife, Jenny, later moved to Gothenburg, Rickard, along with Joachim, became a driver for the Microsoft competence network at Cap Gemini Ernst & Young in Gothenburg. Even though Rickard is a Certified Java Developer, these days he is working more and more with Microsoft technologies, and also holds MCP and MCSD certifications both in Windows DNA and the .NET platform. Nowadays Rickard is working for Know IT Consulting in Gothenburg as architect and developer.

When Rickard has spare time outside of work, he likes to spend it with his wife and their daughter Leah. He also likes to play his guitar and sing Eric Clapton songs.

About the Technical Reviewer

JASON LEFEBVRE is Vice President and one of the founding partners of Intensity Software, Inc. Intensity Software (`http://www.intensitysoftware.com`) specializes in creating boxed products that migrate legacy mainframe applications directly to ASP.NET, with source code intact. Jason uses Visual Studio and the Microsoft .NET framework daily while architecting solutions for Intensity's consulting services clients. He is also one of the developers who created the original IBuySpy Store demo application and its NetCOBOL for .NET translation. Jason has been a participating author in a number of books and has written numerous articles on topics related to Microsoft .NET.

Acknowledgments

There are a lot of people who helped us in writing this book.

Previous Edition

First of all, we would like to thank Phil Pledger, our previous edition technical reviewer, for coming up with great ideas and opinions. Phil's comments and suggestions improved the overall quality of the book. Then we would like to thank our Swedish language reviewer for the previous edition, Johan Theorin, for making us look more fluent in the English language than we really are.

Sten Sundblad at Sundblad and Sundblad (formerly ADB Arkitektur) provided good suggestions for the book. Sten and Per Sundblad's book *Designing for Scalability Using Windows DNA* and *Design Patterns for Scalable Microsoft .NET Applications* are always sources of inspiration and knowledge.

Erik Quist, formerly at Sundblad and Sundblad, was helpful with answering questions we had. We would also like to thank Dell Sweden for letting us use its test lab. This provided us with access to hardware we otherwise could not have gotten our hands on. Thomas Melzer and Marko Rähmö have been of great help.

Thanks to VMware Corporation for providing software so we could test our solutions without ruining ourselves financially with hardware purchases. Allan Knudsen at Microsoft Sweden helped in providing great documents about Windows Server 2003.

Wolfram Meyer, also at Microsoft Sweden, came up with great input for choosing between web services and .NET Remoting.

We also want to thank all at Apress who helped with the previous edition of the book, especially Ewan Buckingham, Tracy Brown Collins, Laura Cheu, and Ami Knox.

This Edition

We would like to thank the technical reviewer for this edition, Jason Lefebvre. Thanks for new input and great suggestions.

Thanks also to Dennis Johansson at Know IT Consulting in Gothenburg. You gave valuable input on the SOA chapter.

Michael Åhs. Thanks for feedback on the SOA chapter.

We also want to thank all at Apress who helped with this book, especially Beckie Stones, Ewan Buckingham, Lori Bring, and Julie Smith.

A special thanks to Gary Cornell at Apress for giving us the opportunity to write both of these editions.

Joachim would like to thank Karin, Opus, and Gaston for their support and for accepting all the hours he spent in front of the computer.

Rickard would like to thank his wife, Jenny, for supporting him through all the work on the book.

Without your help we could not have done it. Thanks a lot!

Introduction

We feel that many designers and architects lack an understanding of how to use Microsoft technology to build and implement large enterprise solutions. Far too often we have found architects shivering at the thought of building mission-critical systems based on this technology—not because they have tried and failed in their attempts, but because they simply do not have a good awareness of what tools are available. We want to change this.

The idea for this book came up in 2002. We first thought about writing this as an internal document at Cap Gemini Ernst & Young. When doing research on the market, we discovered that very few books focused on the IT architect and system designer. Most books were directed toward the developer, and we wanted a book for a broader audience. Because we think many IT architects lack a thorough understanding of what they can actually achieve on a Microsoft platform, we decided that we should extend the intended audience of our document outside Cap Gemini Ernst & Young and try publishing it as a book. Apress has always published great books, so we turned to them first. Gary Cornell became interested, and this book is the result.

Who Should Read This Book

The target audience is primarily designers and IT architects, but we try to cover topics we feel are valuable for developers to have knowledge about as well. First, let us define these three categories. Different companies may have different definitions for these terms, so to avoid confusion we will specify what we mean here.

Architects

An *architect* is a person who, together with the customer (or the decision maker), retrieves the requirements and the data flow for an application or solution. The architect also defines the servers, function blocks, and so on that are needed to make the application work. An architect works with the management of the company to find out how the application should be designed at a high level. He or she also determines the need for integration with other systems.

This person does not have to have deep technological skills; rather he or she designs on an abstract level and produces a blueprint of what the solution should look like.

An architect can be either an application architect or an infrastructure architect. The infrastructure architect focuses on the networking issues—how clusters should be placed and how to secure the infrastructure. The application architect focuses on the application(s) and the design of these. The best result comes when these two types of architects collaborate closely during the design phase.

Designers

A *designer* is a person who takes the map from the architect and from it completes a working design based on, for instance, Microsoft or Java.

This person is probably a developer with a lot of experience in the field. He or she knows the technology very well in contrast to the architect.

There are also designers who design the infrastructure. These people determine the clustering solution to use, which server versions to implement, the security technology to use, and so on.

Developers

Finally we have the *developer*, the person who implements the application design that the designer has created. This "coder" performs the final job. But the developer can also be a person who implements the infrastructure that the architect and the designer have decided on using.

How This Book Is Organized

We want you, the reader, to use this book to inspire you. It is intended to show techniques available to you through Microsoft technologies, and also to demonstrate that you can build great applications on the Microsoft platform these days.

The book gives you an overview of the important parts of an enterprise application and shows some best practices that we have learned over the years for designing such an application. Design is always key to a successful project.

Since the book is focused on design, we do not dive deep into the specifics of enterprise applications. There are other books for that. Instead this book tries to be a bridge between the architect/designer and the developer. Use this book to find the topics that are important to a certain part of an application, and then continue dissecting that area.

■**Note** Even though this book is rather canted toward the Microsoft way, it would be a mistake to think that this is the only technology to use. We ourselves use other technologies, such as Java and Linux, when non–Microsoft technologies provide a better solution (or even the only solution) for our customers.

The following is a chapter-by-chapter overview of the book.

Chapter 1: Introduction to Enterprise Application Design

Chapter 1 is a general introduction to a few important topics associated with enterprise application design and development. Here we give you an overview of enterprise application integration (EAI), Unified Modeling Language (UML), and Object Role Modeling (ORM).

Chapter 2: Windows Server System

In this chapter, we show you what kind of software is available from Microsoft, enabling you to build a good platform for your application. We cover the operating systems and the .NET Enterprise Servers, and see how they fit into the design of an enterprise application.

Chapter 3: Cluster Techniques

Here we give an overview of the two techniques Windows offers that make it possible to cluster servers. Network Load Balancing (NLB) and Microsoft Cluster Service (MSCS) are integrated in the Windows Server family and used to enhance scalability, reliability, and availability.

We also take a closer look at Application Center, which is a .NET Enterprise Server. This server helps you manage your clusters in an easier way.

Chapter 4: An Overview of the Windows Server Family

This chapter dives deeper into the Windows Server operating systems. We show you the Windows architecture and how you can use NLB and MSCS with your platform. We also include a discussion about security in Windows.

Chapter 5: The Enterprise Application Architecture

Chapter 5 looks at the enterprise application itself. We discuss how you can, and should, design it, as well as many other topics vital to the design phase.

Chapter 6: Web Services Design and Practice

Everybody has heard about web services. If you have not, or simply want to know more, this is the place to look. Here we cover design and security issues, and we also discuss when you should use web services and when you should use .NET Remoting instead.

Chapter 7: Service Oriented Architecture (SOA)

In this chapter, we take a look at SOA or Service Oriented Architecture as it is called. We will discuss what SOA and Services are and how the architecture differs from a traditional application.

Chapter 8: Internet Information Services

In this chapter, we dissect Internet Information Services (IIS). We show its architecture, how ASP.NET is used, and how to tune and secure IIS.

Chapter 9: Data Storage Design and SQL Server

Data storage is important in all enterprises. You need to have a well-thought-out storage policy in place so you can reduce cost and double work. Here we show you how you can consolidate your data by designing your data storage properly.

We also cover SQL Server's architecture, performance, and security in this chapter.

Chapter 10: An Example Application

Here we bring it all together. We show you how we would design an enterprise application using the tips and tricks we present in this book. The application we demonstrate how to build in this chapter is a time reporting application for a large enterprise.

What This Book Covers

This book will show you some of the best practices in designing an enterprise application that we have found invaluable in our own work. More and more our customers have asked for integration solutions over the last few years. With the introduction of SOAP and XML, we have found that we could use much of the same thinking when designing these applications as we used before. Of course, we have constantly evolved our thinking and refined our design patterns as new techniques have been introduced. A great source of inspiration and knowledge are Sten Sundblad and Per Sundblad, authors of *Designing for Scalability Using Windows DNA* (Microsoft Press, 2000. ISBN: 0-735-60968-3) and of course its follow-up, *Design Patterns for Scalable Microsoft .NET Application* (published through their own company and available at their web site, http://www.2xsundblad.com). These guys know what they are talking about, so make sure to visit their web site to learn more about their design patterns.

What This Book Does Not Cover

In this book, we will not discuss integration in itself. We will instead focus on a general design that can be implemented for many solutions, no matter what their purpose may be. We will try to cover a broader spectrum than most books do. If there is one thing we have learned, it is that having the big picture is important. If a large project needs to be delivered on time and at the same time fulfill its expectations, developers and designers alike need to have a broad view of it. This obviously means we cannot be as thorough as we would like to be in many areas, but luckily other books are available for this. For example, the Sundblad and Sundblad books we have already mentioned are valuable for their design patterns and modeling suggestions. Other books offer deep coverage of operating systems, databases, web services, XML, and all those areas that are important to us. This book tries to bridge these boundaries so that you can build better applications for your customers or companies.

Building an enterprise application is not an easy task. If you do not design it properly from the beginning, the risk of failure will increase dramatically. Poor design might not be noticed at once, but with time, performance issues as well as extensibility issues are sure to emerge. To avoid this, IT architects and system designers need to have knowledge about what techniques are available and how these can be used.

This book is intended to be a guide in learning more about this subject. We believe you, the reader, will find it useful in your professional life. We hope you enjoy reading it as much as we enjoyed writing it.

We won't cover any non-Microsoft technology. This is not because we don't use anything else but Microsoft (because we do), it is just due to the fact that the book would have been too complex if we had mixed in Java, Linux, UNIX, and all the others.

■■■

CHAPTER 1

Introduction to Enterprise Application Design

Information has been a key part of society ever since humans started living in communities. Early on, it was vital to keep track of the seasons so people could anticipate when it was best to hunt, sow seed, and so on. As human society has grown more and more complex, so has our need for information. Applications and data, in various forms, are important to many companies nowadays. Obviously this has been true for a long time, but with the globalization of the enterprises of today it has become even more important.

In this chapter, we're going to spend some time discussing how enterprises have ended up with their information spread over so many places that retrieval is often difficult. We are also going to have a look at something called enterprise application integration (EAI), a concept developed to bring order to chaos.

Even though integration may involve some techniques and tools unnecessary in an ordinary multi-tier application, the basic design does not change much. This way, developers can still use the knowledge they have.

Another important area is the Service Oriented Architecture (SOA) that so many people are talking about. SOA, and thinking in Service Oriented (SO) terms during design phase, is important not only for medium-large and large companies but also for smaller ones as well. SOA also has a lot to do with integration, as you'll see in Chapter 7. (We will also have a short introduction here in Chapter 1.)

One thing we would like to point out is that designing for scalability is as important to integration projects as it is to all other projects. You will always have to consider this in enterprise applications. Unnecessary delays and bad performance cost time and money, and if you don't pre-plan solutions for these common problems during the design phase, your application will most certainly be considered a failure after it has been deployed. In this book, we'd like to show you some tips and tricks for building more successful solutions that also scale well. We'll also cover some of the implications that having an SOA in your enterprise will have on both scalability and performance.

Note One thing we have learned over the years is that you should always design an application so that it is possible to scale it. Even though a particular application may not be intended for use by more than a handful of people from the start, many such applications have a tendency to grow in popularity, and suddenly hundreds of users want it. If you've designed with scalability in mind, from the beginning, you really won't have a problem when this happens. By simply separating the different layers from each other and then placing them on different computers or clusters, you suddenly have an application that can serve many users without a complete rewrite.

In the Beginning . . .

Back in the eighties, stock traders on Wall Street used stand-alone terminals. But it soon became obvious that they needed a way to link the terminals, asset trading data, and management systems together so that it would be easier to get an overview of all brokerage information, allowing them to make better decisions. This may have been when the concept of application integration was born. After that, many other businesses found they had similar needs.

Many things have pushed the need for integration to the forefront of business concerns. Client-server solutions started taking the place of mainframe systems, for instance, and developers were suddenly able to build more flexible solutions for their companies. In those days, many of the solutions and applications were proprietary to the companies that had developed them. When two companies merged, heterogeneous environments made it difficult to map data. The complexity of all these applications needed to be reduced. A way to get these applications to work together was required, and the answer was application integration.

With the Internet explosion in the nineties, new ways for companies to do their business evolved. Business-to-business (B2B) and business-to-consumer (B2C) opportunities unavoidably led to a need for integration, not only within companies, but also between companies and their customers.

The first generation of EAI solutions was often a hub-and-spoke architecture (where a single integration server, the hub, handles the information exchange and transformation for the spokes, or many applications or data stores) or of an integration bus-oriented one. Suddenly, a logical separation started to appear in applications. Data was separated from transport, requests from responses, publisher from subscriber, and so on. Slowly, standards like CORBA and COM started to introduce themselves. People began talking about loosely coupled communication. A problem with CORBA and COM, however, was that they were still fairly proprietary. It was not easy to integrate these two standards. There were also some performance and scalability problems with these methods.

The constant evolution of business continuously drives a change to EAI. Nowadays the term has expanded to also include message brokering, business process flow management, and workflow. As companies try to reduce costs, it becomes more and more important to simplify the creation, management, and modification of integrated applications. Companies can't rely on technicians and developers all the time when a change has to be made in the IT infrastructure or in the business processes. There is also a great need to reuse business logic to cut costs and reduce complexity. Fortunately, standards like XML, SOAP, web services, and others have been developed that make it easier, more cost effective, and safer to integrate.

Enterprises Today

Let's take a look at an imaginary company that manufactures and sells cars, called R & R Automobile Corporation. R & R has been around for quite a number of years now. During this time, hundreds of data and communications systems have grown up in the company, and so many, in fact, that nobody knows the exact number. These systems reside on different hardware and software platforms: 70 percent of these probably reside on mainframes, while the rest are scattered on client-server and PC systems. Data is transferred between these systems at different times. Some systems transfer or receive data in real-time, while others transfer or receive data in batches, on a daily, or even weekly, basis. A few systems cannot communicate with others at all, and R & R staff has to print information from those systems and manually enter it into other systems.

This chaotic architecture makes it hard for R & R to know all the details about its relationship with its customers (see Figure 1-1). This is obviously a problem for a company, especially if it must be able to respond to changes in the business environment in a timely manner.

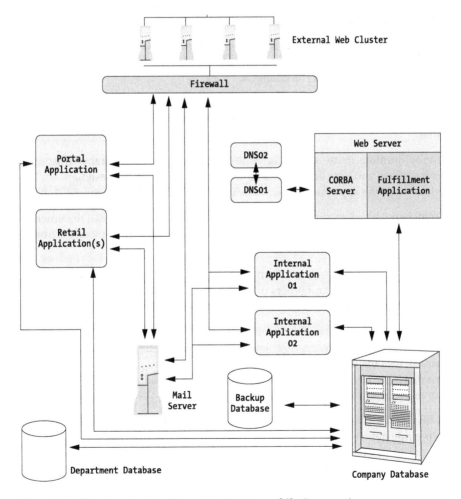

Figure 1-1. *The chaotic situation at R & R Automobile Corporation*

R & R management has discovered the need for a closer interaction with both partners and customers. This means that the supply chain, customer support, and service need to be tuned so that R & R can be an effective, modern company, which management believes can be achieved by providing a better integration between the applications. Obstacles have arisen in the way of achieving this, however. Through all these years that R & R has existed as a company, boundaries have been established between units, including geographically dispersed offices, product lines, and so on, and these factors all diminish the ability of employees to share information within the company. As you might understand, it's hard to give value to the customer if the obstacles within the company are as big as this. Nevertheless, integration across the enterprise probably will provide significant opportunities to show a unified front to the customer. It will also most likely supply more efficient end-to-end processes.

Take a look at some of the problems, or perhaps challenges, that face an R & R integration team:

- R & R uses a mix of technologies. Over the years various technologies have been used to build R & R's applications and databases. As mentioned, some systems provide an interface to the surrounding world, while others do not. The company is rife with customer relationship management (CRM) systems, and other applications, both standard and proprietary. These applications are often run on different platforms.

- New applications at R & R need to extend the features provided with legacy systems. The cost of updating the legacy systems is too great to be considered as a serious alternative, and some of the systems just can't be changed.

- New business workflows need to be developed. R & R needs to find ways to develop new workflows for its business processes, while somehow incorporating its existing applications.

- Many of the applications in use at R & R have no clear separation between their business logic, user interface, and data access. In a modern n-tier application, designers and developers architect the application to separate these items, as shown in Figure 1-2.

- The data transferred between applications is provided in various formats. EDI documents are used, but so are text files and XML files. It is therefore difficult to map the fields from one data structure to the fields in another.

- Different component models are used. Some applications use CORBA (Common Object Request Broker Architecture) and others use COM/COM+. This has resulted in tightly coupled applications that do not easily communicate with each other.

- R & R's systems are not integrated with the outside world, and the issues so far have been within the company. But, at a moment when R & R is about to interact with its customers and partners on the outside, most of these issues remain. An additional problem that R & R must face is that it has no control over these other systems. This means the R & R team has to adjust to the ways the outside world communicates.

- Most of R &R's legacy systems run smoothly. Management knows that changing a legacy system to provide new features involves the risk of introducing bugs and errors. Is it worth the time and money it takes to do such changes? Also, in order to implement any changes, the integration team also needs documentation that often doesn't exist anymore. If this documentation is found, it will take quite some time for the developers to go through it so that they can understand the systems.

- Any new integration solution deployed today must also be open, so that future infrastructure requirements can be supported. To comply with this, a lot of thought has to go into the design of the solution. R & R will also have to carefully consider the technologies the company is using, so that they are based on industry standards as much as possible. R & R cannot afford to fall for the latest hype when choosing a technology, at least not if that technology is relatively unknown or unproven.

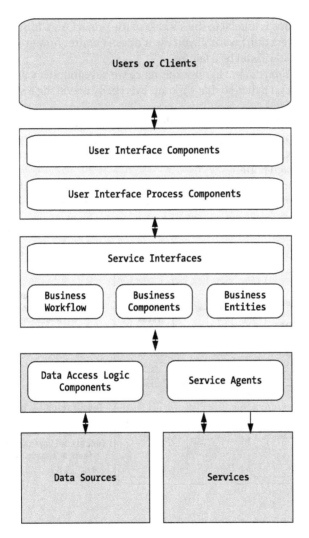

Figure 1-2. *An n-tier application model*

As you clearly can see, integration will not be an easy task for the team at R & R. You can actually think of this as a puzzle. All the pieces are scattered around on the floor. The work ahead of the team is to build a complete picture from these pieces. This is the vision you should strive for in your own integration attempts. As with all visions, you will probably never reach perfection, but if your aim is high, you may come pretty close. And fortunately, there are some tools and techniques available that can help get you on your way.

Before starting any new development project, take a moment (preferably more than a moment, to be honest, especially if you want your project to succeed) and consider a few things. First of all, you should know which problem or problems you really need to solve. Then, you should consider what parts of the development will give the most value to the company. After that, you can start identifying what you need to build and what you need to connect. You also need to be sure to have solicited feedback from management (or whoever is paying the bill) as well, since meeting their expectations is crucial to the success of the project. You don't want to build something that your employers don't want. If you do, it doesn't matter how great an application or system you have built, it will still be a failure.

These points might seem obvious to you, but in our experience we have found it valuable to get answers to all of these questions on paper, so that we know everybody is working towards the same goal.

Once you have answers to your questions, you can start designing your integration solution. One of the things we would like to point out right away is that there really isn't a significant difference between designing an integration project and designing any other enterprise application. You can apply all the same design patterns.

Figure 1-3 shows an example of an application that integrates new functionality with the data from legacy systems. As you can see, the design is still n-tier, in order to provide for maximum flexibility and scalability.

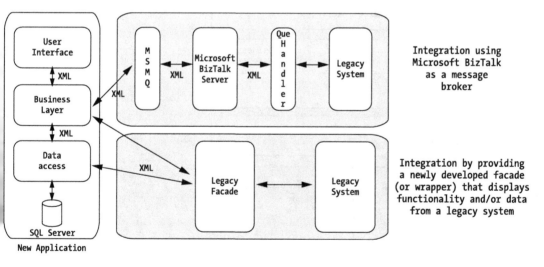

Figure 1-3. *An n-tier application model with integration that includes legacy systems*

Compare this to Figure 1-4, which portrays an ordinary n-tier application without integration.

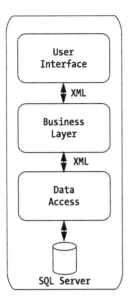

Figure 1-4. *An ordinary n-tier application model*

Types of Integration

As we see it, there are three kinds of integration:

- Integration with legacy systems (within the enterprise)

- Integration with actors outside the enterprise

- Integration of the same business logic, with various end-user interfaces

We'll discuss each of these in more detail in the next sections.

Integration with Legacy Systems

In the R & R case, a lot of the company data and information has been scattered all over the enterprise. The benefits of creating a unified interface for all the systems holding this information should be rather obvious to you. You also may have noticed that it could be quite expensive and difficult to modify existing systems to provide, for example, a web services interface to their features. A common way to solve this problem is to create a wrapper around the system that exposes an interface for existing features, as well as access to some new ones if necessary (see Figure 1-5).

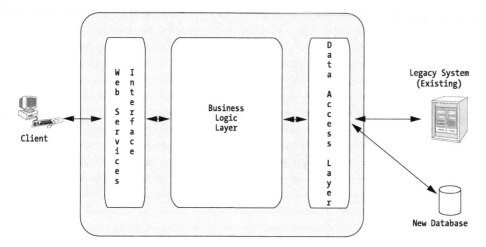

Figure 1-5. *A wrapper to a legacy system built with .NET techniques*

For this scenario, we have built a multilayer wrapper around the legacy system, revealing the features as web services. We could also have exposed them as .NET Remoting objects, COM interfaces, or .NET enterprise applications, but that doesn't change the general design. In cases where the existing system can't hold the new information necessary for new business needs, we'll need to implement a separate database to store this data. An example of this situation is when it is not possible to store new information about customers in the existing database.

Note An important thing to remember is that if response times from legacy systems are slow, you might need to set up a new caching database of your own, and implement replication between them—at least if the legacy system is out of your control, and you can't performance-tune it. The same thing goes for systems you do have control over, but can't possibly tune more.

Integration with Actors Outside the Enterprise

With all the new business opportunities nowadays, it is essential that a company be able to communicate with the outside world. Messages, data, and information are exchanged between companies in an ever-increasing way. To solve this problem, we often use some kind of message broker, like Microsoft BizTalk Server (see Figure 1-6). In the case described here, our partners and customers have a wide choice of ways to transfer (and receive) information. This provides the flexibility to incorporate our own services into the applications of the outside actors.

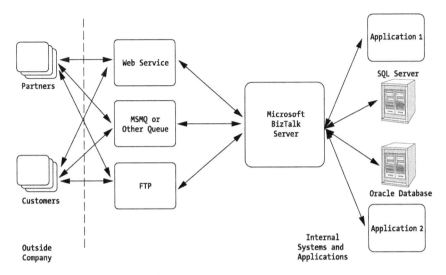

Figure 1-6. *An integration scenario using Microsoft BizTalk Server as a message broker*

Integration of Business logic

When you design your applications, you should strive to make them available for opening by other applications. If you expose your business logic as web services, it's quite easy for other developers to integrate them into their applications. This way you can let various applications and devices use the same business logic, which cuts down the investments necessary to provide a flexible architecture (see Figure 1-7). The only thing that differs between these various end-user interfaces is the way data is presented. Since this solution builds on de facto standards like XML and SOAP, you should also make sure future applications can reuse your business logic.

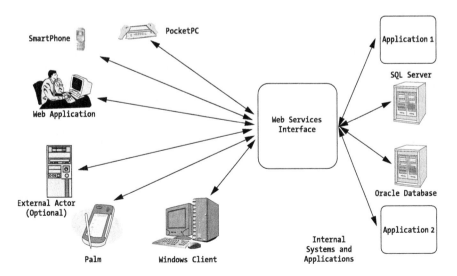

Figure 1-7. *Different clients sharing the same business logic*

One of Our First EAI Experiences

One of the first times we were part of an integration project based on Microsoft technology was in late 1999/early 2000. SOAP was relatively new and XML had just started to make its voice heard. A global company wanted to develop a new web shop for its customers, and wanted a proof-of-concept for doing this on a Microsoft platform. The task was to integrate a web solution with three of the company's legacy platforms: UNIX, VAX/VMS, and AS/400. We developed an application that used the web services SDK to handle communication between the different layers of the application. We chose this design because we had a lot of firewalls to pass through and we did not want to open up too many ports in them.

The solution worked very well. The data sources were scattered in different countries, which caused a slight delay, of course, but the response times were more than acceptable. When a delay occurred that was not due to communication, it was always the legacy system that was the bottleneck. So we were more than happy to present great results to our customer. (Looking back on it now, we are glad to have tools like Visual Studio .NET around nowadays, so we don't have to spend as much time on coding as we did then. We could do the proof-of-concept in half the time now, as compared to then.)

The conclusion we gained from this experience is that integration is here to stay and is important to many companies. Especially in large enterprises, if you can provide a unified interface for the many scattered sources of information that exist, you can gain many advantages. This also means that developers should consider this issue during the design and development stage of all new applications and solutions.

SOA

Over the last few years the acronym SOA, or Service Oriented Architecture as it stands for, has been a popular buzzword used by many people in the industry. But SOA has turned out to be much more than a buzzword and many companies are now exploring the opportunities for implementing Service Orientation (SO) in their organization. This is the reason why we dedicate an entire chapter to SOA and the design of services in an SOA (see Chapter 7). We will briefly cover some SOA topics here in Chapter 1, but if you want to have a closer look we recommend that you go directly to Chapter 7.

But first, let's take a look at services and examine what a service really is. For example, I recently applied for a renewal of my driving license from the Swedish Road Administration (SRA). The SRA's whole procedure for handling this can be said to be a service. The service, in this case, being to process my application and then based on various (and for me, hidden) facts and procedures, they either issue me a new license or reject my application. I don't need to bother about how the SRA processed my information or which routines they followed internally to process my application. In this case, my application is a request to a service which SRA exposes and its answer (whether a new license or a rejection) is the response to my request.

A service in itself is no mystery. Think of it as something that encapsulates a business process or an information area in your business.

CBDI (http://www.cbdiforum.com/) comes rather close to our own definition of Service Orientation (SO), when they describe SOA as "the policies, practices, and frameworks that enable application functionality to be provided and consumed as sets of services published at a granularity relevant to the service consumer. Services can be invoked, published, and discovered, and are abstracted away from the implementation using a single, standards-based form of interface." In short, we might say that SOA is the approach and that web services are only one of the implementations of SOA. Let's see if you agree with this definition after having read the book. A lot of people, however, do think they have an SOA perspective just because they use web services. In some cases this might be true, but often theses services are not Service Oriented (SO), but rather only expose capabilities that live up to the requirements of the protocols used by the web services.

Why has SOA had such a massive impact on IT Architecture during these last few years? Almost everywhere you go you hear this acronym; at conferences, seminars, on web sites, and in news group discussions. Microsoft has also clearly shown their support for SOA, especially with their Windows Communication Foundation (formerly known as Indigo) effort, which we will see more about in Chapter 7.

Don Box (no introduction necessary I hope?) said it well when he claimed that even though we stretched the technologies as far as we could for distributed objects, it turned out that it didn't quite cover everything and that we'd need something else. (This is not a direct quote, but the heart of the message is in there.) Sten Sundblad, of Sundblad & Sundblad, also agrees that this probably is why SOA seems to be springing up everywhere.

This doesn't mean that our enterprise applications will be constructed purely by gathering services from various places, at least not for the time being. But, as you might have understood from our previous discussion about EAI and enterprises, today we most definitely use services from external sources a lot.

This still doesn't mean we will, or should, stop building "traditional" enterprise applications that are tightly coupled within themselves—far from it. But you should keep in mind when building enterprises that in the near future you will benefit from having a service perspective when doing the architecture and design of such applications. Just remember that implementing SOA in your company means that the whole company IT strategy needs to be changed. It is not intended for single applications, so it is quite a big step to take.

The topic is so important that we have dedicated an entire chapter to SOA in this second edition of our book. In the first edition we tried to emphasize the importance of having Service Oriented thinking, but we did not use the term Service Oriented Architecture.

Before we close the discussion of SOA for now, let's take a look at the qualities that a service should posses. Being familiar with these guidelines will help you during your exploration of the book. Sten Sundblad co-author of "Designing for Scalability with Microsoft Windows DNA" and also co-creator of Sundblad & Sundblad in Sweden (both with his son Per) describes it very well, as always, in the Swedish document "Service Oriented Architecture—An Overview" (translated from the Swedish). Unfortunately, this document is only available in Swedish, but makes a good argument for both learning Swedish as well as learning SOA. The following is what he says a service should be:

- Autonomous.

- Have a message-based interface.

- Have its own logic, which encapsulates and protects its own data.

- Clearly separated from and loosely coupled to its surrounding environment.

- Share its schema with its consumers—not with its class.

David Sprott and Lawrence Wilks of CBDI say in the article "Understanding Service-Oriented Architecture" available at `http://msdn.microsoft.com,` that services should have the following characteristics. Note that these go rather well with what Sten Sundblad says.

- Reusable: A reuse of service, not reuse by copying code or implementation.

- Abstracted: Service is abstracted from the implementation.

- Published: Precise, published specification of the functionality of the service interface, not implementation.

- Formal: Formal contract between endpoints places obligations on provider and consumer.

- Relevant: Functionality presented consisting of a granularity recognized by the user as a meaningful service.

We'll take a closer look at this in Chapter 7, where we discuss SOA further. At that time, we'll also go over Don Box's four tenets for designing services, and how his ideas fit into the scope of Sundblad, Sprott, and Wilks. Keep the definitions and characteristics we just covered in the back of your mind while reading this book though. It might be a good inspiration for when you start thinking about your own applications and what you can do with them.

Now we'll introduce you to another important topic in the computer world: content management (CM). The basics will be covered here, but in Chapter 5 you will get a look at some of the tools you can use to manage your web sites. We mention it now because this is a very big issue in many companies. The tools may seem too primitive at this juncture, but you can be sure they are going to evolve quickly during the coming years.

Content Management

Nowadays, content management is crucial for keeping costs down in maintaining sites and for keeping your site up-to-date in an easy manner. Keeping a high-volume web site up-to-date using low cost methods takes more than just a fancy HTML editor. It's necessary to have complete support for reusable components, including plug-in support, easy administration of user groups and roles, and easy administration of the content on the site. These are only a few of the issues that a modern content management tool must handle smoothly.

First, we'll go through some of the basics of content management, since you need to know quite a lot of definitions to understand content management environments. The primary focus for the first content management tools was to manage content. The first versions kept data in simple databases, and the editor was often a simple ASP (Active Server Pages) page with fixed fields for the title, introduction, and body text.

The area where content is displayed on a page is often called a *placeholder* or a *content component*. A placeholder can hold any kind of information. The most common kind of placeholder today is the kind that contains formatted HTML—transformed from XML. But, as you will see later, it can also contain charts, images, or even content retrieved from other web sites. There can be *x* number of placeholders on a page. Objects of a specific type are placed in a content component. These objects can, for instance, be of a particular type, say an article, and contain HTML code. Normally, you have flow layout of the objects in a placeholder, which means that they are added one after the other to the placeholder.

Content management is all about effectively collecting, managing, and making information available in targeted publications. Information is created or acquired, and then put into a master format (like XML). This information is then segmented into chunks, that is, content components or placeholders. Content components serve as metadata containers for the content that make it easier to organize, store, and retrieve the information. The content is then managed in a repository stored in a database and/or in files on the hard disk. To make the content available for the end user, the content management system (CMS) pushes it to target publications such as web sites, web services, e-mails, or newsletters. A good content management system helps organize and manage the publishing process. General reasons behind the need for content management tools are as follows:

- There is too much information to process manually.

- Many publications need to be created from the same source.

- Information is changing too quickly to be handled manually.

- Content and design need to be separated to be able to update the look and feel of the site without rewriting the content.

The Anatomy of a Content Management System (CMS)

A content management system typically has four parts.

The *collection system* contains the tools and procedures. This system is used by the staff to gather content and to provide editorial processing. The collection system often consists of four different areas: authoring, aggregation, conversion, and editorial/metatorial services.

Authoring is the process of creating content from scratch. Authors mostly work with a framework that allows them to fit their content into the structure of the target publication. Authors should be encouraged to change the meta-information, since they often are the best people to determine whether its the right information for the work they are creating.

Aggregation is generally a process for streamlining content from different sources to be included in the CMS.

Conversion occurs when imported information needs to be restructured: tags may be either inserted or deleted, for example. One conversion problem involves identifying structural elements (footers, for example) that only have format codes marking them in the source content. Another problem is transforming formatting elements that do not exist in the target environment.

Finally, the *editorial service* applies the editorial format, while the *metatorial service* adds metadata that connects the current content with other content in the CMS.

Next, we'll move on to some necessary systems.

The *management system* is made up of the database and files of all the content and meta information. It also comprises the processes and tools employed to access, update, and administer the collected content and meta information. The management system stores the content and makes it possible for staff to select content and manage it. A management system must also be able to connect to other systems via web services, for instance.

The *workflow system* contains the tools and procedures that are used by staff to ensure that the entire process of collecting, storing, and publishing runs effectively and efficiently, and according to well-defined timelines and actions. A workflow system supports the creation and management of business processes. In the context of a content management system, the workflow system sets and administers the chain of events around collecting and publishing.

Finally, the *publishing system* consists of the tools, procedures, and staff employed to draw content out of the repository and create publications for a target, such as a web site.

Problems with Content Management Today

Many companies nowadays are installing content management systems. They are often driven by the growing recognition that business currently generates huge volumes of information, and that this information must be made available to staff and customers—when and where they need it. Few companies, however, ask themselves this question: What do we want to achieve with a CMS tool? The fundamental question is how to get the right information to the right person at the right time. To be able to answer this, you need to ask yourself two questions:

- What information does the business need?

- What technology should be used to manage this information?

Presently, most CMS tools only solve (or focus on) the second question—the first question is often overlooked.

The Content Creators

The people who create the content are often the category of users who are most forgotten in the development of CMS tools. Many large CMS tools provide versioning, workflow, and job tracking support, whereas the tools provided for the authors often are weak. This is a critical problem, because if the tools provided for the authors are difficult to use, how will the site be fed with new updated information?

The problems with hard-to-use author tools grow exponentially with the amount of content available. If the authors complain a little in the beginning, you can be quite sure that they will yell at you before too long!

We will now discuss some simple steps for selecting a CMS tool.

Identify the Business Needs

Do not start a CM project without identifying the business problems that the CMS is meant to solve, and figuring out the strategic benefits it will help to achieve. Implementing a CMS tool is not a goal in itself.

Talk to the Users

This is the most missed step, even though it is the easiest! To find out the requirements, simply ask the users. Once you have convinced the users that you will use their feedback, the tips will never stop.

Rewrite the Content

We have seen too many companies that only want to move their current information into a CMS tool. This is far from the most optimal solution. Instead, these companies should focus on rewriting their content on a long-term basis, in order to make it fit the CMS and digital publishing. Many companies also do not understand that it is difficult to write a good technical article or description! The use of good professional technical writers is often absent today. If you were to ask your customers whether they would be willing to let their people code one of the critical applications they are going to hire contractors for, the answer would probably be no. But when it comes to content, these same customers are not interested in investing much. In our view, many companies are taking the design, layout, and content itself too lightly.

Quality Not Quantity

One of the biggest problems, besides the quality of the information that is published, is that too many people publish too much. An intranet or an external site may contain too much information, making it hard for users to find what they are looking for. The solution is to give the user less, but better, information—remember quality before quantity. As mentioned before, you must encourage the customer to rewrite content for the CMS in order to develop the content further, rather than publishing old manuals directly into the CMS tool. Putting old stuff into a CMS tool directly will mostly decrease the organization's efficiency rather than improving it.

Structure and Navigation

Next comes the need for a navigational tool that makes it possible to traverse the information on the site (even if you have reduced the quantity, you still may have thousands of pages to handle). Without an effective tool to navigate this content, the site will be useless. We often use information architects and professional indexers to pinpoint the problems, and from there construct a solution that solves the problem and makes end users happier.

Workflow and Review

Currently, there are two different workflows on the market: centralized and decentralized.

1. *Centralized workflow* is when all workflow passes through one person (or possibly a few), who needs to authorize the information before it's published. This solution is great in that the information published via the CMS can be held to a consistent level.

2. When you are working with a *decentralized workflow*, many authors are allowed to publish information directly to the site. This presents the challenge of ensuring the consistency and quality of the content. The use of templates is one tool you can use to try to help the authors in following the design guidelines set up for the site.

Despite the selected workflow model, you need to ensure that any kind of workflow and review model exists on the site before you take it live. Trying to apply a workflow after the authors have started to work is likely to fail.

Support Authors

Finally, the most important category of users is the one that will publish information via the CMS tool. These people need to have an easy tool that can help them with everything from browsing images for use in the content to approving and publishing complete articles via the CMS tool. If you are using a decentralized workflow model, this is even more important, since more people will be working with the publishing tool, and you will have to provide more support if the selected tool doesn't fulfill the authors' requirements.

The authors should not be required to understand HTML, XML, or other technical stuff. The best solution often is to have a publishing tool similar to some other tool they are using on a daily basis, like a word processor word processor. This makes it easier for the authors to learn the new environment and quickly start producing material for the new CMS.

In Chapter 5 we will show you two different CMS tools and explore the pros and cons when applying the mentioned criteria on them.

The next topic we'll cover is modeling. Our preferred modeling tool is Microsoft Visio or a Rational Software product (like the IBM Rational XDE Modeler). Visio comes with Visual Studio .NET, and to be honest this is the tool we most often use—but we really don't prefer one over the other. To describe our models, we use the Unified Modeling Language (UML), which is supported in Visio as well as in Rational's products.

The Unified Modeling Language (UML)

No matter how good a coder you may consider yourself to be, you still need some structure during the process of building a system. If you want your new solution to be a success, you need to keep the quality high, and make sure it meets the needs of the users. If the designers, developers, and users do not speak the same language, you can be certain you will have problems in the end.

One of the worst things that can happen in a big project is when people think they mean the same thing, but they really don't. Eventually this might lead to disagreement over which features to include in the solution, and thus make a perfectly functional system a failure. As consultants, we cannot afford to let this happen. If our customers are not happy with the result, we will have difficulties getting an assignment from them again. This is why it is so important to agree about the real requirements of the system. For such an agreement to occur in a project, you need to describe the system so that various groups of people involved will understand how it should function.

Take a simple example. Say your friend is building a house. In this process, he has carpenters, painters, plumbers, electricians, you name it, involved. If only one set of blueprints exists and they only showed the exterior of the house, he would have serious problems. Why is this? Well, different workers need different views of what they are trying to build and many of your friend's workers will need to see the *inside* of the house. The same thing is true when it comes to software engineering. To get consensus, you need a technique, and this technique is called *modeling.* Modeling has proven to be a success factor in many projects over the years.

The other day, we saw a TV show about a man in Sweden realizing his lifelong dream. He was building a real Batmobile, the car Batman drives around in, and he and his friends were just finalizing this impressive vehicle. The team started the project by modeling an exact replica of it in Styrofoam so they would have a good view of what to build. The model simplified the reality and made it easier to get everybody on the same page. Even though a model does not have to be this extreme, you are better off creating at least one (or more) model.

In the book *The Unified Modeling Language User Guide* by Grady Booch, James Rumbaugh, and Ivar Jacobson (Addison-Wesley, 1998. ISBN: 0-201-57168-4.), modeling achieves four aims:

1. Helps you visualize the system as it is or how you want it to be.

2. Permits you to specify the structure or behavior of a system.

3. Gives you a template that guides you in constructing a system.

4. Documents the decisions you have made.

As you can see, you have much to gain by using this technique. And large, complex systems are not the only ones that benefit from modeling either. Modeling helps even smaller systems, as many systems have a tendency to grow and become more and more complex as they go along. With a model, you can grasp this complexity, even after a long time has passed since the inception of the first version of the system. So, if you don't model at the start of a project, you probably will regret it later on, when it is too late. A good thing, proven over and over again in many projects, is to have an object-oriented mind-set when designing and building software solutions.

Another thing that having a good set of UML diagrams can help you with is finding bottle-necks early in the design process. The sooner you eliminate them the less they cost to get rid of.

You must also think about modeling at different levels. Sometimes you need a high-level view of the system, and sometimes you need a low-level view. You need, for example, one view when showing the solution to decision makers and another one when talking to developers.

Modeling can be difficult, however. If you aren't careful when you choose what to model, you might be misled by your models and thus focus on the wrong things. Because models are a simplification of reality, it might be easy to hide important details. To avoid this, you need to make sure you connect your models to reality. If you have a weaker connection in one place, you must at least be aware of it.

Don't think that one model is necessarily enough, either. Going back to the example of your friend's house, recall that different workers will need different views. This is true here, too.

By using the Unified Modeling Language (UML), you can achieve all of this. UML is a stan-dard for writing software blueprints, and as the name implies, it is a language. UML can be used to visualize, specify, construct, and document the deliveries (or artifacts) of a software-intensive system. But remember that because UML is only a language, it is just one part of the development cycle.

If you have little experience of UML, here comes our crash course just for you. It is by no means a complete coverage of UML, but it is important to have an understanding of these concepts, since we use them frequently in this book. If you feel you have sufficient knowledge in this area, you can move on to the next part of this chapter, Object Role Modeling (ORM).

Activity Diagram

An *activity diagram* shows the flow of control. Activities are action states that move, or transi-tion, to the next state after completion. In Figure 1-8, you can see these activities as rounded rectangles. Our example shows a simple flow of control for the creation of sales campaigns mailed to registered customers, which are also published on a web site. All transitions between the activities are represented by an arrow. To show activities performed in parallel, we use synchronization bars.

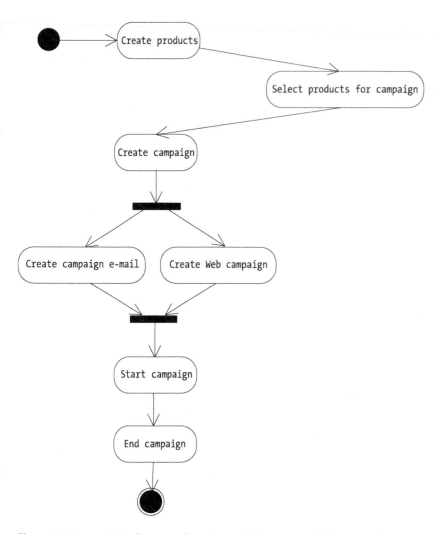

Figure 1-8. *An activity diagram showing activities as rounded rectangles*

These diagrams are really flowcharts used early in the design process to show the work-flow between use cases. You are not required to use them at this point in the process, however. You can use them where you feel they are appropriate, or when you think they explain a flow in a system so that a decision maker can understand what you mean.

In your activity diagrams, you can use something called *swim lanes* to show ownership. In Figure 1-9, we have added a swim lane to our activity diagram to show the responsibilities of sales clerks and sales managers.

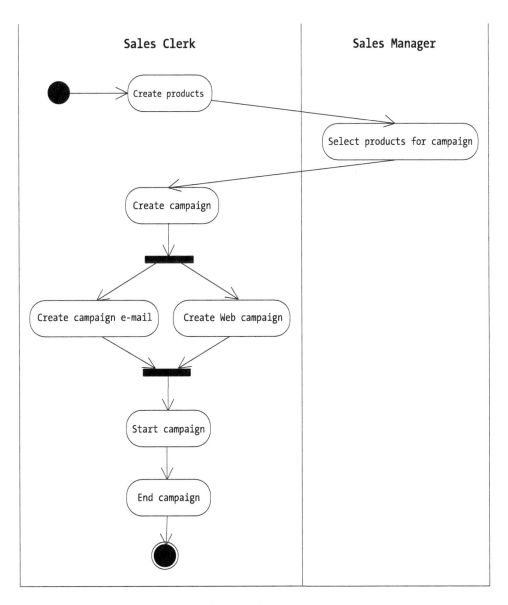

Figure 1-9. *A swim lane added to our activity diagram*

The clerk handles everything but the selection of the products to include in the campaign. That task is left to the sales manager. So now we have shown the responsibilities of all parties in this extremely simple scenario.

Use Cases and Use Case Diagrams

When you create use cases, you first have to decide which actors will participate in your solution. An actor can be a person (or group of persons), but it can also be another system—that is, something that interacts with the system, but is *outside* the system. We represent our actors with stick figures, pretty much like the ones in *The Blair Witch Project,* if you are familiar with that movie (see Figure 1-10).

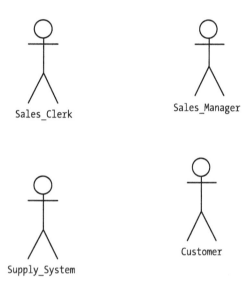

Figure 1-10. *Actors in a use case diagram represented as stick figures*

Let us continue our simple scenario from earlier. We have already mentioned two actors: the sales clerk and the sales manager. Do we have anyone else? One actor that immediately comes to mind is the customer. Another one might be a supply system, that is, a system that keeps track of our products and the information related to them (like stock, price, and description).

The next thing to do is find your use cases. The easiest way for you to do this is by looking at your actors and asking yourself why they want to use the system. A use case in itself is a description of actions that a system performs to give an actor the result of a value. In our example, they are portrayed as ovals, as you can see in Figure 1-11.

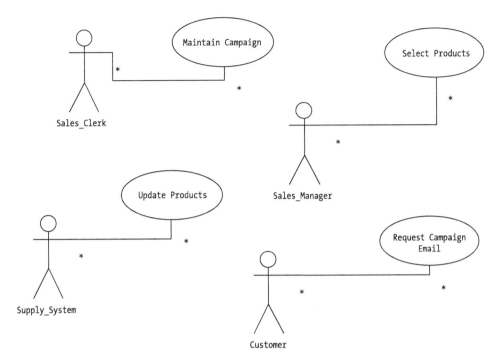

Figure 1-11. *Actions that a system performs for the actors*

In our example, the customer selects a campaign e-mail. The sales clerk maintains the campaign catalogs, and the sales manager requests available products. Finally, the supply system maintains the products.

Now, when you have identified some use cases, you can start documenting them. This is done by describing the flow of events from the actors' point of view. You must also specify what the system must provide to the actors when the use case is executed. The use case should show the normal flow of events, but it should also show the *abnormal* flow—that is, when something goes wrong during execution and an alternate scenario takes place. (The scenarios will be on a high level, so you cannot catch all possible actions.)

Often, use cases will be great for showing the people paying for the system what actually will happen in it. This way, you can be assured early in the process that what you are building is what the customer expects.

Let us take a look at the sales clerk use case for a little while. This starts when the clerk logs in to the system. The system verifies the password and then shows the campaign mainte-nance form. The clerk can choose from various alternatives what he or she intends to do:

- Create new campaign: Create new campaign subflow executes.

- Modify campaign: Modify campaign subflow executes.

- Delete campaign: Delete campaign subflow executes.

- Review campaign: Review campaign subflow executes.

- Exit: Use case ends.

When you've created your use case diagrams, you'll have a good overview of the system. If you are modeling an integration project, you must not forget to consider where you need to deal with legacy systems at this early stage. If you model your use cases thoroughly from the beginning, you will not be surprised by unexpected problems later on, when coding has started.

Sequence Diagrams

Sequence diagrams are used to illustrate the dynamic view of a system. They show the interaction and the messages sent between objects in chronological order (see Figure 1-12).

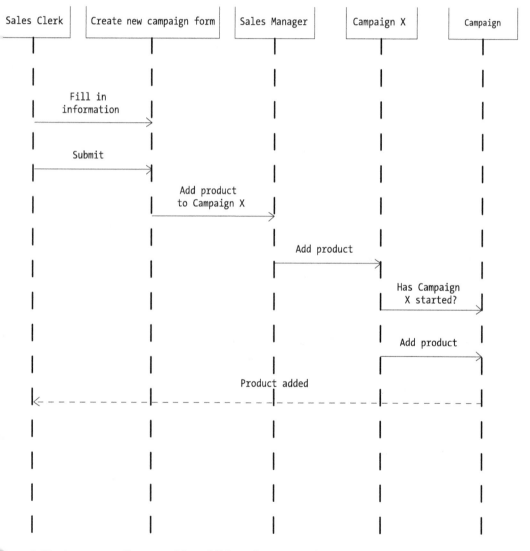

Figure 1-12. *A sequence diagram of the addition of a new product to a campaign*

First, you place the objects that participate in the interaction at the top of the diagram across the x-axis. The object that initiates the interaction is typically placed to the left, and the more subordinate objects to the right. The messages sent are placed to the left along the y-axis (time). Our example here shows the addition of a new product to a campaign.

First the clerk fills in information about the product to be added to Campaign X. She then submits the information to the sales manager to see if the product is valid for this campaign. If the product is approved for addition, the manager tells the campaign object to add the product. The campaign object then checks that the campaign has not started, and if it hasn't, the product is added.

Sequence diagrams are great for showing what is going on in a process. In collaboration with the customer, they can help in mapping out the requirements of the system. We suggest you do a sequence diagram for every basic flow of every use case, and keep doing them until you think you have enough. Enough is basically when you cannot find any more objects and messages. For instance, in our example, we do not have to do another sequence diagram to show how a sales clerk adds a product to Campaign Z. We already have a basic sequence diagram for this flow of events.

Class Diagrams

This is one of the most common diagrams used. Through class diagrams you can model the static design view of a system. A *class diagram* shows classes that are collections of objects with a common structure, behavior, relationships, and semantics. In UML, classes are represented by a rectangle with three compartments, as shown in Figure 1-13. The top compartment displays the name of the class, the middle one lists its attributes, and the bottom one indicates its behavior (or operations).

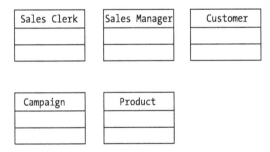

Figure 1-13. *A class diagram*

You can choose to show one, two, or all three of these compartments. When you choose the names for your classes, try to maintain a standard throughout your project. You can, for instance, decide to use singular nouns, like Customer, with a capital letter at the beginning. How you choose, or what you choose, is not important. What is important is that you stick to your standard, so as to avoid confusion later on.

What UML modeling elements do you find in class diagrams? You will probably have many class diagrams in your model, since they show the logical view of your system. They show which classes exist, and the relationships between them. They also show associations, aggregations, dependencies, and inheritance. From your class diagram, you can see the structure and behavior of your classes. You can also see multiplicity and navigation indicators. Figure 1-14 shows the class Campaign and its attributes. In the real world, we would find out these attributes by talking to our customers and looking at our requirements. For the purposes of our example, let us say that the class has five attributes: Name, Start_date, End_date, Discount, and Sales_manager.

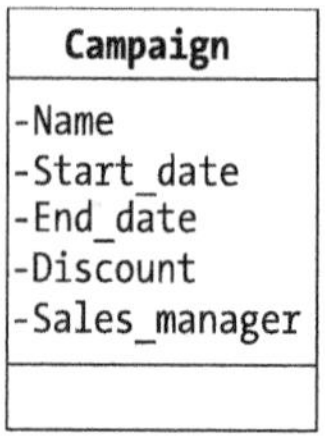

```
Campaign
-Name
-Start_date
-End_date
-Discount
-Sales_manager

```

Figure 1-14. *The class Campaign and its five attributes*

Name is the name of the campaign. Start_date and End_date represent the start and the end of the campaign. Discount is the percentage that prices belonging to this campaign are lowered during the campaign. Sales_manager is the name of the sales manager responsible for the campaign.

Next, you need to find some operations for your class. *Operations* are the behavior of the class. In Figure 1-15, we have hidden the attributes of the Campaign class and show only the class name and operations. Since this is a simplified view of a class, only three are specified: Add, Delete, and Modify. There could, of course, be many more, just as there could be many more attributes. It all depends on your requirements and the input from the customer.

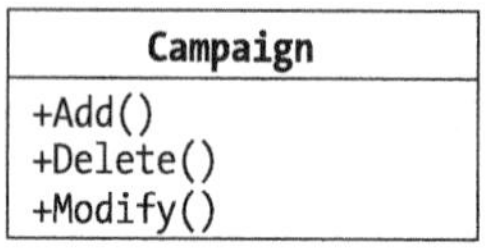

```
Campaign
+Add()
+Delete()
+Modify()
```

Figure 1-15. *The Campaign class and its operations, with the attributes hidden*

Once you have your classes, you can start looking for the relationships between them. Three kinds of relationships exist in UML according to the document "Introduction to the Unified Modeling Language" by Terry Quatrini (http://www.rational.com/uml/resources/whitepapers/index.jsp): association, aggregation, and dependency. They all represent a communication path between objects. One could argue that inheritance should be counted as a relationship; however, we chose to cover it separately a little later.

Association is represented by a line connecting classes, as you can see in Figure 1-16. This is a bidirectional connection, which means that one class can send a message to the other, because if they are associated, they both know the other one is there.

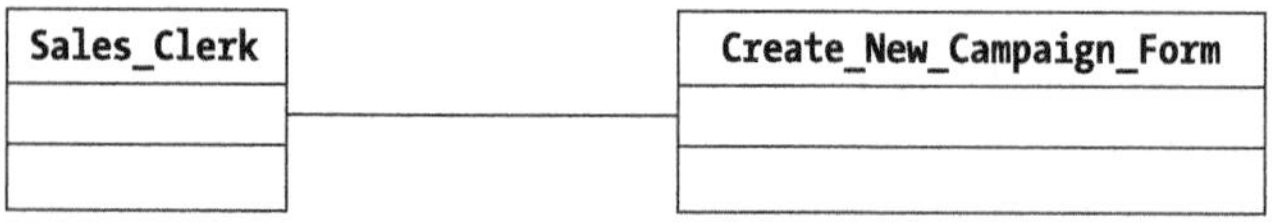

```
Sales_Clerk                    Create_New_Campaign_Form


```

Figure 1-16. *An association between two classes*

A stronger form of relationship is the *aggregation*. In UML, you show this as a line connecting the related classes. The line has a diamond on one end (see Figure 1-17). An aggregation shows the relationship between a whole (the diamond) and its parts. When you, as a developer, see this kind of relationship, you know this means there is a strong coupling between those object classes.

Figure 1-17. *An aggregation between two classes*

Figure 1-18 shows the third kind of relationship, the *dependency*. As you can see in this figure, the dependency is represented by a dashed line. It points from a client to a supplier. The client does not have to have semantic knowledge of the supplier, and so this is a weaker form of relationship. It shows that a change in the specification of one class may affect another class that uses it. Keep in mind that the reverse may not necessarily be true. Use dependencies when you want to show that one class uses another class.

Figure 1-18. *A dependency*

To find your relationships, start by looking at your sequence diagrams. If you find that two objects need to talk to each other, they must have a way of doing this. This way is the relationship. The deeper you analyze your diagrams, the more you will know what type of relationship to use. A parent-child relationship will probably be an aggregation, and so on.

We will now spend a few moments on multiplicity and navigation. *Multiplicity* simply states how many objects participate in a particular relationship. It shows how many instances of one class relate to *one* instance of the other class. Based on this, you need to decide for each end of an association and aggregation what level of multiplicity is needed. Since multiplicity defines the number of instances, you will represent it in your diagram with either a number or an asterisk (*). The asterisk is used to represent a multiplicity of many (see Figure 1-19). In our previous example, we could say that one campaign can only be owned by one sales manager. But one sales manager can own several campaigns. This is known as a one-to-many relationship, which would be represented as 1 - *.

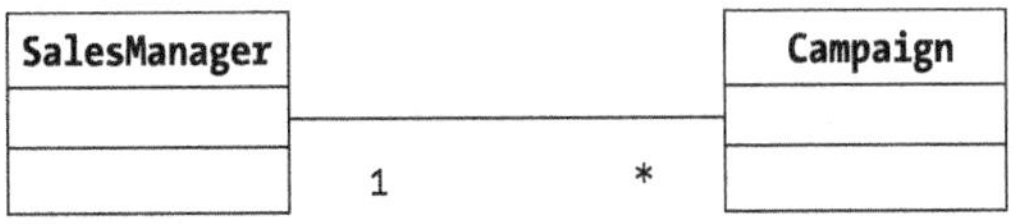

Figure 1-19. *A multiplicity of one to many*

You decide multiplicity by examining your business rules. For our example, we could have a business rule stating that one sales manager can own only three campaigns. Then we would have a one-to-three relationship, as Figure 1-20 shows.

Figure 1-20. *Here we have a one-to-three relationship.*

Navigation is represented by an arrow. You should try to start the arrow at the class that initiates communication between classes. The sales manager in our case initiates the communication with the campaign, which is why the arrow shown in Figure 1-21 starts at the SalesManager class.

Figure 1-21. *An arrow starting at the SalesManager class indicates that the sales manager initiates communication with the Campaign class.*

Inheritance is the relationship between a superclass and a subclass. In our example, if we have a class called Employee, we can have other classes like SalesManager or SalesClerk that are separate classes but still fall under the Employee class. That is, a SalesManager is an Employee. In Figure 1-22, you can see this relationship is shown with a triangle.

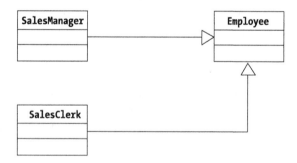

Figure 1-22. *Inheritance between two classes*

Be cautious when using inheritance. You do not want to build too many levels, because if you do, a change in one class will affect many others. This could bring disaster to your products, since you might have to make changes in many places because of this. Build another level only when you are sure there is an inheritance situation, and do not include it just for the sake of having it.

This is all the UML we will cover in this chapter. With the knowledge of the topics you have gleaned in this section, you have come quite some way down the path of designing a great system. A good source of information about UML, and the topics we did not cover here, is the book we mentioned earlier, *The Unified Modeling Language User Guide* by Booch et al.

After this quick UML course, you are equipped to understand the use cases shown in this book. In Chapter 10, we will use these diagrams to exemplify what we mean and how we reason when building our examples.

UML and SOA

In Chapter 7 we will see how we can use UML for visualizing a Service Oriented Architecture. We can tell you right now that you are in for no big surprises, which is a good thing.

Object Role Modeling (ORM)

Another method for conceptual modeling, called *Object Role Modeling* (ORM), has been around since the seventies, but is still relatively unknown to most people. It can be of great use to you in your work, however. While the class diagrams of UML are used primarily for the design of classes and the relationships between them, ORM is used as a tool for information and rules analysis. You use it to analyze and document the information you handle in your system.

In ORM, the application world is represented as a set of objects that perform different roles. You could call ORM fact-based modeling, because the relevant data is verbalized as elementary facts. You cannot split these facts into smaller facts without losing information.

The objects in ORM are shown as ovals, as you can see in Figure 1-23. The objects are connected by *predicates*. These appear as sequence boxes in the figure. Each of these boxes corresponds to a role in the relationship. A predicate is only a sentence with object holes in it. If you include the object types with the predicate, you have a fact type. Let us take an example, such as "SalesClerk created SalesCampaign."

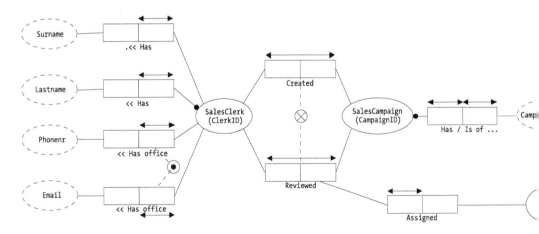

Figure 1-23. *An ORM model*

In our model here, each predicate has two roles; the fact type "SalesClerk created Sales-Campaign" has one role played by SalesClerk (creating) and another role played by SalesCampaign (being created). In ORM, you can have any number of roles in a predicate. An example with three roles, known as a *ternary predicate*, would be "ConferenceRoom at Timeslot is booked for Activity."

A fact type may itself be treated as an object type. That way it can also play a role. Take a look at the following fact type: "SalesClerk reviewed SalesCampaign." This can be objectified as "Review," which can participate in the fact type "Review assigned Rating."

An ORM model can include business rules like constraint or deviation rules. A uniqueness constraint is represented as an arrow-tipped bar over a role. This indicates that each object playing that role only does so once. For example, one SalesClerk has only one Lastname.

A dot on a role connector means that the role is mandatory. In this example, you can see that a SalesClerk must have a Lastname and that a SalesCampaign must have a CampaignTitle.

In Figure 1-23, we also have a constraint on Rating. Rating can only have a value between 1 and 10, which is represented by {1..10}.

To show an inclusive or constraint, you should use a circled dot. In our example, this indicates that a SalesClerk must play at least one role, but can play the other, or both, as well. We also have a circled X in our model, which is used here to show that a SalesClerk cannot review the same SalesCampaign that he or she created. Verbalizing this results in the following:

- No SalesClerk created and reviewed the same SalesCampaign.

- Each SalesClerk has some Phonenr or has some Email.

From our ORM model, we can generate a database class diagram (see Figure 1-24). The ORM model describes the world in terms of sentences (and rather simple ones as well), whereas a relational database schema describes the same in terms of tables and columns (or attributes).

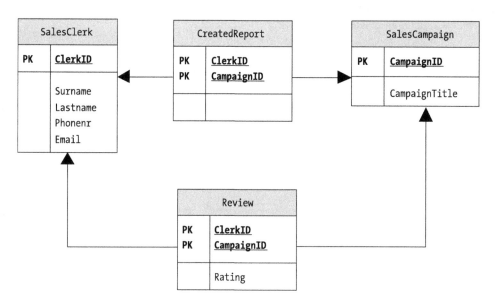

Figure 1-24. *The ORM model mapped to a database schema*

ORM uniqueness is, of course, mapped to primary key constraints in the database. In this example, our mandatory role constraints are enforced by making columns mandatory, which we show by making them bold and adding foreign key constraints.

As you can see in Figure 1-24, our eight fact types in the ORM model map to four normalized tables in the end.

Why Use ORM?

ORM models are attribute-free. They are hence immune to changes that cause attributes to be remodeled as entity types or relationships. Another benefit of ORM is the simple verbalization in sentences. By being non-technical, you can have business experts talk about the model in sentences and sample populations, and thereby ensure that the applications meet their business requirements. You can also use ORM models to capture business rules. These rules, along with the fact types, can be mapped automatically to a correctly normalized database schema. By using the various design procedures of ORM, you get help when modeling to map conceptual models to logical ones.

ORM and SOA

In Chapter 7 we will see how we could use ORM in an SOA architecture. There are some implications we need to consider and we will discuss them there.

Summary

Integration and content management are important to enterprises today, and need special mentioning. Since so many new applications are web-based and often use data from various systems, you need to consider them thoroughly. The Service Oriented Architectural approach also has implications on how we should design our systems.

The importance of designing for scalability cannot be stressed enough. Keep in mind, however, that this does not necessarily mean that performance is the most important thing all the time. In some instances security has to be more important than performance, as this book will show. Unfortunately, security almost always comes with a slight performance penalty—but if you design your applications correctly, you can compensate for this. Another issue that obviously affects scalability and performance is the impact of using external services. If a service response is slow, our own application will suffer. This is something we need to consider during the design phase so that we know how to handle situations like that. A pure SOA perspective affects scalability and performance, and we need to change our way of looking at this subject slightly when implementing such an architecture.

In order to successfully design and develop an application or system, all people involved need to have consensus on what to build. By modeling in UML you can accomplish this. For your own good you *should* use it. If you don't model, there most certainly will come a time when you wish you had. If you are unfortunate, this is when customers question if the system you built actually was the one they asked for.

A great way of ensuring your application maps to the users' requirements is by using ORM. With the simplicity of this method, you can have business experts talk about the model in sentences and sample populations. You can then map your ORM model to a database schema.

Our aim with this book is to help you in designing a good, scalable application that will be a success for the development team. So don't wait around anymore. Dive into the book and good luck with your applications!

CHAPTER 2

■ ■ ■

Windows Server System

When you are designing a scalable solution, it is essential that you choose the right platform for each of the application tiers on which you'll be running. If you make a mistake during the design phase, it might be hard or costly to correct later on.

Prior to Windows 2000 Server, very few companies would ever consider running their business applications on a Microsoft operating system. Microsoft's reputation was not good. But as more and more companies discovered the major improvements Microsoft had made to their server platform, many of these companies, even large ones, reevaluated their opinion on this matter. With the release of Windows Server 2003, Microsoft proved that their dedication to this matter was going to be sustained and they are now known to have a very good foundation for all sorts of enterprise applications. In our work as consultants, we have seen a steady increase in requests for Microsoft-based solutions even in such traditional areas as banking. This has much to do with the enhanced stability of the operating system, but it also has to do with security and standards-based technology playing a larger role. Microsoft has put a lot of effort into building better, more scalable, more available, and more secure platforms. Microsoft has also developed server operating systems that come in different flavors, depending on which use is intended for the system in question.

The first step towards widening the Windows family came with the release of Windows 2000 some years ago. With this edition, it was now possible to have a platform that covered everything from the small, centralized organization to the large, distributed enterprise. Suddenly you could deliver a Microsoft-based solution that could offer 99.999 percent uptime (the five nines).

Windows 2000 Server came in three editions: Windows 2000 Server, Windows 2000 Advanced Server, and Windows 2000 Datacenter Server. Each of these was designed for different uses in the enterprise.

When we wrote the first edition of this book, Microsoft had just released the second release candidate of its next generation operating system, called the Windows Server 2003 family. Now the final product has been out for some years and in Windows Server 2003 many things have been improved when compared to the Windows 2000 Server. The Windows Server 2003 family comes in even more editions than Windows 2000 Server. You can choose from the Windows Server 2003 Web Edition, Windows Server 2003 Standard Edition, Windows Server 2003 Enterprise Edition, and the Windows Server 2003 Datacenter Edition. Two of these also come in 64-bit editions, so the total number of siblings in this family is six.

With all these versions available, it's obvious that in the design phase you must make the best choice for your platforms. A wrong choice might affect performance and scalability, and you could face a time- and cost-consuming process of putting it all together in the end. It would also be bad, for example, if you chose the Datacenter Edition for a simple web server, not because your performance would be degraded, but because of the unnecessary higher cost of this edition.

This chapter will focus on the different server platforms that Microsoft offers. We will also discuss the differences between the various operating systems and show you when and where they are appropriate to use.

When we wrote the first edition of our book, Microsoft was using the term .NET Enterprise servers to describe the line of servers they offered. This name was changed, however to Windows Server System somewhere around the time of its publishing at the end of 2003. But that wasn't all—it was also expanded and it now includes a wider range of products, as seen in Figure 2-1.

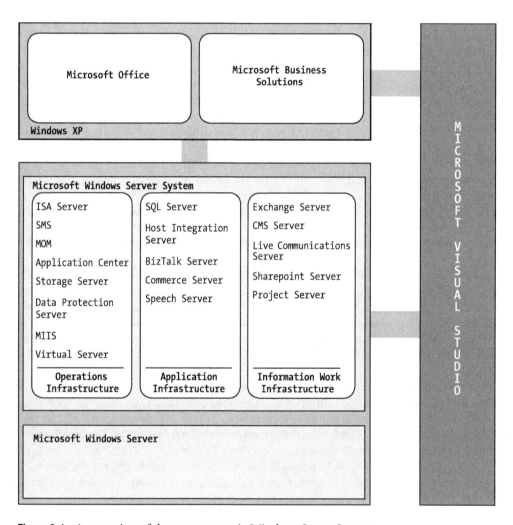

Figure 2-1. *An overview of the components in Windows Server System*

The focus in our book is still on the infrastructure for building end-to-end solutions using Windows Server 2003 as the core platform, but it's a good bet that many companies still use Windows 2000 Server and will continue to do so for some time yet. The operating system is just the platform to build your applications on, and many of these other servers are very useful in helping us build a Microsoft solution. They do this by adding functions we do not have in the operating system from the beginning, which also means that we don't have to develop them ourselves. So if you are to make the correct design choice, you must have knowledge of these as well.

But let us start by looking at the operating system. Since this book focuses on scalability, we won't cover any Windows 2000 features that don't enhance scalability, performance, and security.

Microsoft Operating Systems

Confidence in Microsoft's operating systems, prior to Windows 2000, was not great in larger enterprises, so developers mainly used UNIX and other platforms for application servers and mission-critical systems. Windows NT was mostly used to handle users and the logon process to the network. It was also employed for file and print servers, though not many IT professionals trusted it as a platform to run their business applications on. Some developers saw potential in it, but most people more or less looked at it as a toy operating system on the server side. Unfortunately for Microsoft, this reputation has been hard to shake off. In our work we often meet people who regard anything Microsoft develops as toys. This is too bad, because starting with Windows 2000, Microsoft has convinced us more and more that it really can build stable platforms—platforms that help developers design and build scalable solutions.

A big complaint from IT professionals was that they often needed to reboot the operating system because of errors that occurred. Microsoft was blamed for this problem. The critique was well deserved in many cases, but a lot of the errors that resulted in rebooting the OS were caused by administrators trying new software and installing things they shouldn't have. Also, a lot of these errors came from faulty drivers for hardware that was not supported. Microsoft analyzed nearly 1200 Windows NT 4.0 Servers to find out where to put the most effort in stabilizing Windows 2000. The company found that 65 percent of the reboots were caused by planned outages, such as adding hardware or software. Furthermore, Microsoft found that of the unplanned reboots, more than half were caused by faulty device drivers, antivirus software, and hardware failures.

No UNIX administrator would have tried to install beta software for a new program on, say, a Solaris system—nor would they have tried to install any new cool games. Unfortunately, we have seen such actions on Windows systems (in production) ourselves over the years, mostly on Windows NT servers but also on some Windows Server 2000 systems as well. Fortunately this bad habit has almost completely vanished and nowadays poses no threat to security or scalability on systems that we have been in contact with. Since Windows was easier to handle than some of the other popular systems of the time, many people and companies developed software and hardware for it, and many experimented almost freely. The result was a lot of problems and constant reboots. Many of these errors could have been avoided or solved without rebooting the server: if awareness of the reasons for them had been more widespread.

Microsoft saw these problems and put a lot of effort into building a new system architecture that improved server uptime, increased fault tolerance, and increased availability. Microsoft knew that it was essential to deliver a platform that enterprises could feel confident building their business on to have success in the market.

Microsoft also saw the need for companies to extend their business to the Internet. This required a comprehensive web, security, and communications technology built into the operating system, combined with good scalability and performance for handling the demands of Internet traffic.

Windows 2000 Server Family

All Windows 2000 Server versions come with a built-in web server: Internet Information Services 5.0, also referred to as IIS. In Windows NT 4.0, this web server was called Internet Information Server 4.0 and came with the Windows NT 4.0 Option Pack. Note the difference: Now it is a *service*, before it was a *server*—just like the Microsoft Cluster Service (MSCS). We will take a closer look at IIS in Chapter 7, where we'll compare IIS 5.0 with the new IIS 6.0, released with Windows Server 2003.

Note One thing worth mentioning here though, is the inclusion of better support for Active Server Pages (ASP) in IIS 5.0, which gives you better options for building dynamic web solutions.

Microsoft built native support for XML into its operating system from Windows 2000 Server forward. Nowadays, it is virtually impossible to find a Microsoft product missing XML support. This is a good thing, because since it first was introduced, XML has gained respect as a standardized means of transporting data, and is used extensively in application development.

To enhance scalability and availability, Microsoft also made significant improvements to the core operating system, and added support for more CPUs and more memory. They also improved memory management and the handling of device drivers to reduce unplanned downtime.

We can break these scalability improvements down to enhancements in two areas: scaling up and scaling out.

Scaling Up

The following technologies were improved:

- Large memory support was increased to a maximum of 32GB RAM.

- 32-way symmetric multiprocessing (SMP) support was included.

These improvements are mostly useful in backend database systems, messaging server systems, decision support, and data mining systems.

Scaling Out

Improvements were also made to the following areas:

- Network Load Balancing (NLB) could include up to 32 servers in one cluster.

- Component Load Balancing (CLB) could be included with Application Center 2000.

- Microsoft Clustering Service was rewritten.

These areas prove helpful when building web infrastructure, application servers, and directory and DNS servers.

Other Feature Enhancements

Here are some other features that also were enhanced:

- Improvements to Winsock Direct for efficient interconnectivity within a system area network

- Support for high-performance data sets

- Integration of Microsoft Messaging and Queue Service to Microsoft Message Queuing (MSMQ)

- Integration of Microsoft COM+ Transaction Services (MTS) into the OS

Beside these improvements, a lot of effort went into helping administrators by providing useful tools to handle their everyday work. These tools are often based on a wizard system that aids in administrative tasks step by step.

Let's take a look at the different versions of Windows 2000 Server. The smallest version is Windows 2000 Server. This entry-level version is suitable for use as a file, print, intranet, and infrastructure server. Network Load Balancing and Microsoft Cluster Service aren't included in the Windows 2000 Server, so this product is not intended to be used as a web server for large web sites. Neither is it intended as a database server, unless the load is modest and the demands for availability are small. But this version includes IIS 5.0, which makes it great for smaller intranet or Internet solutions. There is, however, a way to use this server as a member in large web clusters. By installing Application Center on it, you also get support for Network Load Balancing, and suddenly you are able to cluster IIS, which means that you can handle large web sites using Windows 2000 Server as a platform. So as a web server using Application Center, this version is a good choice for running your web sites. The cost of the operating system is also less than its other siblings too, which makes it even more attractive for these solutions.

Windows 2000 Advanced Server includes tools for enhancing scalability and availability from the start. Network Load Balancing is included, as well as Microsoft Cluster Service. This makes it an ideal platform for running e-commerce and lines of business applications. Advanced Server is also a good choice for medium-sized databases, and for messaging servers like Microsoft Exchange Server, providing good availability to these applications. Since the cost of this server version is higher than the Windows 2000 Server, we would not recommend it as a platform for web sites, regardless of whether they are on an intranet, an extranet, or the Internet. If you are building that kind of application, you are better off using Windows 2000 Server with Application Center on it.

Microsoft's flagship when it comes to operating systems is undoubtedly the Windows 2000 Datacenter Server. Upon its release, this was the most powerful operating system from Microsoft ever. This server was designed for enterprises that demand the highest level of availability and scalability. This edition is, however, not available from retailers. The only way to purchase a Datacenter Server is by contacting one of the Microsoft OEM partners. To be able to sell these systems, the OEM companies need to comply with the Datacenter Server program. This means both hardware and software are put under close examination to ensure they meet the high standards that can help enterprises reach 99.999 percent uptime on their systems. No updates to the Datacenter systems, be they hardware or software, are allowed without this close examination. This way it is not possible for an administrator to install insecure code or devices, which was, as you saw earlier, the cause of a large number of unnecessary reboots.

Table 2-1 gives an overview of the feature set included with the different versions of the Windows 2000 Server family.

Table 2-1. *An Overview of the Features in the Windows 2000 Server Family*

Feature	W2K Server	W2K Advanced Server	W2K Datacenter Server
Max CPU	4	8	32
Max memory	4GB	8GB	32GB
IIS 5.0	Yes	Yes	Yes
COM+	Yes	Yes	Yes
MSCS	No	Yes	Yes
NLB	No	Yes	Yes
Process control management	No	No	Yes
Winsock Direct	No	No	Yes
Active Directory	Yes	Yes	Yes
Kerberos/PKI support	Yes	Yes	Yes

Windows Server 2003 Family

With the computing world becoming more and more distributed, the need for integrating IT systems grows with it. Enterprises must offer personnel in various locations the same services as those available at headquarters. For example, with the connectivity possibilities these days, the need to distribute a complete product catalog to every salesperson, regardless of location, no longer exists. This catalog can now reside at headquarters, and each salesperson can use a web-based application to access it, just as if it was located on his own computer. With the introduction of SOAP, XML, and web services, it has become even easier to share services within an organization, as well as with partners and customers. It's now possible to build features based on a web service into a Windows application. The application itself is run on the user computer, but the web service can be run on the other side of the world, if necessary. If you want to learn more about web services and their benefits, please see Chapters 5 and 6 in this book, where we'll dissect web services thoroughly. Web services are here to stay, and they give you great opportunities. Microsoft has realized this, and its .NET initiative is a response to this. By using Visual Studio .NET, it has become fairly straightforward to integrate various web services into your own applications.

The next generation of server operating systems from Microsoft, the Windows Server 2003 family, includes .NET Framework integration. This offers great possibilities to simplify the development of large-scale applications that can exploit XML web services. This way, businesses of all sizes can benefit from the .NET application platform.

■**Note** The .NET Framework is available for Windows 2000 as well, but in Windows Server 2003 it is integrated right out of the box. Performance tests also show great performance gains for running .NET applications on a Windows Server 2003 compared to running the same applications on a Windows 2000 system. In Chapter 9, we will give you a closer look at the performance gains we have found in our tests.

Let's take a look at some selected improvements in the new server family that enhance both scalability and availability. First of all, the new version of Internet Information Services, version 6.0, has been completely re-architected from earlier versions. IIS 6.0 includes a new fault-tolerant process model that definitely improves the reliability of web sites and applications. In earlier versions of IIS, a single application failure could bring down the entire web site. Now, in IIS 6.0, a new feature called the *application pool* provides a self-contained process, consisting of a single web application or multiple sites. If an error occurs in an application pool, only that process is affected, and all the others will still be functioning. You will learn more about the application pool later in the book, but as you can understand from this short description, the availability of web sites has increased significantly.

IIS 6.0 also includes native support of ASP.NET. This is not such surprising news, as the .NET Framework is included in the operating system, and ASP.NET is a part of this framework. But a good thing about ASP.NET is that it gives you better performance compared to the old ASP model.

Web services are deeply integrated in the Windows Server 2003 family. Existing COM+ applications and Microsoft Message Queuing objects can easily be converted and exposed as web services. MSMQ now also uses SOAP and XML natively, so loosely coupled applications can interoperate with a broader range of systems. This lets legacy systems take advantage of the connectivity .NET offers.

Both scaling out and scaling up has had some significant boosts. When it comes to *scaling out*, clusters using Microsoft Cluster Service can now have up to eight nodes. This is twice the number of nodes Windows 2000 offered. Thus, you are provided with the tools to give you many possibilities for deploying applications and setting up failover policies that suit your business. It is also possible to separate nodes geographically, which provides for high fault tolerance. What this really means is that you can deploy an application on an eight-node cluster that is geographically dispersed over two separate locations. If you lose functionality at one location, your application will still function.

All versions of the Windows Server 2003 family now offer Network Load Balancing without the use of Application Server.

Scaling up has also been enhanced. The Windows Server 2003 family can now offer from 2- to 32-CPU SMP support, depending on which version is used. The amount of RAM a system can handle has been improved, giving you the possibility of having as much as 512GB in your system.

The administrative tools have also been improved, with more wizards and options for configuring the system. Figure 2-2 shows the Manage Your Server Wizard starting page, which helps administrators configure the server for different uses.

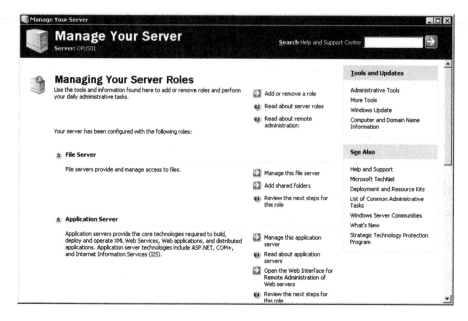

Figure 2-2. *The Manage Your Server Wizard in Windows Server 2003 Enterprise Edition*

Figure 2-3 shows the Server Administration page from the Web Edition.

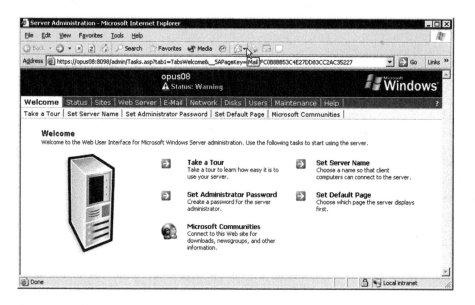

Figure 2-3. *The Server Administration page in Windows Server 2003 Web Edition*

The server family itself has once again grown. Now you have four versions to choose from. (If you want to be picky, you actually have six, since two of these also come in 64-bit versions.)

- Windows Server 2003 Web Edition

- Windows Server 2003 Standard Edition

- Windows Server 2003 Enterprise Edition 32-bit/64-bit

- Windows Server 2003 Datacenter Edition 32-bit/64-bit

Next we will take a look at them separately so you know when and where to use which version.

Windows Server 2003 Web Edition

As you saw earlier, the only way to use Windows 2000 Server as a web server in a cluster was by using the Application Center and the Network Load Balancing features it offers. In the Windows Server 2003 family, one version, the Web Edition, is designed for providing web serving and hosting. Using this edition, it's easy to deploy and manage a new web server, and at the same time get a server that is optimized to be a robust platform for web serving and hosting, as well as functioning as a host for XML web services.

The Web Edition is not intended for any other use but as a web server. This means you cannot install other servers in the Windows Server System on this platform. SQL Server, Exchange Server, and most other enterprise servers will just not be allowed to install, as Figure 2-4 shows.

Figure 2-4. *SQL Server is not allowed to install on the Web Edition.*

The .NET Framework, however, is included so you can take full advantage of this. Since ASP.NET is a powerful way of building your distributed applications, you now have a good platform to deploy your web applications on.

Another aspect of the slimmed down Web Edition is that fewer services are running on it. This allows the web server to concentrate on its tasks without the operating system having to spend CPU time on Windows services that really are not necessary for a web server. This paves the way for increased performance, which is always something you want on a web server. The Web Edition is also an excellent platform for you to develop and deploy your XML web services on. In Chapter 10 you will see how this can be done.

Since the use of the Web Edition is as a web server only, the scale-up capabilities aren't so good (and they don't need to be either). This version supports two-way SMP and only 2GB of RAM. As you can see, it is intended to run on fairly standard hardware, so as to be easy to deploy and manage. This is also what you usually seek for the servers in a web cluster. You want to be able to go out and buy standard hardware when you need more power in your cluster, and easily deploy it in your solution.

Note Keep in mind that the Web Edition can be a member of an Active Directory domain, but cannot run Active Directory itself.

Windows Server 2003 Standard Edition

Like its predecessor, Windows 2000 Server, the Windows Server 2003 Standard Edition is an excellent choice for small businesses, as well as for individual departments. You can use this version as a robust platform for file and print services. It is also a good choice for secure Internet connectivity. Since the Standard Edition can run Active Directory, it offers the possibility of being used for centralized desktop application deployment.

When it comes to scalability, this server version offers up to four-way SMP support and handles up to 4GB of RAM. This means it scales up better than the Web Edition, but if you are looking for a web server solution only, you would still be better off using the Web Edition. As a database server, however, you can definitely use Standard Edition for small to medium-sized databases. If you do this, you must keep in mind that it offers no support for Microsoft Cluster Service, which means you cannot guarantee constant availability for your databases. If you need MSCS, you must move up to at least the Enterprise Edition. The Standard Edition is, on the other hand, a preferred platform for your business logic, with which it will perform well indeed.

Windows Server 2003 Enterprise Edition

This edition of the Windows Server 2003 family, named the Enterprise Edition, is the next version of Windows 2000 Advanced Server, and you probably recognize the name from the Windows NT 4.0 Enterprise Server.

The Enterprise Edition offers many scalability and availability features. First of all, it's provided for both the 32-bit and the 64-bit processor architectures, giving it optimal flexibility and scalability. Besides this, it includes Network Load Balancing as well as Microsoft Cluster Service. Scaling up is possible for as many as eight CPUs. The 32-bit version can handle 32GB of RAM, whereas the 64-bit manages 64GB.

You can use this edition as a web server in one of your clusters if you want, but we recommend it as a database, application, or messaging server. We feel it would be overkill to use it as a web server, given all its features.

You can also cluster this edition in an eight-node cluster, which further stresses the use of it as something other than a web server.

Windows Server 2003 Datacenter Edition

When you need the highest level of scalability, availability, and reliability, Microsoft offers the Datacenter Edition. On this platform you can, without worry, deploy your mission-critical applications and databases. This version offers everything the Enterprise Edition does, only much more of it. It includes Network Load Balancing and Microsoft Cluster Service, and, like the Enterprise Edition, it is also available in a 64-bit version. So far nothing new, but when it comes to scaling up, the Datacenter Edition provides you with 32-way SMP. The 32-bit version manages at most 64GB of RAM, and if that is not enough for you, the 64-bit version handles 512GB.

As you can see here, this is a powerful platform best suited for when you need scalability and availability. Like the Windows 2000 Datacenter Server, it can only be purchased through the Windows Datacenter Program and the OEMs participating in it.

When you build an application that has high demands on availability and needs a stable and well-performing database, the Datacenter is the platform of choice. But it comes with a high price tag, so you need to consider your application demands carefully before running out and getting this system. It could be that the Enterprise Edition offers everything you need instead.

Table 2-2 presents an overview of the different Windows Server 2003 editions.

Table 2-2. *Overview of the Feature Set of the Windows Server 2003 Family*

	Web Edition	Standard Edition	Enterprise Edition 32/64	Datacenter Edition Feature 32/64
Hot-add memory*			X/X	X/X
RAM	2GB	4GB	32GB/64GB	64GB/512GB
SMP	2	4 Way	8 Way/8 Way	32 Way/32 Way
NLB	X	X	X/X	X/X
MSCS			X/X	X/X
.NET Framework	X	X	X/X	X/X
IIS 6.0	X	X	X/X	X/X
ASP.NET	X	X	X/X	X/X
UDDI		X	X/X	X/X

* Depending on OEM hardware

To summarize all this information, Table 2-3 shows our recommended platform for different parts of a scalable application design.

Table 2-3. *Recommended Use of Microsoft Operating Systems in a Multitier Application*

Web Server	Business Logic	Data Layer
W2K Server with Application Center	W2K Server, W2K Advanced Server	W2K Advanced Server, W2K Datacenter Server
Windows Server 2003 Web Edition	Windows Server 2003 Standard Edition, Windows Server 2003 Enterprise Edition	Windows Server 2003 Enterprise Edition, Windows Server 2003 Datacenter Edition

We prefer the Windows Server 2003 family and our experience over the last years has been that this is the right way to go. But many companies still use Windows 2000 Server, so we need to take these editions into account as well. As we have been participating in the official Microsoft beta program for Windows Server 2003 since beta 1, our own servers have been running Windows Server 2003 exclusively in various forms since then. We find them stable and reliable so far, and our testing has shown a great performance increase in our applications, as we will demonstrate in Chapter 10.

Windows Server System

Let's now take a look at the three remaining parts of the Windows Server System:

- Operations infrastructure

- Applications infrastructure

- Information worker infrastructure

As we can see, Microsoft tries to cover all aspects of the IT world, not leaving much room for anyone else to be a part of the process. It doesn't have to be this way, but many companies standardize on a specific platform and then it's easy to get hooked. We have discovered that many of the parts of Windows Server System can help us write better applications, but we definitely don't only use Microsoft products. The focus of the book is the Microsoft way, however, so we will not discuss other platforms or products here.

Before we take a look at some of the individual products we will discuss these concepts a bit. Let us start with operations infrastructure.

Operations Infrastructure

Here's where we find the administrators tools. Everything from the tools that help people maintain the company network to tools for managing security and resources can be found here. According to Microsoft, the range of products they include promotes operational efficiencies through simplified deployments, management, and security. One of their goals has been to provide these things, all while reducing IT infrastructure costs at the same time. You can be the judge as to whether they've succeeded. Some of our customers and colleagues do use these tools and are happy with them, so some truth to these marketing words might exist after all. The products included here are as follows:

- Internet Security and Acceleration Server (ISA)

- Systems Management Server (SMS)

- Microsoft Operations Manager (MOM)

- Storage Server

- Data Protection Server

- Microsoft Identity Integration Server

- Virtual Server

- Application Center

A large focus for Microsoft has been on helping enterprises utilize their servers better by consolidating them. You should also know that it's possible to automate tasks so that management can be more cost-effective. We have also discovered the use of MOM in our application development, but we will tell you more about this later.

Application Infrastructure

Now we're going to look at application infrastructure. As you know after reading this far, the world is a complex, interoperable place and not many applications remain lonely islands anymore. In a service-oriented environment we need tools and extra help to make all this easier to handle. We can no longer rely only on development tools like Visual Studio when we develop applications and services. We need a platform that eases integration with not only a Windows platform but also with UNIX, Linux, and others. The application infrastructure servers are meant to be our saviour for these tasks, and these products are all part of this concept.

- SQL Server

- BizTalk Server

- Commerce Server

- Host Integration Server

- Speech Server

Information Worker Infrastructure

The third part of Windows Server System is the information worker infrastructure. These tools are meant to help the information worker (you know who this is, don't you? You, me, and basically everybody else are included here) get through the day while also being more productive. The information worker infrastructure will help us communicate better and collaborate with others without bothering about how we will accomplish this. The tools here include:

- Exchange Server

- Microsoft Office Live Communication Server

- Content Management Server

- Project Server

- Sharepoint Portal Server

Visual Studio

As you can see from Figure 2-1, Visual Studio runs through the whole of the Windows Server System. It runs all the way from the Windows platform to the information worker's applications (MS Office and such). With its help, we can develop our applications and services in an easy way, using a graphical interface. We won't discuss Visual Studio in this chapter at all, but I'll assume you all are familiar with this tool.

Next, we will cover some of these servers in Windows Server System. Although not all of them have something to do with scalability issues, we feel that it is essential to have knowledge about them when designing a Microsoft solution, since they can be a great help to you when you're designing and building applications. This part of the chapter is only an introduction to these servers. Later in this book you get a chance to take a closer look at a few of them: we have left the others out of our discussions because they do not directly affect the design of a scalable .NET application.

Microsoft Application Center Server

Because this is Microsoft's tool for deploying and managing highly available web applications, you'll find this server is useful for you. So useful, actually, that we have dedicated much of Chapter 6 to it. Please refer to this chapter for more information.

Microsoft BizTalk Server

Most large enterprises have made huge investments in their legacy systems. These could be one of many kinds, such as CRM, SAP, and so on. These investments make it hard to replace these systems if new functionality is required, and it is usually quite expensive to add new features to them. We have noticed an increase in requests for help on integrating new systems with these existing legacy systems. We have also noted that the demands for integration with other enterprises and customers have increased. To help you easily integrate and automate business processes, Microsoft has developed the BizTalk Server—and you do not have to be a programmer to use many of its features. This makes it quite effortless for nonprogrammers to develop business processes in an easy-to-use graphical interface and then let the developers implement them.

Microsoft Commerce Server

Online businesses seem to be ever increasing. More and more possibilities exist for leveraging the business around the world, and the time when business was local are over for many companies. Not only large enterprises, but also small and medium-sized companies are finding a new market globally. This puts high demands on people who have the skills to engage and manage a global network of customers and trading partners. Suddenly, not only do you have to worry about local currency, but you have to do business transactions in multiple currencies and languages. All of this means that your business decisions have to be smarter, and more carefully considered, if you want your company to prosper.

Microsoft Commerce Server is a set of tools that can help you improve your online business. Commerce Server consists of five integrated systems:

- Business analytics system

- Profiling system

- Product catalog system

- Targeting system

- Business processing pipeline system

Commerce Server systems, Business Desk, Commerce Server Manager, and the Commerce Server database are preconfigured and packaged in *solution sites*, which developers can use as a starting point for building a custom site and for integrating third-party applications.

Figure 2-5 shows the internal relations between these five systems. You can also see how these systems interact with databases and administrative tools.

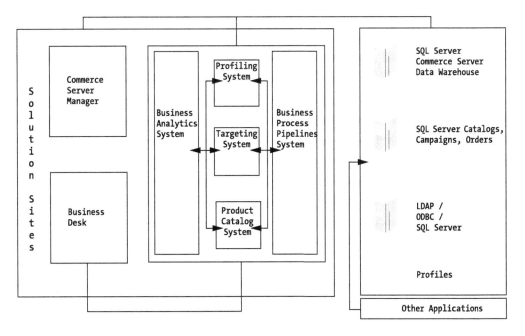

Figure 2-5. *An overview of the internal relations in Commerce Server*

Business Analytics System

With an online business, you often don't get to meet your customer in person. This means that you miss a lot that a salesperson in a store takes for granted. The personal interaction with the customer in a store makes it possible to see purchasing patterns easier. It's also an immediate way to find out which campaigns give the best sales result, since the salesperson is standing in the midst of it, while it's happening. The customer can also tell the salesperson directly what he or she needs, or would buy, if a store doesn't have it in stock. The salesperson can also get valuable feedback from demonstrating upcoming products, and use that information to decide what to carry next.

In the online world, this isn't so easy to get a grip on. The Business Analytics System helps you deliver more effective customer and partner interaction, and also drive increased revenue through sophisticated analysis and predictive business intelligence tools. With these tools, you hopefully can catch new trends and market opportunities, and hence make the correct decisions with the information given.

Profiling System

One important issue in your business is making your customers feel welcome to your web site. Since you don't meet the customer in person, you need to find other ways to attract them. You can do this by personalizing your web pages to better suit your customers' and partners' needs. Commerce Server's Profiling System gives you a foundation for personalization across your online business. You can create customer-specific product catalogs, pricing, and business processing, as well as targeted merchandising and advertising campaigns. Hopefully all this makes your customers feel welcome and special, which gives you a better platform for doing good business.

Product Catalog System

Based on your Profiling System, you can tailor your product categories for different customers. Different customers get different discounts based on rules you set up, and this has to be reflected in your product catalog as they browse through it.

The search capabilities must also be great, or you will definitely lose your customer. The Commerce Server Product Catalog System helps you with providing the catalog with prices in different currencies, and by displaying product details in various languages—all, of course, based on the Profiling System.

Targeting System

You often need to target your merchandising campaigns so that they attract the intended buyer. Relevant content must also be displayed for visitors based on their profile and current context in the business process. Personalized e-mails are often a vital part of online business, and you must have ways to quickly and easily compose them. The marketing campaigns, e-mails, and content must also be displayed in the correct language, so that your Swedish-speaking customers will not receive content in French, for example.

This is where the Targeting System comes into the picture. With the help of its tools, you can achieve this a little easier than without Commerce Server.

Business Processing Pipelines System

When your customers have made a purchasing decision and want to place an order, you need business processes that fit your own business. By providing a series of extensible, prebuilt pipelines that manage the order process and other processes, as well as providing possibilities to interoperate with backend systems via a tight Microsoft BizTalk integration, the Business Processing Pipelines System can be a valuable tool for developing your business. And, if the pre-built pipelines aren't adequate, you can either create new ones or extend the existing ones.

Management

Different management tools are supplied with Commerce Server. The Business Desk is used to update catalogs, target content to users and organizations, and analyze site usage and productivity. This tool is primarily intended for business managers, to allow them to work with Commerce Server systems.

Administrators, on the other hand, primarily use the Commerce Server Manager, through which they can configure system resources and manage applications, databases, and servers.

Scalability

As you can see, Commerce Server does not help you in enhancing scalability. Some of my colleagues also have found that the sites created with Commerce Server have had problems handling heavy loads as well. This may have changed in the latest edition, but we haven't found any of our customers willing to try it, so we do not know if this is true in real life or not. Commerce Server can fully take advantage of a Windows Datacenter Server running up to 32 CPUs per server. It also supports Network Load Balancing, which means it is possible to use in a web farm. You can even use it with Microsoft Cluster Service. All this enables you to build applications for maximum scalability and availability even though the product in it self might not allow it.

Development

Commerce Server is built on .NET technology. It supports the .NET Framework as well as ASP.NET. The server integrates with Visual Studio .NET, giving the developer a more unified and familiar user interface. Commerce Server now also supports XML web services to help you enhance your online business solution further.

But keep in mind that it is also backward compatible, so you don't have to take the leap to .NET yet if you choose not to, even though we strongly suggest you consider this if you haven't done so already.

Microsoft Content Management Server

Web content management is important in any successful online business today. It must be easy to create, publish, and manage the content provided on your sites. This process must never be more difficult than providing the content itself. If it is, too much energy, time, and money will be spent on administration, and your content might suffer as a result of this. And, of course, if your content does not meet a high level of quality, visitors and potential customers might go somewhere else.

A few content management tools are available on the market today, especially for the Windows market. Microsoft Content Management Server (CMS) is one, and EPiServer from ElektroPost is another. In our company we use EPiServer for most projects, but CMS has its benefits as well. CMS integrates smoothly with Commerce Server, Sharepoint Portal Server, and Visual Studio, which gives it an advantage over its competitors, and might be a good choice if you are running an all-Microsoft environment.

The whole process of content management is very important, though. In Chapter 5, we take a closer look at some of the tools you can use, both for deciding when content management is needed, and which tool suits your solution the best.

Microsoft Exchange Server

Microsoft Exchange Server is a product that we will not look into especially deeply in this book. It does not enhance scalability or availability in any way, so you do not have to consider it in the design of a scalable .NET application. Nevertheless, it's important for you to be aware of this product.

Exchange Server is Microsoft's messaging server, and as such it can be used in many solutions. We have not been big fans of Exchange Server in its earlier versions, but after getting feedback from friends and partners who have been using Exchange 2000 for a while now, we must say we've been feeling a whole lot better about it lately.

Exchange Server integrates into Active Directory, making it simpler to administer since you do not have to keep redundant user databases. But, as Active Directory is necessary for Exchange Server to install, you'll need to plan the deployment thoroughly before rolling it out. If you, for instance, use a catalog service other than Active Directory, you must plan deployment of Active Directory at the same time as the planning of Exchange Server deployment.

You can design a scalable and reliable communications platform, including e-mail, scheduling, online conferencing, and instant messaging, using almost all Microsoft technology if you want. Figure 2-6 shows a scenario integrating Exchange Server with Active Directory, Microsoft ISA Server, and Microsoft Mobile Information Server.

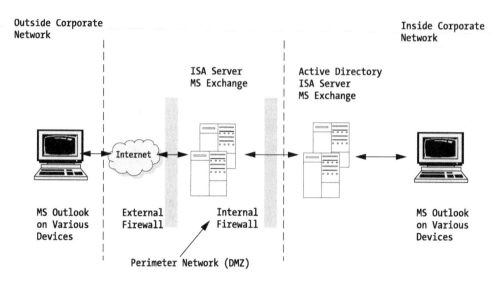

Figure 2-6. *An integrated communications platform using Microsoft technology*

The solution described shows how users in or out of the office can connect to the messaging server using different devices.

Although it might look attractive to be able to integrate so many servers with each other, you should be cautious. You must consider whether it's really such a good idea to leave so much of the infrastructure in the hands of a sole software supplier. The answer to this is not an easy one to give. This is an issue that must be considered internally in an organization, well before a decision is made. There are pros and cons to every solution, and finding the one with the most benefits is tricky. We leave the subject for now, but it will keep coming up here and there throughout this book.

Host Integration Server

Integration is the name of the game these days, as we have stated earlier. Host Integration Server will not be discussed in much detail here, but it is nonetheless a great tool to have on hand on many occasions.

Host Integration Server helps in extending Microsoft Windows to other systems by providing application, data, and network integration. If you have invested a lot of money and resources in your existing infrastructure, you won't want to have done so in vain just because you might want to use newer techniques. Host Integration Server helps you preserve the existing infrastructure, while still letting you quickly adapt to new business opportunities.

This server supports a wide variety of network protocols and network service types. It can offer you great support in accessing various data sources on different platforms like mainframes, UNIX, AS/400, or Windows. You can also integrate Microsoft Transaction Server and COM+ with IBM's CICS or IMS, giving you two-phase commit between platforms.

Host Integration Server offers programmatic access to its features, as well as a MMC-based interface, to suit your needs. When you develop new applications that extend the features of legacy systems, Host Integration Server can be of great help to you by simplifying your integration difficulties.

Microsoft Internet Security and Acceleration (ISA) Server

At first glance, the ISA Server might look like a tool for system administrators only. But if you take a closer look at it, you soon find out that it has some features that help you build your web solutions as well.

ISA Server consists of two parts that together provide secure, fast, and manageable Internet connectivity. What ISA Server offers is integration between an extensible, multilayer enterprise firewall and a scalable web cache. Figure 2-7, a subset of Figure 2-6, shows how the ISA Server in this scenario is placed between the internal and the external firewall. It is not a replacement of firewall hardware, but an addition to security, which is important in your solutions.

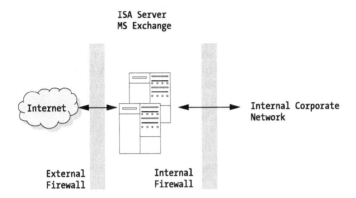

Figure 2-7. *The placement of ISA Server between an external and an internal firewall extends the security provided by the firewall hardware.*

ISA Server helps you in controlling access to, and the monitoring of, your network. If it discovers unauthorized access attempts, or other attacks of the network, it alerts the system administrators so they can respond quickly. The heightened security this offers is something your scalable applications always can benefit from, at least if it does not degrade performance in a drastic way. Since ISA Server scales both up and out, it should be possible to overcome these issues.

The web cache saves network bandwidth by storing and serving locally cached web content to your internal users. This way, requests for Internet web pages that are popular (for instance, news site pages) do not have to travel outside your external firewall, because ISA Server sends the cached page back to the client issuing the request. Some benefits of this are it is faster than fetching the page on the Internet, and you do not have to purchase an unnecessary amount of bandwidth.

Microsoft Identity and Integration Server

In many projects we have seen that user information, as well as resource information from all over the company network, is needed for a new application. This information can be used for logging on to web sites and other applications and is often spread across numerous systems.

For an application, like a web application, it can be great setting up an ADAM (Active Directory Application Mode) and using that to fetch user credentials. The problem is that it takes time and money to manually collect this information from the company information directory (Active Directory, Novell eDirectory, IBM Directory Server, or where ever it may reside). Sure you can script the extraction and insertion if you want, but what happens if information changes after the retrieval? We need a way of keeping the information in our application directory up to date so that it reflects the actual data in the company.

Imagine if our application uses the username and password a user logs onto the network with to also log in to our application. If the user changes her network password, she no longer can log onto the ADAM directory we use. We need a way to avoid this without it taking too much of management's time and effort.

What Is It?

The Microsoft Identity Information Server (MIIS) is here to help us solve these kinds of problems. MIIS is a centralized service that stores identity information from many directories. MIIS uses SQL Server 2000 database to store its information.

It also integrates the information in its storage area so that it will be easier to retrieve. Microsoft has had the intention of letting MIIS provide a unified view of identity information about users, applications, and network resources. It can also be used to synchronize this information between the data sources.

There are currently two versions available to us:

- MIIS 2003 SP1, Enterprise Edition

- MIIS Feature Pack 1a for Microsoft Windows Server Active Directory

The major difference between these two is that the Enterprise edition can synchronize between heterogeneous directories and non-directories (like Lotus Notes and Domino) identity stores while the Feature pack only synchronizes with Microsoft identity stores. The Enterprise Edition also costs money, which the Feature Pack does not. Many people think it costs too much, so the implementations have been limited so far. Some of our customers have backed out after hearing the cost associated with it, and have chosen another solution.

What Can It Do?

The MIIS is not solely developed for the benefit of developers but its main target is obviously administrators. So, besides being able to synchronize MIIS also can be used to

- provision and de-provision accounts. When a user starts working at the company and is being created as an employee in the human resource system, that event can trigger a chain that also creates his or her e-mail account, network account, and so on. Then, when an employee leaves the company we can automatically de-provision his account from all systems.

- synchronize and manage passwords. By offering a web-based interface, both administrators and users can manage passwords from a web interface. With this self-service, users do not have to trouble the help desk with simple tasks like resetting or changing their passwords. The help desk also only needs one application to reset or change passwords through all systems in the network.

- manage groups and distribution lists. MIIS can be used to create groups or distribution lists containing users and resources based on, let's say, organizational attributes (job function, office location, and so on). MIIS can also be used to synchronize these between multiple systems.

How does it work? Well the identity information is collected from the connected data sources with the help of management agents. In Figure 2-8 we can see that these agents store this information in the connector space. Here, the information from a data source is gathered as a connector space objects or CSEntry objects as they are also called. The *connector space* is a staging area basically, containing representations of objects from a connected data source. MIIS uses this information to be able to determine what has changed in the data source and then stage incoming changes.

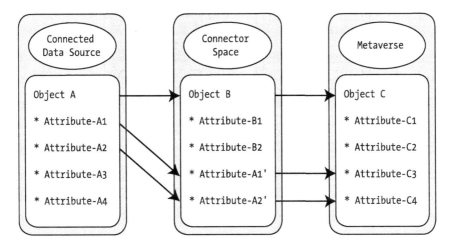

Figure 2-8. *How connected data sources are mapped via the connector space to an MVEntry in the metaverse*

These objects are then mapped to objects called *MVEntry*, in the metaverse. The *metaverse* is a storage area containing aggregated identity information from numerous data sources. This means that information about a user can be collected and updated from many data sources and mapped to one single object in the metaverse (see Figure 2-9).

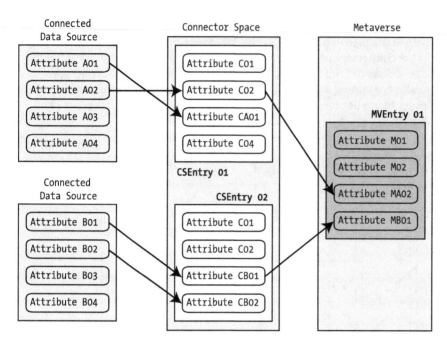

Figure 2-9. *Two connected data sources provide attributes to one object in the metaverse*

All changes from one system to an MVEntry object are then propagated to all the data stores that provided the information in the first place. When an MVEntry has changed, these changes are first propagated to the CSEntry objects. From here they are exported to the connected data sources. If the data source is unavailable at the moment of update, the information is not lost, but is still kept in the CSEntry object and can easily be propagated when the source is back online. This process helps keep all data sources up to date without management efforts.

If you want to learn more about MIIS please refer to the document "Essential concepts for Microsoft Identity Integration Server 2003" available at http://www.microsoft.com/technet/prodtechnol/miis/default.mspx.

Microsoft Operations Manager (MOM)

As we all know, outages in an application cost a lot of time and money. IT professionals must investigate what has happened and find a solution to the problem. The end users can't perform their work during this time and this all adds to the final cost of the problem. As always, time is money, hence the administrators need great tools to help them out. They need the means to catch potential errors before they happen, and if they still do occur, they need tools to help them find the best solution fast, so that the effects of the error can be minimized.

This means that IT professionals need tools to help them monitor different systems, probably based on the role of the system. It doesn't help, however, to only to have monitoring. When specific events occur they need to be forwarded as alerts to the correct person(s) so that they can react. Having such help, administrators can determine the importance of monitoring events and also quickly find their root cause. This way the administrators can also decide which event needs attention first so that they don't fix a subordinate event before the really important one and also so that they can avoid making problems more severe than they have to be.

There are different tools available on the market to help out with these tasks. Microsoft has its own, called Microsoft Operations Manager (MOM). This has now reached version 2005, which was just released as we're writing this.

Overview

MOM has been developed to solve the problems described previously. Microsoft even has the slogan "Get knowledge to avoid the avoidable" attached to their product, so you can see that they set their aim high. Let's take a look at the features of MOM before I explain why we as architects and developers also benefit from this product.

MOM is used to primarily identify issues faster. It does so by monitoring events and based on certain rules generate alerts and solutions to alerts so that administrators can take the correct decision faster. The solutions are fetched from an extensive knowledge database that comes with the various *management packs* that can be added to MOM.

Management Packs

Management packs are central concepts in MOM. They are made for specific products or servers like SQL Server, Exchange Server, or Windows Server, just to mention a few. These packs contain predefined threshold values for monitoring, rules for monitoring, and also a knowledge base for how to resolve issues. You can also create management packs yourself or add additional rules, thresholds, or resolutions to existing packs.

The resolutions in the knowledgebase are linked to an alert that helps the operator by being immediately available when an alert occurs. But to ease the burden of the operator, the packs also include predefined scripts that can be triggered automatically, or by an operator, and therefore resolve an issue directly. If there is a need the operator can add his or her own scripts for other alerts.

Consoles

To identify issues earlier in the process, MOM offers different user interfaces based on the role of the administrator. The *administrative console* is aimed at those people managing MOM itself. That is, the administrative console supports optimization, installation and all other aspects of maintaining MOM. The *operator console* (see Figure 2-10) can be used if you need to identify issues and perform monitoring tasks. Here we also see the alerts generated by the monitored applications or servers.

Figure 2-10. *A screenshot from a production environment (hence the blurred names in some places) showing the MOM Operator Console*

Since operators not always are sitting in front of a system with the operator console installed there also is a *web console* available, where summary information, alerts and events are shown. There is also a fourth console, the *reporting console*, used for, that's right, reports. The reports here are predefined, but if you have skills with the Visual Studio environment you can create your own custom reports for this.

Data

Let us take a look at what kind of data MOM can handle. Four kinds of data can be spotted and are stored in the MOM database:

- Event data

- Performance data

- Alert data

- Discovery data

Event data is the data from the event logs of the computers monitored. The logs include the application log, the security log, and the system log, as we all probably recognize from our own computer. MOM collects this data and can be used as additional information for trouble shooting, for generating reports, and to view operational data and so on.

Performance data comes from various sources, like performance counters and Windows Management Instrumentation (WMI). This data can be used by the operator in different formats from the operator console. They are also used to identify crossings of critical thresholds, so that these problems can be discovered quickly and actions taken immediately.

Alert data contains information about a detected problem. If, for instance, a threshold crossing is discovered, and an alert is generated, lots of information about the alert is gathered. Here we can find information about the problem (name and description for instance), the application or server that generated the alert, the severity of the problem, how many times it has been reported, and basically everything a user needs to know about the health of the managed computer(s). This information is updated as MOM continuously gathers information about the alert.

Finally, we find *discovery data*. This isn't data that is directly available to the user, but rather the snapshots of entities discovered for a certain scope. We'll leave this, as it isn't interesting for us in this discussion.

You might be asking yourself why we're telling you all this information right now. Well, let's say we have a custom application running critical processing in our company. This can be a web application, Windows application, or a distributed application of some kind. Wouldn't you like to have the opportunity to monitor this as well and get alerts when certain events occur? We certainly would. And guess what? We can: using the Microsoft Enterprise Instrumentation Framework (EIF). There is also another tool which we'll discuss in a while but we'll focus on EIF right now.

Note Instrumentation is about the same as tracing, some might say. That's true, but it's also much more at the same time. Nick Weinholt in the white paper "Microsoft Enterprise Instrumentation Framework" uses an analogy of the dials and displays in cars, which I like very much. These instruments provide the driver with the capability to monitor the health of a vehicle. These instruments can give you indications for when an action from the driver is required, such as "Hey you need to fill my gas tank, driver!" They can also give basic diagnostic output in case of a breakdown. For instance, if the driver ignores the low fuel warning, the vehicle definitely will let him or her know this is the cause when the vehicle stops. Instrumentation is supposed to do the same thing for system engineers and allows them to take correct actions so that an application (or server) can operate in a robust manner. MOM anyone?

Enterprise Instrumentation Framework

The EIF has enabled us as developers and architects to plan and implement custom instrumentation in our applications. The framework is a unified API that uses functions already located in the Windows operating system. We have the options to handle events, logging, and tracing, among other things. IT professionals can then use existing monitoring tools, like MOM, to diagnose applications.

Note Please note that we can use other tools than MOM for this as well.

Wait a minute! Aren't there options in the .NET Framework for this already? Yes there are. The System.Diagnostic.Trace class can be used allowing developers to output trace messages which in their turn can be consumed by trace listeners. The DefaultTraceListener routes the output of System.Diagnostic.Trace to Debugger.Log and the Win32 OutputDebugString function.

These functions are good enough when we have a local application(s). They are not good enough, however, when it comes to the instrumentation of distributed applications, since they lack a lot of the features necessary to trace the request flow through a tiered application or to filter events by categories. There also isn't enough structured error information provided. We could probably write our own TraceListener to solve this, but why do that if there is a framework handling this already?

EIF provides an event schema that can be used to separate the various types of events that a system can generate. It can also augment information about events with information about security contexts, process, and thread information.

Remember that the use of .NET Trace functionality doesn't necessarily exclude the use of EIF, or the other way around, and that they can coexist and cooperate.

Let's take a look at some of the parts of EIF. The first we will look at are *event sinks*, which are the big parts of EIF. These are destination stores for event data. There are three defined:

- WMI. This one should only be used for severe, infrequent, or very significant events. The reason for this is that the WMI event sink is rather slow—in fact, it's the slowest of the three. The outputs of WMI are stored by EIF in the catalogue \Windows\system32\ wbem, which is created when you install EIF. A management application like MOM can be used to consume events from the WMI Event sink.

- Windows Event Trace. This is by far the fastest event sink available. This sink writes data to a binary log file. The information can then be viewed either with a viewer supplied by EIF or by a custom viewer. You could, for instance, easily write an ASP.NET application displaying this data. The Windows Event Trace uses a Windows Service called Windows Trace Session Manager to handle its data and buffer it to hard disk. Be aware that if this service is not started first, the output will be written directly to disk. This is much slower than using the service, since the Windows Trace Session Manager uses the RAM to store information before writing to disk.

- Windows Event Log. This event sink is another reason to use MOM. It is slower than the event trace but not as slow as WMI. Still be selective when choosing events written to this sink, since flooding the event log is not particularly popular with the IT Professionals. The Event Log sink can write events to local as well as remote event logs. Since MOM can collect information from the event logs on remote machines it can be used to retrieve information from this log.

Next thing we will look at are the *event sources*. An event is always raised from a specific event source. This can be an application or part of an application. We can define our own source(s) and associate them with a specific event in EIF giving us opportunity to filter output to a particular event sink based on the source of the event. EIF supports for example the following three event sources:

- SoftwareElement event source

- Application event source

- Request event source

The last part we will look at is the *event schema*, which is the schema defining the sets of events an application can raise. The schemas can be of two types: *standard*, which is generated by the developer, such as errors, audits and diagnostic trace events, or *internal*, meaning fired by EIF itself. We can extend the standard event schema so that we can create our own events.

Now we can see that by using EIF to write instrumentation into our own custom application we can raise events that MOM can discover and use. This way, our administrators can monitor our applications, just like any other server or application. This gives us a great way to catch performance and scalability issues early.

But we mentioned there was another tool as well. We'll look at that now.

Logging and Instrumentation Application Block

Microsoft provides a set of application blocks aimed at making life easier for developers. These are ready-made building blocks that you can just add to your project(s) and that will take away much of the boring coding you have to do. These blocks are parts of the patterns & practices Enterprise Library and can be downloaded from the Microsoft web site. In Chapter 5 we'll show you more about most kinds of blocks and how they can make your coding simpler.

One of these application blocks is an updated version of the Logging Application Block, previously available, but now called Logging and Instrumentation Application Block. It also includes functionality from the Exception Management Application Block as well. By using this application block in our applications, we can incorporate standard logging and instrumentation in a simple way. It gives us opportunity to log events to a number of different recipients such as the event log, e-mails, databases, message queues, files, or WMI. As you might now understand, this gives MOM a chance to catch these events as well. In Figure 2-11 we can see an overview of how it works internally. We won't discuss this further here, but if you are interested please look at the product documentation available with the download of the application block.

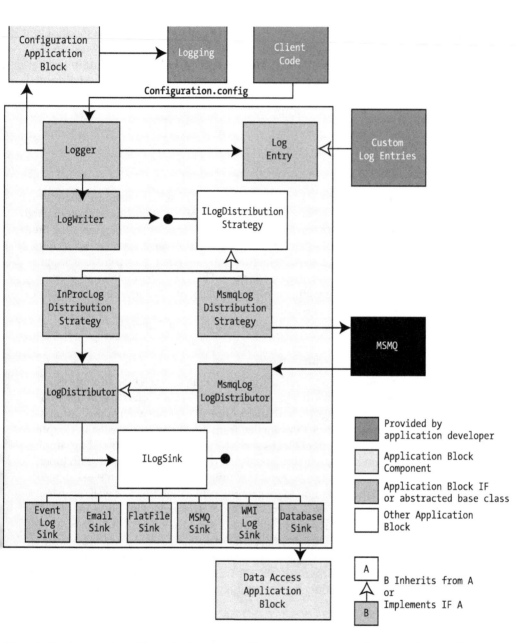

Figure 2-11. *An overview of how the Logging and Instrumentation Application Block works internally*

One of the benefits of the Logging and Instrumentation Application Block is that it makes EIF a tad superfluous. We basically can do the same with this application block as we can with EIF. We also get some new features like an e-mail event sink, support for a database event sink (instead of a specific SQL Server event sink which was available in earlier application blocks), and also the option to configure formatters through the Enterprise Library Configuration Console (see Figure 2-12).

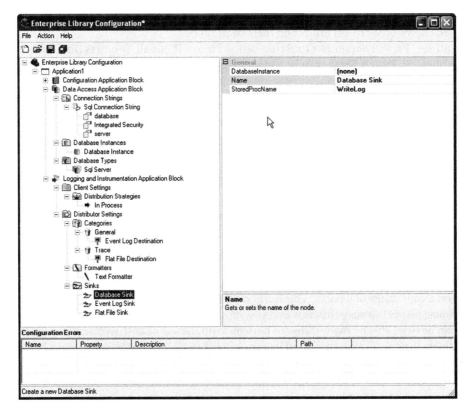

Figure 2-12. *Screenshot from an Enterprise Library Configuration Console*

Whether we choose EIF or the Logging and Instrumentation Application Block is really a matter of taste. So far, we've really only had the chance to try out EIF in real projects—however we have used some of the old application blocks in projects and they also work fine, so there is little doubt that this application block should meet their set standards. This means that the field is pretty much open for any of the two you'd like. Our suggestion is that you try them out in a test environment and then decide in which situations you think they fit.

You now see that we have several ways of instrumenting proprietary applications. You can write management packs for MOM yourself, containing information about what to monitor, threshold values, and actions to take when various alerts occur in our own applications. This is really useful for mission-critical applications especially in a large enterprise environment.

Microsoft Project Server

If you've been doing project management, you know how important it is to be cost-effective and complete your projects in a timely manner. You also know that you need to deliver projects that reach the goals that are set up for them. You've probably used Microsoft Project as a tool to help you sort the various tasks, roles, and steps included in a project.

Microsoft Project Server lets an organization better manage its projects, and share best practices between project teams. The web-based access to Project Server allows entire project teams to stay informed of the latest news about the projects they participate in. This way, the team members can update, view, and analyze project information, without having to have locally installed copies of Microsoft Project on their computers.

As you can see, Project Server is a tool that can aid most, if not all, projects (including your scalable ones). So Project Server can be a great help in organizing your project and letting you deliver what you set out to deliver, without spending all your effort on administration.

Mobile Information Server

One of Microsoft's goals is about bringing information together anytime, anyplace, and on any device. This is not as farfetched as many goals can be, if you think about it. If you are like many people nowadays, you take a PDA, mobile phone, and other mobile devices with you wherever you go. When you are on business trips, you still want to be able to reach your calendars and e-mail. In the past, this kind of connectivity has been a bit of a problem, but recently this has become as easy as picking up the mobile phone. The Mobile Information Server lets you securely gain access to your e-mail, contacts, calendar, tasks, or intranet business applications no matter what device you use. (We are sure there are exceptions to this, but it sounds impressive, does it not?)

By using the Mobile Information Server infrastructure, you can build in access to your applications on a wide range of devices. This is a good thing, and, as you will see in Chapters 5 and 9 of this book, one of our suggestions is that you should design and build your applications so that they can be reachable by many different devices. With the use of XML web services, you can build business logic that can be accessed by various clients, giving you flexibility and a better reuse of the code you have written.

Microsoft Sharepoint Portal Server

In a large enterprise, it's important to share knowledge and information. It is also important to find the correct information when you need it. If you have a good system for this, employee productivity can increase.

By using a web portal, you can create a central access point to all the information available in your organization. Access to files, documents, databases, and so on can be integrated with document management services and search capabilities. It's often as important for effective document handling to keep track of versioning as it is to keep track of code versions. So, if the tool offers good document management capabilities, you should be happy.

A large global medical company is just now, in early 2005, on the verge of taking the final step towards a single portal for all sites across the globe. When a company with well over 50,000 employers chooses to do such an investment, it's really worth considering for you and your (probably) much smaller projects. The company is aware that there are many obstacles in the way of realizing this plan, but they are determined to succeed.

Using Sharepoint Portal Server, you can aggregate information from different data sources into one convenient place. From there, you can control access to the information so that only those you allow can update, view, or create information. It also lets you control versioning and provides extensive search capabilities.

One of our customers has been using Sharepoint Portal Server since it was in its first beta. The company was an early adopter of this Microsoft product, indeed! Their experience, so far, has been good, and now all of the company's documents and files, which were scattered all over the network, have been inventoried, and are accessible from a single starting point. Different departments have their own tailored sites, where they find information relevant to their line of work. The company also has the option to personalize the pages to better suit their individual way of working.

The implementation has not been a walk in the park for them, but now, when all the hard work has been done, it seems most of the customer's employees find that it has been worthwhile. You should, however, be aware of certain weaknesses in the Sharepoint Portal Server, in areas including deployment, backup and recovery, security, and integration with other servers in Windows Server System according to some of our customers. Based on all the feedback we've heard about this product so far, it will definitely be exciting to see what the future will offer.

Microsoft SQL Server

Databases are an unavoidable part of most applications. If you design and build a distributed application that can expect a large number of simultaneous users, it is essential that your database be able to handle the load.

SQL Server is Microsoft's relational database management system (RDBMS). It offers both XML support and the ability to query across the Internet by being fully web-enabled. You'll learn more about the options for providing reliable databases in Chapter 9 of this book. For now, it's sufficient to say that SQL Server fully takes advantage of Microsoft Cluster Service, which gives you great flexibility in providing a data source that is available for as much time as possible. By using Windows Datacenter Edition, you can reach as much as 99.999 percent uptime in your database system.

The current version of SQL Server is SQL Server 2000. The next generation of SQL Server, SQL Server 2005 is expected to be released by the time this book hits the stores, but as always, this may change. This version offers some exciting news for the world of databases that we will cover later in the book. In Chapter 9 we'll take a better look at SQL Server and Data Storage in general.

Summary

In this chapter we've focused on giving you an overview of the different servers offered by Microsoft. You have seen that the Windows Server family has been expanded, with a dedicated web server in the Windows Server 2003 editions, compared to the existing Windows 2000 family. You have also learned about the various servers available in the Windows Server System, and how they can fit into the design of a scalable .NET application.

The point of this chapter is to give you some ideas about where Microsoft's servers are best suited for use. Keep in mind that we don't say that they are necessarily the best choice at all times, but many times they are. Choosing which application to use is something you have to decide when you design your application, based on what you need to accomplish and on the standards that exist in your enterprise. As IT architects and system designers, we feel it is important to have knowledge about the technologies that Microsoft offers to be able to make the correct decisions early in the design process, and thereby avoid poor design that can affect performance and scalability in the end. Microsoft has shaped up in many areas, and nowadays offers good alternatives to what have been more or less de facto standards in the industry earlier. By using an infrastructure that seamlessly integrates many applications with each other, performance, scalability, and manageability gains can be made.

Microsoft has shown that SQL Server is a competitive database alternative, both in performance and price. These results are achieved by using clustering techniques described later in this book.

Our own testing also shows that web sites running ASP.NET on Windows Server 2003 display great performance gains compared to ASP.NET on Windows 2000. Others have made similar results as well.

What this all adds up to is that Microsoft definitely is on the right track, and more and more of our customers are interested in deploying large .NET applications. This means that if we as designers, architects, and developers do not know how, and with what, to build these applications, we might suddenly find ourselves run over by those who do.

CHAPTER 3

■■■

Cluster Techniques

A large organization uses business-critical systems every day. It is essential that e-commerce and other business applications are up and running 24 hours a day, all year round. This could be an expensive task for a company to perform, depending on the solution that it chooses. Therefore, small companies in the past may not have had the resources necessary to protect their applications the way they would like, whereas large companies may have had the resources, but preferred to spend their money on something more productive.

Microsoft has developed tools to solve these problems on industry-standard PC hardware. In the Microsoft Server family, *clustering technologies* have been introduced as an integrated part of the operating system. But what is clustering then? Well, *clustering* basically means linking individual servers with each other and coordinating the communication between them so they can perform common tasks. Easy, is it not? But what is it good for then? The answer, of course, is that if one server fails, clustering allows the other servers to pick up its tasks, so that the service performed by the cluster is disrupted as little as possible (and preferably not at all). Clustering techniques were first integrated in Windows 2000 Advanced Server and Datacenter Server and have been developed further in the .NET Server family.

Note But, you ask, couldn't you do this with Windows NT 4.0 also? Yes, you could, actually. In Windows NT Enterprise Edition, Microsoft introduced Microsoft Clustering Server (MSCS) and Windows Load Balancing Service (WLBS). But since then, these features have been developed further and also renamed to Microsoft Cluster Service (MSCS) and Network Load Balancing (NLB). Note the important but subtle difference in MSCS. Before it was called a server, but now it is called a service, meaning it has become an integrated part of the operating system and not an add-on product.

In this chapter, we're going to cover the basic architecture of clustering. We'll look at the two clustering techniques available in the Windows Server families, and the problems that they can solve. We will also cover Application Center, a tool Microsoft has developed to ease the management of a server cluster, and which also offers other helpful features. Let's start by looking at the problems that clustering is built to solve: scalability and availability.

What Clustering Does

So why is clustering significant? Imagine running a web site on only one server. If that server went down, the whole web site would stop working. A single server also has a limit on how many concurrent users it can handle before the load degrades performance so much that it becomes a real problem. Clustering has been developed to solve these two problems, which we call availability and scalability, respectively.

Availability

Availability means that a service, say an e-mail service, should be available for the users for as much time as possible. Imagine the anger among Hotmail users if the service went down for long periods of time, making it impossible for them to check their e-mail for long periods. That would not be so good for Hotmail's customers. To solve this, the administrators of the service must make sure that no single point of failure exists, because if it does and this point fails, the service also goes down. Often the solution is to distribute the service on several servers, in order to avoid this horror.

Scalability

The second problem is *scalability*, which means that if the workload on a service increases, you must be able to add more power to handle the increase. Imagine the e-mail service again. What if your e-mail service provider got so many new users that the provider's servers could not handle this new load and crashed? That would not be a dream scenario at all. To avoid this, providers often add more CPUs or more computers to the cluster to help carry the load.

Different Types of Clusters

There are two types of cluster techniques in the Microsoft server family. An administrator can use these two types separately, or in a combination. One doesn't rule out the use of the other—rather, both can work together to help an organization provide service for its partners and customers, or its internal employees. Windows clustering technologies include those discussed in the following sections.

Network Load Balancing (NLB)

NLB service balances the incoming Internet Protocol (IP) requests among a cluster of up to 32 servers. This technique helps in solving both the scalability and the availability problems. Several servers can share the workload, and if one server fails, the others handle its work without the users noticing. This technique is often used in large web farms, or terminal server farms, for instance. (You'll learn more about this technique later in this chapter in the "Network Load Balancing Overview" section.) NLB creates a virtual server, so that clients only have to know the name or the IP address of the virtual server, no matter which server actually handles their request.

Microsoft Cluster Service (MSCS)

This service helps primarily in solving the availability problem. A cluster service works by having two or more nodes in its cluster. If one node fails, the other (or others) takes over. This is known as *failover technique*. So, when do you use this? If you have a database like Microsoft SQL Server, you can use this technique to provide availability for the users and to make sure that the data has not been compromised during the failover. You can also use this with Microsoft Exchange Server. Again, the clients only have to know the IP address or the name of the cluster and they don't need to bother with the individual servers in the cluster.

■ **Note** Please note the difference in using the word *cluster* here as it might be confusing. Cluster is used as a term with both NLB and MSCS. The distinction between them, as we use them, is that clustering is something you do with MSCS and NLB is a cluster (collection) of several computers co-operating to solve load balancing issues.

Combining the Two

As mentioned earlier, these two technologies can work together. You can deploy NLB across the front-end web servers and use MSCS at the back end, to cluster the SQL Server that is providing the web pages with data (see Figure 3-1). This way, you make sure that both scalability and availability are as high as possible.

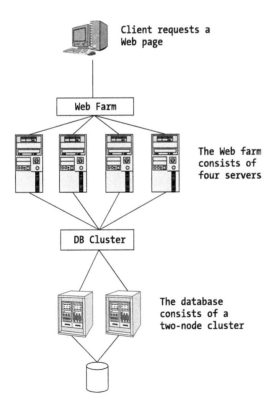

Figure 3-1. *Combining MSCS and NLB*

When to Use What

Now that you have learned the basics about clustering, you might be wondering when to use which technique. Table 3-1 helps you with your decision.

Table 3-1. *Overview of When Each Clustering Technique Is Suitable for Use*

Application	NLB	MSCS	Benefits
Web server farm	X		Enhances scalability and availability
Terminal server farm	X		Enhances scalability and availability
File/Print server		X	Enhances availability and data consistency after failover
Database server		X	Enhances availability and data consistency after failover
Messaging server		X	Enhances availability and data consistency after failover
E-commerce	X	X	Enhances scalability and availability

■**Note** But there is still one problem. With a cluster of 32 servers, or perhaps several clusters, how on earth do you, as the administrator, handle the maintenance of such a number of computers without going completely mad? What we're talking about here is manageability. Well, it might sound difficult, but luckily there are tools available to help you out. These tools present the cluster as one single point of control. And yes, here you definitely want a single point so as not to go crazy. Some of these tools are integrated in the operating system, but Microsoft has also developed a server, called Application Center, to help the administrator with these tasks. Application Center will be presented, along with others of these tools, later in this chapter.

Network Load Balancing Overview

As we mentioned already, one way to increase both scalability and availability is by using Network Load Balancing, which allows you to cluster up to 32 servers to respond to IP requests. This comes in handy when you need to distribute web client requests among a cluster of Internet Information Services (IIS) servers, for instance. The benefit of this is that the client trying to use the service only has to remember one IP address, and NLB hides all the rest of the servers in the background. If the server handling the client's request fails, another server takes its place, and the client should not notice the switch, as illustrated in Figure 3-2.

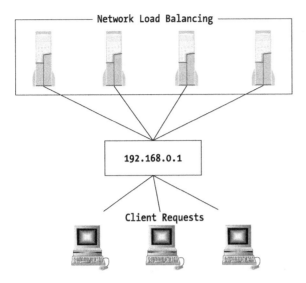

Figure 3-2. *Clients access only one IP address, while several servers actually perform the tasks in the background.*

Of course, you can use web servers other than IIS—NLB works with all the web servers on a Windows system. You can also use NLB with Terminal Service servers for client access, as well as many other applications, such as streaming media and virtual private networks (VPNs).

Concept

All servers in an NLB cluster host a driver called wlbs.sys. You might recognize the first part of the name from earlier in the chapter. WLBS is, of course, Windows Load Balancing Service, and it is a surviving Windows NT 4.0 driver. Or, at least, the name survived. This driver determines which server handles the incoming request by using a statistical mapping algorithm. The wlbs.sys driver runs between TCP/IP and the network driver, as you can see in Figure 3-3.

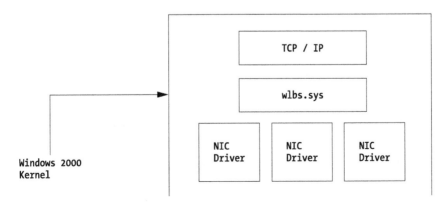

Figure 3-3. *The wlbs.sys driver runs between TCP/IP and the network interface card (NIC) drivers.*

The NLB driver executes in parallel on each member of the cluster. This is called *distributed software architecture* and it's great because it makes it possible to not have a single point of failure. In other words, Network Load Balancing will still function if one or more servers fail. Also worth mentioning here is that our application(s) will not run *x* times faster just because we add *x* number of servers to the NLB cluster. Instead, we're just making sure that at least one server is available to handle incoming requests. The benefit of having the NLB driver running on all servers in the cluster is purely fail-safe reasons. This way we don't have a single load balancing point that can fail.

The cluster has one primary IP address that all of the members can listen on. The cluster members need to be located on the same IP subnet so that they can detect network traffic destined for this IP address. You configure the primary IP address just like you configure any other IP address. But if several servers have the same IP address configured, wouldn't this generate an error? Normally it would, but NLB will take care of this for you, and you'll never get an error if you set it up properly.

You can also allow something called a *multi-homed NLB cluster*. This is simply a cluster with more than one primary IP address configured.

To handle the communication with a specific server in the cluster, all servers have a dedicated IP address. So, if for administrative purposes, you need to connect to a certain server, you just use the dedicated IP address instead of the primary IP address. Otherwise, you wouldn't know which server actually responded to you. This is also the reason why only one dedicated IP address can be configured for each cluster server. But keep in mind that all servers can have several primary IP addresses, as shown in Figure 3-4. Otherwise, you couldn't configure a multi-homed NLB cluster.

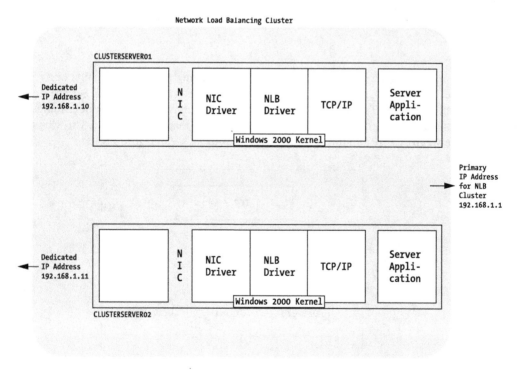

Figure 3-4. *Dedicated IP addresses and primary IP address*

All servers in a cluster send something called a *heartbeat message* to all other servers in the cluster. This happens once every second. If any server, during a five-second period, notices that another server has not sent its heartbeat message, the server will begin a process called *convergence*. This process determines which servers are still parts of the cluster.

Note If you'd like to know more about this, please see *MCSE Training Kit: Microsoft Windows 2000 Advanced Server Clustering Services* by Microsoft Corporation (Microsoft Press, 2001. ISBN: 0-7356-1293-5).

If you add a new server to the cluster, convergence takes place on the first server that notices the newcomer. This happens because the new server sends out a message that says "Hello. Here I am" and starts the convergence process.

Convergence takes about ten seconds to complete. If an incoming request was bound for a server that failed for some reason, the client might experience a ten-second delay before convergence finishes and another server handles the request.

Scalability

One of the advantages of NLB is that, as your applications need more server power, you don't have to shut down the cluster to increase it. You can simply add a new industry standard PC to the cluster and voilà: your power just increased!

But there is a limit to how many servers can be part of a cluster. But, though a cluster can only include up to 32 servers, this really isn't a problem. If your cluster should need more power than that, you can always use a cluster of clusters. That is, behind each of the 32 members in your first cluster you can hide another cluster. And behind every member of these clusters you can hide . . . we think you get the picture. This is a highly unusual set up, however. Though we haven't come across anyone using NLB this way, it's still nice to know that it can be done. What this all adds up to is that NLB is a great way to increase scalability. We know companies that don't need a large web farm most of the year. But when Christmas approaches, for example, the pressure on their web site increases and something has to be done. What these companies do is simply lease some servers from a leasing company, configure them for NLB, replicate all web content, and then insert the servers into the cluster. Now these companies are ready to handle all customers. When Christmas is over, the traffic decreases and the servers are returned to the leasing company.

Availability

As we have mentioned, NLB also helps with increasing availability. You might have many identical servers in the cluster, but it doesn't necessarily matter if one or more of your servers fail. As long as at least one of them is up and running, client requests will continue to be processed. Within ten seconds of the failure of a server, NLB will reroute the requests to a functioning server. But of course, if only one working server remains in the cluster and the load is big, the response times will increase. And, if the load increases even further, the last server might give up from sheer overload. On the other hand, the likelihood of all but one server crashing at the same time is small, so you really shouldn't lose any sleep over this issue.

Note Please note that the number of servers you have left in a cluster will affect response time. In fact, response time will increase if the load is too heavy for the remaining servers. In other words, problems may come long before only one server is left in the cluster.

Manageability

One question that arises if you have a large cluster is how to actually manage the servers. How can the administrator have time to do other aspects of her job when numerous servers need to be handled? If the administrator tries to administer all of these servers locally, there wouldn't be any time left in the day. But have no fear—several tools are available to make life easier. One such tool, which comes out of the box with Windows Server, is called wlbs.exe (recognize this, anyone?). This tool allows an administrator to remotely manage servers in an NLB cluster. Another tool, actually a server in itself, is the Application Center, which can be purchased from retailers everywhere. This product gives you great opportunities for cluster control as well as a lot of added value. Application Center is discussed in more detail in the "Application Center Overview" section later in this chapter.

Pros and Cons

Do you have to use a Microsoft solution to accomplish these benefits of load balancing? The answer is, of course not! There are other ways to handle load balancing. But these might have some drawbacks that NLB does not have.

Round-Robin DNS (RRDNS), for instance, distributes the IP requests among the servers in a cluster. But the difference is that if one server fails, requests are still forwarded to that server until an administrator removes it from the address list. NLB handles this by itself by rerouting the requests automatically.

Third-party hardware products are also available. But these are often expensive and can potentially be a single point of failure. Since NLB in itself is a distributed application, no single point of failure exists, unless, of course, the unlikely event occurs that all but one server crashes simultaneously.

NLB requires no special hardware. This way you can save money by running it on the servers you have already decided to be part of your cluster. You don't even have to use the same operating system on your machines. If you already have an old Windows NT 4.0 cluster running WLBS, you can integrate these machines into a Windows 2000 NLB cluster easily and at the speed you choose for yourself.

But upgrading is the way to go. Why? Well, Microsoft has made some big enhancements to NLB. NLB is not a virtual NIC anymore. Instead, it is an optional LAN service that is automatically installed with the operating system. When you want to use it, you just set the correct properties for it, as shown in Figure 3-5, and you are ready to rock.

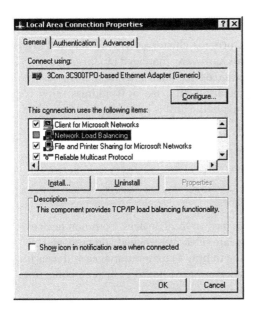

Figure 3-5. *NLB is available under Local Area Connection properties*

Changes to these properties can even be made without causing a reboot of the server. The service will be back up after a short delay of 15 to 20 seconds.

You can also configure NLB when you perform an unattended installation. This helps in deployment of new servers.

MS Cluster Service Overview

As we already mentioned, Microsoft first introduced Microsoft Cluster Service in Windows NT 4.0 Enterprise edition, but then changed the name to Microsoft Cluster Server (but left the acronym the same—MSCS). Since then many enhancements have been made to this product.

In a cluster the individual servers are referred to as *nodes*. This service helps primarily in solving the availability problem. A cluster service works by having two or more nodes in its cluster. If one node fails, the other (or others) takes over.

Windows 2000 servers can provide up to a four-node cluster in the Datacenter Server, whereas the .NET Server 2003 can host up to eight nodes.

The cluster represents itself on the network as a single server and is often called a *virtual server*. The cluster provides access for its clients to different resources, such as file shares, printers, or other services.

The servers in a cluster are connected physically, as well as programmatically, and can coordinate their communication when a client requests a service. The cluster provides a high degree of availability for its clients because each participating cluster server can supply redundant operations should a hardware or application failure occur.

Concept

The collection of components on each node that perform the cluster activities is referred to as *Cluster Service*. The components, whether software or hardware, managed by Cluster Service are called *resources*. A resource can be a physical hardware device, such as a disk drive or network card, as well as a logical item like an application, application database, or IP address.

We consider a resource to be online when it is available and is providing service to the cluster. Resources have the following characteristics:

- They can be owned by only one node at a time.

- They can be managed in a server cluster.

- They can be taken offline and brought online.

In Cluster Service, each server owns and manages its own local devices. Common devices in a cluster, such as disk arrays and connection media, are selectively owned and managed by a single server at any given time. This way of referring to how a cluster manages and uses its local and cluster common devices and resources is called a *shared-nothing* cluster architecture.

Figure 3-6 illustrates how a two-node cluster can be organized.

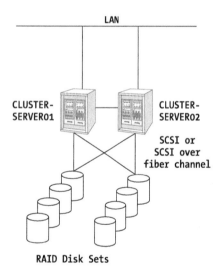

Figure 3-6. *A simple two-node cluster*

The cluster servers communicate with common external disk arrays by using a Small Computer System Interface (SCSI) or SCSI over fiber channel. While each server hosts and manages its own copy of the service provided by the cluster, common resources like files can be placed on a common disk array external to the cluster.

To better understand how this can be helpful, imagine a two-node database cluster. If each server has its own local copy of the database files, constant replication would be necessary to constantly keep both copies an exact replica of the other. To avoid this, the database and its transaction log files are placed on external disk arrays, providing fault tolerance by using different RAID levels. The database server, however, still runs on each node: only the database files are placed on the common disk array. Because only one database exists when a failover occurs (one node fails and the other takes over), the database is not compromised in any way.

In the Windows Server 2003 family, it's also possible to configure a cluster on disparate places. This means you can deploy a cluster with eight nodes in two separate places with four nodes at each place. If an entire building vanishes, the application can still continue to work. We will include more about this Chapter 8.

Availability

Cluster Service can detect a software or hardware failure. When it does, it quickly assigns the responsibility of the application or service to another node in the cluster. This process is called *failover*. After the failing node has been fixed, it can come back online again. This is called *failback*.

If you need to upgrade the cluster—for example, when you want to apply a new operating system service pack or an upgrade to the service the cluster provides—you can easily do this. What you need to do is to manually move the network service that the cluster is providing to another node. This procedure makes sure that client requests will not be interrupted during the upgrade. After the upgrade, you move the service back and take the node online again.

The failover procedure reduces single points of failure on the network and thereby provides a higher level of availability. But keep in mind that Cluster Service alone can't guarantee server uptime; you need other maintenance and backup plans, too. But this is a great tool in helping administrators keep services up and running.

Manageability

Cluster Service makes life easier for system administrators in other ways, too. One thing it does is to provide a single point of control (remember, this is a good thing) for administration purposes. Administrators can manage all devices and resources in the cluster as easily as if they had all been on one server. If necessary, administration can also be performed remotely.

And, because they can take resources offline manually, administrators can perform maintenance and upgrades without interrupting the service. This is also good for the clients, as they still can access the resources they need without being disturbed in their work.

Pros and Cons

So when do you preferably use Cluster Service then? Well, one usage has already been mentioned. When you have an important database that needs to be available almost every second of the day, Cluster Service is a great tool to enhance availability. Imagine the chaos if medical records were only sporadically accessible to hospital staff due to a faulty database. You can also imagine the rage of bank customers if they couldn't withdraw their money when they need to, or access their web-based bank services when they want to.

Cluster Service is also useful is keeping e-mail services online. Microsoft Exchange Server works great on a Cluster Service. The concept is the same as for the database described previously.

■**Note** But keep in mind that Cluster Service is not the perfect technique for enhancing scalability. Other techniques exist to help you there. You have already taken a look at NLB earlier in this chapter, but there are others too, as you'll read later on.

Application Center Overview

As you have seen, NLB is a great way to enhance scalability and availability in a large web server cluster. But as you certainly understand, a large cluster of computers will present some difficulties. And you must overcome these difficulties if you want your applications to work properly. You must address three key issues when building a large web solution. We have discussed them before, but they are very important, so we will go over them again and see what problems they might present.

- *Availability.* You can't accept a web site that isn't accessible to your visitors. Often, you need the site to be up and running 99.999 percent of the time. This doesn't leave much room for the type of maintenance that might require you to take the servers down. Do the math and see. Network Load Balancing helps you reach this goal by letting many servers appear externally as one. But with a large cluster, how can you manage the servers and still keep your sanity?

- *Scalability.* As your web site grows more and more popular, the load increases. Even with a cluster of web servers, you will eventually reach a limit to how much the cluster can take. This is why you need a way to add more power easily, and without interrupting the site. You just don't have the time to take the cluster down, reconfigure it to use more servers, and then take it online again.

- *Manageability.* This topic might seem obvious to you now, after we've presented some of the problems with a large cluster. But there is more to this than managing the servers. You must also find easy ways to update your web site content when you have a large cluster. When you have many servers, you must be able to update every server very quickly, in order to make the same content available on all servers. Doing this manually would take a long time for administrators. You have much more important things to do, trust us.

Microsoft technicians have seen these problems too. They manage one of the world's largest web sites themselves and realized these issues a long time ago. That's why they have developed a great tool to make life easier. Application Center is a management and deployment tool designed to solve these three issues. But, as you will see, Application Center can do wonders for the business tier, too.

A cluster is a set of servers that serve the same content to cluster users. A cluster can handle HTTP requests as well as DCOM requests. Application Center is designed to handle two of the tiers in a multi-tiered solution. We have already talked about the user interface in terms of a web site cluster. The clients accessing this tier can be either thick (that is, a Windows application), or thin (which means a web browser client). Especially with the web services technique (which we'll discuss in another chapter of this book), it is easy to incorporate a web service into a thick client. The clusters discussed so far in this chapter have all been web clusters handling HTTP requests.

But Application Center also handles DCOM clusters, which makes it good for managing the business tier as well. Business logic is often a set of COM+ components or assemblies in .NET. These components serve the purpose of separating the logic from user interface and database access, thus making it more general and accessible to all sorts of applications. The traffic on this tier can be great, especially if it is serving a large web cluster as well as many other applications on the network. Therefore you must find a way to scale this tier. You can do this by using Component Load Balancing (CLB), which is included with Application Center. Figure 3-7 shows a schematic overview of a web site solution using Application Center to handle load balancing.

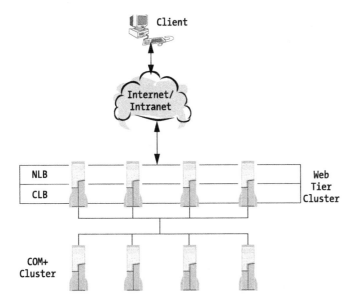

Figure 3-7. *A schematic view of a web site solution*

Application Center clusters are designed for stateless, middle-tier applications, such as web sites and COM+ applications. As opposed to Windows clustering, Application Center clusters don't need to share a common disk array and don't need to use special hardware.

Concept

Let's take a look at the Application Center feature set. It has four major features as we see it:

- Cluster services and load balancing

- Synchronization and deployment

- Monitoring

- Administration

These features all help to solve the problems described earlier. Cluster services and load balancing help in maintaining scalability and availability. Synchronization helps when you need to add new content to (or update content in) your solution. It also helps when deploying a new application. Administration and monitoring provide you with greater manageability, thus making it easier to control all of your servers from one single point.

Cluster Services and Load Balancing

Application Center includes several wizards (such as the one in Figure 3-8) and a user interface based on Microsoft Management Console (MMC). These tools help the administrator by making it easier to create and manage clusters.

Figure 3-8. *The New Cluster Wizard, an example of the wizards provided in Application Center*

Application Center supports the following types of clusters (see Figure 3-9):

- General cluster (web-tier)

- COM+ application cluster

- COM+ routing cluster

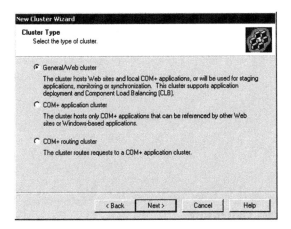

Figure 3-9. *The New Cluster Wizard screen, where you choose the type of cluster you are building*

General Clusters

A *general cluster* is nothing but a group of servers processing client requests. In this category you find the web server cluster, which is the kind of cluster this chapter focuses on, in addition to database clusters, staging clusters (also known as deployment servers), and stand-alone clusters. Yes, you read that correctly. A *stand-alone cluster* is a cluster with only one member, which you will learn more about later in this chapter. A few other clusters also fit in the general category, but these are the most important ones.

The most common cluster using Application Center would be a web server cluster that hosts web sites as well as local COM+ components (or assemblies in .NET). These clusters can use several load-balancing techniques. Application Center doesn't care if you use load-balancing techniques other than Network Load Balancing. In Figure 3-10, you can see that during the setup of a new cluster you can choose the type of load balancing you will use. You'll still get the advantages of clustering several servers that we've already discussed.

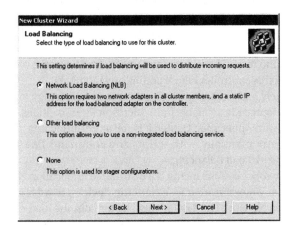

Figure 3-10. *Specifying a load-balancing type for a new cluster*

A typical scenario using Network Load Balancing might look like Figure 3-11. Application Center, in this scenario, eases the task of administering the cluster. Adding and removing (setting members online or offline) is handled through the Application Center user interface.

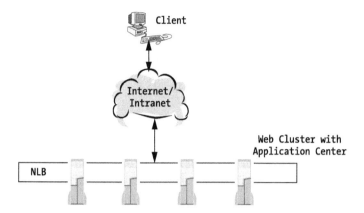

Figure 3-11. *A typical scenario using Network Load Balancing with Application Center*

Because Network Load Balancing dynamically distributes client workload, even when you set members online or offline, the site is available during the whole process. This makes it easy to add more power to your site by adding servers during runtime.

Third-Party Load Balancers in Application Center

As already stated, you do not need to use NLB if you don't want to. Many sites use an external load-balancing device to distribute incoming client requests (see the following illustration). The device is simply a piece of hardware placed in front of the web servers handling the requests.

These third-party load balancers can be monitored and managed through the Application Center user interface. Application Center monitors member status, sets members online or offline, and synchronizes content and configuration for all web sites included in the process. To make this solution work, you need to integrate the load balancers with Application Center. This is achieved by configuring the communication between the device and Application Center. All cluster members are synchronized with a cluster controller, and to avoid problems and unexpected behavior, you need to make sure that all content exists on this controller before adding any members.

To be honest, Application Center is a relatively bad tool for managing these load-balancing devices. Even though the Application Center Resource Kit, available from Microsoft Press, includes tools for third-party load-balancing integration with Application Center, it is still a very crude way of doing things. You will need to do a lot of work manually, with scripts and command-line commands, which you can avoid if you use Network Load Balancing.

One other thing to keep in mind is that Network Load Balancing is a distributed application and runs on all servers in the cluster, whereas an external load-balancing device provides a potential single point of failure. If a server in a Network Load Balancing cluster fails, the load balancing still works because every member runs a copy of NLB. If your hardware load balancer fails, you might have a problem if you lack the right backup solution. So, if you have a Microsoft solution you might do best by just sticking with a NLB cluster and skipping the external devices if you want a load balancing solution. It's almost always the most cost-effective way of doing this.

Single-Node Clusters

We mentioned single-node clusters. You might think they seem strange, since a cluster, by definition, ought to use more than one server. But sometimes it can be useful to operate Application Center on a single server, without the multimember cluster context. If you use Application Center on a single-node cluster, it treats this cluster as a one-member cluster, (which it is). This is typically useful when you need a stager or a staging area—that is, a server where you can publish content before you actually deploy it onto the production cluster. This provides a way of testing quality and functionality within development and testing environments, before going live with your site. Because the stager doesn't need to be as powerful as the production cluster, you can use a simpler cluster but still keep the Application Center functionality.

COM+ Application Cluster

In the web pages of a web application, different components are instantiated to serve the application with data of various sorts. You could, for instance, have an application where a salesperson looks up customer data by calling a COM+ component that has a function named GetCustomerData. It really doesn't matter whether the application is a web application or a thick Windows client, the instantiation is the same. If the GetCustomerData component resides on a different server, than the application itself, and there are many users accessing this component, the workload on the server can be immense. To ease the pressure on the server, you can create a cluster of servers to handle these COM+ components, just as you might do with your web site. The benefits of doing this are the same as for Network Load Balancing described earlier. Application Center COM+ clusters load balance the method calls to instantiate the components across multiple cluster members within the COM+ cluster. A simplified scenario of this is shown in Figure 3-12. This cluster uses Network Load Balancing as a load balancer.

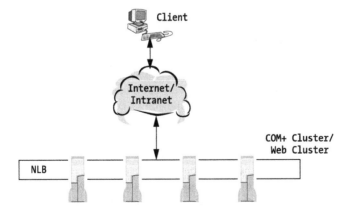

Figure 3-12. *A simplified scenario using Network Load Balancing for a COM+ cluster*

To support Windows-based clients using DCOM, the cluster can understand DCOM calls and use Network Load Balancing to distribute these incoming client requests.

But in a more likely scenario than the one just described, the layering of the application would be different. To ease the load on the web cluster, the COM+ components would probably be moved to their own cluster and Component Load Balancing would be used to load balance the activation requests for the COM+ components, as shown in Figure 3-13.

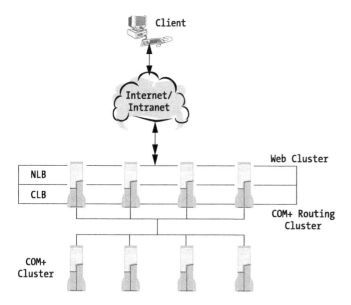

Figure 3-13. *A likely scenario using CLB for distributing the activation requests for a COM+ cluster and NLB for a web cluster*

COM+ Routing Clusters

In the scenario in Figure 3-13, we have also included something called a COM+ Routing Cluster. This cluster is located on the web servers and uses Component Load Balancing to route requests for COM+ components from the general cluster to the COM+ Application Cluster. COM+ Routing Clusters are not really necessary, but serve their purpose when you need to load balance COM+ requests from a general cluster across multiple COM+ Application Clusters. This depends on a limitation in the Application Center 2000 release of Component Load Balancing that makes it possible for CLB to have only a single list of remote servers for every routing server. Otherwise, web clusters can communicate with COM+ clusters over load-balanced DCOM without a COM+ Routing Cluster, since each web cluster member acts as its own router for choosing the right COM+ server to handle component activation.

If you develop a new application entirely in .NET, you would not use COM Interop, of course. In this situation, you would use .NET Remoting with binary formatting, either over HTTPChannel or over TCPChannel. You can scale .NET Remoting hosted in IIS just as you scale your web clusters, and you'll find that performance is high as well. The one thing you need to remember is that this only works when you use .NET Remoting hosted in IIS. When it comes to .NET Remoting outside IIS, we haven't found a way to scale this, but we suspect that future versions of Application Center will solve this limitation.

On the other hand, when you have an integration project and can't change the old components, CLB is a good way to enhance performance.

Component Activation

The fastest way to activate components is by having them on the user's local machine (or web server, if it's a web application). But by using the scenario in Figure 3-13, you get a lot of other benefits that clearly outnumber the use of local components:

- COM+ Application Clusters can accept requests from both thin and thick clients. That is, they can handle both web browser–based clients as well as Windows-based clients. This means you can reuse business logic in many applications.

- If the COM+ components reside on the web server, they could consume resources, making the server unresponsive. You can't let this happen. Otherwise, you may as well abandon the idea of the five nines (99.999 percent uptime). By creating a separate cluster for the components, the web server is relieved of some of its burden and can continue to handle client requests with better performance.

- To gain higher security, you can also place the component cluster behind a separate firewall. By doing this, you will restrict clients accessing the web cluster from accessing the components as well. You will learn more about this later in the chapter.

- Since you isolate COM+ applications on a separate cluster, you accomplish higher manageability. By having two clusters, you make it possible to have different developers and administrators maintain each cluster independently. Of course, this requires a large organization with lots of resources. This isn't for the small web site, obviously, which would not need load balancing anyway.

Network Load Balancing in Application Center

You use a wizard to set up and configure Network Load Balancing in Application Center. This wizard, called the New Cluster Wizard, quickly sets up and configures Network Load Balancing (refer back to Figure 3-8). Remember, this is the same wizard you use for setting up any load balancer, as you saw in Figure 3-10. You don't need to configure anything during this process, because the wizard handles everything. However, if you don't like the default values, you can easily change them by using the Application Center user interface after you've created the new cluster (see Figure 3-14).

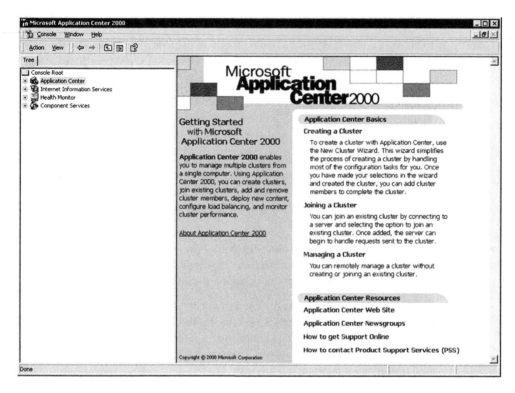

Figure 3-14. *The Application Center MMC*

The user interface makes it easy to add and remove cluster members once you are up and running with the cluster. This is also the place to go if you need to change other aspects of your Application Center configuration.

One thing to do before running the Application Center setup is to make sure that you have at least two network interface cards. You will need to have one card for handling internal communication within the cluster and one for handling communication with clients. The latter card needs to have at least one static IP address that is used as the cluster IP address, or as we refer to it, the virtual IP address. This is the address that clients use to access the cluster.

Synchronization and Deployment

We stated earlier that Application Center helps in synchronizing the cluster and in deployment of an application. First, let's explain what we mean by an application. An *application* in this context can contain a complete web site with all of its content, such as web pages, COM+ components, system settings, and any other content that must exist on each cluster member for the solution to work properly. But it can also be a COM+ application intended only for the business tier. (By the way, guess where the name Application Center came from?)

To synchronize the cluster when, for example, developers make updates to a web page, Application Center uses an image of the application. The image can, of course, contain one or more applications if needed. When a new application with all its content is ready for deployment from the staging cluster, an initial application image is created. This image is copied by Application Center to a cluster controller on the production cluster and then replicated to all member servers. The controller maintains the latest, most accurate content for the cluster. When an update occurs in any of the application content on the controller, changes are synchronized automatically to each of the other cluster members. If you want to, you can manually perform this synchronization.

As you can see, Application Center certainly eases the job for administrators. But keep in mind that what we have been talking about here is not what we usually call content management, even though Application Center does handle content. Content management, in the classic sense, is covered in Chapter 5 of this book, and is more about the administration of the content on the web pages in an application. Content management applications often help in managing who has the access to update a specific web page and the guidelines that exist for the page. Microsoft has a tool called Microsoft Content Management Server to help do this, but other tools, such as EPiServer, might be a better solution in many cases. By setting user rights and client rights, and creating web page templates with the content management tool, you can control the look of the web site and make sure that the design rules are followed by the people allowed to update the pages. You can also restrict who gets to see which page and which parts of a page they are allowed to see. This process is known as personalization of a web page and is often managed with the help of a content management tool.

So as you can see, there is a difference between the content management provided by Application Center and the content management provided by other tools. But the two techniques are often used in conjunction with each other to make life even easier for administrators.

Monitoring

To maintain a high availability of your cluster, you need to know certain things. You need to have a thorough understanding of when your clusters are running smoothly, but you also need to know when they are having a bad day and their performance is compromised. To be able to understand this, you must be able to comprehend events and performance metrics. When some events occur, it might be a clue to a pending failure of the cluster, and if you do not see the signs, you can't prevent it from happening. If you don't know that a constantly high CPU load means it might be time to add more power to the cluster by perhaps adding one or more servers, you are in big trouble. And, of course, if you are a system administrator and let your clusters fail, and thereby let company applications fail, your employer will not be happy.

To prevent this from happening, Application Center provides a rich set of features that helps you detect, analyze, and fix both performance and availability problems.

Application Center continuously records and displays different aspects of the health and functionality of your cluster (see Figure 3-15). These aspects are

- Events

- Performance counters

- Server health

- Member status

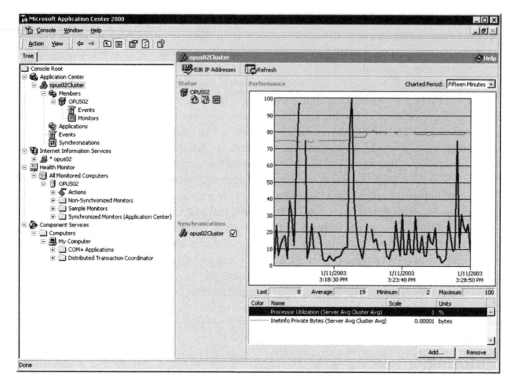

Figure 3-15. *The Application Center UI showing performance counters*

Events and performance metrics are stored on each server in your cluster. You can use performance metrics to view these in real time or aggregated over a longer period. This makes it possible for you to spot immediate problems or to discover long-running trends. Since Application Center is a single monitoring point, you can also use it to collect events from many member servers in a single view and thereby expedite the filtering of events and processing of the same for an administrator.

You can also set numerous thresholds for specific events and information and ask to be notified when a threshold is reached. You can set thresholds on event logs, Windows service failures, HTTP calls, WMI events, and more. This functionality is provided by Microsoft Health Monitor 2.1, which is distributed with Application Center. You can also set up possible actions to be taken when these thresholds are reached. We have mentioned notification already, but predefined scripts can also be run if necessary.

So who or what generates this monitoring data anyway? Well, several actors are involved in this process. Different applications, Windows services, and other objects are responsible. Here are a few:

- *Application Center, itself.* Of course, most events are generated by Application Center, since it is one of the main actors involved. If it didn't keep an eye on itself, it really wouldn't be of that much use to you.

- *The operating system.* For example, Windows 2000 Server or any other OS in the Windows family produces many events that let you know the status of the OS and Application Center.

- *Health Monitor.* If you want to be able to set thresholds for events and respond to them with various actions, Health Monitor must be able to notify you, run scripts, or send other events when thresholds are met. Application Center collects a large amount of data from Health Monitor by default. There are also ways to expand these collectors by creating new ones, or installing Health Monitor sample data collectors. This is useful if you don't find the ones supplied adequate for your situation.

- *Windows Management Instrumentation (WMI).* This is a management infrastructure that provides standardized methods for accessing events and other monitoring and management information across an enterprise environment.

Monitoring Process

So let us look in more detail at how the process of Application Center monitoring is carried out. There are four steps in this process:

- Data generation

- Data logging

- Data summarization

- Data use

Data Generation

Figure 3-16 shows an overview of how Application Center, Health Monitor, and the operating system generate events and performance counters. It also shows how this data is provided to WMI.

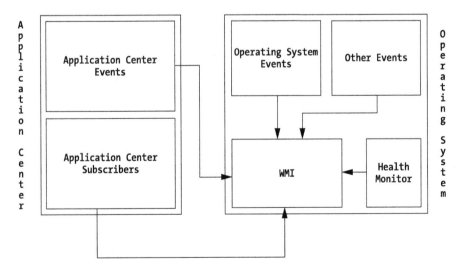

Figure 3-16. *The Application Center data generation process*

Application Center subscribes to some of these WMI events and logs them for later use in the user interface. Microsoft Application Center is also smart enough to provide its own events with extended and troubleshooting information, a feature called *event details*.

Data Logging

During Application Center setup, if you choose to install Application Center Event and Perfor-mance Logging (see Figure 3-17), a SQL Server 2000 database is also installed. This is, as we are sure you have already guessed, where Application Center stores the logged data.

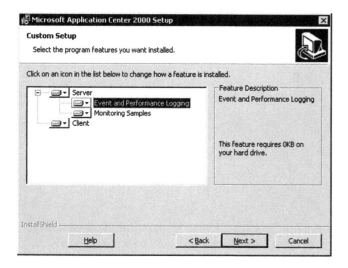

Figure 3-17. *The Application Center custom setup*

Because the infrastructure of this database is exactly like an ordinary SQL Server and also provides the same functionality, you can use the same techniques for accessing this database as you would if you were to access a SQL Server. In other words, this means you can use SQL queries and stored procedures to access data. Other data accessing methods, like ADO.NET, are also possible options, giving you the flexibility to choose for yourself the way you want to retrieve data. If you don't want to go through the trouble of making these queries, you can use the Application Center user interface to display the information you are looking for. The impor-tant thing to remember here is that these other accessing methods are available, so that, when the user interface does not show you what you want, you can find the information yourself.

One benefit of storing the monitoring data in a database is that you can display informa-tion more flexibly. You can also let other applications and services access the data.

In the Application Center Event View, you can choose to view the data points for different time frames (see Figure 3-18). Application Center scans logs for 1-minute, 15-minute, and 2-hour time frames. The older the information is, the less detail it provides. This happens because as data is summarized over a longer period of time, say one day, for example, there is no way of keeping the same level of detail as you can for the 1-minute interval. These logs are cleared by default after a specified number of days. A property called Keep logged events for (days) is available in the Event Properties dialog box.

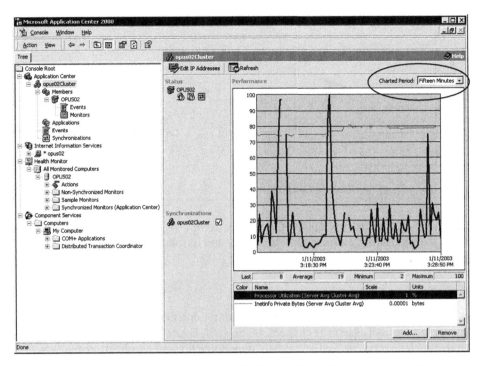

Figure 3-18. *The Application Center UI. Marked is the place where you choose the time frame to be displayed.*

As you have seen, Application Center collects a large amount of data in a detailed format about the cluster and its members. This data quickly grows, and lots of disk space is required to hold it. Application Center therefore summarizes this data periodically and loads it into a summarization table. Two kinds of data sets are summarized:

- *Event data.* Data that is maintained in the log for a specified number of days as mentioned previously. The default is 15 days before any data is removed.

- *Performance counter data.* Data that is collected every 10 seconds. This data is summarized in four intervals: 1 minute, 15 minutes, 2 hours, and daily. The whole cluster is synchronized with these time intervals.

Because the summarization changes the granularity of the data, less and less detail can be shown as the time frame grows larger. If you want to be able to see the data in greater detail later, you must collect data more often. This requires, of course, more disk space, but luckily hard drives are cheap these days. So if you decide you have enough disk space, you can archive the detailed data before it is summarized, and then you can really dive into it when you want to.

Data Use

Figure 3-19 shows different ways of collecting data from Application Center logs and presenting them in a report. By using SQL queries, you can easily import the data into your favorite presentation tool and generate the reports you want to display.

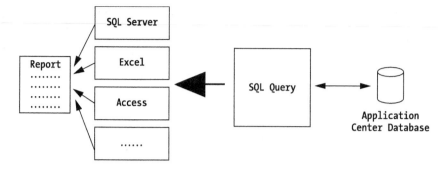

Figure 3-19. *Schematics of Application Center data use*

But of course, you can also use Application Center Event View, Performance Chart, and Cluster Status to display information about the cluster and its members. It is also possible to customize these views.

Administration

The primary administrative user interface for Application Center is the MMC. From here you can administer local as well as remote clusters, as shown in Figure 3-20. You can also choose to connect to a specific server as well as a cluster depending on your administrative needs.

Figure 3-20. *Here you can connect to a remote or local server. You can also choose to connect to a cluster or to a specific server.*

The MMC is not the only administrative tool available, however. There is also a web-based interface, but this only has limited administrative possibilities. So if you are going to administer a remote cluster or server, you should really try to use the MMC. When you do this, you also get a secure remote connection.

If you are really into command-line commands, Application Center is equipped with a set of these, too. You can use these commands to automate administration and management of Application Center.

And, as if this were not enough, there is also a programmatic interface to Application Center that you can use to build administration of clusters in your own applications.

Use of Application Center

Let's have a look at three possible scenarios using Application Center. The point of discussing these is partly to show different ways of taking care of security in your web applications, but also to show where Application Center is useful in a solution. All clusters in these examples are run by Application Center—web clusters as well as COM+ clusters.

Example 1

The first example (Figure 3-21) shows an internal network protected by a single firewall. The web cluster, COM+ cluster, and stager are all behind this firewall. The database is also protected only by this firewall.

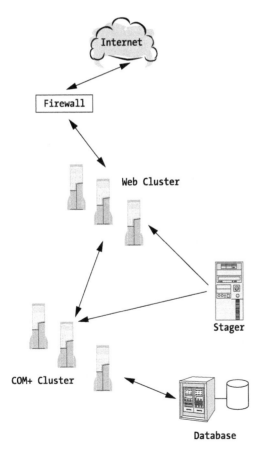

Figure 3-21. *A simple scenario using COM+ and a single firewall*

In a scenario like this, both the database and the business logic in the COM+ cluster as well as the stager are potentially exposed to users from the outside. To prevent some of these security risks, it is very common to add another firewall, thereby creating a perimeter network.

Example 2

Here we have added a perimeter network, as Figure 3-22 shows. This is commonly referred to as a *demilitarized zone* (DMZ). In this scenario, we protect the staging server and database server from being compromised by, say, a Trojan horse attack. But as you clearly see here, we have only partly solved the problem. While the database and staging server are protected behind the second firewall, we may still potentially expose the business logic. The COM+ components often use role-based, or programmatic, security to keep data safe. This could be compromised if the components reside on the web tier of our application. And we do not want to risk our business logic coming into the wrong hands, because this could jeopardize our business. We must do something about this.

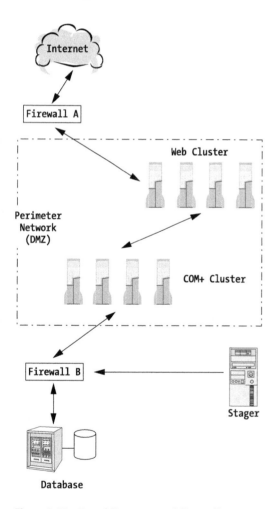

Figure 3-22. *By adding a second firewall, we create a DMZ.*

Example 3

In the third example, we also move the COM+ cluster behind the second firewall, as Figure 3-23 shows. Here we use CLB to even further enhance security in the web site. An unreliable client trying to access the business logic would be prevented from doing so by the second firewall. It would instead only allow COM+ components to be created by calls from the web tier cluster.

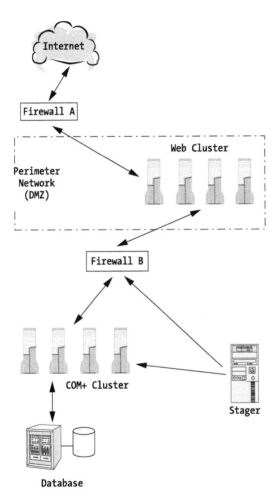

Figure 3-23. *The application logic is moved behind the second firewall.*

But we still have a few problems left in this solution. We can even further enhance security by using web services instead of COM+. If we let COM+ calls through a firewall, it means we must open up the specific ports necessary for this traffic to be let through. Instead, we instead want to keep the firewall as closed as we can and only allow HTTP traffic through. The next example shows how this kind of solution could be designed.

Example 4

Figure 3-24 shows the design of a solution where we have changed from exposing our logic as COM+ components and use web services instead. One thing you need to understand before using this scenario yourself is that the inclusion of web services comes with a certain penalty. Performance is negatively affected by having to use HTTP instead of COM+ calls. COM+ calls are generally faster than HTTP calls, but since in this example we are on our internal network, we have control of bandwidth usage, and we feel it is better to lose a little performance than to have too many holes in our firewall. Our own testing shows such a tiny performance degradation that we believe the move to web services is well worth the effort, just to have better security. But we strongly suggest testing such a method before deploying it.

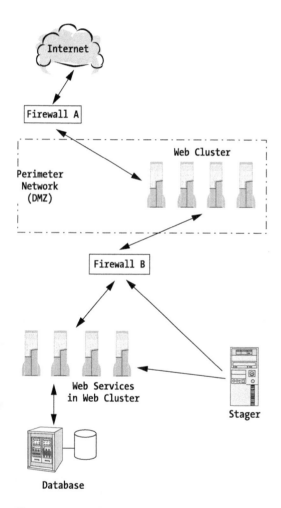

Figure 3-24. *In this scenario, we expose the business logic as web services.*

In all of these scenarios, we could also use .NET Remoting instead of COM+ or web services over an HTTP connection. .NET Remoting is a generic and extensible interprocess communication system. You can use it to create web services hosted in IIS, and therefore have all the security, scalability, and state management (both session and application state) that ASP.NET and IIS offer. If you're interested in security issues over performance, you should use ASP.NET or .NET Remoting hosted in IIS. If you use any other transport protocol, you would have to handle security yourself. The same goes for using the HTTPChannel outside of IIS.

It is not possible to load balance .NET Remoting if you host it outside of IIS. This we suspect will change in the coming versions of Application Center. In the meantime, in our scenarios we must host .NET Remoting in IIS if we want to use it.

If you want to keep the IIS hosting with its security, and still get increased performance, you should definitely use the binary encoding of .NET Remoting. Our own tests, as well as several others, show a performance boost when using the binary formatting, even if we use the HTTPChannel.

To get absolutely maximum performance from .NET Remoting, you should use the binary formatting over a TCPChannel. But if you do so, you must be certain that you are running in an entirely secure environment, behind a firewall. So in this case, we would not recommend it, since you need to expose objects outside of your firewall. The key issue, as we see it, is to keep the firewalls as closed as possible. If you open up ports in them, you have a potential security risk. This is why we recommend the use of only port 80 and HTTP traffic when you need to expose objects outside of your firewalls. This limits you to the use of web services or .NET Remoting over the HTTPChannel, of course, but you should be able to live with that.

If you need to choose between .NET Remoting using binary formatting over an HTTPChannel and traditional web services, you should consider some issues. Both methods are scalable when hosted in IIS, but keep in mind that .NET Remoting using binary formatting over an HTTPChannel is faster than traditional web services. .NET Remoting, however, demands that the client have access to the .NET Framework to give full access to all its features, and if you need interoperability with other platforms, this is not always possible. You could use a J2EE implementation called JNBridge that connects .NET with Java, but we haven't tried this ourselves. You could think of .NET Remoting as a substitute for DCOM, where you make many calls to a component during the session and need more extensible features than you can get from web services. .NET Remoting is very useful, especially when you have communication between .NET applications that do not have to cross a firewall and you can be certain both ends support the .NET Framework in that case.

If you want a client that isn't using .NET Remoting plumbing to access your web services created from .NET Remoting objects, you need to think about some things first. If you carefully pare down your endpoints to bare-bones data types and semantics, you could use them. If you do not restrict parameters to built-in simple types and your own data types, you can't interoperate your .NET Remoting web services with other web services implementations. You also need to avoid client-activated objects and events in that case. What have you really got left then? Not much more than a traditional web service could offer. So if you want to support a wide range of clients, you should use traditional web services.

A good suggestion is to choose web services by default, even in a homogeneous environment, between internal systems and subsystems. Use .NET Remoting only in those special cases where you really need it. This would be when you know that the client supports the full .NET Framework, and you need the extensible features of the full Framework. This could also be when performance is an issue, since .NET Remoting generally is faster than web services.

Our recommendation for using .NET Remoting with some transport protocol other than HTTP is to make sure the client is placed behind the same firewall as the Remoting object. If it isn't, you'll need to open up the firewalls, which gives you a potential security hole. You would also need to implement security yourself, in code, since you can't use the built-in features of IIS in this case.

Now you have come a few steps down the road of security. But there is a lot more you can do. One way to enhance security would require you to dive into the world of Windows and network security, which is beyond the scope of this book. Application Center is based on the services provided by Windows and Internet Information Services. In Application Center, you find very few user-configurable security settings. You must therefore learn and understand Windows security to fully secure your network. It is also essential that you keep in close cooperation with the people who understand these things the best: the system architects and the administrators. But let us not forget the software developers. A lot also can be done to enhance security in the code.

These are a few different scenarios using Application Center. If we personally wanted to choose a solution for our own network, we would definitely choose Example 4, since the benefits are great with this setup. But in the end, it is up to each company and each web site to set its own standards.

Maintaining Session State in a Clustered Solution

Imagine you are handling a large web cluster using Network Load Balancing and Application Center. On this cluster, you run an online store selling books. Customers can browse the products and add interesting items to their shopping carts. Since you are using Network Load Balancing, all client requests are subject to load balancing. When the customer first establishes a session on the web site, he or she is directed to a specific server. It is Network Load Balancing that forwards the request to this server. To maintain *session state*, all coming requests from this customer must be redirected to the server where the session was established. But since Network Load Balancing redirects client requests to different servers, the customer is not guaranteed to end up at the server where the session was started. This means that the items in the shopping cart might disappear suddenly, since the new server taking care of the request has no idea of who the customer is and that he or she has added items to the cart. If this happens, the customer is likely to take his or her business elsewhere, and you'll lose the sales.

So how can you solve this problem? Well, there are several ways to do this. The Application Center solution is to provide a *request forwarder*. The request forwarder makes sure all HTTP requests are forwarded to a particular server so that session state is maintained. It also makes sure the following requests are forwarded to the cluster controller (because if they were not, synchronization of the cluster would overwrite updates):

- Internet Information Services (IIS) administration requests

- Microsoft FrontPage publishing

- Web Distributed Authoring and Versioning (WebDAV) publishing

- Web-based administration requests

Let us concentrate on HTTP requests. How does the request forwarder work? The forwarder is an ISAPI filter and extension. This means it positions itself in front of the IIS and checks incoming requests before they are handled by the web server, but after they have been load balanced by Network Load Balancing. Based on the information in the request, the request forwarder sends it to the correct cluster member. For this to work, you need to have set up a few things. First of all, you need to understand request forwarding only applies to sites that use Active Server Pages (ASP / ASP.NET) session state. This is set up in IIS by enabling session state in the application configuration for the site. To save you time, this is done by default. After that, you need to make sure the clients accept cookies, since the request forwarder uses these to maintain session state by associating clients with a specific cluster member and writing the information to the cookie. Following requests from a client will be forwarded to a particular cluster member based on the information in the cookie.

This scenario presents some problems. What if the client rejects all cookies? It would be hard to use this solution if that were the case.

Performance is also slightly impacted by the request forwarder, since requests are processed after they have been load balanced.

If you want a scalable solution with good performance, our advice is to avoid use of session state with load balancing. Solve the problem some other way.

One other solution might be to keep session information in a SQL Server database. If you choose to do this, you must keep state information in a cookie or in the URL header. This way it doesn't matter which cluster member a client request is redirected to. You can always find session information based on the state information. You should also build a check in your web pages that investigates whether the client accepts cookies: if not, keep state in the URL header instead. This solution is excellent when you need a reliable solution, since you can cluster the SQL Server to handle failure scenarios.

To even further enhance performance, you should disable or even uninstall the request forwarder completely. This way you get rid of the overhead caused by it.

When you use ASP.NET, you can take advantage of the built-in features for session state handling. In ASP.NET, session state is independent from the ASP.NET host process. This means ASP.NET session state is run in a separate process, and ASP.NET can come and go as it likes, while session state remains.

ASP.NET also has better support for handling your web server farms. The new out-of-process session state allows for all servers in a farm to share a session state process, which is what you want when you can't guarantee that a client is redirected to the same server for its entire session. To achieve this, you change the ASP.NET configuration to point to a common server. There are two options for configuring the out-of-process session state: memory-based (using a state server) and SQL Server-based. Cookie handling has also been simplified in ASP.NET. Now you only change a configuration setting to apply cookie-less sessions. This could be complex to achieve in legacy ASP.

Pros and Cons

Application Center is great for handling large clusters. It enhances manageability and presents Component Load Balancing that helps you scale not only the web server, but also business logic. One of its drawbacks is that it might not be the perfect tool if you choose third-party load balancers, since the integration with these devices is not that great yet.

You have also seen that Application Center provides the request forwarder to help you maintain state in a load-balanced solution. But a good rule is this: For better performance and scalability, do not use state in such a solution. For smaller sites, it might be a good way to solve session state, but in a large cluster with heavy traffic, you are better off without it.

One thing that has changed since last edition of our book is that Windows Server 2003 now is supported on Application Center. All you need to do now is to prepare your Windows Server 2003 system by running W2003SrvPostUpgrade.bat from the root of the Application CD before you install Application Center on your system. Read the help files and readme files carefully before you start installing and you'll be fine.

Summary

In this chapter, we have focused on different clustering techniques and some of their benefits and concerns.

In review, clustering is mainly used to solve two things:

- *Scalability.* Being able to handle an increasing load

- *Availability.* Being available for as much of the time as possible

You have seen that Microsoft offers two techniques to help you with this. The first, Microsoft Cluster Service, is great for enhancing availability. The second, Network Load Balancing, is great for improving both scalability and availability.

But with clustering several servers together arises the problem of managing them. Another major issue is updating, for example, a large web cluster, so that all the member servers receive the changed files when new versions are available. To help you with this, Microsoft provides the Application Center server. In this server are tools and wizards that ease the administrative issues involved in having large clusters. Application Center also makes it easy to administer several clusters, local as well as remote, by being a single point of control.

Another great tool in Application Center is Component Load Balancing, which offers the possibility to distribute COM+ activation requests just like you distribute HTTP requests with Network Load Balancing.

You have also seen that using session state in a load-balanced cluster decreases performance and should not be used if you want a scalable solution with optimized performance.

Throughout this book, you will find more tips for creating a scalable .NET solution. We'll continue now with Windows Server System and its contents.

■■■

CHAPTER 4

An Overview of the Windows Server Family

So far, we have presented an overview of the Microsoft server families. In this chapter, we will have a look under the hood of Windows. We will show you some of the architecture and how you can scale it, using the techniques we described earlier. You will also learn how to secure your servers.

We won't include many practical examples: rather, we will focus on the plumbing so that you can decide for yourself which features you want to explore further and implement. Since Windows Server 2003 and Windows 2000 are so similar, we will not separate them in this discussion. We will, however, take a look at the small things that have changed between the two versions of Microsoft's server families.

Let's begin by looking at the architecture of a Windows Server system.

Windows Server Architecture

Any performance monitoring, tuning, or optimization you do on a Windows Server system involves the kernel. Actually *everything* you do involves the kernel. The kernel is the most central part of the operating system, and without it you can't use much of the Windows System at all. Figure 4-1 shows an overview of the Windows architecture, which we will look at more closely later in this chapter. It is very similar to the Windows 2000 architecture.

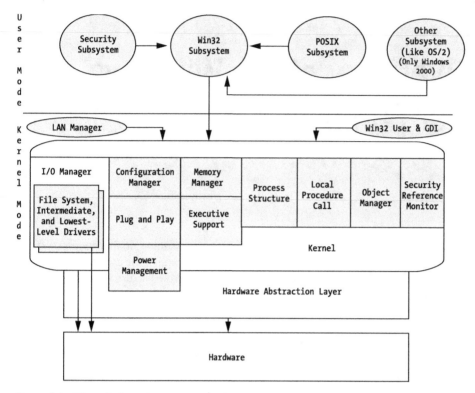

Figure 4-1. *The Windows Server 2003 architecture*

If you want to optimize and secure your system, you need to spend a little time on this piece of operating system machinery. The *kernel* is basically the system32 directory in the Windows catalog on the hard drive. It is made up of many files, including .dll, .exe, and .com files. The executive, shown in Figure 4-2, serves to protect the kernel. This is the part of the operating system that applications access. This way nothing ever accesses the kernel itself, and it becomes harder to sabotage the system.

The executive can be considered the interface to the kernel, in the same way that business logic, in a multi-tier application, should always be exposed by an interface. It adds a layer of protection around what is important to your system, but still allows for others to use it.

The kernel and the executive are closely linked together, so that when we discuss the executive in this book, we almost always talk about it in terms of an interface to the kernel. We will take a closer look at the kernel soon, starting with the executive service. But first we need to make a short detour.

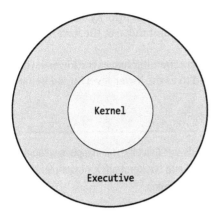

Figure 4-2. *The executive protects the kernel*

Threads

Before we go any further, we need to digress a moment to cover threads, because threads are a central part in any operating system architecture discussion.

A *thread* is a single path of execution within a process. Threads share all the resources that the process has (such as memory). All of the applications running on your servers have one process each. All the threads belonging to the application are contained within this process. There can be one or many threads within a process—thus the terms single- or multithreaded applications. If you open Windows Task Manager and click the Processes tab, you can see the processes running on your computer.

The process contains everything that has to do with the application. Here you'll find the virtual memory space (which you'll learn more about later), system resources, application settings, and the data for the application.

In order to make Windows change the way it processes your applications, you need to change the priority of the process. You can do this by right-clicking a process in Task Manager and then selecting the appropriate priority from Set priority. You can choose from these six priorities:

- Realtime

- High

- AboveNormal

- Normal

- BelowNormal

- Low

The higher you set the priority, the higher the performance of the application should be.

Threads are assigned slices of processor time, based on their priority. This priority is in turn based on the priority of the process containing the thread, so that the only way you can affect the thread priority is by changing the process priority. When the operating system executes threads, the one with the highest priority is executed first. The order of execution is handled by the *thread scheduler*. If you have many threads with the same priority, the scheduler loops through these and gives them each a fixed size of execution time.

When the scheduler has executed all of the threads with the highest priority, it moves to the next lower level and executes the threads waiting there. It will not move to the lower level as long as there are higher-level threads left to execute.

If a higher-level prioritized thread starts running again, the scheduler leaves the lower-level thread to execute the higher prioritized thread. This is referred to as the lower-level thread being *preempted*.

Note The operating system sometimes adjusts the priority of threads dynamically. This happens when an application with a graphical user interface shifts between foreground and background, for example. The foreground application is given a higher priority than the background application.

Executive Service

Most of the Windows executive can be found in a file called ntosknbrnl.exe (see Figure 4-3). This file contains the executive, and also parts of the kernel as well. If you use a tool like the Dependency Walker, usually shipped with Visual Studio, you can see that this exposes more than 1200 functions.

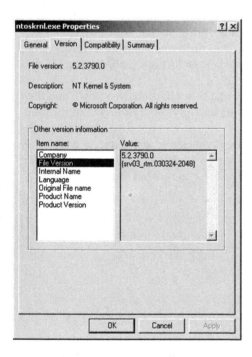

Figure 4-3. *The ntoskrnl.exe file of Windows Server 2003 Web Edition*

■ **Note** The ntoskrnl.exe file exists in various forms for an operating system version. If you run your OS on a single CPU machine, one version of the file is installed. If you run the OS on a multi-CPU machine, another version is installed. Obviously, this means that the file (or rather a version of the file) is important from a performance perspective as well.

Software-Based and Hardware-Based Security

There are two kinds of security in your servers (this applies to workstations as well, but we will mainly talk about servers here). The first is software-based and controlled by the operating system. The other is hardware-based and controlled by the processor. Let's consider the Intel processor architecture for a while. The very simplified view of this architecture, shown in Figure 4-4, includes four rings of protection for software running on the server.

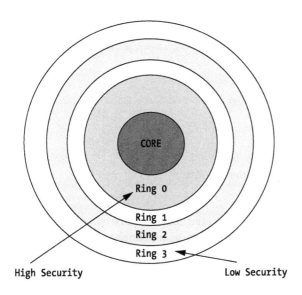

Figure 4-4. *The four rings of security surrounding the core of the system*

These layers can be seen as hardware-based security. The closer you get to the core, the more secure the environment is. You can think of these rings as the walls surrounding the Helm's Deep fortress in *The Lord of the Rings*, which took the enemy a lot of energy and time to break through. The inner ring, ring 0, is where the operating system resides. Not much can touch this ring. Your applications reside in ring 3, on the other hand, and do not have much protection at all.

User Mode vs. Kernel Mode

Now it is time to introduce the terms *kernel mode* and *user mode* and see where they fit into all this. Ring 0 is what is commonly referred to as kernel mode, and as you can see, this is a fully protected environment. This mode allows access to system memory and all processor instructions. Operating system code runs in kernel mode, as do most device drivers.

Ring 3 is referred to as user mode, and is hardly protected at all. This mode is a non-privileged processor mode, with a limited set of available interfaces, and limited access to system data.

In Figure 4-5, you see a simplified view of the kinds of applications and services you can execute in these two modes. The main point of these two modes is to protect the operating system from applications. User applications should not be allowed to access or modify operating system data directly. When an application needs the services of the OS, it makes a system service call instead. The operating system then validates the request and switches the processor from user mode to kernel mode, thereby allowing the request to be processed. After the system service call is completed, the processor mode is switched back to user mode before returning control to the user application.

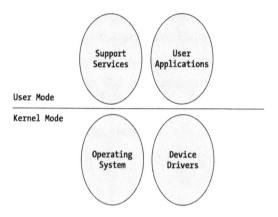

Figure 4-5. *User mode, kernel mode, and the applications within*

All user-mode threads execute in a private, fully protected address space when they are not executing in kernel mode. Because of this privacy, one process cannot view or modify another process's memory without special permissions. This prevents user-mode processes from causing failures to other applications or to the operating system itself. Errors from failing applications are also prevented from interfering with other applications due to this arrangement.

In kernel mode, on the other hand, all operating system components and device drivers share a single virtual address space, and thereby have access to all system data. This is why it is so important that all kernel-mode code be well designed and well-tested, because poor-quality code could violate system security or perhaps corrupt system data (not to mention the trouble that a malicious hacker could cause in this mode).

The key system components of the Windows Server 2003 are basically the same as for Windows 2000. In Figure 4-6, you can see these components, as well as which of them operate in kernel mode and which in user mode.

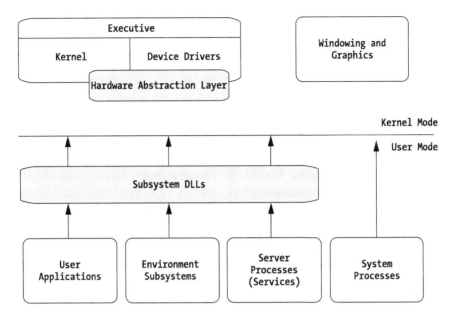

Figure 4-6. *The system components of the Windows architecture*

Kernel Mode Components

These are the kernel mode components:

- *The executive.* This contains the base operating system services, which we will study closer later in this chapter.

- *Kernel.* Here you find low-level functions.

- *Device drivers.* These are file system and network drivers and hardware device drivers that translate input/output (I/O) function calls into hardware device I/O requests.

- *Hardware Abstraction Layer (HAL).* This layer isolates the kernel, the executive, and the device drivers from differences between various hardware platforms.

- *Windowing and graphics system.* This is where the graphical user interface (GUI) is implemented.

User Mode Components

The user mode components are as follows:

- *System processes.* These contain processes that are not Windows services, like the logon process, meaning they are not started by the service control manager. (These are sometimes called system support services.)

- *Service processes.* Unlike system processes, these are started by the service control manager.

- *User applications.* Win32 applications and the like are found here and are supported natively by the OS. Other types of user applications can be supported by installing the appropriate environment subsystem.

- *Environment subsystems*. These expose native operating system services to user applications.

- *Subsystem DLLs*. These translate function calls (such as APIs) into internal system service calls.

- *Core Win32 subsystem DLLs*. Here you find kernel32.ddl, advapi32.dll, user32.dll, and many more.

What Does the Executive Do?

The executive exposes five kinds of functions, or tasks. Perhaps we should call them "collections of functions," since this better describes what they are.

The first one is the *application programming interface (API)*, which operates in user mode. Here you'll find the various functions that a developer can access to get different tasks done. An example of this is the possibility to read or write data to the disk. The interface to these functions is a DLL called ntdll.dll (see Figure 4-7).

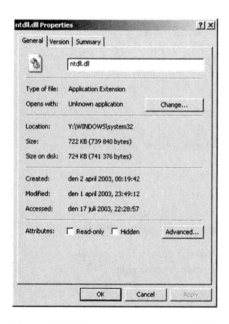

Figure 4-7. *The property page of ntdll.dll*

More than 200 functions are available from this file, but instead of accessing ntdll.dll itself, developers use the Win32 API. The Win32 API in turn makes most of these accessible, without the developer having to make the low-level calls necessary to access them.

The second collection, called the *internal system*, also operates in user mode, and it exposes functions primarily intended for use by the operating system's applications. Another application could call these functions, but that is not very common. In this collection, you find functions that help in:

- Performing local procedure calls (LPCs)

- Creating paging file(s) on disk

- Returning low-level information, like an object security identifier (SID)

The next collection, called *driver*, operates in kernel mode. Developers can use low-level calls to access the functions for this collection, but Microsoft has a driver development kit (DDK) available that you can use instead to access these functions. The functions in this collection operate in kernel mode, since they expose methods to access the operating system directly. Most hardware vendors use these to develop drivers for their hardware.

Now we have reached the fourth collection, *internal system component*, which also operates in kernel mode. Here is where you'll find functions that let various operating system managers communicate with other subsystems. The I/O manager may need to send data to the graphics subsystem in order to display something on the screen.

The final set of functions operates in either user or kernel mode, and is called *internal components*. These functions are designed to let COM components have special access to the operating system. Depending on what the component is designed to do, it can operate in either mode.

The Executive Provides More Than Just Exported Functions

The executive also provides various managers. One of them, the I/O Manager, we mentioned earlier. Before we describe this manager and the others, you need to have an understanding of the two categories they can fall into. The first, referred to as *internal* here, provides internal support for other managers. These are only accessible to components inside the kernel. The other, called *external*, responds to needs *outside* the executive.

We will start with the aforementioned *I/O Manager*. This manager handles all input and output to the operating system. This I/O can, for instance, be between the OS and the hardware devices. The I/O Manager in reality consists of three components:

- *File systems*. This component takes an I/O request and transforms it to I/O calls that a physical device can understand.

- *Cache manager*. The cache manager provides caching services to the file systems. That is, it places recently accessed data from the hard drives into memory, so it can be accessed quicker. This way performance is improved. An example of this is when a document is accessed continuously by users. The cache manager quickly discovers this, and places the document in RAM instead, so that it will be accessed more quickly for future calls. The cache manager provides caching services to file system calls, but also to networking components as well. Not everything is cached, however. You cannot force the cache manager to cache things it doesn't want to cache, either. A file that is continuously accessed is cached, as you saw earlier, but a file that is read sequentially is not. So depending on the type of activity on your server, you always have more or less caching activity going on.

- *Device drivers.* Because some parts of the OS lack the ability to talk directly to the hardware, you need a translator. This translator is the I/O Manager. There are two kinds of drivers when it comes to the I/O Manager: high-level drivers and low-level drivers. The high-level drivers are those that need a translator, because they do not know how to communicate with the hardware directly. An example of such a driver might be the file system drivers like NTFS or FAT. They are depending on the I/O Manager to translate their requests to the device, so they can be processed. The low-level drivers, on the other hand, do not need a translator, because they can communicate with the physical device on their own. The SCSI Host Bus Adapter (HBA) is an example of a low-level driver. Other low-level drivers are those that do not support the Windows Driver Model (WDM). These are drivers that control a physical device directly.

The next manager, also internal, is named the *LPC Facility* (short for Local Procedure Call Facility). This was developed to make it easier to pass calls between applications and the Windows subsystems. To better understand how it works, let's consider a remote procedure call (RPC). This is when you make a remote connection to a server from another computer and ask it to do you a favor by executing a function. When you do this, you have created a *shared resource.* When you have both the client and the server on the same machine, an LPC is established instead of an RPC. When your applications request the services of the I/O Manager, the stub in the application process packages the parameters for the call. After the actual call has been packaged, it's sent to the executive, via the LPC.

The *Object Manager* is responsible for allowing the operating system to create, manage, and delete objects. These objects can be threads, processes, synchronization objects, and other abstract objects that represent operating system resources.

The next manager we would like to discuss is the *Virtual Memory Manager*, or VMM. By using virtual memory, you can trick the operating system into believing it has more RAM than the system actually has. This is done by swapping data between the physical RAM and a temporary paging file on the hard disk called a *swap file.* VMM handles the swapping by determining which data to move in or out of RAM. The data that has been in RAM the longest period of time is the first to be moved to the swap file when the system is running out of physical memory.

The VMM keeps track of all physical memory pages in your system. It stores information about these pages, such as their status, in the *page frame database.* The status of a page could be one of the following:

- *Free.* This page is free but has not been zeroed yet. A page with this status is read-only.

- *Valid.* Such a page is in use by a process.

- *Modified.* A page that has been altered but not yet written to disk.

- *Standby.* If a page has this status, it has been removed from the process's working set.

- *Zeroed.* This page is available to the system.

- *Bad.* If you have a bad page, you also have a hardware error. No process can use this page.

Every time a page is moved in or out of memory, the VMM uses the page frame database, and if necessary, updates the status field.

The page frame database associates pages with each other, based on their status. So instead of searching the entire database for all free pages, it only has to find the first, and all the others will follow behind. So, we can actually say that the page frame database consists of six different lists, based on the status.

VMM must make sure a minimum number of pages are available to the system at all times. It does so by processing both the modified and standby lists, and moves pages from these to the free list (changing their status to Free). Before moving modified pages, VMM writes their changes to disk. Before the system can use a page (for other than read-only activity) it must change the status to Zeroed, and it is VMM that handles this, too.

Each process created in RAM is assigned a unique virtual address space. The VMM maps this virtual address to physical pages in memory. It thereby eliminates the chance of one process, or its threads, accessing memory allocated for another process.

When a process requires a page in memory, and the system can't find it at the requested location, we say that a *page fault* has occurred. Page faults can be one of two kinds:

- Hard page faults

- Soft page faults

Hard page faults mean that the requested data has to be fetched from disk. When this happens, the processor is interrupted and you will lose performance.

Soft page faults occur when the requested data is found elsewhere in memory. The CPU can handle many soft page faults, as opposed to hard page faults, without losing performance.

The *Process and Thread Manager* is external, and provides functions to both create and terminate processes and threads. It is the kernel that manages processes and threads, but the executive provides an interface to these functions via the Process and Thread Manager.

Security policies on the local computer are enforced by the *Security Reference Manager*, which is an external manager. Policies are enforced at both the kernel-mode level and the user-mode level. One of this manager's functions is to prevent users from accessing processes running in kernel mode. Another is to restrict them from accessing data or objects they are not allowed to access. The Security Reference Manager checks with the Local Security Authority, or LSA (which we will discuss in more detail later in the chapter) to find out if a user has the right permissions to the object he or she is trying to access.

The next manager is the *Run-Time Library*. This manager is internal, and provides the arithmetic, string, structure processing functions, and data conversions for the operating system.

The last manager, also internal, is called *Support Routines*. These routines allow the executive to allocate paged and non-paged system memory. They also allow the executive to interlock memory access. The Support Routines are also used to let the OS create two synchronization types: resource and fast mutex.

How to Work with the Executive Objects

Windows applications, like Win32 applications and OS/2 applications, act as an environment for other applications. These application environments, or *subsystems* as they are also called, allow Windows to emulate other operating systems. The executive provides generic services that all environment subsystems can call to perform basic operating system functions. The subsystems build on the services of the executive to provide environments that meet the specific needs of their client applications. Each application (user mode) is bound to only one subsystem and can't be bound to more.

Windows 2000 provided support for Win32, OS/2, and POSIX subsystems. In Windows Server 2003 there has been a slight change. Now only Win32 and POSIX subsystem support remains. To check which subsystems are installed and the operating system files that they use, open the registry editor and look at the following registry key (also, see Figure 4-8):

```
HKEY_LOCAL_MACHINE\SYSTEM\CurrentControlSet\Control\Session Manager\_SubSystems
```

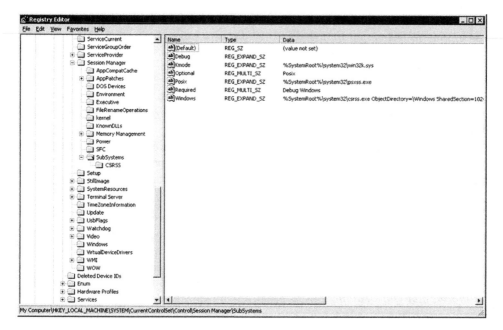

Figure 4-8. *Here are the subsystems on our system.*

Windows has been designed to natively run Win32 applications, of course, which gives it several benefits over other applications. To be honest, most applications running on a Windows system are Win32 applications these days, and the support for other subsystems is not that vital.

You can't run your Windows system without the Win32 subsystem, however. The code to handle windows creation and display I/O is implemented in the Win32 subsystem. So when an application needs to perform display I/O, other subsystems call on the Win32 subsystem to handle these tasks.

What the subsystems do is to act as translators between the application environments and the executive. This is necessary because the executive can't provide the services needed for each environment. The applications call the functions in the operating environment, which in turn calls the executive objects. This way the applications can receive a result they expect and can understand.

Table 4-1 shows the available object types and a short description of each.

Table 4-1. *Objects Made Available by the Executive*

Object	Description
Access token	An access token is used to determine the rights an object has to access resources.
Event	An event is used to notify objects of a system occurrence, or to synchronize two objects' activities.
File	A file is a universal object that allows you to work with data on the hard drive.

Object	Description
Key	If you open the registry editor, you can see these keys for yourself. They hold data that define the properties for a resource or object. A key can contain zero or more values (properties).
Mutex	The mutex is a synchronization object used to serialize access to some resource.
Object directory	The object directory is a container, and as such is used to hold other objects. Windows Explorer shows a hierarchical directory created with the help of the object directory.
Port	This object is used to pass messages between processes.
Process	A process can be described as an application. It contains a set of threads (described in the Thread entry, later in this table). A process contains at least one thread, but can contain many as well. The process also contains the virtual address space and control information.
Profile	This measures the execution time of a process within a given address space.
Queue	A queue in real life is a waiting line, and so is this queue. It is used to notify threads about completed I/O operations.
Section	Memory that is shared by more than one thread or process is called a *section*. In Win32 this is referred to as a *file-mapping object*, and is used for file caching, among other things.
Semaphore	Every time an object is requested by another one, a counter is incremented. The counter is a part of the semaphore. When the object is no longer needed, the counter is decremented. When a set access count level is reached, the semaphore restricts access to the object.
Symbolic link	A symbolic link is an object pointer, which is a shortcut, or indirect link, to another object.
Thread	A thread is an element of execution within a process.
Timer	This is basically an alarm clock for threads.

Synchronization

Because Windows is a multitasking, multiprocessing operating system, more than one application can try to access some part of the executive's memory at the same time. The Memory Manager uses the page frame database every time an application accesses memory, wants more memory, or releases memory. Because only one such database exists, two applications could possibly try to access it at the same time if they perform memory-related tasks. This could, of course, cause problems.

Note The page frame database keeps track of whether a page frame is in use by a certain application and whether the page frame is currently in memory.

This is why the operating system needs to synchronize access to resources like the page frame database. Synchronization access includes maintaining a queue for accessing the resources needed, which means a performance penalty. So if you want to optimize the amount of system resources that your applications use, you need to make sure they spend as little time as possible accessing a synchronized resource. Table 4-2 lists the various synchronization methods the executive can use.

Table 4-2. *Synchronization Methods the Executive Exposes*

Method	Description
Spinlock	The spinlock locks access to a resource so the accessing process has sole access to it. It is used by operating system components and device drivers to protect data. Since the spinlock locks the processor, it should be used for something short and very specific to the current process.
Dispatcher objects	These synchronization objects are provided by the kernel to the executive. They can be used in either kernel or user mode. The Win32 API exposes these as different functions, like WaitForSingleObject() and WaitForMultipleObjects(). This way an application developer can use them to make sure resources are available to an application, and that no one else uses them.
Executive resources	These are synchronization methods that only kernel-mode applications, such as drivers, can use.

■**Note** Do not confuse application spinlocks with kernel spinlocks. The kernel spinlocks are used internally by the Windows executive and I/O drivers to avoid many processes accessing the same resource at the same time.

Hardware Abstraction Layer (HAL)

From Windows NT and later, Windows has been designed to function on a multitude of hardware and CPU versions. The operating system should not need to know anything about the platform it is working with, at least not within reason. To provide this functionality the Microsoft constructed HAL. The OS uses the HAL to access devices that the machine provides, and this includes the processor. If you examine your machine, you will find a file named hal.dll, as shown in Figure 4-9, in the system32 catalog in the Windows directory.

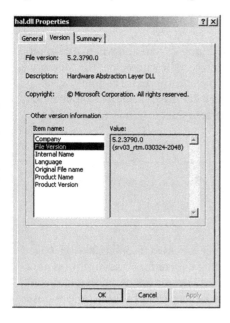

Figure 4-9. *The hal.dll property page*

Every hardware platform has a different HAL, which makes it possible for Windows to operate on various platforms with minimal need for rewrites of code. In short, Windows talks to the device drivers, which in turn talk to the HAL. The HAL in its turn talks to the hardware.

The HAL always provides the same interface, so the operating system does not really care on which platform it resides, as long as the HAL is correct for the platform. Device drivers are, of course, still needed, as they are a part of the communication chain just mentioned.

Note Even though this might sound good, it still does not make it effortless to move software from one platform to another. It reduces the amount of code you need to write when you must move an application between platforms, however. With .NET applications this move will be easier, since you only need to know that the new platform uses the same .NET Framework version as you used on your earlier platform.

Windows Subsystems

We mentioned earlier in the chapter that Windows includes environment subsystems. These operate in user mode. In Figure 4-10, you see an overview of the components included in the Windows architecture.

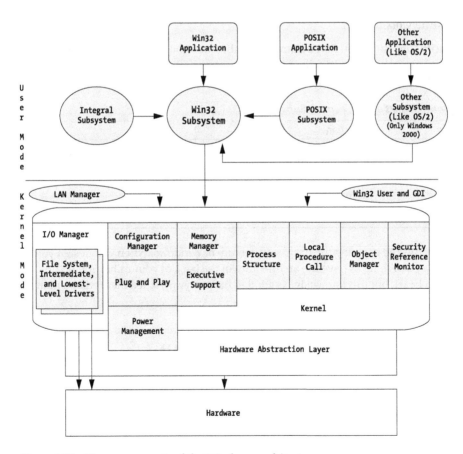

Figure 4-10. *The components of the Windows architecture*

Since we have already covered the most important aspects of the subsystems, it is sufficient to say that performance is negatively affected when running applications like OS/2 or POSIX applications on Windows systems. This is due to all the overhead added by emulating another operating system. You can see the same thing happening when you run Win32 applications on a 64-bit Windows system.

The *Integral subsystem*, which we will take a look at here, is not a subsystem in which applications run, nor is it an emulator of another operating system. What it does is handle a multitude of other tasks. Among these you find functions that control the overall security of the local computer. Other functions that you find here are the *server service, workstation service*, and the *security subsystem*. Anyone who has looked through the service MMC recognizes the server and workstation service. Now you know where these two functions come from, so let's take a closer look at them:

- *Server service*. This is a component that makes it possible for Windows to provide network resources, which could be something as simple as sharing a directory on the network. This service is important to Windows, since many other services, like Message Queuing, depend on it.

- *Workstation service*. The workstation service lets your computer access other computers' shared resources on the network. That is, it lets you access a resource that a server service provides on another machine. It also provides an API so you can programmatically access the network redirect.

In the security subsystem you find a number of subcomponents. These enable the security subsystem to control access to Windows and its resources. Table 4-3 shows the functions of the security subsystem and the components behind them.

Table 4-3. *Subcomponents of the Security Subsystem*

Subcomponent	Function
Logon process	Initial logon authentication. It also accepts local as well as remote logon requests from users.
Security Reference Monitor	Keeps an eye on rights and permissions that are associated with user accounts.
Local Security Authority	Monitors which system resources need to be audited.

Now we have finished covering the basic architecture of Windows. When you design your applications, it is a good thing to have the architecture in the back of your mind. You do not need to know it by heart, but this knowledge is good to have anyway, since there will be many times it will be a benefit to you.

Next, we will explore scalability, availability, and reliability.

Scalability, Availability, and Reliability

In order to provide a scalable and reliable platform, you can adopt various strategies. *Scale up* and *scale out* are the two common categories that these strategies fall under. Scale up basically means adding more hardware, or better performing hardware, to a single server. You could add more RAM or more and stronger CPUs, for example. Scale out means that you distribute your workload on many servers. Here you find Network Load Balancing (NLB) and Microsoft Cluster Service (MSCS), as we described earlier in the book.

Scaling Up Windows

Let us start by looking at ways of scaling up Windows. Before you simply add more RAM or more CPUs, you need to consider the Windows version you are using or planning to use. It would be a waste to add four CPUs to a Windows Server 2003 Web Edition system, for instance, since it only supports two CPUs in the first place. As you can understand, this is also why it is so important to carefully consider the platform you are going to use for the different parts of your system, early in the design process. You want to neither under- nor over-dimension it. It is also important to consider future needs of the system so you can easily scale up later on, with minimum cost and without the need to purchase a new license for the operating system.

With the addition of the Windows Server 2003 family, Microsoft offers a wide assortment of operating systems that can scale from 1 CPU all the way to 64. Table 4-4 shows an overview of the basic scaling-up possibilities in the Windows 2000 Server and Windows Server 2003 families.

Table 4-4. *Basic Scaling-Up Possibilities of the Various Windows Server Versions*

Server Edition	Max RAM	Max CPUs
Windows 2000 Server	4GB	4
Windows 2000 Advanced	8GB	8
Windows 2000 Datacenter	64GB	32
Windows Server 2003 Web	2GB	2
Windows Server 2003 Standard	4GB	4
Windows Server 2003 Enterprise	32GB	8
Windows Server 2003 Enterprise 64-bit	64GB	8
Windows Server 2003 Datacenter	64GB	64
Windows Server 2003 Datacenter 64-bit	512GB	64

Scaling Out Windows

In some cases, it's not enough just to rely on scaling up. It might not even be the best way to increase performance. Your web clusters, for example, benefit more from scaling out than from scaling up. It is better to let more web servers handle client requests than to have one huge server become a single point of failure. Database systems and messaging systems can benefit from both ways of scaling, as you will see later. Table 4-5 shows how you can scale out the Windows Server families.

Table 4-5. *Scaling-Out Possibilities in Windows*

Edition	NLB Nodes	Cluster Support	Cluster Nodes	Comments
Windows 2000 Server	32	NLB		Only with Application Center
Windows 2000 Advanced	32	NLB/MSCS	2	
Windows 2000 Datacenter	32	NLB/MSCS	4	
Windows Server 2003 Web	32	NLB		

(Continued)

Table 4-5. *(Continued)*

Edition	NLB Nodes	Cluster Support	Cluster Nodes	Comments
Windows Server 2003 Standard	32	NLB		
Windows Server 2003 Enterprise	32	NLB/MSCS	8	
Windows Server 2003 Datacenter	32	NLB/MSCS	8	

You can see that you have to carefully consider which Windows version to use during the design phase. We have said so before, but this is more important than many developers and designers think it is. You need to estimate the load, and the possibility of the load increasing over time, early on. Although the scaling features make it easy to add more power, you don't want to plan to have more expensive license fees in your system than you have to, at least from the beginning. You do not want to implement a web cluster based on Windows Server 2003 Standard Edition, unless you really need one of its features. The Web Edition is sufficient in most cases. It would also be unfortunate if you implement your database server on the Windows Server Standard Edition, and later on found out you need to cluster it with MSCS. Then you would have to spend money on an upgrade of the operating system and would probably end up with the completely unnecessary cost incurred by having both the Standard and the Enterprise Editions. That is just a waste of money that you can avoid if you spend time on the design.

You should really consider the level of reliability and availability you need. If you are implementing a database system, can you possibly accept several minutes of disrupted service while you do a restore of a backup? If the answer is yes, go with the Windows Server 2003 Standard Edition. If the answer is no, you need something more powerful, like the Enterprise Edition or Datacenter Edition.

Do you need your services up and running constantly? That is another crucial question, since it affects the choice of both platform and cluster solution.

Server Clusters Using MSCS

A cluster with MSCS is often used for a database or messaging system. There are several ways of setting up such a system. This kind of cluster consists of two or more nodes—that is, two or more independent servers. A node can be either active (meaning it is handling requests) or passive (the node is standing by in case an active node fails).

You need to carefully consider whether a node in your cluster should be active or passive. Why? Well, if an active node encounters an error and fails while a passive node is available, you can let that node take the failing node's place without many problems. (This is based on the assumption that the passive node has the same, or better, hardware configuration as the failing node.)

You can also have a situation where all nodes are active in the cluster. If one node fails, applications and services can be transferred to another node. Then the load on the failover node will increase, because it needs to handle the load of the failing node as well as its own. You do not want to under-dimension the hardware in this case, because if you do, the failover node might give in to sheer pressure and fail as well.

To better understand how you can use active and passive nodes, have a look at Figure 4-11. This figure shows two nodes, of which is active (Active01), with Passive01 standing by in case Active01 fails.

The average workload on the active node is a maximum of 45 percent CPU and memory resources. If Active01 fails, Passive01 takes its place and still has the resources left for peaks in the workload. This gives you time to fix the problems on the failing node, take it back online, and then fail back from the failover node.

Active01

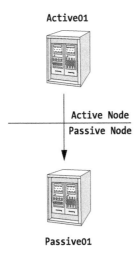

Active Node
Passive Node

Passive01

Figure 4-11. *A cluster with one passive node and one active node*

In a scenario such as Figure 4-12, you don't have a passive node that awaits a failing node. To make sure failover is successful in this case, you must configure the servers so the workload is proportional on the average. In this scenario, the failover has been configured to go from Server01 to Server03. Let us say Server01 has an average workload of 50 percent and Server03 has an average workload of 25 percent.

Server01

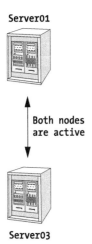

Both nodes
are active

Server03

Figure 4-12. *A cluster with two active nodes*

In this example, all servers have identical hardware configuration. If Server01 fails and Server03 takes its place, the new load on Server03 would be 75 percent. This does not leave much room for workload peaks. An even worse scenario would be if both servers averaged 50 percent of the workload. Then a failover server would have a 100 percent workload in case of a failure. The server could quite easily give in, giving you limited use of your cluster solution.

Another scenario to consider would be if you configured your nodes to be able to failover to any of the other servers in the cluster (see Figure 4-13). If they each had a workload of 35 percent, you could easily handle one failing server. The failover node would be working at 70 percent, but it could still handle requests. If another node fails and the same failover node had to handle this load too, it would be working well over 100 percent capacity, which would bring it down. The last node would probably die of a heart attack, even before it could try to handle the load. This would leave you with a nonworking cluster.

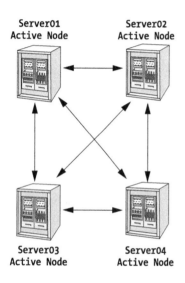

Figure 4-13. *A four-node cluster where all servers could fail over to all others*

The scenario shown in Figure 4-14 is a common setup in many enterprises. In this case, you have set up your four-node cluster to have one passive node only. You have configured it to be at least twice as powerful as any of the other three servers. The workload on the three active nodes is 35 percent on average. If any of the active servers fail, the passive node would step in to take its place. Since it is a powerful server, it would have less workload than the failing node, making it prepared to handle one or more failing servers.

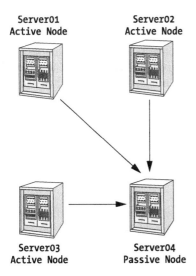

Figure 4-14. *A four-node cluster with only one passive node*

Most companies do not even have a more powerful passive server, since the likelihood of more than one server failing is small. But be aware that this is a calculated risk. The worst-case scenario could make the whole cluster fail.

These examples try to illustrate the importance of designing the cluster solution in a good way. The solution will be different depending on what problems need to be solved. You must consider the following, however:

- How many nodes should you use?

- What hardware configuration do you need?

- How should you use active/passive nodes?

- How much workload should the nodes have?

Handling Data in a Cluster

When you have a server cluster like the ones described in the previous section, data must be shared between applications running on the nodes. You would not have much use of a failover cluster node if it was unaware of the updates made by the failing node before the failure. This is often solved by using what is called a *shared-nothing database configuration*. This means that each server in the cluster owns a subset of the resources, and no server in the cluster owns the same subset at the same time as another. If there is an error, and one server goes down, you can configure the cluster so that another (predefined) server takes ownership of the resources that the failing server owned.

All the data is placed on a common disk array, which could be connected over a SCSI cable or a fiber optic cable, or via a Storage Area Network (SAN). If a node fails, the data is still accessible to the failover node.

When you have many active nodes, often each node is set up with a specific view into the database. This allows the various nodes to handle specific types of requests. Say you have a cluster handling the database of customer accounts. One server would have a view into the database for all accounts between A through F, another would handle G through K, and so on. The only node that could update an account is the active node responsible for this section of the database. This setup eliminates the possibility of having multiple nodes updating the same account.

You might still encounter an error to the shared data, however. So you need to plan the redundancy of this as well. The most common solution is to use a RAID disk configuration, which would provide fault tolerance of various levels, depending on which RAID was chosen. This book will not cover RAID configurations, as this is out of the scope of our topic.

Architecture of a Server Cluster

When a node is active, its resources are available. The clients, however, do not access the node in itself. That would not be a good solution, because if the node should fail, you would have to change the configuration of the clients so they access the failover node instead. The solution to this is to configure *virtual servers*. As long as the clients access the virtual server, it doesn't matter whether node A, B, C, or D services its requests. That is an internal cluster problem instead, and this solution is much more preferable than changing all clients.

A virtual server specifies groups of resources that fail over together. When a cluster server fails, all the groups of resources on it that are marked for clustering fail over to another node. When the failed server has been fixed, you take it back online again. If you have configured your server cluster to do so, failback to the original server takes place. You could also configure the current server to continue processing requests, however, and make the fixed server become a passive node instead.

Let us take a look at *resource groups*. In a resource group, you collect, or associate, resources that are related to or dependent on each other. When you choose which applications you want to be a part of a resource group, you should consider its need for high availability. If your users require the application constantly, it should be a part of a resource group. If it isn't, it can still run on the cluster server, but you would not have high availability for it.

Unfortunately, just adding any application to a resource group will not do. The application needs to be able to handle a cluster environment: otherwise it would not benefit from clustering. Applications that can work within a cluster environment are said to be *cluster aware*. They have built-in features that let them register with the server cluster, so that they can receive cluster status and notification information. SQL Server and Microsoft Exchange Server are both cluster-aware applications.

Even some *cluster-unaware* applications can be assigned to a resource group, and therefore take advantage of failover technique. A few criteria must be met by such an application to allow this. The application must be able to store data in a configurable location—that is, it must be able to store data on a shared storage device, since this is how cluster nodes access application data. The application must also use an IP-based protocol for network communication. Cluster communication uses IP-based protocols: other protocols are not suitable. When a failover occurs, a temporary loss of network connectivity occurs. The application clients must be able to handle this loss by being able to try again to get access to the resource, and thus continue to function normally when failover occurs.

If the application can provide this, you can add it to a resource group. This way you add high availability to applications not designed for clustering in the first place. But be sure to check the applications thoroughly, and test them before adding them to a production cluster. Testing is, as always, a key part of all implementation.

Microsoft Cluster Service in Windows Server 2003 is built on three key components:

- Cluster service

- Resource monitor

- Resource DLLs

The cluster service is the core component, as you can see in Figure 4-15, and runs as a high-priority system service.

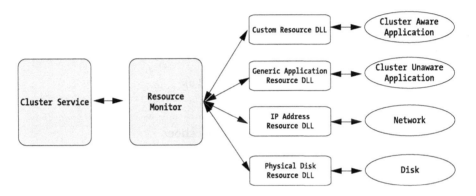

Figure 4-15. *The architecture of MSCS in Windows Server 2003*

The *resource monitor* is an interface between the cluster service and the cluster resources. This is run as an independent process. By using the resource API, the resource monitor and the resource DLLs communicate with each other. The API exposes a collection of entry points, callback functions, and related structures, as well as macros to manage resources.

You have built-in tools to manage your clusters. The primary tool is the Cluster Administrator (see Figure 4-16). From this you can manage your cluster objects, perform maintenance, and monitor cluster activity.

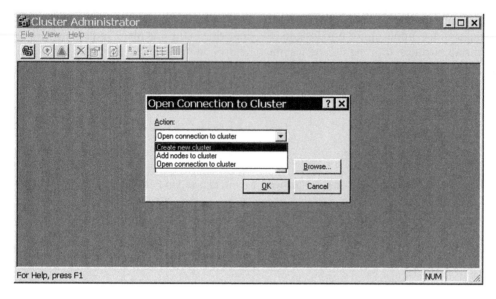

Figure 4-16. *The Cluster Administrator before any cluster is set up*

Geographically Dispersed Clusters and Multiple-Site Applications

The clusters you have seen so far all have one common denominator: The servers reside at the same place. What happens if the entire site disappears? Naturally you would lose all data, and your applications would vanish. This is perhaps a highly unlikely scenario, but the last few years of terrorist acts have taught us it that it *could happen*. A similar calamity does not have to be the result of something as dramatic as terrorism, either. Your office could catch fire and crumble to the ground. These are the things you need to at least consider when designing a highly available application anyway.

■**Note** Keep one thing in mind though. You cannot protect yourself from everything. But, you should strive for minimizing the possibility of everything going wrong at the same time.

This reminds us of an experience we had at a Swedish company. Just to avoid embarrassing anyone, we won't mention any names. We were sent to a customer to help with an application. The company's server hall had two large steel safes in the middle of the room. When we asked what they were for, we were told that the company had duplicates of its most important servers in these safes. When one safe was opened, the room was not left unguarded. Someone was required to be there—otherwise the safe had to be closed. The administrator was, understandably, very proud of this solution, and we could bet someone could nuke the building and the servers would still be okay.

When we set to work on the application, we had to look through the event logs of one of the servers. We noticed a lot of warnings originating from the backup software. We asked if the company was aware of this and were told it was, and that the problem was going to be solved soon. But when we looked a little more thoroughly, we noticed that no backup of the servers existed at all. So, even if the servers were protected in safes, no backup was available. If an error in the data sneaked in that had to be corrected, this could not be fixed with a restore operation. Talk about a waste of money on the safe!

The point of this little anecdote is that you have got to plan carefully when you try to protect your data and applications. You don't want to make such a mistake yourself.

To avoid problems with a server hall vanishing, you could use multiple sites or separate parts of your clusters in different physical locations. The latter solution is called *geographically dispersed clusters*. Figure 4-17 shows an example of a *multi-site solution*.

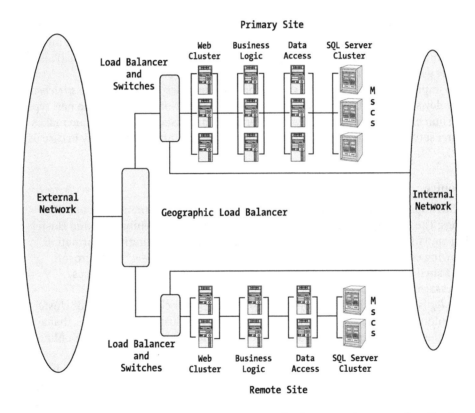

Figure 4-17. *A multi-site cluster solution that uses both NLB and MSCS to handle clusters*

When you implement a multi-site solution, you configure one location as the primary site, and the other (or others) as a remote site(s). The architecture at the remote site should mirror that of the primary site. The components that are mirrored, or any other considerations you might have, must be decided by your Service-Level Agreements (SLAs).

There are different ways to implement this kind of solution, and your choice depends on what level of security you need. When you have a *full implementation design*, you mirror everything at the remote site. This way the remote site can handle everything the primary site can. It can operate independently or, if necessary, handle the entire load. If you select this design, you need to set up real-time replication and synchronization of your databases and applications, so that you do not have sites that lack information. If you cannot set up real-time replication, you need to make sure you replicate as often as possible. You must then also be aware of the discrepancies that can occur in the data.

A *partial implementation design* is one that only mirrors specific components to the remote site(s). This solution obviously can't cover for the primary site. What it can do is handle peak hours. It can also maintain limited uptime if the primary site fails. You could even use it to provide limited services as needed. If you choose a partial implementation, you need to consider how often you must replicate data. Is it necessary with real-time replication, or could you manage with less, and live with a certain latency?

To implement any of these two designs, you could use *geographically dispersed clusters*. This is a technique supported by MSCS. Instead of having a shared-nothing database on the same LAN, you must find a solution that works over long distances with this technique. This is most often done with the use of Virtual LANs (VLANs) that let you connect to SANs.

One of the improvements to geographically dispersed clusters (sometimes called *stretched clusters*) in Windows Server 2003 is the introduction of the *majority node set*. This is a new type of quorum resource, and it changes the way cluster quorum is used. This technique makes sure that cluster servers that are geographically dispersed still maintain consistency in case of a node failure.

Quorum Resource

Each cluster has a special resource called the *quorum resource*. A quorum resource usually does two things: The first provides a means for arbitration leading to membership and cluster state decision, and the second provides physical storage to store configuration information.

The following comes from "Server Clusters: Architecture Overview" by Microsoft Corporation, March 2003 (see http://www.microsoft.com/_windowsserver2003/docs/ServerClustersArchitecture.doc for further information):

A *quorum log* is simply a configuration database for the server clustering. It holds cluster configuration information, such as which servers are part of the cluster, the resources that are installed in the cluster, and the state that those resources are in (for example, online or offline).

There are a few reasons why the quorum is important in a cluster:

We will focus on one of them here and that is consistency—since the basic idea of a cluster is multiple physical servers acting as a single virtual server, it is critical that each of the physical servers has a consistent view of how the cluster is configured. The quorum acts as the definitive repository for all configuration information relating to the cluster. In the event of the Cluster Service being unable to read the quorum log, it will not start, since it is not able to guarantee that the cluster will be in a consistent state—one of the primary requirements for a cluster.

Note The quorum is used as the tie-breaker to avoid "split-brain" scenarios. A *split-brain scenario* happens when all of the network communication links between two or more cluster nodes fail. In these cases, the cluster may be split into two or more partitions that cannot communicate with each other. The quorum guarantees that any cluster resource is brought online on only one node. It does this by allowing the partition that "owns" the quorum to continue, while the other partitions are evicted from the cluster.

Figure 4-18 shows that an ordinary cluster configuration lets the quorum resource write information on all the cluster database changes to a recovery log(s). This way you can recover cluster configuration and state data, if needed. The quorum resource is placed on a shared disk array. The information on the shared disks can be used to see if other nodes in the cluster are functioning.

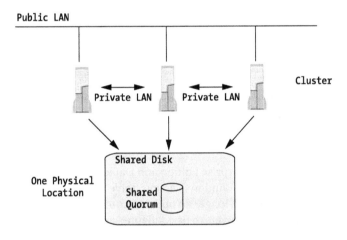

Figure 4-18. *An ordinary quorum placement on a shared disk array*

Figure 4-19 shows a geographically dispersed cluster running Windows Server 2003.

In this scenario, quorum data, including cluster configuration and state data, is stored on the system disk of each node in the cluster. This way, a dispersed cluster can maintain a consistent state, without the trouble of setting up quorum information on storage located on the interconnect.

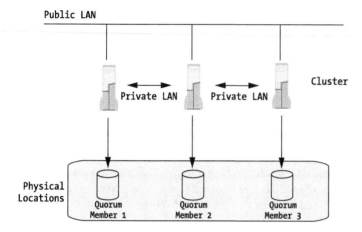

Figure 4-19. *A Windows Server 2003 MSCS configuration where the quorum resource has been configured as a majority node set*

■**Note** The name *majority node set* comes from the fact that the majority of the nodes must be functioning for this configuration to run normally. This could obviously be a problem if for some reason many nodes fail.

New in MSCS for Windows Server 2003

In Windows Server 2003, MSCS is available in the Enterprise Edition and Datacenter Edition. Several changes have been made to MSCS in this new Windows version. Table 4-6 lists a few of these new features. Most noticeable is that MSCS is no longer an optional component. Now it is integrated into the operating system, enabling the servers to be configured as a cluster node, without access to installation media. Other benefits are that you can create and change clusters from a remote computer using cluster administration tools. You do not have to reboot your server after installation or change of the cluster configuration either.

Table 4-6. *New Features and Improvements to MSCS in Windows Server 2003*

Feature	Description
Larger clusters	In Windows 2000, the Datacenter Edition allowed support for four-node clusters. Now you can support eight nodes, using Windows Server 2003 Enterprise Edition or Datacenter Edition. This provides many more options for configuring your clusters. Take one of the examples shown in the "Server Clusters Using MSCS" section earlier and try it for yourself.
Better manageability	The management tools have been polished and extended. Among these is Diskpart, a new tool that lets you expand cluster disks dynamically online. Applications can now be made cluster-aware using scripting languages like VBScript and JScript. This way your developers (or administrators) can write add-ins for applications, thereby making them possible to monitor and control in a cluster. MSMQ support has been enhanced. It now includes support for triggers, allowing applications with high availability to be built and still have access to all the features of MSMQ.

Feature	Description
Active Directory	Virtual servers can be registered in Active Directory. This integration means you now can use Kerberos authentication and delegation when your applications are run in a cluster. You don't have to know the exact location of the cluster either, but can instead look in the directory to find it.
Quorum resource	As mentioned, beside the traditional cluster quorum improvements mechanism, you now have the majority node set. As described previously, you can get great help from this in building your multi-site, geographically dispersed clusters.
EFS support	Encrypting File System (EFS) is now supported on clustered disks.
64-bit support	Of course 64-bit support is included, and it lets applications take benefit of larger memory capacity. This will be pretty cool when the next version of SQL Server will be released.
Storage capabilities	Optimizations have been made in the support of Storage Area Networks. Worth mentioning here are targeted device resets and storage interconnect requirements. Distributed File Systems (DFS) has been improved. Now you find multiple stand-alone roots and independent root failover support for active/active configurations. You can now also support offline files on a clustered file share, meaning clients' cached data is stored on a clustered share.
Various improvements	The cluster service account password can now be changed or changes dynamically, without needing to take nodes offline. WMI support has been added to cluster control and management, cluster state change events, and application and cluster state information, just to mention a few changes. Log file handling and logs have been improved. There have also been improvements to the logic for a failover in the event a complete loss of internal communication within a cluster has occurred.

Some Good Tips for MSCS

Now you know more about the architecture of MSCS. Let us take a look at a few of the general requirements for clusters before examining some best practices.

To determine if your hardware is supported by the operating system, you can navigate to the Microsoft web site and have a look at the Hardware Compatibility List (HCL). You can build your cluster on hardware that isn't on the list, but then such a setup would not be a qualified configuration, and support from Microsoft would be limited.

Strive to use identical hardware whenever possible on the cluster servers. Use the same NICs, switches, and so on, to avoid problems.

When you plan your cluster, the object is to avoid a single point of failure. That is the whole idea of clustering, after all. To avoid problems with network connectivity, you should use two or more independent networks that connect the nodes of a cluster. You cannot allow these networks to have a common physical component, either. You must make sure they do not share switches, and so on, to avoid any single point of failure.

What else do you need to think about? When it comes to communication settings, there are a few important things to consider. The first thing would be to manually configure the NICs to use the same communication settings. You must also make sure the port settings on the switches match these settings.

Tip Do not use automatic detection, as some NICs drop packages while negotiating the network settings.

The subnets used for the cluster must have distinct subnet numbers that separate them from each other. For example, if you have two subnets, you could use the following addresses:

- *Subnet 1*: 10.1.x.x mask 255.255.0.0

- *Subnet 2*: 10.2.x.x mask 255.255.0.0

This way you have two separate subnets available. You could use DHCP on your subnets, but we strongly recommend manually configuring the IP addresses with static values: otherwise failure to renew a lease would disrupt cluster operations. To further avoid a single point of failure, you should use at least two of the subnets for internal cluster node communication. You can configure two settings here: One is Internal Cluster Communications only, and the other is All Communications in Cluster Service. Of these, subnet 1 should be used exclusively for internal communication between cluster nodes. This is called the *private network*. *Public networks*, on the other hand, are those networks that clients use to communicate with the cluster.

All nodes participating in a cluster must belong to the same domain. To avoid a single point of failure, the domain also has to fulfill some requirements. The easiest way to do this is to duplicate everything. That is, use at least two domain controllers for a start. If you use DNS, you must make sure you have at least two DNS servers that support dynamic updates. All nodes in the cluster and all domain controllers must be configured with a primary and at least one secondary DNS server. Do not forget to have at least two global catalogs as well.

You also might want to address a few other issues:

- Do not configure DNS, WINS, or default gateway servers on the private NICs. WINS and DNS servers should be configured on the public NICs, however.

- If your public NICs are used for communication with clients or services on remote subnets, you should configure them with default gateways.

- The private subnet should be isolated, so do not connect anything beside the cluster nodes. Do not implement any WINS, DNS, DHCP, or anything else on these subnets.

When you have geographically dispersed clusters, you should also think about the following:

- You can let nodes in a cluster be on different physical networks. If you do, the private and public networks must appear as single, non-routed LANs. You can accomplish this by using techniques such as including VLANs. Remember to make sure all VLANs fail independently of all other networks if using this technique.

- Latency for round-trip communication between cluster nodes must be less than 500 milliseconds. This value is also true for communication between the nodes and the SAN.

Network Load Balancing

Network Load Balancing provides failover support for IP-based services and applications that need high scalability and availability, as you saw in Chapter 3. An NLB cluster, like a MSCS cluster, exposes a virtual IP address that clients use to access the services of the cluster. The architecture of an NLB cluster is much simpler than that of a MSCS cluster, however. NLB runs as a network driver, as you can see in Figure 4-20. This means it does not require any special hardware to function.

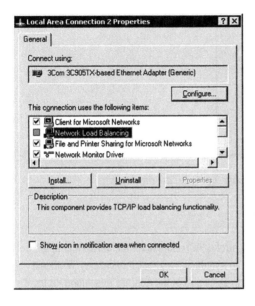

Figure 4-20. *The properties of a local area connection*

What you need to consider is having IP networking installed on all load-balanced servers. This, of course, is because Network Load Balancing is IP-based.

You do not have to have common data storage configured as in MSCS either. All nodes in the cluster are equipped with the same information—for instance, exact copies of a web site.

The normal scenario when setting up NLB is to use at least two NICs. One is set up as a cluster NIC and is used to handle network traffic for the cluster. The other is set up as a dedicated adapter and handles traffic outside the cluster, like client-to-cluster communication.

NLB can operate in two modes, as Figure 4-21 shows: unicast and multicast. The default mode is unicast, to ensure it operates properly with all routers.

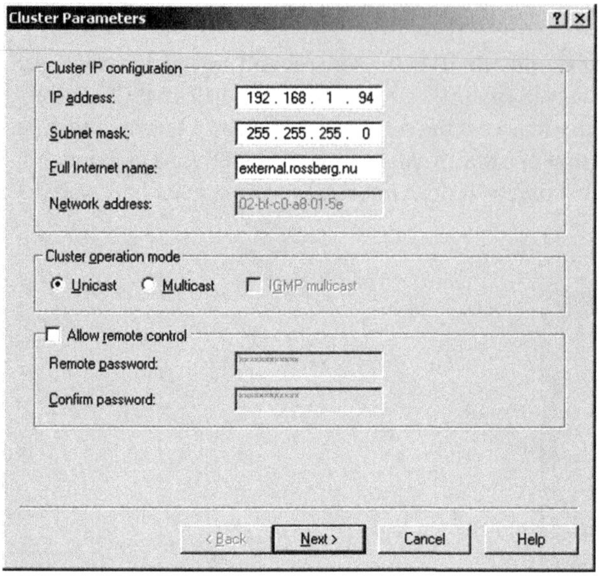

Figure 4-21. *An NLB cluster can operate in either unicast or multicast mode.*

Note *Unicast* means that NLB assigns a Media Access Control (MAC) address for the network adapter, and *multicast* means NLB converts the cluster MAC address to a multicast address if necessary. Multicast also ensures that the cluster IP addresses resolve to this address as part of the Address Resolution Protocol (ARP). The NIC NLB is bound to retain its original MAC address.

The NLB driver acts as a filter between the cluster adapter and the TCP/IP stack. This makes it possible to allow only traffic bound for the designated host to be received. Keep in mind that Network Load Balancing only controls IP traffic (TCP, UDP, and GRE) on special ports. You must therefore configure the port that you want NLB to listen to. If NLB encounters traffic on a port not configured with NLB, it simply lets it pass through, without any modification to the IP stack.

One of the benefits of using Network Load Balancing to load balance your web servers is that you don't have to rely on any specific hardware. The point is that you could take an off-the-shelf server and simply add it to your cluster without much hassle. You just add the data you need for your applications, like web pages and other web content, and you are ready to rock. You aren't dependent on any fault-tolerant hardware in any particular way. You don't have to have any fancy RAID solution configured, because if the server fails, all its requests are rerouted to another server within ten seconds. You can then correct the error and add the server back to the cluster again. This cuts the hardware costs for an NLB cluster.

What you do have to spend some time and effort on is synchronizing data. No participating cluster server should contain old information. Luckily, there are tools that help you with this, so you do not have to manually update all 32 servers in your cluster. (For more information about content management, please see Chapter 5.)

New in NLB for Windows Server 2003

Even though NLB is much simpler than MSCS, there is room for improvements in the Windows Server 2003 family. One thing that strikes us is that NLB is now supported on *all* the server members. The introduction of the Web Edition is a step in the right direction when it comes to building web clusters. The cost of this edition is not much higher than the cost of Windows XP Professional, making it an excellent choice in these situations. Since one of the objectives with NLB is to keep costs down, and making it simple to implement is another, this is a good thing. You can now order a simple pizza-box server preconfigured with the Windows Server 2003 Web Edition, have it delivered to you, and quite easily add it to your cluster in practically no time, at a cost of about $2000. There is no need for expensive Microsoft Web solutions any longer.

■**Note** Windows Server 2003 Web Edition is only available as an OEM-installed OS. You cannot buy the software from the shelf without ordering a server at the same time, as with other Windows Server versions.

One of the problems with having a large NLB cluster involves administering all the servers. Tools like Application Center have made life easier in the past, but now quite capable management applications are coming out of the box. One of these tools is the Network Load Balancing Manager (see Figure 4-22). With this tool, you can create new NLB clusters and configure existing ones. You can also use it to add and remove cluster members.

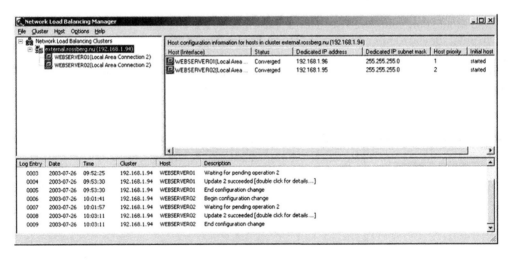

Figure 4-22. *The Network Load Balancing Manager in Windows Server 2003*

Another benefit with the Network Load Balancing Manager is that you can use it to diagnose improperly configured clusters easily.

You can use this tool not only for the clusters on the server Network Load Balancing Manager is run from, but also for remote administration of other NLB clusters. This way you have a single point of configuration and management for your NLB clusters.

Another feature of NLB in Windows Server 2003 is the introduction of *virtual clusters*. This feature can be used to configure different port rules for different cluster IP addresses. In this case, each IP address corresponds to a Web site or application hosted on the NLB cluster. You can also use it to select which host in a cluster should be used to service traffic sent to a specific web site or application on the cluster.

In Windows Server 2003 you have the possibility of binding NLB to multiple NICs. By doing so, you can host multiple clusters on the same hosts, despite the fact that they are on independent subnets. This also lets you use NLB for firewall and proxy load balancing in those cases where you need load balancing on multiple fronts of a proxy or firewall.

When NLB is running in multicast mode, you can enable Internet Group Management Protocol (IGMP) support on it. This allows you to limit switch flooding to only those ports on a switch that have NLB machines connected to them. This is done to conserve network resources.

■**Note** Switch flooding is caused by the NLB algorithm. This algorithm requires all hosts in an NLB cluster to see every incoming packet addressed to the cluster.

Some Good Tips for NLB

Now we will introduce you to what we consider some of the best practices for NLB based on our experience over the years.

When you operate your clusters in unicast mode, NLB can't distinguish between single NICs on the hosts. This is why you need a separate NIC for internal cluster communication.

You should only configure TCP/IP on a NIC where NLB is enabled.

In order for you to more easily manage troubleshooting, you should enable NLB logging. In Figure 4-23, you can see where this should be enabled in the Network Load Balancing Manager. When you do this, you need to specify a log file, since this logging doesn't use the Event Viewer.

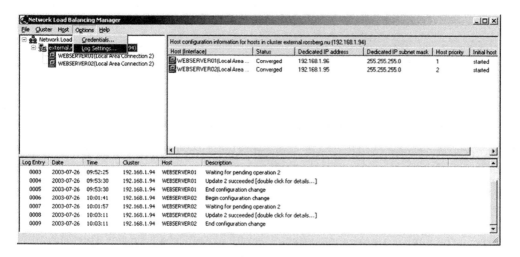

Figure 4-23. *Enabling logging in Network Load Balancing Manager*

Make sure that all cluster parameters and port rules are set identically on all cluster nodes. Check so that all ports used by NLB have port rules set. That means you should make sure FTP traffic is directed to port 20 and 21 or any other port of your liking. After a port rule is set, *always* click Add: otherwise the rule will not take effect.

Since NLB doesn't stop and start applications, you must make sure the applications are started on all the cluster hosts that they are installed on. You need to ensure the applications are started so that your cluster gives you the best benefits.

One thing that might seem obvious is nevertheless worth mentioning. Make sure that the same IP addresses are entered in the TCP/IP properties as in the NLB setup. Also make sure that the dedicated IP address is listed before the cluster IP address in the TCP/IP properties box (see Figure 4-24). Otherwise, you can't ensure that the responses to the connections originating from one host will return to the same host. (In our case, 192.168.1.96 is the dedicated IP address, and 192.168.1.94 is the cluster IP address, as you can see in Figure 4-24.)

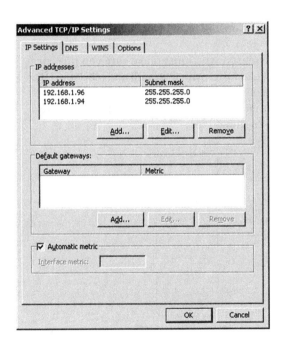

Figure 4-24. *The dedicated IP address should always be listed before the cluster IP address.*

Caution Keep in mind that you should configure both the cluster IP address and the dedicated IP addresses as static. Do not use DHCP here, the same way you would not use it for MSCS.

The hosts in a cluster should belong to the same subnet. All clients must then have access to this subnet, unless, of course, you do want the cluster to be idle. (But then you would not have set up a cluster in the first place.)

You cannot enable NLB on a server that is part of a MSCS cluster. Or rather you could, but Microsoft doesn't support it. We haven't tried it, however, and really can't say what the result would be.

When you configure your NICs for load balancing, you should configure a default gateway for the NLB NIC in case you have two (or more) NICs on different subnets. You should also update your routing tables so that all traffic will go through this gateway. The gateway settings on the other NICs should be blank. If your NICs are on the same subnet, you do not need to hack the routing tables. (Remember that this last point only applies to Windows 2000 systems and not to Windows Server 2003 systems.)

If you do not want to use the graphical management tools for NLB, you could use the command-line–based nlb.exe, which lets you configure NLB through the command line.

While we are talking about management tools, it might be worth mentioning that you can control your clusters remotely. You can choose if you want to allow this during setup, but based on our experience we do not recommend this. Using the remote control option presents too many security risks. Some of the possible risks if you allow this are more exposure to data tampering and denial of service attacks, so use the Network Load Balancing Manager or WMI instead.

If you don't to enable this option for some reason, you must make sure you provide a strong password. You should also protect the NLB cluster with a firewall and block the UDP control ports necessary for remote control. (The default values for these ports are 1717 and 2504 at the cluster IP addresses.) Only access the cluster with remote control from a secure, trusted computer, behind a firewall, as Figure 4-25 shows.

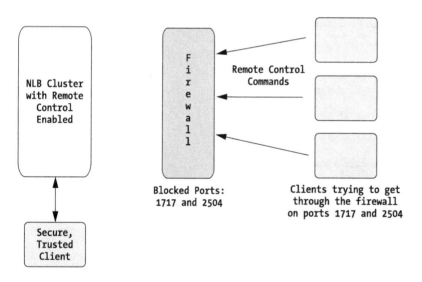

Figure 4-25. *Setting up remote control for your NLB cluster*

Caution Please don't use the remote control option unless absolutely necessary.

Troubleshooting NLB Clusters

Finally, we will show you some ways to troubleshoot NLB. There are various tools to help you with this. An old favorite is, of course, the Event Viewer. Check this to see if any unexpected errors have occurred. The ping command is useful for checking if the cluster is alive and responds to requests. Don't forget to enable NLB Manager logging. as shown previously. The logs can be useful in troubleshooting.

You also might want to keep an eye on a few performance monitors:

- CPU load

- Network interface: packets/sec

- Web service: connection attempts/sec

The nlb.exe command-line tool also has a few commands that might come in handy. Check out the Display and Query commands to find out whether you might prefer to work with this tool. You can also find more information at http://www.microsoft.com/windowsxp/home/using/ productdoc/en/default.asp?url=/windowsxp/home/using/productdoc/en/nlb_command.asp or by just typing **nlb /?** at the command prompt.

Performance Comparisons

In mid-2003, Microsoft published a document called "Visual Basic .NET on Windows Server 2003: A New Benchmark" (http://msdn.microsoft.com/library/_default.asp?url=/library/ en-us/dnbda/html/ws03perfbench.asp). In it, Microsoft compared an application running on Windows NT 4.0 Enterprise Edition, Windows 2000 Advanced Server, and Windows Server 2003. The application was written in Visual Basic 6 and Visual Basic .NET. We will focus only on the Visual Basic .NET benchmarks here because VB 6 is not an option in our solution. This also means we will not discuss the NT 4.0 benchmarks either, because .NET is not supported on this platform.

The benchmark tests shown in Figure 4-26 clearly indicate that a .NET application on Windows Server 2003 outperforms the same application on a Windows 2000 platform. This comes as no surprise to us, since this is what we have noticed in our own projects. What is more interesting is that the .NET Framework 1.1 offers a significant performance boost compared to version 1.0 on both operating systems.

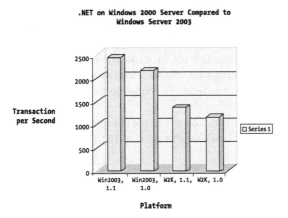

Figure 4-26. *The same application is executed on two platforms and comparisons are made*

The tests show that the best Windows 2000 benchmark only achieves 55 percent of the transactions per second that the best Windows Server 2003 provides. That's a good argument for choosing Windows Server 2003 as a platform for building applications.

Since we never trust these kinds of benchmarks without trying them ourselves, we decided to rerun the tests in our own lab. We wondered, would we see the same or bigger difference in our own tests or would it be less?

We decided to do the tests in VMware 4 on our workstation first, just to get a feel for how the results would be. VMware graciously provided us with licenses to its virtual machine software, so that we could avoid buying expensive hardware for these tests.

Since we also wanted to try this in a real environment, we turned to Dell Sweden and asked if they could help. This way we had a chance to run more extensive tests. Fortunately, they not only allowed us time in the lab, but also granted us professional help through their technicians as well. In Appendix A, we show a complete list of the hardware made available to us by Dell.

We decided to do two test runs of our own:

- Replicate the tests in VMware on our own machine.

- Replicate the tests in the Dell test lab.

As an option, we thought it would be a great idea to try one of our own applications in the Dell lab, if time permitted.

We also decided to only test version 1.1 of the .NET Framework, since that is the version we use daily anyway.

Tests on VMware

The VMware tests were run on a Compaq Presario 8000 workstation with a 2.2 GHz CPU and 768MB RAM. We used VMware to create our virtual servers.

The database server was the same for both scenarios: a Windows Server 2003 Standard Edition running SQL Server 2000 Developer Edition SP3. We installed the database with the scripts Microsoft provides for the test application, and then inserted some data with other scripts.

For our application servers, we used two virtual servers—Windows Server 2003 Standard Edition in scenario one, and Windows 2000 Server in scenario two. This way we tried to have versions that were as equal as possible from the two server families. They both included Visual Studio .NET 2003 Enterprise Architect with .NET Framework 1.1. We also made sure all the latest available patches were installed. We then installed the application according to Microsoft's installation instructions.

On our client computer, we used Application Center Test (ACT), a tool in Visual Studio 2003 Enterprise Architect, to create a test script. The script was created by recording navigation in the test web application (through which we pretended to purchase some books) and then logging out.

Since we used a VMware solution, everything really ran on the same computer. We hence decided to limit the number of simulated connections, so we set this value to 10 (see Figure 4-27). All test runs were 300 seconds long.

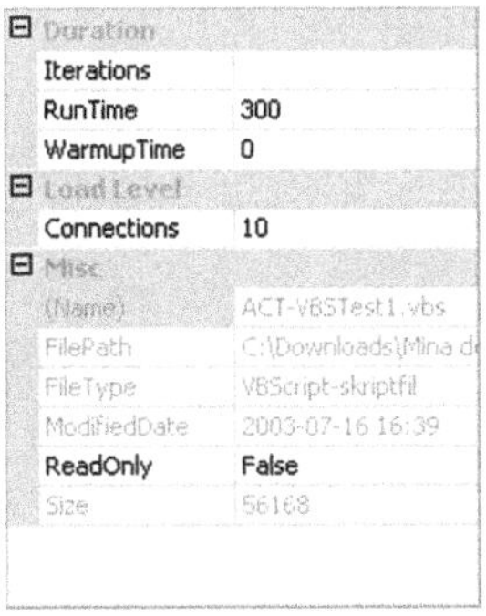

Duration
Iterations
RunTime 300
WarmupTime 0
Load Level
Connections 10
Misc
(Name) ACT-VBSTest1.vbs
FilePath C:\Downloads\Mina d
FileType VBScript-skriptfil
ModifiedDate 2003-07-16 16:39
ReadOnly False
Size 56168

Figure 4-27. *We simulated 10 connections on the first test runs.*

We were then ready to do some testing. We started the database server, and then we started the Windows Server 2003 application server. When they were both up and running and we had verified that the application worked, we started the first test run.

When the test was finished, we found that we had managed to get 119 requests per second. The total number of requests was 35,764. We received no HTTP or socket errors. We ran the test again, and the results were similar (see Figure 4-28)—117 requests per second and no errors.

Windows Server 2003
Request per Second
119
118.5
118
117.5
117
116.5
116
W2003 Test 01 10 Req
W2003 Test 02 10 Req
Test Run

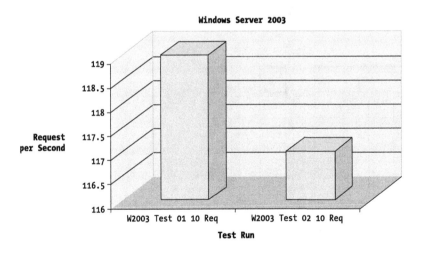

Figure 4-28. *First two tests on Windows Server 2003*

We then shut down the application server and started the Windows 2000 version instead. When we had verified that the application worked on this platform too, we ran two sets exactly like the ones just shown. The results were a bit different (see Figure 4-29). We managed to get 83 requests per second, but we also got close to 900 HTTP errors and nearly 20,000 socket errors on the exact same hardware.

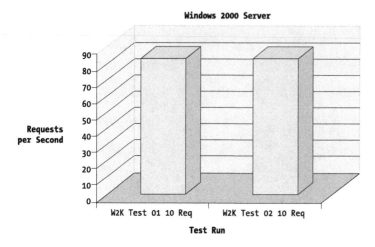

Figure 4-29. *First two tests on Windows 2000 Server*

The Windows 2000 platform managed only 70 percent of the requests per second that the Windows Server 2003 did (see Figure 4-30).

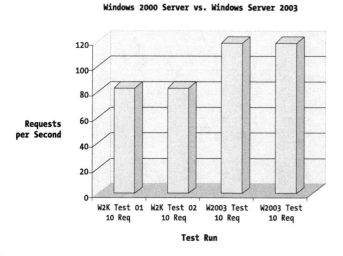

Figure 4-30. *Windows 2000 versus Windows Server 2003*

We ran the test ten more times on each platform, but the results were the same, give or take a few requests per second. Next we decided to lower the number of simulated connections to five instead of ten and see if the results were any different. The results were not much different in the outcome (see Figure 4-31). The Windows 2000 virtual server managed 80 requests per second, which was 74 percent of what the other platform managed. To be certain of our results, we ran the tests ten more times on each platform, but nothing significant changed.

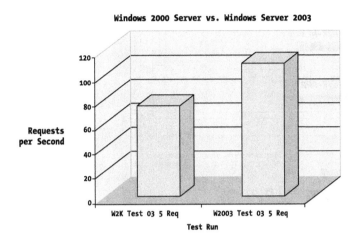

Figure 4-31. *Windows 2000 versus Windows Server 2003 with five connections*

Now we couldn't wait to get to the Dell test lab and run the tests on some "real" hardware, which would allow us to increase the load on the test system.

Tests at Dell

The equipment that Dell provided us is shown in Figure 4-32 (a detailed list of this hardware appears in Appendix A). We were very happy to be able to run our tests on this hardware. Since running virtual machines always costs performance, because they're all running on the same physical machine, we were curious to see if the results would be the same on real hardware.

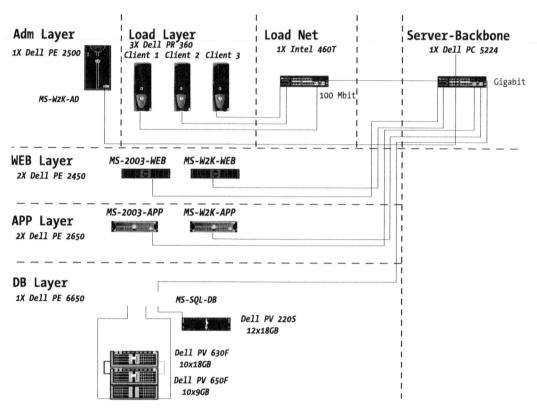

Figure 4-32. *The equipment Dell provided us*

The first thing we decided to do was to run the exact same tests as we did in VMware. We decided that was our most important task during the days we had access to the lab.

Here is a closer look at what systems we had available to test on:

- The database server was the same for all tests, a Dell PE 6650.

- The application servers were Dell PE 2650 machines. One of them ran Windows 2000 Enterprise Server, and the other ran Windows Server 2003 Advanced Edition.

- The web servers were Dell PE 2450 machines. One of them ran Windows 2000 Standard Server, and the other Windows Server 2003 Web Edition.

- The three clients were all Dell PR 360 computers running Windows XP Professional.

- We also had an Active Directory Server running Windows 2000 Server. The machine we used for this was a Dell PE 2500.

One of the first things we became aware of at Dell was that ACT did not support multiple test clients. That meant we could not load balance the requests on multiple clients like we could in ACT's predecessor, the Web Application Stress Tool. Since the Web Application Stress Tool could do this easily, we really expected ACT to do the same. After several phone calls to our contacts at Microsoft, we were informed that the full version of ACT should be a part of

Application Center Server. Alas, to install the server the clients needed to be running at least Windows 2000 Standard Server, and ours ran Windows XP Professional. So, unfortunately we couldn't verify this, and we did not have enough time to reinstall the clients. Instead, we had to find another way to accomplish the same thing. The question we asked ourselves was why Microsoft had chosen to limit ACT this way. We still don't know the answer.

What we finally did was we used the same scripts on each of our three clients and started them simultaneously. We could perhaps get out of sync by a second here and there, but we had no choice if we were going to put a heavy load on our servers.

The script we used was recorded the exact same way we recorded the one for the VMware tests. We started out with only three connections on each client, and a total of nine connections against the server. The duration of the tests was five minutes for each test run. Then, we ran the tests five times against both application servers.

The results were almost the same on every client. We did see that client 1 achieved slightly more requests per second than the others did, but this was due to a better CPU on that machine. In Figure 4-33, you can see the results for each client on the Windows Server 2003 platform, and in Figure 4-34 you can see the Windows 2000 Server results.

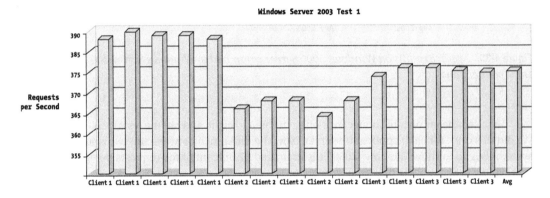

Figure 4-33. *Results on Windows Server 2003 with three connections*

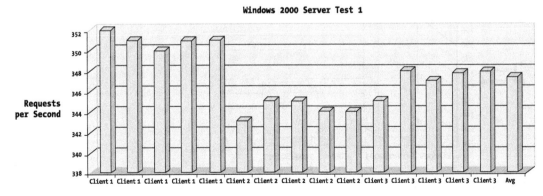

Figure 4-34. *Results on Windows 2000 Server with three connections*

When we ran the Windows 2000 Server tests, each client managed to get an average of 347 requests per second, and on Windows Server 2003, the result was 380 requests per second (see Figure 4-35). This meant that Windows 2000 Server managed 91 percent of the requests that Windows Server 2003 did. We had actually expected the difference to be larger, but so far the load was moderate.

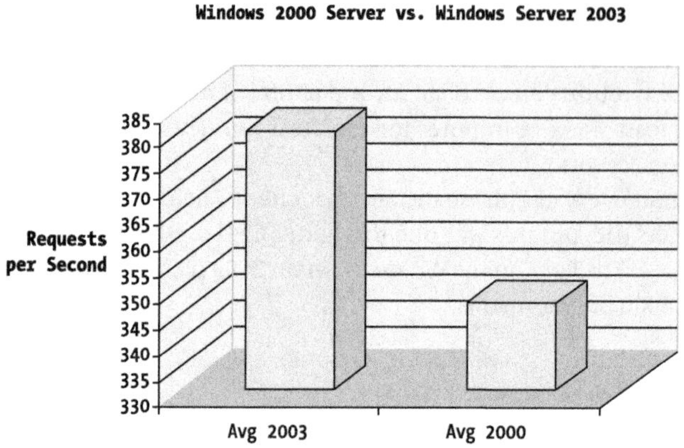

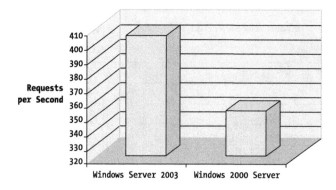

Figure 4-35. *Average results on Windows 2000 Server compared to Windows Server 2003 with three connections*

We raised the number of connections on each client to eight, and ran the tests for 60 minutes. We did this once for each application server. Now the difference between the two operating systems began to show. Windows 2000 only managed 87 percent of the requests per second that Windows Server 2003 did (see Figure 4-36).

Windows 2000 Server vs. Windows Server 2003, with 8 Connections

```
        410
        400
        390
        380
Requests 370
per Second 360
        350
        340
        330
        320
            Windows Server 2003   Windows 2000 Server
```

Figure 4-36. *Average results on Windows 2000 Server compared to Windows Server 2003 with eight connections*

To see if we could find more of a difference between the platforms, we slowly increased the number of connections until we reached 30 connections on each client. This means we had 90 simultaneous connections to the servers.

What we saw clearly during this test was that Windows 2000 showed virtually no signs of being able to increase the number of requests per second it could handle. Windows Server 2003, on the other hand, handily served the increased load without giving up. As Figure 4-37 shows, Windows 2000 still handled 347 requests per second, whereas Windows Server 2003 averaged 417.

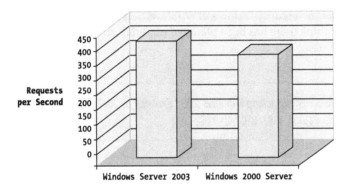

Figure 4-37. *Average results on Windows 2000 Server compared to Windows Server 2003 with 30 connections*

■**Note** During these live tests, the error count was close to zero on each platform. Based on this, we conclude that we should be careful with using VMware as a test application for stress tests. It is preferable to use real hardware for these types of tests.

We ran a few more tests after this, but our conclusions did not change. Windows 2000 simply could not handle an increasing load, whereas Windows Server 2003 could. This was as we expected, so we were not surprised.

.NET Framework 2.0 is coming to its RTM as we're writing this and though we would have wanted to see how performance will change, unfortunately we don't have access to this equipment anymore. The only thing we can say is that some testing we have done indicates that performance has been improved further, but we need to do some more tests before we can be certain of this.

Security in Windows

Now you know plenty about the Windows architecture and ways of making the OS scalable and reliable. So far so good, but one more important topic exists: security. Throughout this book we try to stress the importance of this. Because most businesses today have expanded well beyond their local area network, increased system security is more important than ever. Microsoft has put a lot of effort into making Windows Server 2003 its most secure operating system so far. At first we thought this was just sales talk, but as the betas have evolved into a final product, we must say that Microsoft has succeeded fairly well. One of the drives for this has been Microsoft's Trustworthy Computing Initiative, a framework for developing devices powered by computers and software that are as secure and trustworthy as the everyday devices and appliances you use at home.

The rest of this chapter will cover the security features of Windows Server 2003. We will not cover Windows 2000 here, as we think there has been plenty of material written on this platform. Let us start with authentication.

■**Note** A good book on Windows 2000 security is *Hacking Windows 2000 Exposed* by Joel Scambray and Stuart McClure (McGraw-Hill Osborne Media, 2001. ISBN 0-07-219262-3).

Authentication

One fundamental issue in security is the process of verifying that an entity or object really is what, or who, it claims it is. How can you be sure it really is Opus Rossberg who is trying to read a file on one of your servers? (As a matter of fact, we would be surprised if it really was Opus Rossberg, since one of us has a cat with this name, so christened after penguin Opus in the comic *Bloom County*. But the point is still valid.) Authentication confirms the identity of any user trying to log on to a domain or access network resources.

In Windows Server 2003 you find the following types of authentication:

- *Kerberos version 5*. This is the default network authentication method for network services. The Kerberos protocol can use either a smart card or a password for interactive logon, so it is quite flexible.

- *Digest authentication*. When using this method, credentials are transmitted across the network as an MD5 hash or as a message digest.

- *Passport authentication*. You have probably used Passport authentication to access Microsoft's web pages. When you use this user-authentication service, you can get a single sign-in for your web site or network, just to mention two examples. This means you only have to log on once; and all other authentication is done transparently.

- *NTLM*. This protocol is provided for backward compatibility with Windows NT 4.0–based systems.

- *Secure Sockets Layer/Transport Layer Security (SSL/TLS)*. This protocol comes into play when a user is accessing a secure web site.

Note Two-factor authentication is included in the Windows Server families. This means you can integrate stuff like smart cards to provide a secure solution for client authentication, logging on to a domain, code signing, and securing e-mail. Support for cryptographic smart cards is a key feature of the Public Key Infrastructure (PKI) that Microsoft has integrated into the Windows Server families and Windows XP. When logging on to a domain using a smart card, you do not have to press Ctrl-Alt-Del to log on. When you insert the smart card, the computer simply asks for your pincode, instead of the username and password you normally supply.

Object-Based Access Control

When a user is authenticated, other issues arise. What can a user do? What resources does he or she have access to? Since you never want to give all users access to everything, you need to let your administrators control this. They can do this by assigning security descriptors to objects stored in Active Directory (AD). This means they can control which user accounts and groups in Active Directory have access to a specific object. The administrators can even control access to specific attributes of an object, giving them quite a lot of power.

Note If Active Directory is not installed or the server is not a member of a domain, you can use the same technique with local users and groups on the machine.

To secure a computer or computers, you can grant users or groups specific rights. You can also grant certain rights to specific resources on the computer, like files, folders, or even services. These rights determine the actions that the user or group can perform on the object.

What kind of rights can you assign? The first one is *permissions*. Permissions define the type of access a user or group is granted to an object and its properties. You can assign permissions to files, Active Directory objects, or registry objects. The permissions you can grant depend on the object they are set to. For a file, you can for example grant *read, write, modify,* or *delete* permissions.

Another right you can assign is *ownership* of an object. When an object is created, the creator is assigned ownership of the object. This right can easily be transferred to another user or group.

You can also let objects *inherit permissions* from other objects. The easiest way to illustrate this is by imagining a folder in Windows Explorer. You can let the files in the folder inherit the permissions applied to the folder, but only permissions marked for inheritance will actually be inherited.

Access control is a major tool when securing your servers. The rule of thumb is this: Do not give anyone or anything more rights than they actually need—not even to yourself! You will seldom need to log on as administrator and have all the rights associated with that account. Remove the Everyone group from all objects and only give those who need access to the objects the permissions they need.

A cool feature in Windows Server 2003 is shown in Figure 4-38. It used to be difficult to try to guess the permissions assigned to an object. Now you are presented with a tab that displays the *effective permissions* for objects. You can select a user or a group, and see the effective permissions for that specific object. To try this, open Windows Explorer. Next, right-click any file or folder. Select Properties. On the Security tab, click Advanced. Now you can select any user or group and see its effective permission on this object, a very welcome feature to Windows.

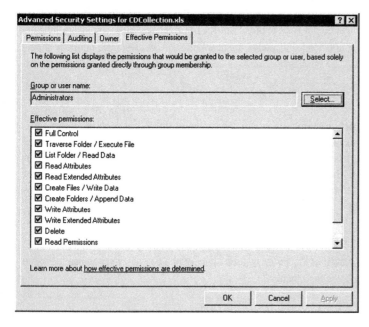

Figure 4-38. *A display of the effective permission of a user or a group for a specific object*

Auditing

To see what is happening to your system, you need a way to track various events. By carefully selecting the behaviors you want to watch, you can track potential security problems. Of course, you want to configure your security so it will take some time for an unwanted guest to get through. When he or she gets through, you can use auditing as evidence for the security breach. Hopefully you can learn from these breaches to tighten security more.

One thing you need to understand when it comes to security is that you should not for a moment believe that you can stop anyone from getting past your security walls. If somebody wants to get through, that person will. It is just a matter of time. What you can hope for, and what you should strive for, is presenting the intruder with so much trouble that the he will be slowed down. Because if you can slow intruders down, you have a better chance of discovering them before they get all the way through.

To audit effectively, you need to establish an *audit policy*. When you do this, you choose which categories of events, objects, and accesses to audit. You must also have a strategy with your policy. What do you want to achieve? Do you want to record those who have accessed the system or data on the system? Do you want to record all failed logon attempts? Do you want to detect unauthorized attempts to mess with the operating system?

When you set up an audit policy, you should usually try to audit the following:

- Access to important data, like files, folders, or both.

- Logon/logoff to the system. You should monitor both the successful and unsuccessful attempts.

- User accounts/group management, to see if anyone has done something they were not allowed to do.

These are just a few options, and there are many more. When you deploy your audit policy, you can use the local security policy tool, if you are auditing a stand-alone machine, or a group policy if you have a domain. When the policy is deployed, you must not forget to regularly check the log files; otherwise you have wasted your time setting up the policy.

Another thing you should not forget is *testing* your policy before deploying it. Does it really catch the events you want it to catch? You might need to tune it before you deploy it. You should also not forget to keep on tuning it as it is deployed. Based on the logs, you might notice if you audit too much or too little, so you may need to change it regularly.

Active Directory Security

Beside the obvious benefits for administrators and users of having a directory where you can store data, objects, and resources, Active Directory also enhances security. All information about user accounts and groups is stored in a protected way in Active Directory. This makes it harder for an unauthorized user to gain access to your information. Another benefit is that AD both authenticates and authorizes users that log on to your domain. This way you can more easily control access to system resources. When a user logs on to the domain, the security system authenticates the user with information stored in Active Directory. When the user then tries to access a service on the network, the system checks the properties defined in the Discretionary Access Control List (DACL) for that service.

EFS, Digital Certificates, and Data Protection

One important aspect of security is protecting your data on disk. Windows now has a very easy way of doing this, with the Encrypted File System. Another way is by using digital certificates.

Let us have a look at EFS first. EFS is extremely easy to use. To see for yourself, open Windows Explorer and create an ordinary text file in a folder of your choice. Right-click the file and select Properties from the menu. Click the Advanced button. A form like the one you see in Figure 4-39 is shown. To encrypt the file, simply check the "Encrypt contents to secure data" option and click OK.

Click OK again and you are done. (Notice the change of the file's color in Windows Explorer.) This procedure works on folders, too. If you encrypt a folder, all files in it will be encrypted as well.

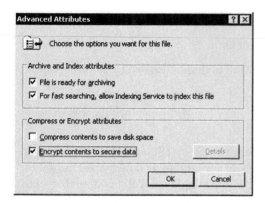

Figure 4-39. *Encrypting your files and folders*

Note By using the cipher command from a command window, you can also encrypt/decrypt files and folders. Type **Cipher /?** to access all options for this command.

Digital signatures are also a good way of securing data. By using them you can ensure the integrity and origin of the data. Digital signatures provide strong evidence that the data has not been altered since it was signed. They also confirm the identity of the person or entity that signed the data. When you have systems involved in e-commerce, digital signing is a good way of enabling integrity. Keep in mind that digital signatures do not protect the data per se—they just tell you it is the same data that the creator generated, and that no one has altered it.

Public Key Infrastructure (PKI)

A rapidly growing and constantly evolving technology is PKI, or Public Key Infrastructure. PKI helps you in verifying the identity of a person accessing information. It also helps in controlling which information a person has access to, once his or her identity has been established. You can use PKI to distribute and manage identification credentials easily and securely over your organization.

When you use PKI, you verify and authenticate each participant involved through the use of public key cryptography. PKI basically consists of three parts:

- Digital certificates

- Certification Authorities (CAs)

- Other Registration Authorities (RAs)

The digital certificate is a digital statement issued by an authority. The authority vouches for the identity of the certificate holder. The identity can be bound to a person, a computer, or a service. The object the certificate is bound to holds the private key used in the identification process. Many Internet banks use certificates to identify account owners, thereby giving them access to their accounts when they access the bank over the Internet. You can use digital certificates for other things like secure e-mail, Internet Protocol Security (IPSec), and Transport Layer Security (TLS) as well.

■**Note** When a host, such as a secure web server, designates an issuer as a trusted root authority, the host implicitly trusts the policies that the issuer has used to establish the bindings of certificates it issues. In effect, the host trusts that the issuer has verified the identity of the certificate subject. A host designates an issuer as a trusted root authority by placing the issuer's self-signed certificate, which contains the issuer's public key, into the trusted root Certification Authority certificate store of the host computer. Intermediate or subordinate Certification Authorities are trusted only if they have a valid certification path from a trusted root Certification Authority. (For more information, see Technet white paper "Windows 2000 Security Technical Overview" at `http://www.microsoft.com/technet/treeview/default.asp?url=/_technet/prodtechnol/windows2000serv/deploy/confeat/_sectech.asp`)

A certificate can hold many pieces of information, but these are the most common:

- Validity information (valid from [date and time]–valid to [date and time])
- The subject's/holder's public key value
- The subject's/holder's identifier information (name, e-mail, and so on)
- Issuer identification
- Digital signature of the issuer so you know the validity of the binding between the holder's public key and its identifier information

There are several reasons for deploying a PKI using Windows. The first is its support for strong security. You can have a strong authentication by using smart cards. To be sure of the confidentiality and integrity of your transmitted data, you can use IPSec on public networks. The data you store on your servers can be protected with EFS. As you see, you can combine techniques to strengthen your security.

Secondly, PKI also helps in simplifying management. You can set up a certificate infrastructure that lets you issue certificates, and by integrating these with other technologies, like smart cards, you remove the need for password.

If you need to revoke a certificate, you can easily do that using the Certification Authority MMC. If you use Active Directory, you can integrate PKI with this, and then get the ability to control certificates through group policy. It is also possible to map certificates to specific user accounts.

■**Note** Certification Services is the component in Windows Server used to create and manage Certification Authorities. Certification Services is managed through the Certification Authority MMC console.

As all this shows, you have many ways to keep your solutions secure. One of the most obvious things Microsoft has done is not mentioned here, but has been covered in a previous chapter. What we are referring to is the way Windows behaves after installation. As opposed to previous versions, practically nothing is enabled by default. This is a very smart move on the part of Microsoft. To get your system up and running, you need to know what you are doing.

You must enable the services you need, since the number of services enabled by default has been cut drastically. There is no way that you can install IIS by accident, for instance. Even if you did, it still would not serve other than static content. ASP and ASP.NET support will have to be enabled manually.

So we can confidently say Microsoft has taken gigantic leaps forward in making a secure environment for applications.

Note In this book, in particular with the demo application in Chapter 9, we will not use all of the features, of course. You need to be aware of them, though, so you can make the right choice when the moment comes. This is one of the cornerstones of good design.

Summary

In this chapter, we have given you a closer look at how Windows works. You have seen the architecture of Microsoft's operating system and hopefully now have a better understanding of what goes on under the hood—enabling you to build better, more secure, and more scalable applications.

■ ■ ■

CHAPTER 5

The Enterprise Application Architecture

As professional developers, it's quite frustrating to realize that we are making the same mistakes over and over again. It is hard enough to develop applications, let alone develop reusable and scalable solutions. Like most programmers, you have probably worked on a project that had you banging your head against the wall because of a problem and thinking, "Ugh—that *must* have been dealt with before." You've probably had a similar feeling when you talked to the architect of a project about some good patterns and all you got back was "Hmmm, if we had some more time, we could have constructed this part of the application better. But since we already have coded this section, we can't change it now."

In this chapter, we will discuss how you can avoid most of these negative experiences when creating an enterprise application. We will examine what an enterprise application needs and how you can meet such requirements with a common architecture. The following text will sometimes get a bit technical, but we suggest you read it through so that you have an understanding of the problems that face developers daily. The ideas and architectures, together with the coding conventions and the design patterns that we cover, will allow you to achieve a robust enterprise application architecture in your applications. We have used all the patterns and conventions found in this chapter with good results for a while now and therefore we can recommend you use them as well.

What Is an Enterprise Application?

A well-designed enterprise application requires several important things, but most crucial are the following:

- *Availability.* Every enterprise application has a solution or strategy to achieve high availability. Rather than measure the ability in terms of the five nines, the goal is to develop high-availability infrastructures for meeting unique customer requirements. Each customer has a different definition of availability: some common obstacles to availability exist in most applications, however. In this chapter, we will show examples of architecture that best combat downtime and meets business requirements. This will mostly be achieved by scaling out the architecture.

- *Security.* Security in an enterprise application is of high importance, since the system information contained therein is probably vital for the company that owns it. The architecture of an enterprise application should be of a defensive nature, which means that security is applied throughout the infrastructure—from transport security to data security. In this chapter, we will show how you can incorporate web service security in your Façade layers.

- *Scalability.* Scaling out and scaling up lets the enterprise application grow with an orga- nization's needs in a controlled and safe way. Scaling out is mainly used on web servers and in application layers, where load balancing can be employed in an easy manner, whereas scaling up is often used on the database layer where replication of data between different servers will sometimes introduce complex administration issues. The architecture we study in this chapter makes it possible to scale up and scale out on all layers therein.

- *Manageability and administration.* When you are scaling out and scaling up, it is easy to forget the people who will be administrating the application for years after you've left the playing field. It is important to work with an architecture that makes it easy to trace, monitor, deploy, and debug. The key here is to plan and lay out the foundation of the architecture before the realization of it begins. In our experience, this is one of the main problems in many projects.

- *Reliability.* An enterprise application needs to be reliable. To achieve this, you need to keep a standardized architecture that can be deployed on several servers (a web farm, for instance) in an easy manner.

- *Supportability.* An application without support is likely to make its users frustrated. Soon or later those users will start asking questions that need to be answered by some- one—probably you. Support for incorporated third-party controls is also important to be able to maintain the application in a correct and safe manner.

- *Repeatability.* When you design your enterprise applications for availability and scala- bility, you need to be able to rapidly deploy such applications across your web farms and clusters. With .NET, you have this capability.

- *Standardization.* No customer likes "Bob's hack" or "Steve's fix" in the long term. By the time some new functionality needs to be implemented, Bob might have moved to the Caribbean and taken the source code with him. The use of standardized infrastructure components through well-known architectural specifications creates predictable and reliable solutions, and also provides a basis for an organization to manage change and growth. The structure for handling the source from a project often has low priority, which can jeopardize the future maintenance of the application.

To achieve these goals, you need to have an architecture and enterprise infrastructure that can support you in the creation of your enterprise application. Microsoft has developed several servers that can help you with the different "bricks" from the preceding list.

The application blocks in Figure 5-1 are used in the enterprise application architecture. SQL Server helps you to store permanent data for the application in a safe way, making it possible to scale up and scale out when necessary.

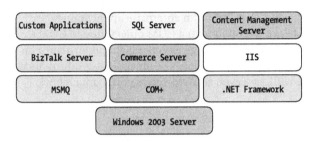

Figure 5-1. *Building blocks for an enterprise application*

BizTalk Server serves as a gateway to other applications, providing you with a graphical, designable interface to the world outside your application. BizTalk Server is also used for orchestration and maintenance of business flows.

Commerce Server, from Microsoft, provides you with a commerce architecture designed to handle the common tasks in a commerce application. Commerce Server is discussed in Chapter 2.

Content Management Server is similar to the Commerce Server in the way it provides enterprise applications with a framework for handling content in a web-based application interface. We have often found that the architecture from a Content Management Server system is a wise choice for developing web-based interfaces for enterprise applications instead of developing the content handling from scratch. Later in this chapter, in the section "Content Management," we will talk about two different content management systems that will boost the development of content-based web applications.

The application infrastructure elements include five items of high importance in the enterprise application, and we discuss these next.

Internet Information Services

The first application infrastructure element, which we will only mention briefly here, is Internet Information Services (IIS). Through IIS you can host your interactive client interface (web-based user interface) and also your interfaces with other applications in the form of .NET Remoting objects or web services. Chapter 8 covers IIS in more detail.

COM+

As mentioned earlier, two of the requirements for an enterprise application are scalability and performance. To achieve this, enterprise architecture requires COM+ for object pooling and transaction support. COM+ also provides you with services to handle the following:

- *Distributed transaction coordination.* This ensures the integrity of your databases.

- *Queued components.* These provide asynchronous execution and can help applications to handle network failures.

- *Object pooling.* This allows applications to support larger numbers of users than would otherwise be possible.

COM+ uses the notion of *COM+ application,* which is the place where your components are hosted to take advantage of COM+. If you are developing an enterprise application based on .NET, the hosted .NET objects in COM+ are wrapped with a COM object, due to COM+ being written in unmanaged code in the current release. This gives you a slight performance hit due to the interoperation between the COM object and the real .NET object. This performance hit is something you should be able to live with, however, as COM+ gives you so much back.

Microsoft Message Queuing

Microsoft Message Queuing (MSMQ) is used to support an enterprise application with asynchronous calls that will, for instance, give you reliability even if the network connection to your database server breaks down. (At least you will not lose any incoming data.) It is also used in decoupled enterprise applications, where the client interface is not connected to the data source all the time. The default behavior for MSMQ is shown in Figure 5-2.

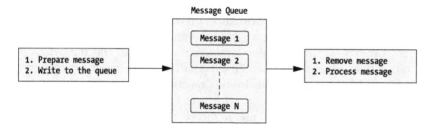

Figure 5-2. *The normal flow when using message queues for asynchronous communications*

The sending application or component prepares a message and writes it to a message queue. The message queue system handles the queue. The queues in MSMQ can be handled either as persistent queues or as in-memory queues. The in-memory queues are faster from a performance point of view because no disk access is necessary to access the queue. From a security performance perspective, however, they are hazardous. If the system goes down, the content in the queues disappears, since it was only stored in memory. If you need the content in the queues to remain there for a long period, use persistent queues, as the content in a persistent queue will be stored to disk instead of in memory.

Queues can be private or public. Public queues are published in the Active Directory. Applications running in the same network but on a different server can retrieve information about the queues via Active Directory. Private queues are only accessible locally on the machine and are not published via Active Directory.

To take advantage of MSMQ from a component, you need to do the following:

- Create a queue that should be used for your messages.

- Add code to the component in order to write to the queue and to read from it.

The System.Messaging namespace contains classes that you use when working with message queues. In Chapter 10, we will demonstrate how you can use these classes to create a queue and post messages. There we will also look at how to use queued components.

Note You don't need to use Enterprise Services to take advantage of MSMQ. Since classes are exposed via the System.Messaging namespace, you are free to use them outside Enterprise Services.

Windows Server 2003

Finally, a platform is available on which to run all the previously mentioned blocks for your enterprise applications—the Windows Server 2003 and the .NET Framework. We won't talk so much about the new stuff found in this Windows version here (refer back to Chapter 4 for more information), but one change of great importance has been made for enterprise applications in terms of performance. When COM was "upgraded" to COM+, it was also more closely integrated to the Windows 2000 operating system. The difference in performance test results conducted on Windows NT 4.0 with COM objects in the MTS—compared to similar tests with Windows 2000 and COM+—is dramatic. A significant improvement has been made in the number of requests per second that can be handled by an enterprise application developed with COM+ instead of only COM objects hosted by MTS.

We witnessed a similar performance boost when we moved from Windows 2000 Server to Windows Server 2003, in which many improvements have been made. In Chapter 9, we will compare Windows 2000 Server running with .NET Framework 1.1 and the new Windows Server 2003 running with the .NET Framework 1.1 and IIS 6.0.

For more information about the Windows Server families, please see Chapter 2.

.NET Framework

The .NET Framework is the final toolbox that the enterprise architecture relies on. It's a computing platform aimed at simplifying application development. Microsoft has put a lot of effort into this, so that it would fulfill the demands of a distributed application environment like the Internet. Another goal has been to use industry standards in communication (like SOAP, HTTP, and XML) so that integration with other platforms, and the code written on them, would be possible. With the use of web services, it is now quite easy for developers to reuse logic written in another language on another platform. Correctly used, this could save enterprises money in the long run. Many companies nowadays offer services, both internal as well as external, built on the .NET Framework.

The .NET Framework is being developed for platforms other than Windows, too. Versions for Linux and UNIX (mostly for FreeBSD) are available or under development right now. Take a look at the open source project lead by Novell called Mono.

■**Note** A good source for news on .NET Framework development for other platforms is http://c2.com/
cgi/wiki?DotNetForLinux. The Mono project can be found at http://www.mono-project.com/
Main_Page.

The .NET Framework consists of two main components:

- The class library

- The common language runtime (CLR)

The class library offers an object-oriented collection of types that you can use (and reuse) to build your applications. Since the class library exposes a set of interfaces that you can use to extend the library, you can build your own classes so that they blend seamlessly into the .NET class library.

The common language runtime (CLR) is the heart and soul of the .NET Framework. It manages code at execution time by providing memory management, thread management, Remoting, and other system core services. One of the principles of the runtime is code management. Therefore, code that targets the runtime, as shown in Figure 5-3, is called *managed code*, and code that does not is called *unmanaged code*.

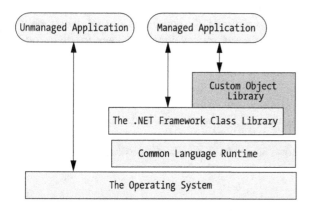

Figure 5-3. *Managed code in .NET*

In Figure 5-3, you see that the CLR is more or less an interface to the operating system. The class library and your own custom libraries sit on top of the CLR, and the managed applications either use these libraries or call the CLR directly.

Unmanaged applications access the operating system directly. IIS, for example, calls the OS without going through the framework.

In Figure 5-4, you see that an unmanaged application (in this case ASP.NET, but it can also be IIS or SQL Server, for example) can host the CLR. Unmanaged applications can load the common language runtime into their own processes. From there, they initiate the execution of managed code. This way, both managed and unmanaged features are available in the environment the unmanaged application has created.

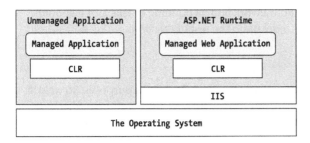

Figure 5-4. *Unmanaged code in .NET*

There is also a third part of the .NET Framework we have not yet mentioned. The Common Type System (CTS), shown in Figure 5-5, describes the data types and the programming constructs available to the .NET languages. Every language does not have to implement them all, so you need to be aware of this when you build applications that offer services to other platforms built on other .NET languages.

Common Language Runtime

Common Type System

Figure 5-5. *The Common Type System (CTS) is a vital part of the CLR.*

To overcome this, all .NET languages should implement a subset of these types and constructs—you should consider these minimum requirements for what these languages must support. This subset is included in the Common Language Specification (CLS), as you see in Figure 5-6. If you build .NET applications that only use the CLS, you can be certain all other .NET applications can understand them.

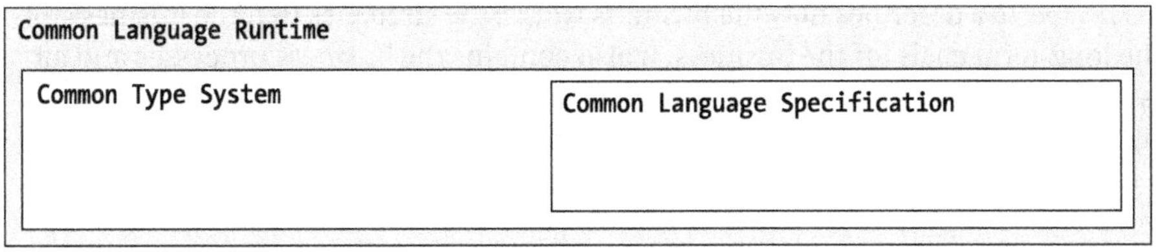

Figure 5-6. *The Common Language Specification is a subset of the Common Type System.*

To enhance performance, managed code is never interpreted. When you compile a C# program (or any other .NET language program), the code is compiled to an intermediate language. At execution time, this is compiled by the Just-In-Time (JIT) compiler, and the managed code then runs in the native machine language of the system it executes on.

This was a short overview of the .NET Framework and its building blocks, but it should give you enough background to be able to understand the rest of this book.

The Enterprise Architecture

Microsoft describes enterprise architecture in a way that is useful for our purposes, so we will base this section on its definition and usage of enterprise architecture. For more information about how Microsoft defines this topic, please visit http://msdn.microsoft.com/library/ default.asp?url=/library/_en-us/dnea/html/eaarchover.asp.

Understanding your customer's business structure, and the way information flows, is of great importance if you're going to be able to deliver the right application. The *enterprise architecture (EA)* exists to help you in this analysis. ANSI/IEEE Std 1471-2000 defines an enterprise architecture as "the fundamental organization of a system, embodied in its components, their relationships to each other and the environment, and the principles governing its design and evolution."

In clear English, the enterprise architecture is a way to analyze business and from the collected information create a map of the company's dataflow. The map will be used as basis for business and technology changes in the future. Enterprise architecture can be drawn in many ways—despite the target audience—but common to any depiction of enterprise architecture is the inclusion of a comprehensive set of cohesive models that describes the structure and model of an enterprise. The different models in the EA are arranged in a logical manner and provide deeper and deeper levels of details about the enterprise, in particular the following:

- Objectives and goals

- Organization and processes

- Systems and data

- Technology used

We divide the different models in enterprise architecture into four different areas: the business perspective, information perspective, application perspective, and technology perspective.

The Business Perspective

The *business perspective* describes how the business works, the strategies that the business follows, and the long-term goals for the business. It also contains the business processes and all the business functions performed. A rough picture of the different organizational structures is also encompassed by this perspective, together with the relationship between all the previously mentioned blocks that comprise an enterprise application.

The Information Perspective

The *information perspective* describes what the organization needs to know to run its business processes and operations. It contains the data models controlling the organization of the data together with the data management policies that should be used to maintain the data. The information perspective also describes how the information is created and consumed in the organization. This includes information about how the data fits into the workflow for the organization, and how the data is stored for all kinds of media.

The Application Perspective

The *application perspective* defines the enterprise's application portfolio and is application-centered. Here you describe the different automated services that support your business processes as well as the interaction and dependencies of the existing application systems. The application perspective also contains a plan for developing new applications and modifying old applications based on the enterprise goals, technology platforms, and objectives.

The Technology Perspective

Finally, it is the *technology perspective* that lays out the hardware and software support in the organization. It includes descriptions of the desktop and server hardware. The technology perspective also specifies the operating systems used and external equipment such as scanners, printers, and modems. This is a never-ending granularity that starts with a rough map, which is then refined until the organization can make decisions based on the information.

Enterprise Terminology

To understand subsequent discussions of enterprise application architecture in this chapter, you need to know the various terminology used to describe enterprise applications, which we will quickly cover here.

A *component* refers to a logical software module, mainly a .NET or COM component. A collection of components makes up an application. These components may be further grouped into various types that determine the layer to which each component belongs.

A *Layer* refers to a logical partition of an application. This partition consists of components of a given type. The model we present here partitions an application into the following four layers, according to the application duties performed by the component types of each layer:

- *UI layer*. Also known as the presentation layer, this includes component types such as user interface (UI) and UI process components, which deal primarily with the creation of UI elements and encapsulate the logic that handles the user's navigation of the UI.

- *Façade layer*. Contains Façade objects that make it easier to request information from the business layer. The Façade layer also makes it easier to handle processes such as wizards, since the wizard flow will be coded in a process component.

- *Business layer*. Includes component types such as business workflow, business component (BC), business entity, and service interface (SI), which encapsulate the business processes and rules that form the core of the application.

- *Data access layer*. Includes component types such as data access (DA) logic and service agent (SA) components, which encapsulate the complexities of dealing with data access for specific data sources (DS) and web services, respectively.

A *tier* is a logical entity, composed of one or more physical hosts or devices to which the logical layers are deployed. Sometimes the physical tiers correspond directly to the logical layers (for example, the web tier could correspond to the UI layer, the application tier to the business layer, and the data tier to the data layer), and sometimes multiple layers are deployed to a single tier.

Figure 5-7 depicts a hypothetical scenario where the UI layer, or presentation layer, is deployed to the web tier and the business and data layers are deployed to the application tier.

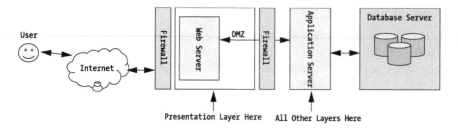

Figure 5-7. *A hypothetical setup of an enterprise application*

OOP

To be able to create an enterprise architecture that fulfills the mentioned requirements for an enterprise application described earlier, you need to work with *object-oriented programming (OOP)* in mind. The enterprise pattern we are going to talk about here is based on general OOP functionality. We are not going to discuss the complete scope of OOP, but will mention the four major building blocks in OOP that make the EA more stable, robust, and easier to maintain.

Abstraction

Abstraction is "information hiding." The user of a module/component does not have to know what is going on inside, just how to use it. The Façade classes in the EA hide the complex structure of the business layer, and instead expose the Façade classes based on the use cases.

Encapsulation

Encapsulation occurs when you separate the public interface to a module from private, internal data, making it clear what users of a module are supposed to know about and what they should not mess with. In C# and VB .NET, this is done by specifying which members of a class are public and which are private. The compiler will not permit code outside the class to refer to the private members. The encapsulation does not serve as protection against fraud or malice; rather, it clarifies what a class should do. An author of a class can say, "I can guarantee the public behavior of my class, since I have kept its internals private—outsiders cannot interfere with my class meeting its public obligations."

Inheritance

A class inherits the behavior (functions and methods together with properties) of another class, and thereby makes reuse programming easier. If A is a class, and B is a class, and B inherits from A, then an object in class B has all of the data members and functions defined for class A as well as those of B.

With a good design, it is possible to reuse large quantities of code quite simply. The EA presented in this chapter uses inheritance for the data access layer, so it inherits some base functionality that should be the same for all data classes. .NET supports inheritance from one base class only, which is a change from the former environments (like C++) where it was possible to have multiple inheritances.

Polymorphism

Through polymorphism, you can use objects without having to know their exact types. For instance, you can iterate a couple of objects and tell each of these objects to "print itself" by calling the "print" function, and each object takes care of the printing itself. How each object responds to the print request depends on what kind of object it is.

Polymorphism can be of three types—inheritance polymorphism, interface polymorphism, and polymorphism through abstract classes. *Inheritance polymorphism* is when each class is inheriting the same base class with functionality. Then we can iterate all different kinds of objects that inherit this base class and call the print function no matter what kind of object it is. Polymorphism by using interface is similar, but here we declare an interface that all classes should implement. The third way to go is to declare abstract classes that must be inherited and define all of the abstract class's methods. The third way is quite similar to the interface solution.

Design Patterns and Layers

Design patterns represent solutions to problems that may arise when you are developing applications within a particular context. Patterns represent a reuse of successful software architectures and designs. Patterns are often language-independent, in contrast to a framework, which is an implementation of many different patterns. Patterns are a solution to common problems in a specific context. A framework, on the other hand, is an implementation of many patterns that functions as a reusable, "semi-complete" application. The last step is to develop class libraries containing "fully completed" classes that you can plug into your applications.

We divide the different patterns on the market today into three types: creational patterns, structural patterns, and behavioral patterns. The creational patterns deal with creation, initialization/deinitialization, and configuration of classes and objects.

The structural patterns take care of the structural issues, such as interface implementation between classes. The behavioral patterns describe how you handle dynamic interactions between classes and objects.

Figure 5-8 shows some of the most well-known patterns divided into these three categories.

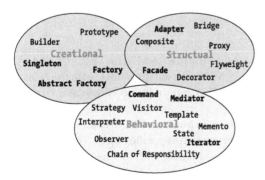

Figure 5-8. *Some well-known patterns divided into categories*

The bold patterns in Figure 5-8 are the ones used in the enterprise architecture presented in this chapter. We will, however, briefly describe all of the patterns in the figure and tell you roughly what they are intended to solve. We will start with the creational patterns that you use to solve creation-related problems in your enterprise application. Secondly, we will look at the structural patterns that help keep a structure easy to maintain and exchangeable. Finally, we will look at the behavioral patterns that help you with the different behaviors that you want your enterprise application to perform.

■**Note** For more information about design patterns, we recommend *Design Patterns: Elements of Reusable Object-Oriented Software* by Eric Gamma et al. (Addison-Wesley, 1995. ISBN: 0-201-63361-2).

Creational Patterns

In this section, we will describe the creational patterns that solve creation-related problems in your enterprise application: the Abstract Factory, Factory Method, Singleton, Prototype, and Builder patterns.

Abstract Factory

The function of the Abstract Factory is to provide a creation interface for related objects. The Factory Method is the "concrete factory" that actually creates the object. For example, our enterprise application in Chapter 10 needs to be able to work with different data providers. For instance, we need to be able to create an Oracle connection if we want the application to work with an Oracle database. We also need to be able to create a SQL Server connection if we want to work with Microsoft's SQL Server. However, we do not want to have to use different codes depending on the data provider we are using. The Abstract Factory simplifies the interface for the data access component by grouping all these different create methods within a single class. In Chapter 10, you will see the Abstract Factory pattern in action, together with the Factory Method, to ensure that our example enterprise application can easily switch between different data providers.

Factory Method

This is the pattern that serves as the "Concrete Factory" to the Abstract Factory pattern, and it defines an interface for creating an object. The Factory Method itself does not create the class, but passes the creation of the object down to subclasses. This pattern is also known as a *Virtual Constructor pattern*.

Instead of creating an object directly, you ask the Factory Method class to create the object for you. By doing so, you don't need to know how you created the specific object. The strength of this approach is that you can easily switch between related classes without changing the code that uses the class, as long as the different classes that the Factory Method returns to you support a known interface. The Factory Method in turn lets subclasses decide which class to instantiate. The Factory Method lets a class defer instantiation to subclasses. For example, in a data access layer, you can use the Factory Method pattern together with the Abstract Factory pattern to create data connections and data commands. For example, instead of creating a SQL Server connection directly in the data access component, you ask the createConnection method (Factory Method) to create an IdbConnection interface of type SQL Server. The createConnection method creates the connection and returns it via the interface IdbConnection. By using this abstraction, the data access component does not need to know how to create a database connection.

Singleton

The Singleton pattern is used to ensure that only one instance of an object exists, and that you have a global point of access to it. Sometimes it is important to be sure that you have only one instance of a class and that instance is accessible throughout the system. The Singleton pattern solves this by making the class itself responsible for keeping track of its own instance.

Prototype

A Prototype is a factory for cloning new instances from a prototype. This pattern is useful when a system should be independent of how its products are created, composed, and represented, and when the classes are instantiated at runtime. This pattern can also be used when you want to avoid building class hierarchies of factories that parallel the class hierarchy of products.

Builder

A Builder separates the construction of complex objects from their representation so the construction process can be used to create different representations. All you need to do as a user of the Builder class is feed it with types that should be built and the content. This is a pattern for step-by-step creation of a complex object so that the same construction process can create different representations. The methods that are used for constructing complex objects are put together into a single class called a Director. This Director class is responsible for knowing how to create the complex objects.

The Builder pattern is similar to the Abstract Factory. The main difference between them is that when an Abstract Factory class method creates its own object, the client of the Builder class instructs the Builder class on how to create the object and then asks it for the result. How the class is put together is up to the Builder class.

Structural Patterns

Structural patterns focus on how classes and objects are constructed to work together in larger structures. Rather than composing interfaces or implementations, structural patterns describe ways to compose objects to realize new functionality.

Adapter

The Adapter pattern is intended to provide a way for a client to use an object whose interface is different from the one expected by the client.

This pattern is suitable for solving issues such as the following: You want to replace one class with another and the interfaces do not match, or you want to create a class that can interact with other classes without knowing their interfaces at design time.

Let's take a look at an example: A client wants to make a specific request of an object (MyObject). This is normally accomplished by creating an instance of MyObject and invoking the requested method. In this case, however, the client cannot do so because the interfaces do not match. The client is working with an interface named IClient and MyObject has an interface named IMyObject. The Adapter pattern helps you address this incompatibility by providing classes that are responsible for redefining the interface and data types on the client's behalf. What the pattern does is actually work as a translator between the client and MyObject. To achieve this, you create a custom Adapter class that defines methods using the interface IClient, which is what the client expects. Also, the Adapter class subclasses the MyObject class, and provides an implementation of the client requests in terms that the MyObject expects. Adapter overrides the method and provides the correct interface for MyObject. By using the Adapter pattern, you do not need to modify the client to be able to talk to the MyObject class via the interface.

Adapter is a structural pattern, and you can use it to react to changes in class interfaces as your system evolves, or you can proactively use the Adapter pattern to build systems that anticipate changing structural details.

Bridge

The Bridge pattern is used for the abstraction of binding one of many implementations to a class. Normally, an interface inheritance is tightly bound to the class that has implemented the interface. When you implement an interface, the class then needs to implement all methods and properties in the interface. This is the conventional way to reuse an interface, but sometimes you will want to do stuff that you can't do with traditional inheritance. The Bridge pattern breaks the direct and permanent link between the interface and the class that implements the interface, which results in plug-and-play functionality for either the interface or the class that implements the interface. This can give you serious trouble if you are not using it the right way, but if you can control it (and know what you are doing), the main benefits of using the Bridge pattern instead of a traditional interface implementation are as follows:

- You can implement only parts of interfaces.

- You can provide an implementation that isn't restricted to only one class module.

- You can assign an implementation to an object at runtime.

- You can easily modify, extend, or replace an interface during the Application Management (AM) phase without needing to mirror all the changes to the interface wherever the interface is implemented.

Composite

The Composite pattern is intended to allow you to compose tree structures to represent whole-part hierarchies, so that clients can treat individual objects and compositions of objects uniformly. Tree structures are often built where some nodes are containers for other nodes, and other nodes are "leaves." Instead of creating a separate client code to manage each type of node, the Composite pattern lets a client work with either, while using the same code.

Decorator

A Decorator pattern extends an object transparently and makes it possible to add extra functionality without having access to the source code.

Extending an object can be done with inheritance and by subclassing the object. This is, however, sometimes impractical, and the Decorator pattern is intended to give you an alternative way to extend the behavior of an object, without needing to create a new subclass. By using the Decorator pattern, you can easily add behaviors to specific instances of objects, which is difficult to do if you subclass your components directly. Examples of Decorators are the custom attributes in .NET. The attributes you will be using for your serviced components, like object pooling, are actually Decorators to classes—they extend the classes' behavior.

Façade

The Façade pattern simplifies the interface for a subsystem and decouples the client from the underlying subsystem. With the many classes and subsystems you use in the enterprise application, it is important to isolate the different layers and reduce coupling. The Façade pattern is intended to provide this, via a unified interface, to a set of interfaces in a subsystem. The Façade defines a higher-level interface that makes the subsystems easier to use. There are several benefits to using Façade patterns. First, this pattern provides developers with a common interface for the underlying layers in the enterprise application, leading to more uniform code. Since the Façade object controls access to the underlying layers, the underlying system is isolated and provides a layer of protection from complexities in your subsystems as they evolve. This protection makes it easier to replace one subsystem with another, because the dependencies are isolated. This pattern is used in the enterprise architecture illustrated in this chapter.

Flyweight

Many fine-grained objects can be shared in an efficient way by using the Flyweight pattern. The Flyweight pattern maintains the state of fine-grained objects internally or retrieves the state for the objects from the outside when they should be used.

This pattern is useful for situations in which you have a small number of different objects that might be needed a large number of times—each with slightly different data that can be externalized outside those objects. The Flyweight pattern is intended to enable sharing to support large numbers of fine-grained objects more efficiently and to reduce resource usage. The pattern references the intrinsic data of an object that makes it unique and the extrinsic data that gets passed in as parameters. This pattern is useful for applications in which you may need to display icons to represent folders or some other object and don't want to add the overhead of creating new icons for each individual folder.

Proxy

One object approximates another. *Smart proxies* represent an implementation of the Proxy pattern, and you use these when you are creating distributed applications in which the calls will pass many address spaces,, keeping the performance at a high level. One implementation of a smart proxy is actually a wrapper around the object you want to use, which organizes write and read operations from the real object in an effective way.

Behavioral Patterns

Behavioral patterns mainly focus on describing and solving complex communications between objects. The behavioral patterns are designed to take care of difficult control flows through the application and let you focus on the way objects are connected instead of on the flow of control between different objects. In this section, we will discuss what we consider to be the most important behavioral patterns.

Chain of Responsibility

The Chain of Responsibility pattern is very useful when you want a workflow for the incoming requests that x number of objects should be part of. The idea with this pattern is to decouple the sender from the receiver(s). This pattern is useful for help and print functionality in your enterprise application, because the call will be raised higher and higher until a handler is found for the particular action.

Command

The Command pattern is intended to encapsulate a request as an object. For example, consider a Windows application with menu items that need to make requests of objects responsible for the user interface. The client responds to input from the user clicking a menu item by creating a Command object and passing this object to an Invoker object, which then takes the appropriate action. The menu item itself makes the request to the invoker without knowing anything about the action that will take place. By using this pattern, you are able to later change the action of the clicked menu item without changing the client itself. Practical uses for the Command pattern are for creating the mentioned dynamic menus, toolkits for applications, queues and stacks for supporting undo operations, configuration changes, and so on.

Interpreter

The Interpreter pattern is a language interpreter for a defined grammar, which uses the representation to interpret sentences in the language. This pattern is useful in search queries, for instance. Instead of defining complex algorithms, you define a grammar that the user can use (such as AND/OR queries). Then you define a language interpreter that will interpret the sentences the user is writing.

Iterator

The Iterator pattern provides a client with a way to access the elements of an aggregate object sequentially, without having to know the underlying representation. An Iterator pattern also provides you with a way to define special Iterator classes that perform unique processing and return only specific elements of the data collection without bloating the interface with operations for the different traversals. The Iterator pattern is especially useful because it provides the client with a common interface, so that the caller doesn't need to know anything about the underlying data structure.

Mediator

Applications with many classes tend to become fragile as the communication between them becomes more complex. The more classes know about each other, the more they are tied together, and the more difficult it becomes to change the software. The Mediator pattern is intended to define an object that encapsulates how a set of objects interacts. This pattern promotes loose coupling by keeping objects from referring to each other explicitly, and lets you vary their interaction independently.

Memento

Client code often needs to record the current state of an object without being interested in the actual data values (for example, supporting checkpoint and undo operations). To support this behavior, you can have the object record its internal data in a helper class called Memento. The client code uses the Memento object for storing its current state, and restoring the previous state of the client is done by passing the Memento object back to the client object. The Memento object supports the client object with functionality to store its internal state, and it does this by violating encapsulation without making the object itself responsible for this capability.

Observer

The Observer pattern is useful when you need to present data in several different forms at once. This pattern is intended to provide you with a means to define a one-to-many dependency between objects, so when one object changes state, all its dependents are notified and updated automatically. The object containing the data is separated from the objects that display the data, and the display objects observe changes in that data.

This pattern is also known as the *Publish-Subscribe pattern* and is used frequently in SQL Server, as well as between components in Component Services, allowing such components to subscribe to events and publish events to each other.

State

The State pattern is useful when you want to have an object change its behavior depending on its internal state. To the client, it appears as though the object has changed its class. The benefit of the State pattern is that state-specific logic is localized in classes that represent that state.

Strategy

The Strategy pattern is very useful for situations in which you would like to dynamically swap the algorithms used in an application. If you think of an algorithm as a strategy for accomplishing some task, you can begin to imagine ways to use this pattern. The Strategy pattern is intended to provide you with a means to define a family of algorithms, encapsulate each one as an object, and make them interchangeable. Strategy lets the algorithms vary independently from clients that use them.

Template Method

The Template Method is a simple pattern. You have an abstract class that is the base class of a hierarchy, and the behavior common to all objects in the hierarchy is implemented in the abstract class. Other details are left to the individual subclasses. The Template Method pattern is basically a formalization of the idea of defining an algorithm in a class, but leaves some of the details to be implemented in subclasses. Another way to think of the Template Method pattern is that it allows you to define a skeleton of an algorithm in an operation and defer some of the steps to subclasses. Template Method lets subclasses redefine certain steps of an algorithm without changing the algorithm's structure.

Visitor

The Visitor pattern uses an external class to act on data in other classes. This is a useful approach when you have a polymorphic operation that cannot reside in the class hierarchy. This pattern is also a useful way to extend the behavior of a class hierarchy, without the need to alter existing classes or to implement the new behavior in every subclass that requires it.

Phew! We just covered a lot of patterns, and even more exist on the market.

The Enterprise Application and Its Layers

All enterprise applications have problems that will recur. All of them also require many steps to complete their tasks, so therefore we will show you how to use patterns in your enterprise applications to make them stable, robust, and changeable. Later in this chapter, and also in the next one, we demonstrate how to implement some of these patterns.

The architecture pattern and the framework we will describe next have many parts in common with the patterns from Sten and Per Sundblad. Their architecture has a common rule for all layers: Keep chunky calls rather than chatty ones. This is something we highly agree with because it results in less overhead between calls in layers, especially when the different layers are in different processes. (For more information about architectures for other kinds of application, please visit Sten and Per's homepage at http://www.2xSundblad.com.)

Here we will look at an enterprise application pattern. The enterprise architecture is based on *chunky interfaces*, which means that a call to an object is returning a chunk of data. This kind of approach is sometimes called *services-based architecture*, and is not as resource-intensive as a chatty interface. A chunky interface returns chunks of information back to the caller, whereas a *chatty interface* follows a more traditional object model, in that you have objects with properties you can read and set. A chatty interface is more resource- and time-consuming than a chunky one, because each call to the object results in a round-trip to the server, and possibly to each layer in the application. See Figure 5-9 for examples of both a chatty- and a chunky-designed object.

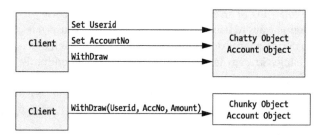

Figure 5-9. *An overview of the chunky and the chatty techniques*

The architecture we are describing here is based on the chunky approach. In all communication where functions are returning data (more than a single value), datasets are used as the carriers. Figure 5-10 shows an overview of the enterprise architecture and the different building bricks you should use to achieve a flexible and scalable architecture for an enterprise application.

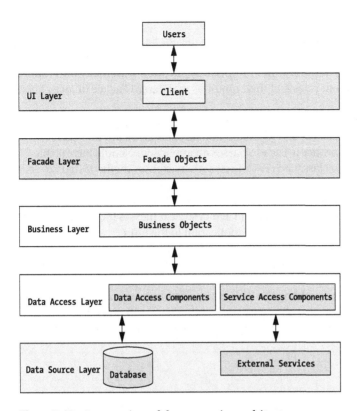

Figure 5-10. *An overview of the enterprise architecture*

The following sections describe the layers for this architecture.

UI Layer

The layer closest to the end user is the UI layer. This layer contains UI controls to handle inter-actions with the user. Here is where all the web controls in a web application will be located. These controls take care of rendering the data to suit the client. They also take care of validating the input from the user, such as checking for valid dates in a date field. The rule is to catch data errors as soon as possible, and this layer helps to do so.

Sometimes we also use an UI Process layer. This layer contains general functions for communicating between the UI layer and the underlying Façade layer.

Façade Layer

The next layer, the Façade layer, has two main purposes for the enterprise architecture.

The first is to encapsulate and isolate the business layers for the clients. By making clients independent of the internal structure in your application, you can change the internal structure in the future, as long as you are keeping the same interface to your clients, via your Façade classes.

The second is that the Façade class acts as a guardian for the application. It should authenticate all users who are calling the Façade methods in the application. When a Façade has granted access to a user, the rest of the application should be able to trust the Façade calls. We recommend that when you are designing an enterprise application with many different roles that you try to keep the different roles and their methods in different Façade objects. This setup is easier to maintain.

One of the most difficult tasks when designing Façade classes for an application is to specify how many Façade classes you will have and what functionality should be put into each of them. A good rule when deciding how many Façade classes an application should have is that every use case generates one Façade class. Each Façade class then exposes methods that cover all the actions the actors on the use case require. This is not always true, however; sometimes the same Façade class is used for several use cases and sometimes a use case employs many different Façades. The latter scenario is one you should avoid, since it messes up the internal structure and makes it more difficult to maintain the application in the future.

The Façade class can either be a traditional class or a class that has been enabled for use as a web service Façade. We believe that all Façade classes should be developed in a web service project in .NET, to ensure that you can easily switch on the web service support for a particular method by adding an attribute to it. By adding the Webmethod attribute, you are still able to call the method as a standard call and also able to call the method as a web service, as shown in Figure 5-11. This makes it easier to scale out the application to meet future needs with as little impact as possible.

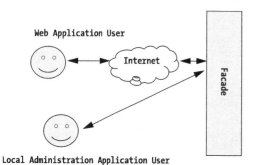

Figure 5-11. *The Façade layer can handle direct calls and web service calls*

Business Layer

Even if you know that an incoming request is validated and granted by the Façade layer (all incoming calls pass a Façade layer), you often need to apply business rules to the request to decide if it is a valid action from a business perspective. The business layer contains code for verifying business rules and taking action with them.

Handling transactions in an easy and secure way is of high importance in enterprise applications. An enterprise application deals with data that is important to a particular company, and it would be dreadful if data integrity is jeopardized by lack of transaction support. .NET supports transactions via .NET Enterprise Services, which in turn uses COM+. Transaction support is also started here if the requested method requires it. You separate transaction-related business rules from the other business rules and place them in their own classes to ease the maintenance. It is also crucial that all starts and stops of transactions are collected in the business layer. Transaction support on classes managed as .NET Enterprise Services should only be enabled when necessary, because it is a performance hit. Figure 5-12 shows the dataflow in the business layer.

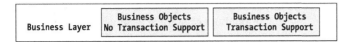

Figure 5-12. *The dataflow for the business layer, including transaction support*

Data Access Layer

The closest of the layers to the data is the data access layer. This layer contains the functions that are doing the fetching and storing in the database. Data passing in .NET can mostly be done in two ways: by using data readers as data carriers between the layers and the client, or through datasets. The difference between these techniques from a performance point of view is not so big, but is of importance from a scalable and distributed point of view. The data reader is marshaled by reference. The actual data is not returned to the caller; instead a reference to the data reader is returned. Each time the client moves forward in the data, a request is sent back to the server. You can easily imagine how the response time can be affected if we have slow performance on the network between the client and server, or between the application layers.

The dataset, on the other hand, is marshaled by value. The data is returned to the client based on XML. This makes it more suitable for distributed applications and also fit to be used for web services. We strongly recommend only using datasets for transporting data between the client and the server. You should also use datasets between the different layers, even if you have installed all layers on one machine initially. You never know when you might need to scale out an enterprise application on more machines, and thereby introduce cross-process problems, which will give you performance hits if you were using data readers between the layers. This would also be true if you needed to separate the different layers due to security reasons—for instance, placing the web server in the DMZ, and the application layer and data layer on the inside, as you see in Figure 5-13.

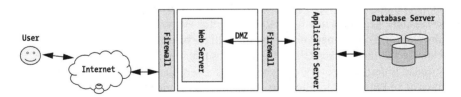

Figure 5-13. *The enterprise architecture divided among different machines*

Specific Data Access Components

The data layer contains data access components that are based on an abstract database class that makes it easy (or at least easier) to switch between different database providers. The abstraction from the specific calls that are for SQL Server or Oracle doesn't matter for your data access components in the data access layer. They are working towards the same data factory. In our example in Chapter 10, you will see that we have database classes for SQL Server and that we can switch easily to a database class for Oracle. The database class for SQL Server will use stored procedures in the data source layer, whereas our database class for Oracle will use plain SQL strings. Since the base classes are quite easy to exchange, we can later implement a class for using MySQL, or some other database engine.

■**Note** The use of exchangeable data access components versus vendor fixed data access components has a price in performance. If you try to keep the data access components exchangeable to use different data source providers, you can't, for instance, use stored procedures in the data source layer to achieve better performance compared to plain SQL queries. Instead, you need to write the code that does the retrieval and storing of data from the data source layer as plain SQL, so that you can more easily switch between different providers. However, we seldom change an Enterprise Application's datasource types, so we might decide to use, for instance, Microsoft SQL Server, and thereby be able to use stored procedures and T-SQL. More frequently an Enterprise Application uses several different types of datasources (such as Oracle, SQL Server), and by using the data access blocks we can use the same technique to access them all. This minimizes the time you need to learn how to access a new datasource.

With the architecture of the enterprise application as we have outlined it in this chapter, you will be able to start with all layers on the same machine, with the possibility to scale the application by adding extra servers to the cluster (see Chapter 4, which discusses the different techniques to scale an enterprise application). If the need arises for you to place different layers on different machines, you can easily do that too.

The Enterprise Library

Many of the problems that the developer or architect faces today aren't project-unique. For instance, data access and logging functionality is something that every Enterprise application uses.

Instead of developing a component library (which will unfortunately be a burden to keep up to date) we can use a library package that Microsoft has released for the .NET platform.

This library, called Enterprise Library, contains several assemblies that will target the most common problems in an Enterprise application, in order to dramatically ease and shorten the development phase.

The Enterprise library (version 1.0) contains the flowing blocks.

Caching Application Block

Often there is a lot of data that can be cached between requests to an Enterprise application. The ASP.NET cache can fulfill many of the simplest requirements, but when we need to have a more complex caching functionality in place, the Caching Application block is the right one to do the job. The Caching block allows us to incorporate a local cache that can cache any kind of data for us.

Configuration Application Block

The Configuration block is one of the main blocks that is used by all of the other Application blocks. The assembly contains functions to allow allows applications to read and write configuration information.

Data Access Application Block

As you will see in our example later in the book, the Configuration block, together with the Data Access Application block, is used frequently. This is probably one of the most common Application blocks that developers try to use from the Enterprise Library. But why? Because here we have a powerful solution to reduce the code to a minimum and the performance to a maximum. The Data Access Application block contains functions to perform tasks towards most common databases.

Cryptography Application Block

When using the Data Access block, a configuration file is created with all database information, such as username and passwords. By default, this file is saved as a text file without any kind of encryption. This is not an acceptable solution for an Enterprise Application. Therefore Microsoft has implemented the Cryptography Application block that allows developers to include encryption and hashing functionality in their applications. This can be used for encrypting the configuration files to prevent unauthorized access to the data.

Exception Handling Application Block

A general approach for handling exceptions is the Exception Application block, which allows developers and policymakers to create a consistent strategy for processing the exceptions that occur throughout the architectural layers of enterprise applications.

Logging and Instrumentation Application Block

When an exception occurs, it might be a good idea to log it, in order to allow the developer to easily figure out what was going wrong. To do this in an Enterprise Application we suggest that you use the Logging and Instrumentation Application block. By doing this, you can incorporate standard logging and instrumentation functionality in your applications.

Security Application Block

The Security Application block allows developers to incorporate security functionality in their applications. Applications can use the application block in a variety of situations, such as authenticating and authorizing users against a database, retrieving role and profile information, and caching user profile information.

For more information about the Enterprise Library, please visit Microsoft's homepage.

Coding Conventions

Projects are far too often driven without good coding conventions and rules for the developers involved to follow. The results of these kinds of projects are often undesirable, with inconsistent layouts of code, implementations of error handling, and so on. Next we'll give you an overview of some of the areas of coding convention that you can use out of the box in your own projects, in order to ensure that the code produced is similar regardless of the developer behind the created class. Many of the conventions that follow are common sense, but we will list them here anyway, to emphasize their importance. Appendix C in this book is based on Microsoft's coding conventions, and extracts the most important rules for enterprise applications. The complete coding conventions can be found at http://msdn.microsoft.com/library/en-us/vsent7/html/ vxconCodingTechniquesProgrammingPractices.asp.

Below is a short summary of the most frequent problems that we have seen in Enterprise projects.

Comments

Commenting in the code is very important for spreading the knowledge of what the code does, and for the maintenance of the code in future releases. Many programmers have problems reading their own code after a couple of months, so imagine what might happen if someone other than the original programmer reads the code after the same amount of time has passed? It is better to spend an extra minutes commenting in a class than spend ten *hours* six months later, figuring out what the class does. Even worse, what if you aren't able to figure out what the class does and you have to write a new one?

If developing in C#, use the XML Documentation feature. There are a couple of ways you can document your code. The first one, which is traditionally used, is standard templates. If you are using C#, you can use the built-in standard documenter—similar to Java's Javadoc— which gives you the ability to extract comments automatically.

Memory Management

It's good practice to create required objects as late as possible and then release them as soon as possible. Hanging onto a resource for as short a time as possible helps you to keep the memory footprint down. Use the Dispose method (shown in Listing 5-1) to tell the garbage collector that you have finished working with component objects. Try to avoid using the Finalize function, because you don't know exactly when it is run during the dispose process of the object and the release of the object's allocated memory. If you are using the Finalize function, make sure to use the Dispose method to trigger the Finalize function:

Listing 5-1. *Using the Dispose Method and the Finalize Function*

```
public void Dispose()
{
    // Clean up unmanaged resources
    GC.SuppressFinalize(this);
}
protected override void Finalize()
```

```
{
    // Clean up unmanaged resources
    base.Finalize();
}
```

Another good practice is to use .NET Enterprise Services for good housekeeping of the resources on the server. By using .NET Enterprise Services, you will be able to define the size of the object pool that you want used objects to reside in until clients need them. As soon as a call to an object is invoked, the object from the pool is returned to the client (for example, the layer). When the method finishes, the object is returned to the pool, and won't be destroyed if the AutoComplete attribute is set. A small number of objects are then used between different client requests, thereby reducing the resource usage on the server. Remember to call the Dispose method on the component to tell the garbage collector that the object can be cleaned up.

Data Access Strategy

Data access strategy deals with the performance optimization, deployment, and scalability of an application. The strategy focuses on a design in which all data is passed to the client in a method call and all database resources are held for a set period of time. (This is also true for all your objects in all layers—you should hold them alive as short a time as possible to reduce the resources in use.)

Pass All Data Back to the Client in a Method Call

In general, stateless objects produce highly scalable solutions. The data access classes are stateless; that is, they do not keep state in instance data members. The client passes all data required for a particular action to a method, and the method passes all resulting data back to the client.

This approach simplifies resource management by freeing every data access object following any method call. As a result, the client can use any data access object to make a method call, because all the required inputs are passed to the object with the call.

As a consequence, you need to keep transaction lifetime longer than any of the connections to the database. The standard transactional support in Component Services (COM+) that uses the Distributed Transaction Coordinator (DTC) will be employed to accomplish this (see the section "Transaction Strategy"). By using the JIT and the object pooling support found in COM+, you can reduce the overhead to create new objects for each call.

Hold Database Resources for a Minimum Length of Time

Database resources are limited and expensive. The data access layer postpones database resource allocation as long as possible and frees database resources as soon possible. The data access classes implement Finalize/Dispose semantics to close the active database connection. The data access objects are allocated and released at the point of a database call in the scope of either a using or try-finally block.

Transaction Strategy

Transactions are initiated in the business layer using the transactional support in COM+. Often, nested local transactions yield better performance than distributed transactions executed by serviced components running under the control of the Distributed Transaction Coordinator (DTC). However, that performance is marginal compared to the increased complexity of the implementation, so use the support for transactions found in COM+.

Security

The key message regarding security is this: Find security issues in development, not in production. Try to run the development environment without administration privileges on your machine—you will be stunned at how many times the application will hang.

You can either use imperative or declarative security. Declarative security is implemented as custom attributes on the class or method level. This kind of security check is often an acceptable solution, since many classes and methods should only be accessed by certain groups of users. Listing 5-2 shows how a declarative security check is added to the DoWithdrawAlot method to only allow users of the role Clerks to execute it:

Listing 5-2. *PrincipalPermission Attributes Added to the Function*

```
[PrincipalPermission(SecurityAction.Demand,Role="Clerks")]
void DoWithdrawAlot()
{
        // Do the transaction...
}
```

Declarative security can also be added on the class level. If you have declarative security added on the class level and method level, the declarative security on the method level overrides the class level's security. Since these attributes are accessible via the Reflection API, you can read the permission sets for your classes and methods and print them out. An accurate documentation of the existing permission sets on the classes and methods in the enterprise application is a very useful thing to have. Any changes in the permissions can be extracted out to documentation by using the Reflection API and thereby keep the documentation up to date.

When you have a class with a method that needs fine-grained security check (for example, you need to verify that the user has access to parts of the code inside a method), the declarative way is not flexible enough. Instead you should use the imperative security check.

When using the imperative security check, you need to call the Demand method on the PrincipalPermission object to demand a verification of the current user. When you call the Demand method, the CLR does a verification that either the current user belongs to the requested role or is the requested user. Next we show you Listing 5-3, a short example of using the PrincipalPermission object to verify that the current user belongs to the correct role.

Listing 5-3. *Using the PrincipalPermission Object*

```
public void DoWithdrawAlot ()
{
    PrincipalPermission permission =
        new PrincipalPermission(null, "Clerks");
    permission.Demand();
    // Now do the transaction...
}
```

If the calling user doesn't belong to the Clerks role, a SecurityException will be raised from the Demand method.

.NET Enterprise Services

.NET Enterprise Services expose all of the functionality you know from COM+. .NET Enterprise Services makes it possible for your enterprise applications to take advantage of object pooling, data connection pooling, and other functions found in COM+. Many developers avoid using .NET Enterprise Services, since it uses COM+ (see Figure 5-14), which is actually built on the unmanaged code, thereby resulting in slight performance overhead when used. Interoperability gives you this overhead, no doubt about it, but if you compare this to creating the pooling by yourself and also handling the transaction support, this overhead is a small sacrifice for having a smaller amount of code generated and an ease of maintenance. The next version of the Component Services will hopefully run as managed code, so that the overhead associated with Component Services disappears. We saw the development and performance boost that happened when MTS was integrated closer to the core and renamed COM+. We hope that a similar boost will occur when Component Services is rewritten in .NET and the .NET Framework is more closely integrated with the system. As you will see in Chapter 10, the move from Windows 2000 Server with .NET Framework to Windows Server 2003 boosts the performance dramatically.

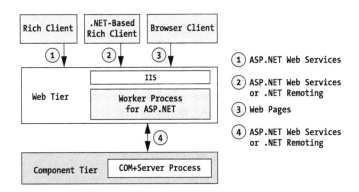

Figure 5-14. *An n-tier architecture using Enterprise Services with COM+*

In order to use .NET Services from your application, your classes need to derive from ServicedComponent and use various custom attributes (the common way to customize the behavior of your classes and methods in .NET) to specify the actual services required. Here we will discuss the major benefits for using .NET Enterprise Services and show you how you can improve scalability and reliability by using it in your enterprise architecture.

Tip Try keeping the serviced components as library applications, since the performance hit that results from running them in a separate context as a server application may sometimes be too high. When you need to run the components on remote machines, or want to run them under specific security context, you need to run them as server applications.

Transactions

Transaction support is only one of the benefits of using .NET Enterprise Services. Other benefits are object pooling, role support, and queued components. Enterprise applications work with sensitive data, and therefore transaction support is of great importance. Without transactions, data will sooner or later be corrupted, when a cascade update or change to the data server is interrupted by mistake. By using the transaction support found in .NET Enterprise Services, you don't need to develop the transaction support yourself. This means that you save time in the development phase and also during the maintenance phase because the code will become less complex.

Assume that you have an enterprise application that deals with bank accounts and their information. Transactions between bank accounts need to be handled to avoid loss of information. A simple server class in your application may look like Listing 5-4.

Listing 5-4. *A simple server class*

```
using System.EnterpriseServices;
[assembly: ApplicationName("BankComponent")]
[assembly: AssemblyKeyFileAttribute("Demos.snk")]
namespace BankComponent
{
        [ Transaction(TransactionOption.Required)]
        public class Account : ServicedComponent
        {
        [ AutoComplete]
                public bool Post(int accountNum, double amount)
                {
                // Updates the database, no need to call SetComplete.
                // Calls SetComplete automatically if no exception is thrown.
                }
        }
}
```

To make this component work, you first need to reference System.EnterpriseServices. Secondly, the Account class needs to derive from the ServicedComponent in the EnterpriseServices. The configuration of the COM+ application that will host the managed code can be controlled via attributes. The first attribute here is the attribute on the class ([Transaction (TransactionOption.Required)]), which specifies that a transaction is required for this class. The [AutoComplete] attribute tells you that the function Post will auto-commit the changes when the function exists (there is no need to explicit call setComplete). If an exception is thrown in the function, the transaction is automatically rolled back. The ease of implementing the transaction support is obvious—you do not need your own transaction code, which makes the application easier to read and to maintain.

The client that calls your server class looks like Listing 5-5.

Listing 5-5. *Client Class Calling Your Server*

```
BankComponent Client
using system;
```

```
using BankComponent;
namespace BankComponentClient
{
    class Client
    {
        public static int Main ()
        {
            Account act = new Account();
            act.Post(6, 90);
            act.Dispose();
            return 0;
        }
    }
}
```

The client looks like any normal client, and the call to your server component account is like any normal object call in .NET. A reference to the BankComponent namespace, the System.EnterpriseServices assembly, and the final call of the Dispose method, is a general .NET requirement when a derived class doesn't override all the base class methods (see Figures 5-15 and 5-16).

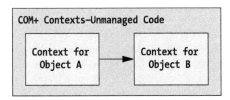

Figure 5-15. *The general context for an unmanaged application and its components*

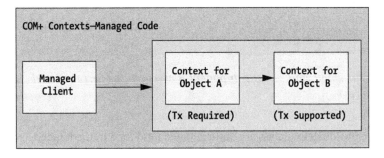

Figure 5-16. *The context for the example managed application*

Deployment

So far you have a server component and a client component. The next step is to deploy your server component on the server, so that you can access it from the client. In a traditional COM+ world, you would have registered the component by yourself in Component Services.

In .NET, you can do this in three different ways—the manual way, which we recommend for production environments in order to control the installation process, the dynamic way, and the programmatic registration way.

Note If the components are to be accessible from old COM components, dynamic registration cannot be used. Dynamic registration can only be used when you have a managed client.

When deploying the dynamic way, the COM+ application that hosts your managed components is configured based on the custom attributes in the code. With custom attributes, you can specify the services that are required, such as the transaction attribute in your server class. The attributes are stored in the assembly metadata. When the components are executed for the first time and you want them installed in Component Services, the metadata and the attributes are read by using EnterpriseServices.RegistrationHelper (see Figure 5-17). In order to make the process of registration easier, all forms of registration use the component EnterpriseServices.RegistrationHelper. This component is accessible as a managed class as well as a COM+ object.

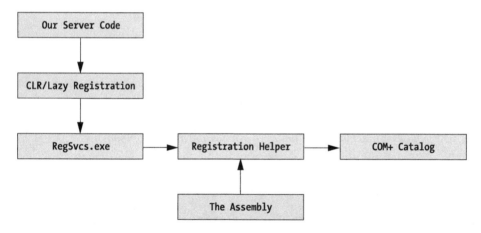

Figure 5-17. *The calls that occur when your server component is executed the first time and registered in Component Services*

The workings of the RegistrationHelper class are quite detailed (and for a more detailed explanation of what is going on behind the scenes, please visit http://msdn.microsoft.com/library/default.asp?url=/library/en-us/_dndotnet/html/entserv.asp). But we want to mention some things that might otherwise confuse you when working with Enterprise Services.

Your .NET classes are registered by the RegistrationHelper and appear on the machine as COM components. If your components do not implement any extra interfaces beside the default interface, the method names will not show up when browsing the components via the Component Services Tool. To be able to see the methods that are in the standard interface, you need to add the ClassInterfaceAttribute to all methods.

When the RegistrationHelper registers your .NET classes as COM components, it generates GUIDS for the COM components. If the assembly is not signed, the GUIDs are generated based only on type and namespace names. This can result in non-unique GUIDs.

Note Assemblies that use COM+ services must be signed. Registration will fail if assemblies are not signed.

You should also verify that you aren't using the ApplicationID attribute in your assembly. If you are using it, your components won't install into different COM+ applications to allow different configuration data for the components. COM+ requires unique application IDs.

As you already know, dependency files are installed either in the same directory as the client or in the GAC.

Note Assemblies that use serviced components in COM+ server apps should be placed in the GAC. Assemblies that use serviced components in COM+ library apps may not need to be placed in the GAC (unless they are located in different directories). The only exception is when hosting with ASP.NET, assemblies should not be placed in the GAC to enable shadow copy to operate correctly. To remove a .NET application that uses serviced components, remove the assembly from the GAC (if it has been registered with the GAC), deregister the assembly from COM+ using regsvcs.exe, and then delete the assembly and the associated type libraries. Assemblies that are dynamically registered do not need to be placed in the GAC.

Next, the RegistrationHelper tries to find out if you have already installed a previous version of the component in a COM+ application. A new COM+ application is created if no existing application is found.

Finally, RegistrationHelper reads all of your attributes on the classes and methods in the component and then applies them to the installed component in COM+.

Since the RegistrationHelper accesses the registry and adds new COM+ applications to Component Services, the user who is executing the RegistrationHelper needs to have administration rights on the machine. This is a common mistake people make when using Enterprise Services from an ASP.NET-based application. The components are initialized from the ASP.NET account, so dynamic registration of the components will fail because this account does not have the right permissions by default. We always recommend to do the registration and creation of the COM+ application manually, in order to have control of the process.

Note Since attributes are coded by the programmer in the class, these attributes might be in conflict with each other. Some attributes can't be listed together with other attributes. These mismatches will not be detected until the RegistrationHelper tries to apply the attributes to the registered component. To avoid these errors, always make it a habit to register your components manually, so you can catch these attribute mistakes before going live.

If no attributes are found in the class, the default values are used for the component in the COM+ application. For instance, if a component is registered and does not have a Transaction attribute specified, the unconfigured default value for the transaction setting in the catalog is set to TransactionOption.Disabled.

When the component has been registered, you can change some configuration parameters, such as object pooling, timeouts, and JIT. However, changing some of these parameters can prevent your code from running correctly. For instance, disabling the object construction for a component that requires getting a constructor string will probably result in an error.

Although some configuration parameters are configurable through the Component Services Tool, others are only read from the class itself and not from the configuration in Component Services. These are JIT, AutoComplete, and object pooling (except for the size of the pool that is configurable through Component Services). Changing these parameters for the component via the Component Services Tool doesn't affect the component at all.

Versioning

Anyone who has ever worked with the Windows DNA environment knows that versioning can be a huge problem and a nightmare—especially when users call you and say that the application doesn't work after the version 1.1 release. .NET removes the reference problems known as *DLL Hell* and helps you to manage your different versions of the application in a more convenient way. In .NET, you can isolate a specific version of an application, because you can put all dependent files into the application directory together with the version and it's not necessary registered globally on the machine. This makes it possible to have many different versions of the same application installed on the machine and running concurrently.

To be able to install a package into COM+, the package must have a unique ID. It is possible to generate a unique ID by applying a GUID in your server class. However, it is better to use versioning of your package instead of applying new GUIDs. As always, you need to increment your version number on the assembly as soon as you change anything in the application. When the incremented assembly is installed in COM+, COM+ generates a new GUID for it, and installs it parallel with the old version in the same COM+ application. By default, the Visual Studio Environment adds the attribute [assembly: AssemblyVersion("1.0.*")], which will increase the version number of the assembly for every build.

Tip We advise you to change the * in the AssemblyVersion attribute to the current minor version you are working on, and manually increment the number when you are going to release a new version to the server. This will give you better control over when new minor release numbers are generated as well as prevent you from accidentally incrementing the minor version just because you test-built the assembly.

You may be wondering what happens when you install a new version—will the old clients stop working? No, the old clients will still work and bind to the old assembly by using the CLR version policy. The version policy differs depending on whether the involved application is managed or not.

- With a managed client and managed server that are running in managed scope, the client will load the right assembly based on the version policy on the machine. This is true if versioning is used in the assembly.

- When you are using a fixed GUID in the managed client, and you create a class using the version policy to get to an old version of the assembly, the fixed GUID in the code will be used during activation to extract the service information from the catalog. The service information returned will be the latest registered assembly using this GUID. This service information will be used to create the object, which may be a newer version than the client requests. The client will get a typecast exception when attempting to cast from the actually created object (version 2) to the referenced object in the client (version 1).

- Consider a situation with a managed client, managed server, and no fixed GUIDs, and you change only the build number. If you are using .NET Framework 1.0, the following will happen: New GUIDs will be generated, but the type library will still have the same version number since type libraries only have two numbers for the version. The client may still be able to work, but if version 2 is installed over version 1, version 1 is then uninstalled, and the type library for version 1 will be unregistered.

- The solution to this is to use .NET Framework version 1.1. In this version, the type library is versioned independently of the assembly. This implies that when changing the assembly version number, the type library version should be changed. If you cannot install version 1.1 of the .NET Framework, you can solve this problem by using only major and minor version numbers.

- Here's another scenario: unmanaged client with a managed server, no fixed GUIDs used. The client will use a GUID to create the component. Interoperability will resolve the GUID to a name, and then version policy gets applied. If version 1 and version 2 of an assembly are on a machine, and the policy is used to get to version 2, the unmanaged client will get version 2.

- Install version 1, install version 2, then uninstall version 1. Now the client cannot create the component unless there is version policy to redirect to version 2. In addition, registry entries must exist for version 1 registration information. One way to create registry information for an uninstalled version 1 is to use the COM+ aliasing feature on Windows XP.

Serviced Components

A serviced component is a component that uses the functionality from Enterprise Services. A serviced component uses, for instance, transaction support, JIT, or object pooling that Enterprise Services handles for you. To be able to access these features, you need to derive your components from the System.EnterpriseServices.ServicedComponent class. To configure your serviced component, you can apply custom attributes to your class. There are three important factors about attributes to remember: the scope, the unconfigured default value, and the configured default value.

The scope of the attributes added to the class can apply to methods, classes, or the whole assembly. It depends on where you put the attribute.

The configured default value is the value that the attribute will be given if you omit to specify a value for the attribute. An example of this is the attribute JustInTimeActivation, which has a configured default value of true—for example, [JustInTimeActivation=True]. If the JustInTimeActivation attribute is omitted completely from the code, its default value will be false. This is an unconfigured default value.

There are many attributes that can be used to configure the COM+ application, but in the following sections we outline the more or less mandatory attributes that we have found quite useful for scalability issues. We also show a simple example of how each of the attributes can be used.

ApplicationActivation

This attribute tells the configuration of the COM+ application if the COM+ application should run in the same process as the client (library) or in its own process (server). The attribute does not have any unconfigured default value, and the configured default value is true, which means that the assembly will run as a library in COM+. This is the optimal solution when you want performance, since running the assembly in its own process forces the application to marshal over boundaries that are quite expensive, as seen from a performance point of view in Listing 5-6.

Listing 5-6. *An ApplicationActivation attribute added to the class*

```
Using System;
Using System.Reflection;
Using System.EnterpriseServices;
[ApplicationName("MyTimeReportComponents")]
[ApplicationActivation(ActivationOption.Library)]
public class TimeReport:System.EnterpriseServices.ServicedComponent
{
        public string GetSubmittedReports(string Userid)
        {
        //Code here
        }
        public string SaveReport(string Userid,string TimeReport)
        {
        //Code here
        }
}
```

ApplicationQueueing

To be able to read from message queues, the serviced component needs to define this attribute. The scope is for the assembly, and it has no unconfigured or configured values:

```
 [assembly: ApplicationQueuing(Enabled=true, QueueListenerEnabled=true)]
public class TimeReport:System.EnterpriseServices.ServicedComponent
{
...
}
```

AutoComplete

When intercepting in transactions, the attribute AutoComplete can be used on methods to tell the serviced component to automatically commit the transaction if no error occurred in the method. If an error occurs, the transaction will be aborted. The unconfigured default value for this attribute is false, and the configured one is true. For example, if the attribute is not specified, the AutoComplete is false, and if the attribute is specified, the default is true:

```
[AutoComplete]
public string SaveReport(string Userid,string TimeReport)
{
    //Code here
}
```

ConstructionEnabled

This attribute makes it possible to specify a constructor string that is editable from the COM+ application catalog via the Component Services Manager Console. By adding this attribute to the class, you do not need to hard code the database connection in the data class, for instance—instead you can specify it in the catalog:

```
[assembly: ConstructionEnabled(Default="myDefaultValue")]
public class TimeReport:System.EnterpriseServices.ServicedComponent
{
    ...
}
```

Transactions

As mentioned before, this attribute gives you the opportunity to specify the kind of transaction the class needs. The unconfigured default value for this attribute is false, and the configured default value is either TransactionOption.Required, TransactionIsolationlevel.Serializable, or Timeout. If you specify TransactionOption.Required, a new transaction will be started; if not, the caller already has a transaction you can participate in:

```
[Transaction(TransactionOption.Required)]
public class TimeReport:System.EnterpriseServices.ServicedComponent
{
    //. . .
}
```

JustInTimeActivation

This attribute applies to the class and allows you to create an object as nonactive and context only. What you get is only a "faked" object—the real object is created the first time you try to access a method or property on the object. When the method returns, the object is deactivated. When the object is deactivated, it will be returned to the pool if the ObjectPoolingAttribute is used; if it is not, the object is destroyed. All resources that the object was using are released:

■ Note When you use the JustInTimeActivationAttribute, do not turn off the JIT compiling by using the
Component Services Admin tool.

```
[JustInTimeActivation]
public class TimeReport:System.EnterpriseServices.ServicedComponent
{
    ...
}
```

ObjectPooling

This attribute makes it possible to define, for a class, the number of objects that should be
pooled (cached) for later use. If this attribute is used, the objects are not created from scratch
when a client requests a specific object. COM+ looks into the object pool to find an existing
object and returns a reference to that object to the caller. The object is returned to the pool
when the caller has finished working with the object. This is an important attribute that is
used, for instance, to limit the number of concurrent connections to a database by specifying
how many objects of the data class may exist in the pool. The CreationTimeOut parameter is
the time (in this case, 25 seconds) that the process will wait for a free object from the pool,
before the creation will timeout and generate an exception:

```
[ObjectPooling(Enabled=true,MinPoolSize=1,MaxPoolSize=8,CreationTimeOut=25000)]
public class TimeReport:System.EnterpriseServices.ServicedComponent
{
...
}
```

Windows/Web Forms

When designing an enterprise application, the architecture behind the UI is of great importance.
Without a good application structure, it does not matter if the UI is fancy or not—the application
is probably a nightmare for users and developers.

The enterprise application we are building later in this book has a user interface that is
web-based. Because most enterprise applications are used by many employees, and you want
the upgrade/installation to be as pain-free as possible for the administrators, such applications
usually have a web-based interface. Since the release of .NET, you can also easily create *smart
clients*—Windows-based applications updated or upgraded via web services on the local intranet.

■Note Microsoft has released an updating application block that can handle the update support for your application. See http://msdn.microsoft.com/library/default.asp?url=/library/en-us/dnpag2/html/updaterv2.asp for more information.

We aren't going into great depth on the user interface here: instead we are going to focus on the elementary principles for having a good UI.

The normal flow for your eyes, when you read something, is from the upper-left corner, moving from left to right, and down to the lower-right corner—at least for those of us in the West (see Figure 5-18). This should also be the normal flow in your application. This means that the information that the user needs to complete the tasks on the page should be presented at the top, and the data the user needs to fill in should be presented thereafter.

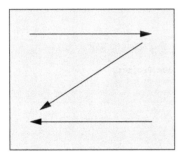

Figure 5-18. *The normal flow in an application window*

Windows Forms

Windows forms are preferred when an application, for instance, is going to take a huge amount of processing on the client side or when you want to put the working load on the client instead of the server. Due to this, the Windows form-based application relies on the client computer's performance more than a web-based application does. We will show you how to apply this "read-flow" rule when we create our example application in Chapter 9.

Regardless of whether you choose a web-based application or a Windows-based application, the way you code behind the graphical controls is the same. The code behind the controls on the web page (if it is a web-based application you develop) is called a *controller function*. The controller function calls the Façade object to implement the desired action and retrieve the required data. Behind a user event, you place a call to the controller function, which in turn calls your Façade class, as illustrated in Figure 5-19.

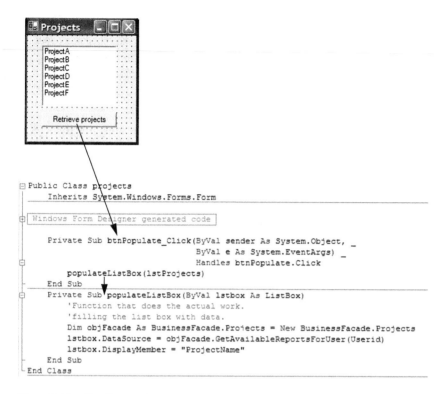

Figure 5-19. *The flow in the UI*

So, what should you do and what shouldn't you do in the user interface? You should not invoke, vote, or participate in any transactions—the transactions should be handled from the business layer and further down in the architecture. When you are working with user input, you should validate the user input so that you know the data is valid. But a good rule of thumb is to validate and detect errors as early as possible in the data flow to avoid round-trips to the server.

When you render data, your user interface will retrieve the data from the Façade objects and perform final formatting of values (such as formatting dates to the local formatting standard at the client). You can also perform any other localization work on the retrieved data.

The user interface in a Windows application can be of different types. A standard Windows application has full support for all kinds of user interaction that gives your users a rich experience. The drawback with this type of application is that you are tied to using the Microsoft platform because Windows is the only operating system, so far, that has the complete .NET Framework implemented. One other drawback is that the application needs to be deployed. Another type of Windows application actually embeds HTML, to allow for more flexibility, as the HTML can be fetched from external resources or even a database in a connected scenario. The drawback with this approach is that you need to protect yourself from malicious script being implemented in the HTML. You also need to include some additional coding to load the HTML and display it, and hook up the events from the application.

Another solution might be to develop the application as a plug-in to a host application such as Microsoft Word or Excel. This is one of the approaches taken for the publishing tool found in the Microsoft Content Management Server we will talk about later, in the "Content Management" section. The benefit of this is that the user can use an application that he or she is already familiar with, making productivity high from start.

No matter which one of the mentioned Windows application types you decide to use, the need for a common approach to access your Façades and the enterprise architecture is the same.

When developing Windows-based applications, you can rely a lot on data-bounded controls. This means that a control, for instance, a list box, can bind to data that will be automatically updated when changes are made to it. This removes the need to write complex data synchronization code.

Always implement error handlers in the code, as we mentioned previously in the section "Error Raising and Handling." You should also take care of errors and present them to the user in a friendly manner. Remember—a friendly manner does *not* mean presenting a stack dump to the user, saying "Oops! Something went wrong—please reboot your computer and have a fresh cup of coffee while you are waiting."

Web Forms

Our example application in Chapter 10 will have a web-based user interface created in ASP.NET. When you develop a web-based user interface, you may want to create a custom error page and a global exception handler in the global.asax file for your application. By doing this, you will catch all exceptions that are not handled by the application and thereby prevent the user from seeing a stack dump or something even worse.

ASP.NET has many great controls for validating user inputs, so it behooves you to take advantage of them. When you work with user input, you should validate the user input so you know that the data is valid. (You may want to validate the data in the Façade layer too, since the client may not be able to validate the data input—this is also true for a web application in which client script has been disabled by the user.) A good rule to follow is to validate and detect errors as early as possible in the data flow to avoid round-trips to the server.

If you create your own web controls, you should use the "abstraction" from OOP—which only shows the properties and methods that you used. This improves the maintainability, since the developer does not need to see unused properties and methods.

States can be handled in different ways. You can employ hidden fields in the page, using the view state functionality (which is quite similar to using hidden fields), or you can employ a separate state server that controls your states. The hidden field solution is not used so much nowadays; it's much more common to use the view state functionality found in ASP.NET.

■**Note** Remember to turn off the view state if no state is needed between calls from the page. The view state generates a lot of text in the page that needs to be transferred between the client and the server in each call.

Implement your controller functions as separate functions instead of putting them directly in the event from where they are started. Doing so enables you to use the same controller function from different places in the page.

Web Services

Web services are used in the Façade layer to expose the Façade methods as web service methods as well.

The integration of web services in the same class as the Façade class has both benefits and drawbacks. The major benefit is that the same code serves as both the web services exposed method and the traditional method. The major drawback is that you cannot easily apply rules or validations that you may want to have specifically for the web services, and not for your direct calls.

Therefore, it can sometimes be wise to have the web services in a separate project, working as a web service–Façade in relation to the real Façade. This solution makes it possible to apply web service–specific rules to each method. The drawback with this solution is that now you have some extra code to maintain.

We have found that in most cases the use of one Façade layer, both for direct calls and for web services, is enough. There is seldom a need for a separate web service project to host a web service Façade. See Chapter 6 for a more detailed description of web services.

.NET Remoting in the Enterprise World

When you design your enterprise application, you need to consider many issues, as you have discovered, and then decide how your system architecture should look. The communication between the different layers in your enterprise application and the communication between different enterprise applications and services can be done in two different ways—either as web services or as remote objects.

All of our real-life solutions so far have used web services by default for exposing functionality to other systems and to retrieve information, mainly because they are simpler to both implement and use and they are not limited to a consumer that needs the complete framework installed (as is the result when using .NET Remoting). Another important aspect is that a web service client proxy can be invoked from code running in a sandbox under the default security policy.

The .NET Remoting system provides you with the functionality to activate objects, control the lifetime of each object, and transport messages to and from the client and the server using communication channels. Communication channels are the items that transport the data between the remote object and the server. The data that is sent via communication channels are serialized using the native .NET serialization formatters, such as SOAPFormatter and the BinaryFormatter. The data that is sent between the client and the server is transmitted over either TCP or HTTP.

■**Note** Serialization is a process by which the state of an object is stored on disk or transferred on a network. *Deserialization* is the reverse—the incoming byte stream is converted back into an object. It is possible to choose the serialization type independently from the transport type. For example, an HTTPChannel can serialize data with the BinaryFormatter.

To achieve the best performance, you should use the BinaryFormatter together with the TCP transport protocol. Where you need interoperability with remote systems, the SOAPFormatter is the preferred choice. Even if the best performance is achieved by using the BinaryFormatter together with the TCP transport protocol, we recommend using web services with the SOAPFormatter and HTTP, because they aren't as complex and their output is pure XML, which is supported on all platforms.

The .NET Remoting Architecture

To be able to choose between using web services and .NET Remoting objects, you need to know how .NET Remoting works. To communicate between a client and a server object in .NET Remoting, you need to use object references of the server object in the client application.

When you create a server object in the client application, you receive a reference to a server object via .NET Remoting. You can then use the object as a traditional local object—similar to how you use web services via SOAP.

Remotable objects can be exposed in two different ways: marshal-by-value or marshal-by-reference.

Marshal-by-value objects are server objects defined as Serializable and implementing the ISerializable interface. When a client calls a method of this object, the Remoting system creates a copy of the server object and passes back the whole object to the client. The client can then work with the object locally and thereby avoid expensive round-trips over the network and application boundaries.

Note When choosing the marshal-by-value approach, remember that some types of functionality cannot be used in the client process. For instance, a server object working with files will likely fail, since the resource pointers to the file system are application domain-specific and the pointers that the copied object receives from the server are not the same in the client process.

If you have a large server object with many properties and methods, it is not suitable to use the marshal-by-value approach. Instead, you can create a small remotable object that can be published or copied to the client application. This small remotable object makes a direct call to the larger non-remotable object on the server.

The other way to expose a remote object is via *marshal-by-reference*. Instead of copying the object to the client process, a proxy object is returned to the caller by the .NET Remoting infrastructure. This proxy object contains references to all the methods and properties in the real server object. When you call a method on your proxy object, the request is encoded and serialized to a message using the preferred techniques and then the message is sent to the server. When the server receives the message, it traverses back to an object call and executes on the server. Figure 5-20 shows the flow between the client proxy and the real server object when using the marshal-by-reference approach.

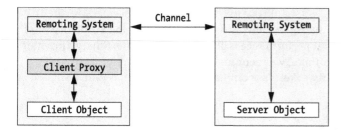

Figure 5-20. *The message flow between the client proxy and the server object*

■ **Note** .NET Remoting is quite clever. If the marshal-by-value object exists in the same application domain as the client, no marshaling will take place. This is the same for the marshal-by-reference object, if it is in the same application domain as the client. In this case, a direct reference is returned to the client instead of a reference to the proxy object.

When you are working with an enterprise application, communication over application domains will likely occur. (An application domain exists between two different applications or between two machines, for instance.) This will happen when you split your enterprise application layers and place them on different servers (web server, application server, and data server). To be able to choose the right technology, web service or .NET Remoting, for your enterprise application, you need to know more about the communication channel between the client and the server when you use .NET Remoting.

Channels make it possible for a client application to send messages to another application running in a different application domain, process, or computer. Channels work with transport protocols such as TCP, HTTP, and others, in order to send messages. Nowadays developers mainly work with TCP and HTTP as transport protocols for channels. A channel works as the message carrier between the client and the server and converts the method call into the selected encoding, such as binary format or XML. Choosing between TCP- or HTTP-based channels depends on which features of the two you need to use. The HTTPChannel transports the messages to and from the client by using the HTTP transport protocol. It also uses the SOAPFormatter by default to serialize the method call before it is transferred.

The maximum number of channels that can be simultaneously opened to a given server is configurable via the clientConnectionLimit attribute in the application configuration file. By default two channels are allowed. All channels that a process has registered are unregistered automatically when the process terminates.

The TCPChannel uses TCP as its transport protocol. It also uses, by default, the BinaryFormatter class to serialize and deserialize messages. One new connection for each client call is created. The connections are closed if they remain inactive for 15 to 20 seconds.

Choosing .NET Remoting Objects or Web Services

So how do you decide when to use web services and when to use .NET Remoting? It's not possible to give a clear answer that will suit all possible solutions. For example, if you have a homogenous environment with machines that all run .NET Framework, and you need the extra performance boost that the use of .NET Remoting currently gives you compared to web services, you should use the .NET Remoting functionality. .NET Remoting gives you a traditional distributed object model with full support of CLR type fidelity. However, when you use .NET Remoting, try to host the objects in IIS to take advantage of the process life cycle management and the security support found in IIS. In a homogenous environment with a .NET client, you can use the BinaryFormatter instead of the SOAPFormatter to achieve better performance (no serialization occurs).

Though both the .NET Remoting infrastructure and web services can enable cross-process communication, each is designed to benefit a different target audience. Web services provide a simple programming model and a wider reach, because they do not require the .NET Framework on the client machine. .NET Remoting provides a more complex programming model because the complete .NET Framework is supported.

In the described enterprise application architecture, we are mainly working with web services in our examples, due to their simplicity and their portability to other platforms.

Content Management

Most of the enterprise applications developed today either handle content internally or present their content to an end user.

Building a content management system from scratch is time consuming, and it will seldom be what it was meant to be—the information flow of the content is often too complex, and mistakes will often occur. Instead of developing a content management system from scratch, you can choose from several systems on the market that have been developed with scalability and maintainability in mind. However, the cost and the complexity of an existing system requires you to analyze your requirements for such a system carefully, in order to ensure that the customer will get the most suitable content management system that represents the best value for his or her money.

Analyze the Requirements

The different problems that we outlined in the introduction to content management presented in Chapter 1 will be investigated more closely here. We will go through a couple of different factors that can help you to decide if your company or your client should invest money in a content management system. Remember that it's not always obvious whether you need to install a content management system. To recap, a content management system is designed to solve the following sorts of problems:

- There is too much information to process manually.

- Many publications need to be published from the same source.

- Information is changing too quickly to be handled by hand.

- Content and design need to be separated in order to allow the look and feel of the site to be updated without rewriting the content.

But when does a customer have too much information to process manually? To answer that question, you need to be able to calculate the amount of content. The content becomes unwieldy for a customer to handle mainly when a lot of content exists and many content types need to be incorporated into the site. When we say "a lot of content," we are referring to the number of pages here, an approximate maximum being 800 pages. This is a rough number because the amount of content is only one part of the problem. (In fact, this approximation applies to sites where most of the pages are static pages that do not change on a frequent basis. If you have an active site, the number is more likely to be closer to 200.) Even if your site has just a few pages, you may also have many placeholders or content components that need to be updated. Every content component involves a user interaction that takes time. To calculate content throughput, you need to know how many placeholders are modified in some way per unit of time. If you intend to create 40 content components per week, and you need to modify 20 of these per week in some way (that is, you must delete or update them), your content throughput is 60 in this example. A rough maximum here is 400 content components for one person to handle a week (in a manual way).

The number of different publications is also an important factor to calculate when determining whether a manual system needs to be replaced by a content management system. Whether you have one simple brochure or three different ones on your site is an important distinction to make. Obviously it takes more time to manage three different layouts, and sometimes even the content on three different sites, than one layout. The personalization factor of the content on the web site is also important—more personalization requires more effort. If you also decide to make your brochure available in three different languages, the amount of work to keep them up to date rises dramatically. Something else you must consider: The previously mentioned factors are not the only ones you need to take into account. Just as each site is unique, each will have its own combination of content issues—the variations are far too many to address in a book. As with many things, experience is the best teacher. However, here we will try to give you a formula that can help you decide whether a customer needs a content management system or not.

To be able to measure the needs and benefits of introducing a content management system to a company, use our *content management formula*:

$$\text{Placeholders} \times \text{Placeholder Types} \times \text{Publications} \times \text{Personalization} \times \text{Redesigns} \times \text{Throughput}$$

■**Note** We want to emphasize that this formula only gives you a hint as to whether the customer will benefit from a content management system or not.

Let us take a look at each of the pieces of this formula:

Placeholders represent the number of places where information will be published (or are published today in a manual system). This number is the total number of placeholders divided by 1000. Adjust values below 0.5 to 0.5. Use values above 0.5 without modifications.

Placeholder Types is the total number of different types of placeholders that exist—for instance, you might have chart placeholders, HTML placeholders, and financial information placeholders from the legacy system. This value is the total number of placeholder types divided by a factor of 5. Again, adjust values below 0.5 to 0.5. Values above 1 use as is.

Publications define the total number of different publications that you need to create.

Personalization is the degree of personalization you have or plan to have in the new system. A factor of 1 indicates that you are not intending to have any kind of personalization. A factor of 2 is for sites with a little personalization (such as e-mail newsletters, simple login features, and a simple page where the users can change their membership properties). Factors 3 and 4 are for sites where personalization occurs on most of the content components. Personalization is also based on statistical information collected from persons browsing on the site (factor 4) and whether publications exist in different languages.

Redesigns stands for the number of major design changes that you are planning to do to the site per year. Divide this number by 2. This factor can never be smaller than 1, however— so for one redesign per year the factor will be 1 and not 0.5.

Throughput is the number of components that are changed in some way during a week. Divide the total number of components by 50, round values up to the nearest half value, and adjust values —below 0.5 to 0.5 and values above 0.5 to 1. Use values 1 and above as they are.

The breakpoint of the formula for recommending a content management system is 1. If the result from the formula is less than 1, the company in question will not gain much by installing a content management system.

Let us look at some examples to clarify how to use the content management formula. Company MyLittleComp does not have a web site—the only publication the company has is a brochure in two languages (Swedish and English) that it distributes as 200 leaflets to its customers. This company changes the brochures once a week and redesigns them twice a year. Inserting these numbers into our formula results in the following:

200 Placeholders × 1 Placeholder Type × 1 Publication × 2 Personalizations × 1 Redesign × 1 Throughput

Based on the previously discussed factors, the value for Placeholders works out to 0.5 (200/1000 = 0.2, which is adjusted to 0.5), and Placeholder Types equals 0.5 (1/5 = 0.2, which is adjusted to 0.5). The other values can be used as they are to calculate the result as follows:

$0.5 \times 0.5 \times 1 \times 2 \times 1 \times 1 = 0.5$

This indicates MyLittleComp does not need a content management system today, but might in the future if it continues to grow.

Company LittleBigger is a travel agency that already has a web presence. This company's site has 600 different placeholders of two different types. The content of 30 different components is changed each week. Since this company is only using the latest technology, it only has a web site that it says it will change three times a year. Using the previous factors for figuring out the values to plug into our formula, we get the following:

$0.6 \times 0.5 \times 1 \times 1 \times 3 \times 1 = 0.9$

This company is a bit tricky. Although the value is quite close to the magic number (1 in this case), close is not enough. LittleBigger doesn't need a content management system in theory, because this company's business is web-based, but there may still be some benefit to using a content management system versus its current manual system.

Finally, our friend's company HeavyComp produces motorbikes and needs to produce a new site with information about its new models and spare parts. Today, HeavyComp's site incorporates 1200 placeholders of eight different types. This company changes the content of 200 different placeholders each week. An e-mail newsletter and a catalog are sent out to members. A new web site will be developed that allows member information to be personalized based on the local area of each member. The site will be redesigned once a year. Plugging in the numbers, we get the following:

$1.2 \times 1.6 \times 2 \times 2 \times 1 \times 4 = 30.72$

This company really needs a content management tool!

Table 5-2 provides a general framework for evaluating your own situation.

Table 5-2. *Evaluating the Results*

Complexity Level	Need for a Content Management System
Below 0.3	You have little need for a content management system.
0.3–.05	You could begin thinking about a content management system if you believe that your needs will grow.
0.5–.075	You should begin thinking about a content management system if you believe that your needs will grow.
0.75–1.0	This is the beginning of the gray zone between needing a content management system and making do without one. In this range, go with your intuition. Consider whether the complexity will grow. If it will, this is a good time to begin a content management analysis preparation. If the complexity will not grow, a content management system may well be more effort than it is worth.
1.0–1.75	This is still in the gray zone for investing in a content management system. However, a content management system is more likely needed in this region than not. Even if the site complexity will not grow, a content management system may save you more money in the long run than it costs to implement.
1.75–10.0	A content management system is recommended. You may be able to start slowly or cover the factors that have the highest values, but eventually you will want to implement a content management system.
Above 10.0	A content management system is definitely needed. The company is likely experiencing content management problems already. If the complexity is well above 10 and still growing, you may need to act quickly to either control complexity growth, or implement the parts of a content management system that relieve the most pressing problems on the site.

Remember that the level of complexity as dictated by our content management formula is not the whole story. If a content management system is very expensive, a complexity of 5 may not be enough to warrant obtaining the content management system—the costs to implement the system may be higher than the savings. On the other hand, you could implement an inexpensive content management system for a site with a complexity level below 1 and see benefits. When you have gained experience from your own projects, feel free to make adjustments to formula values to fit a particular situation.

Some of the Content Management Tools on the Market

There are two types of content tools today that both claim they are perfect for business: document publishing tools and content management systems. Remember, document publishing tools and content management systems are two different items intended to solve different problems. Document publishing tools such as Documentum take care of document versioning and document handling in a large company, whereas content management systems take care of publishing information on intranet, extranet, and Internet sites. However, the trend these days is for document publishing tools to implement more content management features in their latest versions, and for content management tools to include some document handling functionality. There are many different content management tools and document publishing tools on the market today, such as Story Server, Microsoft Content Management Server 2002, EPiServer, Dynamo, and Documentum. We will focus mainly on two content management tools here—Microsoft Content Management Server and EPiServer.

Microsoft Content Management Server 2002

A well-functioning content management system requires more than a simple HTML editor to work efficiently for the customer. You need a system like Microsoft's Content Management Server 2002, where you can plug in new content components and where user roles and authorization is easily handled via a user-friendly interface.

Microsoft Content Management Server, or CMS, is an enterprise-wide web content management system based on .NET technologies, XML, and IIS. Microsoft Content Management Server relies, of course, on other Microsoft server products such as IIS for content publication and management. CMS also requires a Microsoft Server operating system like Windows 2000 Server or Windows Server 2003. You'll also need to install the latest Microsoft Data Access Components (MDAC) and a SQL Server 2000 database that is used as the repository for the CMS. If you want to use CMS, you should do so in a homogenous Microsoft environment— Microsoft tools work best together with other Microsoft tools.

What Is New in CMS 2002 Compared to CMS 2001?

Since the release of .NET Framework, all applications and server environments from Microsoft are moving toward including .NET Framework as one of their building blocks. The inclusion of .NET as part of CMS 2002 empowers this latest version of CMS with new features and extensibilities that were not present in the previous versions. For instance, it is possible, from an ASP.NET project, to author web services and templates for CMS and reuse them in other areas of a site. One thing that was missing in version 2001 was the ability to include CMS projects easily in Visual SourceSafe for source-code version tracking—something that is necessary if you want more than one person to work on the same project.

A good content management system requires a good administration tool. CMS now comes with a great Site Manager utility. Here you can define channels (used in CMS to define a web site's structure) and resource/template galleries. Through the use of channels (which function similarly to the placeholders and content components mentioned earlier in this chapter), you can control where specific content is to be published and when. You can also define when content should be removed from the channel, and also specify groups of users who should be able to see the channel.

Another crucial feature of a content management system is the ability to feed new content into the system. CMS provides two ways to allow authors to publish their articles. First is a new web-based tool that runs in Internet Explorer 6 and allows users to view and edit page content directly in predefined templates. The great thing about this is that no extra application tool is needed on an author's computer. Authors can also sit at home and update and publish their information via an Internet connection (after authentication, of course).

Secondly, you can use a plug-in to MS Office that allows you to publish content directly from Microsoft Word XP! This is a great way to encourage more people to create new content. Many people today use Microsoft Word, so no extra education is required to start publishing information for an intranet, extranet, or Internet site through CMS. The author just fills in some meta-information, and then the plug-in packages the content and sends it to CMS.

So far so good—but does CMS have any drawbacks? From what we have experienced so far, CMS has two big drawbacks: the workflow support and the price. The workflow is a bit too simple to be used in a fairly complex environment. There is a basic workflow system in CMS that enables your users to create page content, but not publish it until it's approved by a designated manager. However, the workflow model is rather static and inflexible. You are not able to split the workflow or to change the approving flow in an easy way. We should all read the label before buying anything—even with a content management system. Microsoft has priced this system at approximately five figures per CPU. With this price, it's obvious that the product is not intended for small and medium-sized businesses, but for larger companies. That said, it's a great tool to control content flow to different sites in the company.

EPiServer

EPiServer is a content management system tool created by a company called ElektroPost. EPiServer is based on Microsoft products such as IIS for content publishing, and SQL Server, which serves as a repository. The latest version of EPiServer, version 4, is written totally in C# and runs as a managed application. This gives developers great opportunities to extend EPiServer to fit their needs better.

EPiServer is based on different building blocks, shown in Figure 5-21, to make the application as flexible as possible for the developer.

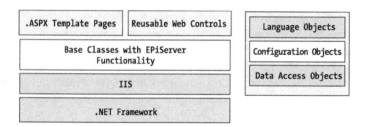

Figure 5-21. *The building blocks of EPiServer*

EPiServer provides several ASPX template pages that the developer can use. These templates can host reusable web controls such as calendar controls and vote controls. The controls and the code in the code-behind page on the ASPX page use EPiServer's base classes to access the data. Besides the aforementioned reusable web controls, this product includes several objects for handling language support, configuration, data access, and security programmatically.

The typical workflow for an administrator to create a new page is as follows:

- The administrator selects a particular type of page to create.

- The administrator fills in the information that should be presented and this information is stored in the database.

When a user requests a page, EPiServer authenticates that the user is allowed to view the page, and it also checks whether the user has administration rights for the requested page. If the user is allowed to view the page, the template is filled with the information from the database, and a cascading style sheet (CSS) is applied to give the page the right look and feel. If the user has administration rights for the page, support for direct editing in the page is enabled (see Figure 5-22).

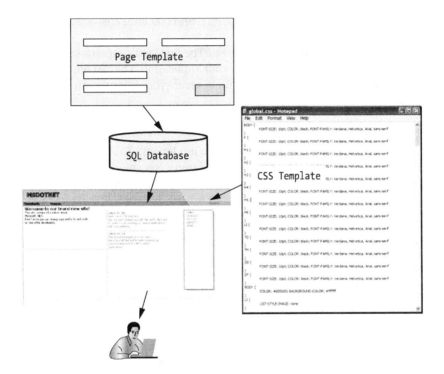

Figure 5-22. *The construction of a requested page in EPiServer*

Content Management Systems Wrap-Up

In the preceding sections we have looked into what comprises content management and the problems related to it. We have shown you a formula for roughly calculating whether a company will benefit from investing in a content management system. Finally, we looked at both the Microsoft Content Management Server and EPiServer and pinpointed some benefits for the different products. We can say that due to its lower price, EPiServer makes a good content management system for small and medium-sized companies—and even bigger companies can use it, since EPiServer seems to scale quite well. CMS is for larger companies, due to the price being a little bit higher, which in turn makes its Return on Investment (ROI) span a longer timeframe than EPiServer's ROI. For the time being, we strongly advise you to compare these two content management systems, and at least one other, with an eye toward user requirements, in order to pick the best content management system for your customer.

Security

The topic of security issues could fill a whole book in its own right. Here we will try to cover some of the main issues you need to be aware of when you design an enterprise application. The following is based on the security guidelines from Microsoft, and the complete guidelines can be found at http://msdn.microsoft.com/library/default.asp?url=/library/en-us/dnnetsec/html/THCMCh04.asp.

Security issues can be divided into three different areas. The first area concerns securing the network. The second involves securing the hosts for your application. The last block deals with securing the application itself. The measures you take to secure your information can also be divided into four categories:

- The first category is the *critical information* you try to secure.

- The second category is the *physical protection* that you implement. To strengthen any security weaknesses you might have missed in your system, you should always start with your hardware. Reduce the number of open ports in the firewall and verify that the firewall is correctly configured.

- The third category is the *operating system*. After you have made it more difficult to sneak into the system by "hardening" the physical environment, you will make it even harder for an intruder to invade your system if you clean up the operating system on your servers. The first step is to reduce the number of administration accounts on the web server and the application server. Do not allow anonymous access to the web server.

- The fourth category involves *information access*. Before you give someone access to data, you need to be sure that person is authenticated, authorized, and audited. A simple and effective way to prevent unauthorized persons from accessing the system, via a computer that has been left wide open, is to verify that all clients in the system have screensavers that automatically lock the client computers when they haven't been used for a while.

A web-based application has many different points where attacks may occur. Because of this the browser needs to authenticate users. When the browser has authenticated a user, the communication between the browser and the server needs to be secured. You need to be able to protect the communication and its data from being altered, and the communication itself from being hijacked or used in a replay attack.

When information has passed the first firewall and entered the web server (see Figure 5-23), you need to be able to secure the configuration so that no unauthenticated person on the server will be able to see important configuration strings. You also need to take care of exceptions and interpolate error messages before you send them back to the user, mainly for helping the user, but also to hide stack traces and other important information a hacker can use to get information about your system.

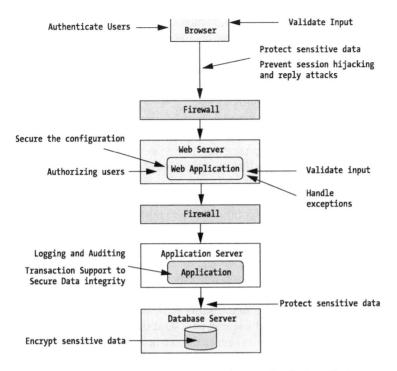

Figure 5-23. *The different security issues that need to be handled*

Authentication

Authentication is the process of determining caller identity. When implementing authentication, you need to consider a few things:

The first is that you need to identify where you want to use authentication. In general, you need to perform authentication when a trust boundary is crossed—such boundaries usually consist of assemblies, processes, and machines.

When you have identified where you need authentication, you must next validate who the caller is, in order to be able to authenticate him or her. The normal way to do this is by having the user authenticate themselves by giving you a username and password. The validation is not a one time thing—you need to do it every time a user comes back and requests information from your application. This requires some form of authentication token.

The most common approach to authenticating users in a web-based application is to use the form authentication support found in ASP.NET. There, you ask the user to supply you with a username and password in an HTML form. To make this secure, you can't use the standard HTTP protocol, since it's wide open for anyone who knows how to monitor network packages. The solution here is to secure the communication by using HTTPS and SSL.

Another threat to the users' credentials is the storage of their information in your server. You need to ensure that no one can read the usernames and passwords in plain text on your server. Therefore, you must encrypt and hash your user credentials in the database to prevent Dirty Harry, who is serving out his last day at your company, from dumping the user table to a file and taking it with him.

OK, so now you are using SSL to secure the communication channel from the web form into your server. You have also encrypted the user credentials in your database—but how are the credentials verified against the input from the user? If you only intend to verify that the user knows the password value, you don't need to store the actual password in your database. Instead, you can calculate a hash value in the database and recalculate the hash using the supplied information from the user during the logon process.

The user has been authenticated, and seems to know the right password, but how do you authenticate the user next time he or she requests some information from your enterprise application? You don't want to bring up the login page every time a user tries to add a new line to the current time report, right? Normally, you give the user some kind of authentication ticket— for example, an authentication cookie. This cookie is sent to the user via some kind of transport protocol. If you are using HTTP, this leaves your system wide open for a hacker to retrieve information from, or "tap," the cookie, and use it for his or her own purposes.

To make it more difficult for anyone to tap your enterprise application for important data, you should try to "harden" the security on the web server and the application server as mentioned previously.

The first step is to log any login failure that occurs in your enterprise application. When the user has entered the wrong password x times, you should disable the user account automatically to prevent any further attacks and be sure to inform the administrator. (It might be a valid, possibly just disoriented user who has entered the wrong password three times, but in that case, he or she just needs to call the administrator to unlock the account.)

The operating system will take care of this disabling automatically for you if you are using Windows authentication, such as NTLM or the Kerberos Protocol. In the example application in Chapter 10, where we use form authentication, we handle these policies in the application.

Note If you are using this approach, you need to be sure that important accounts like IUSR_MACHINENAME are not locked out because of a denial-of-service attack. Try to use other accounts instead of the IUSR_MACHINENAME account.

The second step is to ensure that no password will last forever. Passwords should expire on a regular basis, and a dictionary of the last five passwords for a particular user should be created so none of the last five passwords can be used when it is time for the user to change his or her password. Unfortunately, people are lazy by nature, and we have seen many change their passwords by bumping up an appended numeral; for example, the password mysecret-password1 is changed to mysecretpassword2, and so on—which is not so difficult to figure out. A good approach is to also enlighten users about security issues before an application is delivered, in order to try to lift the security level a little bit. (How many of you have a screen-saver that is password protected and is turned on after a couple of minutes of inactivity?) Many companies today have a policy that says that the user should always lock his computer when he leaves it. Hereby, we prevent other users from getting access to our system in an unauthorized way.

Normally an enterprise application might have different areas with different levels of access. Some areas may be accessed anonymously, whereas other areas require authentication.

It can be wise to portion the site into a public area and a restricted area to make it easier to maintain and to avoid the performance overhead with SSL for the restricted area. A good rule of thumb is to limit the use of SSL, because it takes a lot out of your system's performance. For instance, do not run a whole retail application under SSL—let the anonymous users browse the products—but as soon as they would like to add stuff to the shopping chart, require authentication via a secure transport protocol.

Require Strong Passwords

We have already shown the "increment example" of old passwords by lazy people. Try to teach users to use strong passwords, which have a minimum of eight characters with at least one number in it. We recently ran a brute-force hack tool on one domain controller—it took about two hours to crack the administration password for the machine. Do not make it easy for attackers to crack passwords. Many guidelines are available on the Internet for creating strong passwords. It is also possible to configure the Windows operating system to not let the user use a too short or to easy to crack password. To make it even more secure we can configure the system to not allow reuse of old passwords too.

Do Not Send Passwords over the Wire in Plain Text

Even if you are using strong passwords, you need to secure the communication channel when you send passwords over the network, in order to prevent hackers from tapping passwords out of a message. It's easy for a hacker, when he has gained physical access to your network, to tap your network traffic on confidential information that might damage your company's image even more (besides the fact that your network is already wide open for hackers). To prevent hackers from gathering your unsecured data, you can, for instance, use SSL to encrypt the communication. For SOAP messages, you can use the WSE toolkit.

Do not let a colleague borrow your username and password

Never give out your username or password to someone else. Even if your friend has forgotten his password and " just needs to get that document out quickly," give him your regrets and point him to the administrator instead. (Of course if the person asking you is your boss you could consider to let him use your account—but really just consider that it's never a good idea.)

All intrusions start when the owner of the account doesn't know that someone else knows his username and password. You never know when someone might accidentally see the username and password that your friend wrote down on a piece of paper and then unfortunately left lying visible on his desk when heading home late Friday afternoon.

Protect Authentication Cookies

Protect authentication tickets using encryption and secure the communication channels. Also limit the time interval in which the authentication ticket remains valid, in order to reduce the chances of a hacker decrypting the message and using the authentication cookie. Reducing the cookie timeout does not prevent replay attacks, but it does limit the amount of time the attacker has to access the site using the stolen cookie.

Input Validation

Input validation is of great importance to your enterprise application, for preventing malicious data from entering the system. It's also one of your strongest defenses against application attacks. Proper input validation can easily prevent hackers from doing SQL injection, buffer overflows, and other input attacks. Input validation is challenging, because it differs among applications and even within an application itself.

Do Not Trust Input Until Proven Safe

The best way to prevent your application from input hacking is to assume that all input is malicious until proven otherwise, and that the input needs to be verified not once but twice, no matter where it comes from.

Centralize Your Validation

To make validation efficient and to be able to change it easily and quickly when bugs and new requirements occur, centralize the validation code in the enterprise application. Put the validation code in shared assemblies to be able to reuse them from the whole application. This ensures that you are using the same validation rules everywhere, and that no missed validation somewhere could possibly let malicious input in.

Do Not Rely Entirely on Client-Side Validation

You need to capture invalid data as soon as possible to avoid extra round-trips to the server and/or between the different processes on the server side. However, you can't rely entirely on client-side validation—even if it's easy and quite fancy to use the validation controls in a web application. The reason you can't trust the validation on the client side is because the validation controls are using client scripts to do their validation in the browser. A hacker may turn off the support of client scripts, and thereby bypass your validation! In our example application later in this book, and in the proposed enterprise architecture, we include both client-side validation (to reduce the number of round-trips to the server) and server-side validation (to prevent the aforementioned types of attacks).

Constrain Input and Reject Data

The preferred approach for validating input is to constrain what you allow from the beginning. It is easier and safer to validate data from specific known valid types and ranges than to validate unspecified data. When you design your enterprise application, you normally know the range and the type of data that can be entered by the users. Everything that does not fit into your defined types, lengths, formats, and ranges is rejected as bad data. For instance, you should use stored procedures for fetching and sending data to the database instead of building the update or insert query based on the user's input.

Identification numbers, post office boxes, and zip codes are data that can easily be verified as correct or not. The length of string fields should also be checked, since there will normally be a maximum length for string fields that can be stored in the database. Rejecting "bad" data is in general less effective than checking for valid data. This is due to valid data seldom changing, whereas the "bad" data may change over time.

Testing

When your enterprise application is in the design phase, you should also plan for testing. There are many different ideas about how testing should be conducted in the life cycle of the application. Our suggestion is to continuously perform testing; from unit tests up to complete scale tests. The latter type will obviously be done later in the development cycle of the application. To succeed with tests and achieve the goals you set with testing, you need to follow these seven rules:

Rule 1: Testing Should Begin in the Planning Phase

Don't leave the testing to the end of the application development, when there little or no time left. Plan the various tests from the beginning of the project and schedule these tests incrementally during the entire development phase. A good practice is to have roughly the same time for testing as you have for development—though few projects include that much time for testing. The earlier an error is found, though, the less expensive it is to correct.

Rule 2: Test Against Measurable Criteria

Good tests have realistic and clear criteria to test for. The collection of measurable criteria already starts at the requirement stage. As each requirement is defined, it should be evaluated: Is the requirement correct? Is it objective, measurable, and therefore testable? It is not enough, for instance, to specify that a certain action be fast. You must establish performance criteria that defines what "fast" means.

Rule 3: Testing Is for Experienced Developers—Not for Rookies

Too often we've seen unskilled people or new developers being put into the role of testers. Testing is not a good training ground for new developers. Being a tester requires unique skills—not only the discipline to work through a problem systematically, but also the business knowledge and programming knowledge to recognize problems when they occur.

Rule 4: The Test Environment Should Be Identical to the Real Environment

We've also seen a test environment placed on an old server, which is already shared by a couple of other projects. The disks are nearly full and the performance of the server is bad. Although this scenario may reflect the project environment, the major problem is often that the wrong software and/or version is installed on this "test server." Try to make the test server mirror the production server both in hardware and software. How can you otherwise be sure that the application will run in the production environment, when you have tested in a test environment with different versions of DLLs and software? For a browser-based enterprise application, be sure to test the different browsers that could be used with the application under different operating systems.

Rule 5: Security Concerns Will Continue to Increase

The attacks on systems that are exposed to the Web are not likely to lessen in the future. As Internet use continues to evolve into a mainstay of daily life, the threat from the Internet in the form of worms and viruses presents a major problem to enterprise applications. With the increase in the available functionality and interconnectivity comes a corresponding increase in the necessity to build security into the code at all levels of a system.

Rule 6: Approach Automated Testing Tools with Caution

Even if it sounds great to have a tool that can make all the dreary unit tests for you, such tools are seldom 100 percent accurate. Even if a testing tool manages to automatically test your code, you may end up having written many pages of test code in order to guide the testing tool properly. What we're saying is that successfully introducing automated testing in a project requires time. If you are developing an enterprise application that will last for years, it can be wise to at least use some kind of automatic testing such as the free NUnit (which we cover in more detail in the next section), but, in most cases, manual testing is faster than automatic testing (at least if you count the time to set up the tool and incorporate scripts in the initial testing phase). Only in the long run can the benefits of an automated testing tool be determined.

Tip If you want to break this rule, see the section "Testing Tools" later in this chapter.

Rule 7: Complex Today—Even Worse Tomorrow

If your enterprise application proves complex to test now, it will probably be even worse later when your managed enterprise application talks with unmanaged code. The solution is to arm yourself with caution and skepticism. Test your prototypes and applications for basic flaws early on, particularly in the areas of security and performance. We never believe people who tell us we should test later when more of the "real" application is built—and neither should you.

Testing Tools

If you are going to develop an enterprise application and want to break Rule 6 and use an automatic testing tool, which tool should you choose? Microsoft has developed a stress tool for web-based applications that can be used for testing performance during peak times, but how do you test your Windows form-based applications for both performance and logic?

There is a freeware tool on the market called NUnit that helps you to do unit tests and code tests automatically. When we say "automatically," we mean that you first need to set up a bunch of attributes in your classes that should be tested, specify a reference to the profiling DLL, and finally run the utility. NUnit is written entirely in C# and can be found at http://nunit.org/.

NUnit works with custom attributes on test methods that are used to test specific units. To enable a class for automatic unit testing, you need to follow the procedure we discuss next. Earlier in this chapter we used a banking component, as shown in Listing 5-7.

Listing 5-7. *The Banking Component*

```
namespace bank
{
    public class Account
    {
        private float balance;
        public void Withdraw(float amount)
        {
            balance-=amount;
        }
        public void Deposit(float amount)
        {
            balance+=amount;
        }
        public void TransferFunds(Account destination, float amount)
        {
        }
        public float Balance
        {
            get{ return balance;}
        }
    }
}
```

To test this account class, you need to create a test class. Listing 5-8 shows a test class that tests the method TransferFunds to see that it handles the deposit and withdraw correctly.

Listing 5-8. *Test Class and Test Method to Test the TransferFunds Method*

```
namespace bank
{
    using NUnit.Framework;
    [TestFixture]
    public class AccountTest
    {
        [Test]
        public void TransferFunds()
        {
            Account source = new Account();
            source.Deposit(100.00F);
            Account destination = new Account();
            destination.Deposit(200.00F);
            source.TransferFunds(destination, 80.00F);
            Assertion.AssertEquals(220.00F, destination.Balance);
            Assertion.AssertEquals(80.00F, source.Balance);
        }
    }
}
```

The test class has an attribute named [TestFixture] that tells NUnit that this is a test class. The methods in the test class that should be used for tests have an attribute named [Test]. The TransferFunds test method simply creates an account object and uses the object as normal. The source code itself is not tampered with in any way.

When you have compiled your test class and your source code, you simply start the NUnit GUI and browse for your DLL. When the DLL is loaded, you will see a test structure on the left-hand side in NUnit. When you run NUnit, all tests that pass will be listed in green text, the failed tests will be listed in red.

To learn more about NUnit, we encourage you to visit the NUnit homepage at http:// www.nunit.org. It's quite easy to implement unit test code and run it with NUnit. This is a great tool when you are doing several releases with changes to the code and want to be sure that no new bugs have been introduced.

Summary

In this chapter, we have shown you an enterprise application architecture that can be used to ensure scalable and robust applications. We have talked about patterns and demonstrated how web services fit into the suggested architecture. The internal structure of an enterprise application is of high importance, and therefore we've included a section on coding conventions that can be used in real projects. We also talked about general exception handling and memory management that can make enterprise applications even more robust.

Finally, we introduced you to two different content management systems and compared them to each other. The use of a content management system can boost the development time of a content-based enterprise application and give developers time to focus on the business-critical parts in the application, instead of spending time on the boring tasks that the content management system can handle for them.

In Chapter 9, we will implement an example application based on this architecture to show how it looks in reality. We think this is the best way for you to really learn how to use the enterprise application architecture we outlined in this chapter.

CHAPTER 6

■ ■ ■

Web Services Design and Practice

You have probably heard about web services—you may have even already read a lot about them. Today, nearly every published computer book has something to say about web services, and this book is no exception. So, what are web services? Web services are, by rough definition, functions that serve someone else with information of any kind. This may sound vague, but we will try to explain and exemplify this definition in this chapter. Figure 6-1 shows an overview of web services.

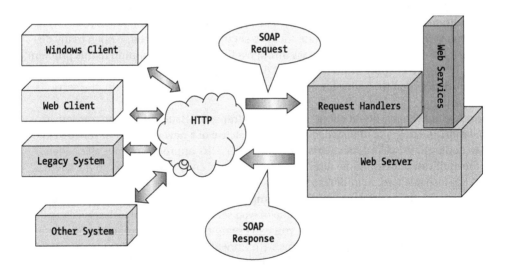

Figure 6-1. *Web services environment*

Unfortunately, most of the current publications and coverage of web services just tell you how wonderful web services are, and don't clearly explain why you should use them. In this chapter, we will focus on two things: explaining what web services are and why you should use them. We will also show you the scenarios for which you should use web services and the scenarios for which you shouldn't use them. In addition to this, we'll also explore the different components and specifications necessary for you to create a complete web service.

First, we will look at where web services fit in with today's application design. It's very important for you to uncover the areas where using web services can ease the burden of integrating different kinds of systems on different platforms, thereby reducing your costs for implementation and maintenance. It also shows you what you need from a web service, and where problems might occur in using such a service.

Web Services and Distributed Applications

In the past we used to develop *rich clients* (often called *fat clients*) to access central data. However today, most of the newly developed applications are so-called *thin clients*. These thin clients are often implemented in a web-based application working with a web server. Obviously the reason is not because thin clients supply a richer user interface/experience, but because it costs less to maintain thin clients than it does rich client installations, which reside on the user's computer.

This is due to client dependence on many different files. A centralized application (web-based) is easier to maintain, because it consists of only one server or web server farm (as discussed in Chapter 3) that needs to be updated when new patches are released. Another benefit of a web-based application is that the client often only needs a web browser to be able to connect and run the application. No specific configuration on the client's machine is necessary. You can let Linux-based, UNIX-based, and Windows-based clients connect to your application, as long as they can communicate via HTTP.

The traditional rich client often uses the Distributed Common Object Model (DCOM) to communicate with the server. This is quite tricky to set up, and you'll need to open many different ports if the communication is to pass through a firewall. A nice solution to this problem is to use HTTP as a transport protocol instead of using DCOM. The familiar HTTP protocol port 80 is normally open through a firewall by default, and communication with the server is easier to maintain.

One other drawback with fat clients (besides the transport issue mentioned previously) is the installation and upgrade of installed fat clients. Release of a new application version can be hard to deploy to thousands of clients. However, with .NET approach to have all needed files for the application in the same directory we can simply copy the directory to the client. Microsoft has also released an updater application block which makes the deployment of fat clients much easier than in the past. With these improvements, the use of fat clients is seeing a renaissance, but this doesn't change the value of web services. The use of web services will be important even for fat clients, because you can create rich clients that access business functions remotely without having problems with firewalls and the like. The update and installation process is also managed via web services for a rich client, though it's installed on the client's computer, which eases the burden on system administrators when installing patches and updates to your applications.

What Can You Do with Web Services?

If you are like most developers, you probably know of a couple of areas where you can use web services, but maybe you are still asking yourself, "What can I really do with web services?"

The easiest, or most obvious, use of web services is to export information that you could conveniently incorporate into applications, such as stock quotes, weather forecasts, sports scores, business information, and so on. It is easy to imagine applications that could be built to analyze and aggregate the information you care about and then present it to you in a variety of ways. For example, you might have a Microsoft Excel spreadsheet that summarizes your company's financial picture—stocks, bank accounts, loans, and so on. If this information is available through web services, Excel can update it continuously. It will also be possible for your colleagues to easily retrieve and access this information—no matter where they are located in the organization.

Some of this information will be accessible to everyone, and some of this information might require a subscription to the service. Most of it may already be available on the web, but web services will make programmatic access to this information easier and more reliable.

The ability to programmatically access the information makes it possible to expose existing application functionality as web services. This allows developers to build new, more powerful applications that use web services as building blocks. For example, a developer might develop an authentication web service that automatically checks the username and password from the company's Active Directory. The authentication web service can then be used to authenticate users in the time reporting application we will present in Chapter 10.

Another example of the strength of web services is when a developer exposes an old legacy system, such as a financial system, so that other developers can easily retrieve information about specific orders or billing information. This web service can be used to do a report for the time reporting application, such as the one we discuss in Chapter 10, where we compare the reported time from the user of the application with the time billed to the customer.

The latter example shows that old legacy systems may be exposed with web services, orders can be read and placed in the legacy system directly, and the different products that were ordered can be reserved from the stock. You could also retrieve discounts from the legacy system for the customer and include them in the order. Many companies today expose their old legacy systems via web services, thereby making it easier for developers to access business information in a controlled way.

In the section "Using SOAP," later in this chapter, you will study some examples of web services, in particular an example of using web services to collect error information. In the section "WSE and Security," we will show you how to encrypt the content of your web services.

Deciding When to Use Web Services

Even if you know what web services are and what they can do, you need to determine when you should use them. Too many new techniques flood the IT market today, without any critical analysis of their business usage and business payoff. It might be easy to say that you should always use web services when you expose functions that you want to be accessible from other applications, but there are some concerns with web services that you should know about before making your decision.

When to Use Web Services

You should use web services in the following situations:

- *When you need to connect different platforms and be able to exchange data between them.* Web services are powerful tools for overlapping the gap between different platforms. The simplicity of web services and the human readiness of the result make web services less error prone than such predecessors as CORBA and DCOM.

- *When you want to expose functionality from an old system and use it in new applications.* For instance, by exposing functionality that exists in the business legacy AS/400 applications, a company can boost usage of business-critical information. This makes it far easier to program toward web services than accessing the AS/400 directly from new applications. It is also quite easy for administrators to configure access to the web services. By using web services with such old systems, you can reuse both code and data.

- *For general functions not used frequently.* Examples of such include central error reporting, application updates, and order and billing information, which can be made accessible through web services.

- *When you need to send data through firewalls—for instance, in business-to-business (B2B) communication.* HTTP is often allowed to pass firewalls by default. This makes it easier than before to tie different systems together, and yet still have firewalls between different parts of an intranet to make it harder for intruders to access a system. Since HTTP is the standard protocol for Internet, it proves to be no problem to integrate.

  Microsoft wants you to use web services everywhere—and we agree for the preceding scenarios. Their ease of use and natural isolation between layers and machines compensates for the little overhead you get when you use web services instead of other Remoting techniques.

When Not to Use Web Services

You should *not* use web services in these situations:

- *When response time is critical to your system.* Today the performance of web services is quite slow due to the standard protocol they use and the packing and unpacking of data. With the HTTP design, no package can be given priority over another, and no guarantee exists that the pages will arrive in a certain order. Even if you could use a binary version for transporting data, it is not recommended for real-time applications, where time is critical.

  Also be aware that a slow network can have impact on the response times. When retrieving many requests, long network distance can cause long response times. It is better to pack different requests into a larger one when communicating with a web service over a distance, in order to reduce the impact of a slow network. (Using chunky calls on methods, rather than having a chatty interface, will boost the performance of web services.)

- *For single-machine solutions.* When you are developing an application running on a single machine, the use of web services will not give you anything extra. In our opinion, it is wise to create the underlying business layers in a way that makes it possible to scale the application in the future by using web services. This way you can meet new demands from the business further down the road. In Chapter 10, we will show you how to create the facade layer, making it possible to expose methods as web services easily.

- *When homogenous applications exist on your LAN.* When you have only one platform (Microsoft, for instance) in your LAN, you will have better performance and ease of use if your applications speak with each other via DCOM (for old Windows DNA applications) or by using .NET Remoting (for new .NET applications). An interesting aspect of .NET Remoting is the ability to use .NET Remoting over HTTP, similar to the way a web service does. With .NET Remoting, you also have the possibility of using a BinaryFormatter with SOAP to allow remote procedure calls (RPCs). Binary format is more efficient than the standard SOAP format due to lower serialization/deserialization overhead.

These are probably the only times when web services should not be used. Even if the performance of today is not as quick as if we were using a direct object relationship between the start and end point, in the future, the standardization of new kinds of transport protocols can change this situation. We employ web services frequently, and find them very useful for reusing existing business values in a cost-effective and easy way. Microsoft itself also recommends web services as a primary choice and .NET Remoting only in specific situations.

Most of the scenarios we mentioned earlier for when you should use web services involve integration. We'll start to look into how integration and interoperability problems can be solved using web services in the next section.

Interoperability

One major problem in the solutions that are created today is interoperability with other platforms. It would be great if all applications were written in the same language and ran on Windows XP, but as you know they aren't. Most interactions with old legacy systems are done by using file transfers or message queuing, and frequently vary from case to case. Often the specification of this interface is stored in some place other than the interface itself. One of the major computer-related costs for companies today is the integration between different systems and applications. We believe that web services will cut this cost dramatically, if they are used well.

Integration is easier with web services because all systems can communicate with each other over HTTP, regardless of platform or programming language. There are many good examples of companies that have exposed legacy functions via web services, thus receiving a reuse boost because functions were suddenly easily accessible to the organization. The interface of a web service is also accessible through a web Services Description Language (WSDL) file, and thereby the specification of the interface matches the interface itself, making it even easier for others to use the web service.

Web services expose an API via a web-based protocol like HTTP or HTTPS. (They can also use other protocols, but we will mainly talk about web services in conjunction with HTTP and HTTPS here.) When we say that web services use HTTP, we mean that web services can invoke functions via HTTP, and get results back via HTTP. (HTTP is in this case the transport protocol that the web service uses.)

For instance, if you would like to build a web service that returns local weather information, you can create an ASP page that takes a city name as a parameter and returns the local weather forecast. To invoke this web service, you can call it by sending an HTTP GET request to a web server such as http://www.myserver.com/weather.asp?CityName=Gothenburg. The return result may look like this:

```
Degrees: 23 C
Humidity: 67%
Precipitation: 45%
PrecipitationType: Rain
```

This simple ASP page is a kind of web service, because it exposes an API based on a standard protocol (in this case HTTP). But web services can do much more than just tell you what the weather will be today. The following sections discuss what else web services can do.

Business-to-Business Integration

By using web services to integrate applications, you can better automate business processes within a company. But what happens when business processes crossing company boundaries attempt to integrate your company's applications with those of your suppliers and/or customers? Integrating business processes across multiple businesses is commonly referred to as *business-to-business integration*.

Web services are a technology that enables B2B integration. By using web services, your company can expose vital business processes to authorized suppliers and customers. For example, you can expose electronic ordering and invoicing, thereby enabling your customers to electronically send you purchase orders, and your suppliers to electronically send you invoices.

This is not a new concept: Electronic Data Interchange (EDI) has been around for a while. The key difference is that compared to EDI, web services are much easier to implement and operate over the Internet, and is widely available to businesses all over the world at a relatively low cost. However, unlike EDI, web services do not provide a complete solution for document interchange or B2B integration. Instead, web services are a key-enabling component in B2B integration, with many other components typically needed to complete the picture. The primary advantage of using web services for B2B integration is low-cost interoperability. By exposing your business functions as web services, you enable any authorized party to easily invoke those services, regardless of the platform and programming language a particular party uses. This reduces the time and effort it takes to integrate a business process across company boundaries, and ultimately saves time and money. The low cost of integration opens up the playing field for smaller companies that find the cost of implementing EDI prohibitive.

Software Reuse with Web Services

Software reuse can be implemented in many ways. The most basic form is code reuse through classes and modules. Compiling the classes into a binary component that is reused extends code reuse. We would say that web services are one more step further down the reuse path. With web services, it's not only possible to reuse the code base, but also the data itself, because the data is located on a server where it can be reached from different applications.

An example of this is an address verification web service. Instead of having a local database with address information that you need to keep updated, you can have a central database and a web service that exposes the address information to you. You send an address to the web service, and it checks the street address, city, state, and zip code to make sure the address exists. If the service is hosted by a provider, the service provider might charge you a periodic fee, or a per-use fee, for the service. A service like this is not possible with component reuse; for this kind of functionality, you need to have a database of street addresses, cities, states, and zip codes.

The Building Blocks of Web Services

In addition to representing functions that serve information of any kind, web services can also be defined as a standard platform for building interoperable, distributed applications.

As a developer, you have probably built component-based distributed applications using COM, DCOM, or CORBA. Although COM is an excellent component technology, in certain scenarios it does not work very well.

The web services platform is a set of standards that applications follow to achieve interoperability, via HTTP, for instance. You can write your web services in whatever language and on any platform you like, as long as those web services can be viewed and accessed according to the web services standards set by ECMA.

To enable the different web services implemented on different operating systems to communicate with each other, there must be agreement as to a common standard. A platform must have a data representation format and a type system. To enable interoperability, the web services must agree to a standard type system that bridges current differences between type systems of different platforms. web services must also be able to find other web services that have been developed . So how can you achieve this? By using XML, XSD, SOAP, WSDL, and UDDI. If all these protocols make you feel panicky, do not fear! In the next sections we will briefly go through these different technologies that make web services so powerful.

XML

Extensible Markup Language (XML) is the basic format for representing data in web services. XML was developed from CXML, an old markup language from the sixties. Its strength was its simplicity when it came to creating and parsing a document, and XML was chosen for web services because it is neither platform nor vendor-specific.

Being neutral is more important than being technically superior. Software vendors are much more likely to adopt a neutral technology, than one invented by a competitor. A noncomplex language will probably also result in noncomplex problems.

XML provides a simple way of representing data by using tags, but says nothing about the standard set of data types available or how to extend that set. To enable interoperability, it is important to be able to describe, for example, what exactly an integer is. Is it 16, 32, or 64 bits? The World Wide web Consortium (W3C) XML Schema Definition Language (XSD), which we will take a look at in the next section, is a language that defines data types.

Here is a simple example of an XML document taken from the weather report example previously found in this chapter:

```
<WeatherReports>
    <WeatherReport>
        <Degrees Scale="C">
```

```
        23
     </Degrees>
     <Humidity>
        67
     </Humidity>
     <PrecipitationPossibility Type="Rain">
        45
     </PrecipitationPossibility>
   </WeatherReport>
</WeatherReports>
```

This XML document contains something called *tags*, or *elements*. Each item appearing in angle brackets (such as Humidity) is a tag. There are many rules that an XML document should follow. One of the most important is that each start tag needs to have an end tag. In the preceding example, WeatherReport is a start tag, and its corresponding end tag, which starts with a slash, is /WeatherReport. The XML document also needs to have a root element into which every child element is placed. The root element in the preceding XML document is WeatherReports.

Each element can either be a complex type or a simple type. The Humidity element is a simple type—it contains only a value. When an element contains other elements or has attributes, it is said to be a *complex type*. The WeatherReport element is a complex type, because it has other element tags beneath it.

These "sub-elements" are considered *child elements* to the WeatherReport element. Child elements to WeatherReport are Degrees, Humidity, and PrecipitationPossibility.

An XML document can have two different states: well-formed and valid. The XML document is well-formed when it follows XML standards regarding start and end tags, and so on. An XML document is said to be valid when it is well formed and conforms to the rules in the XSD document to which the XML document is linked.

XSD

Without the capability to define types, XML would be less useful in a cross-platform world. The World Wide Web Consortium finalized a standard for an XML-based type system known as *XML Schema* in May 2001. The language used to define a schema is an XML grammar known as *XML Schema Definition Language*. Since web services use XML as the underlying format for representing messages and data, XML was a natural choice to represent the definition types for XSD as well.

The W3C XML Schema standard consists logically of two things:

- A set of predefined or built-in types such as string, date, and integer

- An XML language for defining new types and for describing the structure of a class of XML documents such as an invoice or a purchase order

To help you understand the role of XSD in the world of XML, consider this analogy to your favorite programming language: The programming language you use to define application classes (e.g., VB 6 or VB .NET) is an analogue to XSD. When you define a class named COrder, this would correspond to a type definition for a COrder type in XSD. Finally, when you instantiate an object from the COrder class, this object instance is analogous to an XML document that represents an order—that is, an XML instance document. The instance follows the definitions (rules) of the class (meaning that it has the properties and methods defined in the class).

Another way to view the relationship between the XML document and the XSD document is by looking at the use of XSD together with the XML document, which exists in a *Simple Object Access Protocol* (SOAP) message sent to or from a web service.

When an XML document agrees to an XSD and is verified against an XSD document, the XML document is said to be *valid*. (It has been validated with respect to its XSD document and has not broken any of the rules/types defined in the XSD document.) The XSD document is used to validate the information in the XML document so that it occurs in the right order and has the right data types. The XSD document can also be used to verify that certain elements are present, and that they don't go beyond a maximum or minimum limit in the XML document.

When you build a web service, the data types you use must be translated to XSD types so that they conform to the web services standards. The developer tools you use may automate this, but you'll likely have to tweak the result a bit to meet your needs. Therefore, we will give a brief tour here of the XSD type system.

XSD types are either of a complex or simple nature. The simple ones are scalar, or unstructured values. Examples include integers, strings, and dates. Complex types, on the other hand, contain a structure. An example of a complex type is the aforementioned XML element WeatherReport, because it contains child elements and types. An easy rule for determining whether a type is a simple or complex is that an element with attributes and/or child elements is a complex type. Here is an example to clarify the difference:

```
<examples>
<!-- This element is of a complex type because it has child elements -->
<example>
<childelement1>some child text</childelement1>
< childelement2>more child text here </childelement2>
</example>

<!-- This element is of a complex type because it has an attribute-->
<example exampleid="2">some text</example>
<!--This element is of a simple type since it
has no attribute nor child elements-->
<example>some text</example>
</examples>
```

The XSD system is similar to the type system found in .NET, as every type derives from a base type, regardless of whether it is a simple type or a complex type. In .NET the base type is System.Object, and in the XSD type system it is the built-in type anyType. The complex types in XSD derive directly from anyType, and the simple types derive from anySimpleType, which in turn derives from anyType.

When building web services, you need to create XSD schemas to define the structure and the types that are contained in the request and the response messages from the web service. In the weather example previously shown, the WeatherReport element will contain one Degree element of type integer. To declare this in the XSD, write the following:

```
<element name="Degree" type="int"/>
```

This line says that the Degree element is of type integer and will occur only once in the XML document, which is the default for a type. By changing the minOccur and the maxOccur values on the element, it is possible to specify that Degree is optional:

```
<element name="Degree" type="int" minOccurs="0"/>,
```

or that it should be between one and two measurements of the temperature:

```
<element name="Degree" type="int" minOccurs="1" maxOccurs="2"/>
```

If you want at least one measurement of the temperature, but do not want to set a maximum number, you can do so by including the unbounded value as shown here:

```
<element name="Degree" type="int" minOccurs="1" maxOccurs="unbounded"/>
```

SOAP

When you finally have created your web service, other developers or systems will need to be able to connect to it in an easy way. SOAP allows this.

As we mentioned earlier, SOAP stands for Simple Object Access Protocol, a tool which makes it easy for you to use a web service. SOAP provides the standard remote procedure call mechanism used for invoking web services. You can look at SOAP as a proxy for the web service. The SOAP SDK from Microsoft will create a proxy object of your web service that exposes functions for each web service function you have declared. The proxy object finds this information in the WSDL file that we will look at later in our discussion of WSDL. SOAP then takes care of the packing and unpacking of messages sent and received from the web service. SOAP uses HTTP as a carrier of the data and packs the requests or responses to the web service in a SOAP envelope using XML and XSD.

Since 1993, the web has grown tremendously, and it continues to grow. The Internet itself provides basic network connectivity between millions of computers using TCP/IP and HTTP, as shown in Figure 6-2. This connectivity is not of much value unless applications running on different machines decide to communicate with one another, leveraging the underlying network and exchanging information.

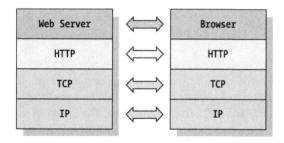

Figure 6-2. *The Internet protocol stack for browser/server communication*

Traditionally each type of application has invented and used its own application-level protocol that sits on top of TCP. For example, HTTP and HTTPS are application-level protocols designed for use between the web browser and the web server, as shown in Figure 6-2. The arrows in Figure 6-2 show the logical communication between peer layers on different hosts. The actual information flow goes down the stack on one host and then up the stack on the other.

Despite the huge success of HTTP as the Internet's main application protocol, it is limited to fairly simple commands centered on requesting and sending resources—for example, GET, POST, and PUT. The result is that we have millions of interconnected computers today, which leverage the Internet primarily for browsing the web, but can't, despite the connectivity, freely exchange data between applications. SOAP proposes to solve this problem by defining a standard protocol that any application can use to communicate and exchange data with any other application. Figure 6-3 shows how SOAP can be used over TCP/IP, leveraging the current Internet infrastructure. Because SOAP is an application-level protocol, it can work directly over any transport protocol such as TCP.

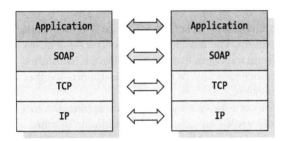

Figure 6-3. *SOAP over TCP/IP*

Today's Internet infrastructure is unfortunately scattered with proxies and firewalls that typically allow only HTTP traffic. In order for Internet-connected applications to communicate, SOAP must be able to flow over the current Internet infrastructure including these firewalls and proxies. To achieve this, SOAP can be layered over HTTP as shown in Figure 6-4.

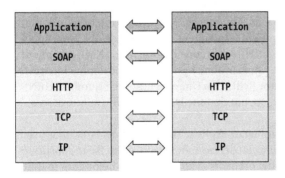

Figure 6-4. *SOAP layered over HTTP*

Layering SOAP over HTTP means that a SOAP message is sent as part of an HTTP request or response, which makes it easy to communicate over any network that permits HTTP traffic. Since HTTP is pervasive on all computing platforms, it is a good choice for transport protocol. To achieve platform independence and maximum interoperability, SOAP uses XML to represent messages exchanged between the client and the web service. Like HTTP, XML is also well-known, and you can find an XML parser for nearly any computing platform on the market (or write your own, if necessary). By leveraging HTTP and XML, SOAP provides application-to-application communications between applications running on any platform and connected over the existing Internet infrastructure. The SOAP SDK and the web services in .NET from Microsoft by default use HTTP as its transport protocol.

We'll talk about using HTTP/HTTPS for SOAP later in the section "SOAP over HTTP," but first we'll take a closer look at the SOAP architecture and the different ways you can manipulate a SOAP message to see the benefits of using SOAP.

SOAP Architecture

The strength of the SOAP architecture is its simplicity. The goal of the SOAP architecture is not to solve all the problems with distributed applications you have today—instead SOAP focuses on using the minimum of standards needed to send messages from one application to another. Older, distributed applications require secure connections and/or transaction support—neither of which is supported by SOAP in its standard version.

You can really think of SOAP as a method for sending a message from one application to another application—and nothing more. Items like RPCs are actually a combination of more SOAP messages, with different contents. Security is often provided by the protocol used for SOAP, but can also be integrated into the SOAP message through WS-Security—as we'll discuss later in the section "WSE and Security."

The SOAP Message

Let us take a look at the SOAP message in Figure 6-5. This message is constructed with a SOAP envelope, a SOAP header, and a SOAP body. A basic SOAP message is a well-formed XML document consisting of (at least) an envelope and a body that both belong to an envelope namespace, defined as `http://schemas.xmlsoap.org/soap/envelope/`. The header and the SOAP fault parts are optional. Since the tags Envelope and Body may exist in the XML document that is to be transferred, the tags use namespaces. A *namespace* is a collection of names that can be used as element or attribute names in an XML document. The purpose of a namespace is to make the combination of the namespace and the tag name unique in the XML document. You need to be able to identify the namespace, which is done by a Universal Resource Identifier (URI). A URI is either a Uniform Resource Locator (URL) or a Uniform Resource Number (URN). The important thing is not what the URI points to, but that the URI is globally unique across the Internet.

A namespace can be declared as either implicit or explicit. The explicit declaration is used in the SOAP message. With an explicit declaration, you define a shorthand, or prefix, to substitute for the full name of the namespace. You use this prefix to qualify elements belonging to that namespace. Explicit declarations are useful when a node contains elements from different namespaces.

We will refer to SOAP elements using soapenv as the namespace prefix for the examples later on in this chapter.

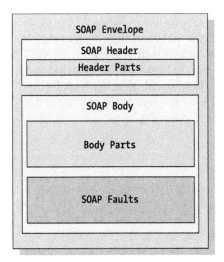

Figure 6-5. *The architecture of the SOAP message*

A simple SOAP message will look like the following:

```
<soapenv:Envelope xmlns:soapenv="http://schemas.xmlsoap.org/soap/envelope/">
  <soapenv:Body>
    <SubmitInvoice
      xmlns="http://mycompany.com/shop.net">
      <invoiceData>
          Data goes here!!
      </invoiceData>
    </SubmitInvoice>
  </soapenv:Body>
</soapenv:Envelope>
```

Envelope

The envelope is the container for the entire SOAP message. This is actually the root XML of the XML document and it has the name Envelope. In the beginning Envelope tag, the namespace is specified. The xmlns is the definition for namespace, and the text following the colon is the namespace prefix that will be used in this XML document. It's possible to include many different namespaces in the same XML document by adding them one after another like this:

```
xmlns:soapenv="http://schemas.xmlsoap.org/soap/envelope/"
xmlns:economy="http://mycomp.com/soap/economy/"
```

This example will often occur, because the information sent in the SOAP message may use different namespaces to separate the same tag name.

Header

The header is optional and can contain information about the SOAP message, such as expiration date, encoding information, and so on. It's possible to include your own information in the header, and later in the section "SOAP Extensions" you will see how the header can be used for security verification and RPC calls. Here we'll show you how to add some header information to a SOAP message. In Listing 6-1, some general information is sent in the header: in this case, the date when the SOAP message was posted.

Listing 6-1. *Header Information in the SOAP Message*

```
<soapenv:Envelope
xmlns:soapenv="http://schemas.xmlsoap.org/soap/envelope/">
  <soapenv:Header>
<postedDate>
12th of May 2002
</postedDate>
  </soapenv:Header>
  <soapenv:Body>
    <SubmitInvoice xmlns="http://mycompany.com/shop">
      <invoiceData>
      Data goes here!
      </invoiceData>
    </SubmitInvoice>
  </soapenv:Body>
</soapenv:Envelope>
```

Fault Part

The last part of the SOAP message might be a *fault part*. This is a child element to the body parts of the SOAP message. The information is generated on the server when an error occurs in the processing of the request. A fault message is easy to create inside a web service, as you will see in later examples. The SOAP message is put back into the response message, and the fault part tells the user of the web services what kind of error has occurred. A typical fault message looks like this:

```
<soap:Fault>
        <faultcode>soap:Client</faultcode>
<faultstring>System.Web.Services.Protocols.SoapException:
A validation error occurred:
The 'http://www.mycompany.com/info.net/schemas/invoice:ItemTotal'
element has an invalid value according to its data type.
</faultstring>
        <detail>
          <Procedure xmlns="http://services.mycompany.com/Invoice/">
                Validation
          </Procedure>
          <Line xmlns="http://services.mycompany.com/Invoice/">13</Line>
          <Position xmlns="http://services.mycompany.com/Invoice/">15</Position>
        </detail>
      </soap:Fault>
```

SOAP Message Formats

Today, many different kinds of SOAP-message formats exist. These formats differ by the way the body element and the data in the header elements are formatted or encoded.

To send a SOAP message, you need to serialize the data into a format that can be understood by the recipient of the SOAP message. If you serialize the data to an XML document and send it in a SOAP message by putting the XML document inside the Body tag, the SOAP message that you end up with is said to be a *document-style SOAP message* and has a literal payload. This is more often called a *document/literal SOAP message*. Normally the use of SOAP is separated into two different areas: document/literal use and RPC use.

In document/literal use, the document usually contains one or more children called *parts*. There are no rules for what the body part of the SOAP message should contain in a document/literal SOAP message—it can contain anything that can be serialized and that you and the recipient agree upon. In RPC use, the SOAP body contains a method name that should be invoked on the receiver's server and an element for each parameter that the remote procedure needs. Section 7 in the SOAP specification defines exactly what the body should contain when it is used for RPC. In addition to the two previously mentioned SOAP-message styles, there are two formats for serializing data into XML. The format you choose determines how your data is serialized into the soapenv:Body and soapenv:Header elements.

When the serialization method is literal, the data is serialized according to an XML Schema. No specific encoding rules dictate how the data should be serialized in a literal SOAP message. With the literal format, the communication is relying on XML documents rather than objects and structures, and the documents may contain anything.

The second serialization method is the *encoded* format. The data in this case is serialized according to rules that dictate the internal structure of the message. The most common rules are the Section 5 rules of the SOAP specification, which define how objects and object graphs should be serialized. Using section 5 encoding results in the data between the client and the services being based on objects and structures.

The decision of which format to use in a communication between a client and a service is open. In theory, the choice of using document or RPC format is unconnected to your selection of literal or encoded format. This gives you four possible combinations to choose among: document/literal, document/encoded, RPC/literal, or RPC/encoded. In the real world, the choice is reduced down to two—document/literal or RPC/encoded. Why? Because normally you would break down the use of web services and SOAP into two groups.

The first group is the one that deals with document exchanges between different applications. Our example application in Chapter 10 exposes web services that send complete time reports (in the form of documents) back to the caller. Such solutions need to describe the data in XML, and the content often doesn't have complex types in it. The preferred choice for these solutions is the document/literal combination.

The second group uses SOAP for invoking remote objects. These solutions normally use RPC/encoded SOAP messages instead of document/literal SOAP messages, since the information in the SOAP message is of a more technical nature and includes complex types.

In the beginning, SOAP mainly functioned as a replacement for DCOM. Because SOAP was easy to use and less error-prone than DCOM, the market became saturated with implementations of SOAP that mainly focused on its DCOM-replacement aspects. SOAP became popular because of its use of the HTTP protocol for transporting information between a remote object and a server. There was suddenly no need for altering the firewall to allow RPC calls to go through, as there was with DCOM.

In .NET you have two ways you can use web services: either as Remoting services or as .NET web services. Remoting, the replacement for DCOM, mainly focuses on remote access to objects on a server. Remoting services are based on RPC/encoded SOAP. The other option, .NET web services, incorporate document/literal encoding intended to be used for message-based web services, such as transferring information back and forth between a client and the server.

Document/literal is the format of choice when working with message-based web services, because you have full control of the format of the message. By using the document/literal format in a business-to-business communication, in which orders and invoices are sent between different companies, you can ensure that the documents are valid to a predefined and agreed XML Schema.

So when do you use the RPC/encoded SOAP messages?

The only time we recommend that you use RPC/encoded messages is when you expose objects on your server that the client should be able to run (invoking as RPC). This may, for instance, be a calculation object that calculates a customer's price for items at the current time. If the server-side objects are based on COM, you'll want to use SOAP messages that are RPC/encoded. If you have developed them in .NET, you would use .NET Remoting.

SOAP is very easy to use. All you need to do is write a request as an XML document and put that document into a SOAP body encoded in the document/literal format. SOAP is mostly used when the need for message communication between different programs arises. This feature of SOAP is very important, since it makes it possible for you to tie different applications together, and reuse and extend legacy information in your business environment in a simple way—no matter what environment the legacy system is running in. One of the strengths of SOAP and web services is the use of standard communication protocols as a carrier for the data. In the next section, we will talk about the benefits of using HTTP for SOAP messages.

SOAP over HTTP

SOAP over HTTP gives you a benefit that many of those who have used DCOM or CORBA sometimes wish they had—free access through firewalls. Since HTTP is a standard protocol that is mostly allowed to pass through firewalls using port 80, the use of HTTP as a protocol for SOAP messages mostly gives you access through the firewalls and proxy servers.

When using SOAP over HTTP, you need to set the HTTP content type header in a SOAP message to text/XML to identify to the receiver of the HTTP request that it contains XML. Also, when sending a SOAP request, you'll need to set the SOAP action header, which always contains a quoted value and communicates additional information about the SOAP message at the HTTP level. This can be useful for firewalls that filter SOAP/HTTP traffic based on certain values of the HTTP SOAP action header. In this way, it is quite easy for the administrator of a firewall to redirect different SOAP requests or even deny access for specific requests.

One example of this technique is to use the SOAP action header for extra customer information that validates the request to access the web. In this way, access to the web services is filtered at an early stage. (This is not always the best solution, but we mention it merely as an example of the use of a SOAP action header.) Normally you should not design your web services to rely on information located in the Action header, as there are other places to put it—for instance, in the SOAP header. Another use of the SOAP header is to block the SOAP message from passage through a firewall and only allow "standard" HTTP traffic. This enables a company to make sure that no web services are accidentally invoked from outside the firewall. Here is a short SOAP message sent via HTTP:

```
POST /msyhop/orders/orderWS/
orders.aspx HTTP/1.0SOAPAction: "urn:OrderAction"
Content-Type: text/XML
Accept-Language: en-us
Content-Length: 800
Accept: */*
User-Agent: Mozilla/4.0 (compatible; Win32; WinHttp.WinHttpRequest.5)
Host: localhost
Connection: Keep-Alive
<soapenv:Envelope xmlns:xsi=http://www.w3.org/2001/XMLSchema-instance
xmlns:xsd=http://www.w3.org/2001/XMLSchema
xmlns:soapenv="http://schemas.xmlsoap.org/soap/envelope/">..</soapenv:Envelope>
```

SOAP over HTTPS

HTTP is perfect to use as a transport protocol for SOAP, but SOAP has no built-in security. This means that the SOAP message is transferred via HTTP, and is open for anyone to explore—not the best solution for critical business information. Anyone who knows how to sniff for TCP/IP packages can easily collect your business-critical information, or even worse, manipulate it and then send it to its destination! One solution is to use HTTPS. HTTPS employs Secure Sockets Layer (SSL) over port 443 (normally).

The encryption of the packages prevents most people from decoding your information. The strength of the security of your communication depends on the length of the encryption key you use. The length is described in bits, and longer the length the better. The key is based on prime numbers and is quite safe to use. This security solution will work fine in regards to point-to-point communication—that is, if the sender and the receiver are aware of each other and are the only ones interacting with the SOAP messages. This security solution can also be very fast, because it's possible to buy hardware that handles the SSL encryption. However, without hardware that handles the SSL encryption, the decision to handle the SSL encryption with software can bring even the fastest server down to its knees. If you are going to use SSL, ensure that you're only using it when necessary and that you have calculated whether or not your server can handle the load.

When there are more actors involved on the SOAP message path, using WS-I specifications such as WS-Security, WS-Policy, and WS-Routing are better choices than relying on HTTPS security for rerouting your SOAP messages. In a more complex application, the web services architecture can't rely on Transport Layer Security because a SOAP intermediary node may need to process the document before forwarding it on to the endpoint. This means that SSL can only be deployed in peer-to-peer environments. The important thing to note is that the number of potential SOAP intermediaries increases as the deployment scale increases.

This decreases the likelihood of encrypting your data successfully at the transport layer, increases the amount of access to each SOAP envelope, and increases the possibility of a passive sniffing attack against your text-based SOAP messaging framework. Message layer encryption and digital signatures are a must for a secure deployment. By using WS-Security, you ensure that the message itself is encrypted—no matter what kind of transport protocol is in use.

Later on, in the "web Services Enhancements (WSE) SDK" section, we will show you examples of how to use the WS-Security specifications from VB .NET via the web Services Enhancements (WSE) software development kit (SDK), from Microsoft. This is an implementation of the WS-Security, WS-Policy, and WS-Attachment specifications.

RPC and SOAP

Rewriting an existing application to move from DCOM to SOAP is often too arduous, since many parts in such an application would need to be changed. You would have to make changes to the server side of the application in order to receive and process incoming XML documents as well as send responses as outgoing XML documents back to the client. You would also have to rewrite the client side of the application to format and send requests as XML documents and receive and parse responses.

Not only that, but most difficult of all, you would have to adopt a programming model that is probably very different from the one you are used to. This model would require you to serialize all data to XML, send it as a request to the server, and, when the answer arrives back from the server, deserialize the incoming XML document and process the return values. Finally, if the existing application architecture doesn't lend itself to messaging (by using stateful server objects for example), you'll find that replacing DCOM with SOAP messaging requires a major rearchitecture and/or some custom SOAP extensions.

To ease the transition process from DCOM to SOAP in an application, you could add an extra layer to the client application. The purpose of this layer is to simulate the previously used DCOM object, but instead of calling the object via DCOM, this proxy makes a SOAP message of the request and sends it to the server. A similar proxy resides on the server side that receives the SOAP message and deserializes it. The server then calls the object on the server, serializes the result, and returns it to the calling-client proxy.

The specification for using SOAP for RPC (Section 7 of the SOAP specification) defines a standard format for communicating this kind of information. In addition, the SOAP specification contains many definitions, including one that defines a standard way of serializing/deserializing native application types (arrays, strings, and the like), which is important for enabling interoperation among clients and servers from different vendors. This standard serialization format is commonly called *Section 5 encoding*, after the SOAP specification section where it is defined. Although the SOAP specification indicates that you can use SOAP for RPC without necessarily using the standard Section 5 encoding, we don't recommend this because Section 5 encoding ensures your application will be able to operate with other applications. Common sense is to stick to a standard if one exists. Most SOAP stacks and SOAP tools combine RPC with Section 5 encoding. Instead of writing your own proxy layers, you can use existing third-party proxies, like those found in Microsoft's SOAP SDK. These proxies enable remote communication via SOAP messages in old Windows DNA environments, where applications are built on COM objects.

We will not continue to talk about older technologies here: instead we will focus on all of the new features in the Windows .NET architecture that make web services and SOAP even simpler to use, yet more powerful than they were in Windows DNA.

Note Previously we mentioned that Section 5 encoding is named after the section that defines it in the SOAP specification. Most of the specification for SOAP is found in Section 5 (which has approximately 40 percent of the total number of pages in the SOAP specification). Section 5 also includes detailed rules for how application information should be serialized and deserialized, including elements such as arrays and objects. In this book, we won't dive into the encoding specification—if you use mostly .NET Framework for your web services, as we recommend, the .NET SDK takes care of the encoding.

Error Messages in SOAP

Sometimes things don't work out the way they should, and you need to report an error back to the caller. This is possible to do by using the fault part in the SOAP specification. In .NET this part is populated with error information from the thrown error object, which makes it easy to return an error message. All you need to do is throw an error inside the called web services method. The fault message contains a fault code, fault string, fault actor, and detail element, as described in the following list:

- *Fault code.* The fault code element is intended for the software to provide a number that identifies the error. It must be present in the SOAP fault element, and the fault code value must be a qualified name.

- *Fault string.* The fault string is provided to give you a chance to see what kind of error has occurred and is not intended for algorithmic processing. For processing, use a fault code. The fault string is similar to the description string found in the error object in VB 6, in that it contains a description of the reason why the error occurred.

- *Fault actor.* The fault actor element is intended to provide information about what caused a fault within the message path. It contains a URI that identifies the source. Applications that are not the final destination for the SOAP message must include the fault actor in the response. The final destination may use it to indicate that the fault actor caused the error itself.

- *Fault detail.* The fault detail element is intended to carry detail error information related to the body of the SOAP message. It must be present, or processing of the message body will not be successful. The detail part may not carry information about faults that have occurred in the SOAP header. To return information about errors in SOAP headers, a fault message should be carried within header elements in the detail part. In the section "SOAP Exceptions," we will give you a more extensive look into SOAP and SOAP errors and how you can use them to return fault information to the caller.

WSDL

Say you now have a web service that communicates by using SOAP. The request and the result are described in XML, and the internal structure of the XML document is defined in XSD. But how do your users and customers know which functions your web service exposes and the parameters that they take? You can easily write this information down in a Word document, but such a document will probably not be possible to parse programmatically. Even worse, a developer might not find your specification document and have to spend a couple of days figuring out what your clever web service is suppose to do, and how he or she can use it!

The answer to this problem is web Services Description Language. WSDL describes web services and the functions that they have in plain XML. It also tells the user of such web services the parameters for each function, as well as their data types and return types. One of the benefits of using this formal approach is that both humans and machines can read the WSDL file. In addition, the WSDL file can be auto-generated from a web service and parsed programmatically. By auto-generating the WSDL file, you can avoid errors that may be introduced by humans in a manual translation. The SOAP proxy also uses the WSDL file to decide what methods the proxy should have.

UDDI

The last link in the web service process chain is Universal Description, Discovery, and Integration (UDDI), which lets you publish your web services and makes it possible for potential customers or users to find them.

UDDI should be viewed as a means of finding particular web services. UDDI categorizes and catalogs providers and their web services. A developer can find WSDL files and access points in UDDI, and then incorporate those web services into its client applications. The UDDI servers that host information about all web services conform to the specification governed by the UDDI.org consortium. Today, one UDDI server hosted by Microsoft, one hosted by IBM, and one hosted by HP. The replication between them occurs on a 24-hour basis, but will probably be more frequent in the future, as more applications will depend on accurate UDDI data. You need to perform a couple of steps if you want to add your web services to UDDI and make them searchable. We will walk you through these steps in the next sections.

Step 1: Modeling the UDDI Entry

The first step is to model your UDDI entry. Several key pieces of data need to be collected before establishing a UDDI entry.

First, you'll need to determine which WSDL files your web service implementation uses. Similar to a traditional COM or CORBA application, your web service has been developed based on an existing interface or a proprietary one. The WSDL file can be generated in .NET by adding the WSDL parameter to the query string on the web service as in this example: `http://www.mycompany.com/_SampleWebService.asmx?wsdl`.

You'll then need to specify the name of your company and give a brief description of it, as well as its central contacts for its web services. This gives companies that would like to use your web service the ability to get in touch with your support team if they need to.

Next, define the categories and identifications that are appropriate for your company. To do this you might browse, for instance, Microsoft's UDDI server (`http://uddi.microsoft.com/default.aspx`). The currently supported taxonomies are North American Industry Classification System (NAICS), ISO 3166, Universal Standard Products and Services Codes (UNSPSC), Standard Industry Classification (SIC), and Geoweb Geographic Classification. Here you can choose which categories best represent your company and allow others to narrow their searches for your web service.

At this point you'll need to determine the web services that your company should provide through UDDI. Add the web services you want to publish and define the different access points they may have (a web service may have different access points). It's important to realize that registering a web service in UDDI doesn't mean that everyone will have access to it. Security, authorization, and authentication can exist in tandem with a UDDI registry entry. Just because someone knows your web service exists does not mean he or she can actually invoke it.

Finally, categorize the web services you would like to publish, just as you previously categorized your company, so that it will be possible for potential users to find your web service by searching on a category.

Now you have a complete UDDI registry entry. The next important step is to register it in the UDDI server.

Step 2: Registering the UDDI Entry

All communications with the UDDI publishing server holding information about your web services use authenticated connections, and therefore you need to register to get a username and a password. The registration contains simple data about you and your business or organization, including the name of the business and an optional description of it. You must also agree to the terms of use statement, so this step cannot be done programmatically. Microsoft requires a Passport for authentication, so you'll need to have one before you can proceed to register your UDDI entry in the UDDI server.

The main purpose of this registration is to let others know your web service exists. There are two ways to do the registration—either by using a web-based registration form or performing the registration programmatically.

If you are making frequent updates to your UDDI, you should use the UDDI .NET SDK to do so programmatically. After downloading and installing the SDK, it is quite easy to register your information in the UDDI server. But if you do not need to update the information frequently, you can use a web-based registration form.

Due to space constraints, we won't show you the complete registration process here: instead, we suggest you take a look at Microsoft's copy of a real UDDI registration at `http://test.uddi.microsoft.com/default.aspx`.

Twenty-four hours after you complete the registration of your UDDI entry, Microsoft's UDDI server will replicate your registration to the other UDDI servers around the world, and your web service will be searchable and ready for others to use.

Transactions and Web Services

Transactions are not supported by SOAP today; however, the WS-I specification group is working on designing transactional support for web services. Transaction support will not be a traditional two-phase commit. (A *two-phase commit* occurs when a transaction coordinator keeps track of all updates to several databases in the network. If all updates are successful, they are committed; otherwise all transactions are rolled back.) Transaction support in web services will be more of a coordination issue in most cases. The WS-I specification group is currently designing WS-Attachment and WS-Coordination to help in handling transactions via web services.

Putting It All Together

Finally, in this section we'll describe the complete flow for a request of a web service. Imagine that a third-party company, called Good Products Inc., would like to get information from your company regarding your inventory, in order to make special offers that suit your company.

Having agreed to this, you install a web service that exposes one function—GetProductStatuses (Optional ProductID as long). It takes one optional parameter, which means that if you do not send in a particular product ID you'll retrieve all products and their statuses. This is a simple web service that only returns an XML document containing the different product numbers and the quantity.

Good Products Inc. is running a Windows service that regularly polls its internal list of subscribing partners. When it reaches your company's server in the list, the following will happen:

1. The Windows service creates a SOAP message (see Listing 6-2). The first element in this SOAP message is an envelope. It identifies an XML document as being a SOAP message, and encapsulates all the other parts of a message within itself. The envelope contains the version number of the message and the rules used by the application to serialize the message.

   A SOAP header element may be placed after the envelope, but this is optional. It can contain authorization information and transactional information. It may also contain extra information for the receiving application, such as priority and so on. If a header exists, it must follow directly after the envelope.

   The last element is the body element. This area contains application-specific information. In Listing 6-2, which also shows a complete SOAP message, an RPC call to a web service requests GetProductStatuses.

Listing 6-2. *A Complete SOAP Message*

```
<SOAP:Envelope
     xmlns:SOAP='http://schemas.xmlsoap.org/soap/envelope/'
     SOAP:encodingStyle='http://schemas.xmlsoap.org/soap/encoding/'
     xmlns:p='http://www.GoodProducts.com/productInfo/'>
    <SOAP:Header>
        <p:From SOAP:mustUnderstand='1'>
            info@goodproducts.com
        </p:From>
    </SOAP:Header>
    <SOAP:Body>
        <p:GetProductStatuses>
            <productid>123-4567-890</productid>
        </p:GetProductStatuses>
    </SOAP:Body>
</SOAP:Envelope>
```

2. After you create a SOAP message, the next step is to send this message via some kind of protocol. Normally you use HTTP or HTTPS, but SOAP doesn't dictate what kind of transport protocol you should use. You could print out the message and send it by ordinary mail if you wanted (but we don't recommend doing this). In our examples we use HTTP, since it is well suited for SOAP messages.

   At this point, you should create a SOAP proxy, as mentioned earlier in this chapter. This proxy will expose the functions of the Web service found at your company as functions on this SOAP proxy object:

```
Dim c As New MSSOAPLib.SoapClient
c.mssoapinit ("http://www.yourcompany.com/productinfo/
services/productinfo.XML")
Dim strProductInfos As String
```

3. Invoke the method GetProductStatuses that the WSDL file describes and that is exposed as a function on the SOAP Client:

```
strProductInfos = c.GetProductStatuses ()
```

4. The productinfo.XML file specified in the SOAP proxy is the WSDL file that contains information about the Web service, so that the proxy (the SOAP client) can create an interface for you with all the functions visible. The result from the Web service at your company is found in the strProductInfos variable in the preceding code line. Now you are ready to parse!

It is possible to create a request to a web service without using Microsoft's SOAP Toolkit. All you need to do is parse the incoming request stream to the web page, extract the information, and execute the requested method. However, this takes some work and requires a lot of code, so we will not show this process here. Figure 6-6 contains a simple schematic of the flow of actions for invoking a web service via HTTP and SOAP.

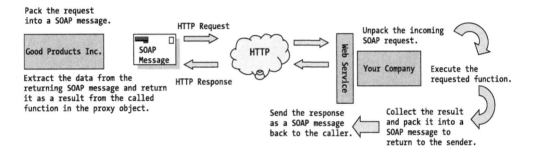

Figure 6-6. *The flow for a web service request*

As Figure 6-6 illustrates, the steps for the web service request flow are as follows:

1. First, the request is packaged into a SOAP message. The SOAP body is then filled with the appropriate information that the client will send or request to/from the server.

2. The SOAP message is sent via HTTP to the server, where the web service receives the message.

3. The server unpacks the incoming messages and executes the requested function.

4. When the server has received the result from the function, the result is packed into a new SOAP message and returned to the caller.

5. The response in the form of a SOAP message from the server is unpacked by the SOAP client, and the client parses the result.

Using SOAP

So far we have looked at SOAP and web services from a technical point of view. When it comes to working with SOAP messages and web services, you need to know how to debug the messages that are sent from and received by the web service. Here we will show you how to create a simple web service and trace the SOAP communication between the client and the server to see what is going on behind the scenes.

Tracing SOAP Messages

To make it easier to understand how a SOAP message is built and what it consists of, an application that traces SOAP messages is helpful. Many freeware tools for tracing SOAP messages exist on the market, and the SOAP SDK kit also contains such a tool, called *trace utility*. It listens on a port that you specify and then forwards all incoming traffic to its destination web server and port, which you also specify. Figure 6-7 shows the trace utility configured to listen to port 8080 and forward the incoming messages to the server localhost.

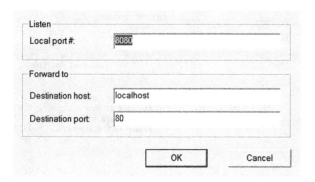

Figure 6-7. *Configuring the trace utility to listen for SOAP messages*

Once you have configured the trace utility to listen to a port, you must make your client send all requests to this port on the destination host. Therefore, for this example, instead of sending a SOAP request to `http://localhost/myservice.asp`, it should be sent to `http://localhost:8080/myservice.asp`. If you want to capture SOAP messages while running code, simply run the trace utility and make it listen on port 8080, and then replace the service URL in the code to point to port 8080 on the destination host. The trace utility will intercept and capture the request and response messages, and display them in the trace window.

The Web Service Example

It is time to see a web service in action. Here we'll walk you through the steps for creating a .NET web service that exposes a couple of functions. After that, we will show you how to create a client that consumes the web service.

The web service exposes functions from a financial legacy system. It will be able to report an account's status, add an amount of money (we wish this were a real web service!), and draw from the account. The web service itself also verifies that the account contains enough money before it allows the business to charge the account. If the sum is not enough, the web service will return a SOAP fault-error message the client has to deal with.

To follow along with this example, perform the following steps.

First, open Visual Studio .NET. Next, select ASP.NET web Service under Templates, and also specify where the web service should be located on the server (see Figure 6-8). For this example, we specified EconomyWS.

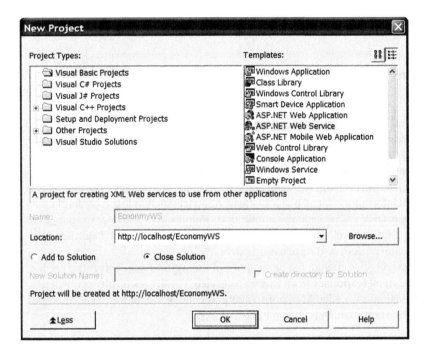

Figure 6-8. *Creating an ASP.NET web service*

Click OK, and VS .NET will set up an empty ASP.NET web service project.

After the project has opened your first action should be to change the name of the created web service page from Services1.asmx, as shown in Figure 6-9, to something more suitable. Since the web service will expose functionality for accounts, rename the project as Account.asmx.

Figure 6-9. *Renaming the default web service*

We assume that you are probably familiar with the VS .NET development environment, so we'll only give you a short overview here. The Solution Explorer contains the projects that are loaded in the solution (a *solution* is a group of files gathered from different projects). This ASP.NET web service project sets up one empty .asmx page (which is the actual web service) and a global.asax page (because this web service is an application in the web server). The global.asax page can contain global information for all pages in the web service, such as logon credentials. It also contains the old events that will occur in this application—Application_Start, Application_End, Session_Start, Session_End—as well as some other events such as Application_BeginRequest, Application_AuthenticateRequest, and Application_Error.

The next thing you will do is change the namespace of the web service. This is the namespace that will be used in all responses from this web service. For this example, you will use the name of a fictional company called My Comp. After you change the namespace, you input the complete web service code, which is shown in Listing 6-3.

Listing 6-3. *The Complete Web Service Code Imports System.Web.Services*

```
<WebService(Namespace:="http://localhost/WebServices", _
Description:="This Web Service exposes account functionality.")> _

Public Class Account
    Inherits System.Web.Services.WebService

    <WebMethod(Description:="Obtains the Salary on the specified account.", _
        EnableSession:=False)> _
    Public Function GetSalaryOnAccount(ByVal AccountID As Long, _
                                       ByVal StrUserID As String) As Integer
        Select Case AccountID
            Case 1
                Return DateTime.Now.Second * 100
            Case 2
```

```
                Dim rnd As New Random(DateTime.Now.Second)
                'Seed value to ensure another pseudo random series.
                Return rnd.Next() 'Return the random number
            Case Else
                Return 0
        End Select

    End Function

    <WebMethod(Description:="Obtains the Name of the specified account.", _
        EnableSession:=False)> _
    Public Function GetAccountName(ByVal AccountID As Long, _
 ByVal StrUserID As String) As String

        Select Case AccountID
            Case 1
                Return "My public account"
            Case 2
                Return "My secret account"
            Case Else
                Return "Unknown"
        End Select
    End Function
End Class
```

Two functions are created: one that returns the name of an account, and one that returns the amount in the account.

To test the project, right-click Account.asmx, choose Set as Start Page, and then choose Start from the Debug menu or press F5 to build and run the project. This will launch a service documentation page in Internet Explorer that should look like the one in Figure 6-10.

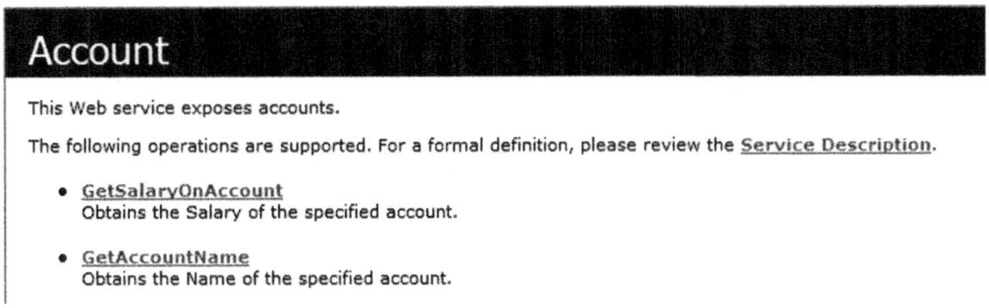

Account

This Web service exposes accounts.

The following operations are supported. For a formal definition, please review the Service Description.

- **GetSalaryOnAccount**
  Obtains the Salary of the specified account.

- **GetAccountName**
  Obtains the Name of the specified account.

Figure 6-10. *The generated service description page*

This is a default page that is automatically generated. If you click GetSalaryOnAccount, you will be transferred to the test page shown in Figure 6-11. On this test page you can invoke the selected method on the web service and also pass it the different parameter it requires.

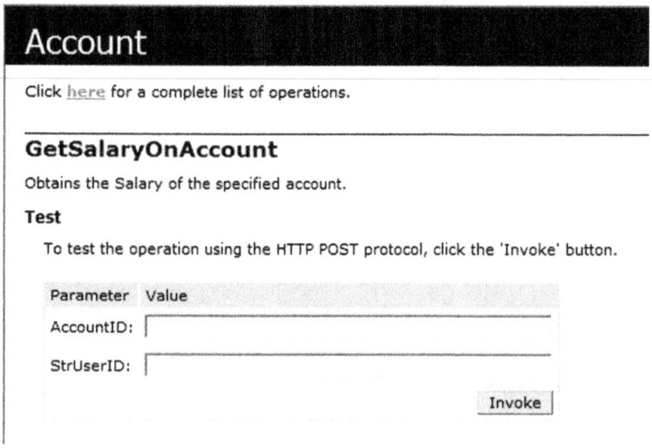

Account

Click here for a complete list of operations.

GetSalaryOnAccount

Obtains the Salary of the specified account.

Test

  To test the operation using the HTTP POST protocol, click the 'Invoke' button.

Parameter	Value
AccountID:	
StrUserID:	

Invoke

Figure 6-11. *The parameter page for the GetSalaryOnAccount function*

Fill in some valid parameter values (1 for the AccountID and a username) and click the Invoke button. The request is sent to the web service and processed on the server, and a SOAP response message like the following is returned:

```
<? XML version="1.0" encoding="utf-8" ?>
  <int xmlns="http://localhost/WebServices">3000</int>
```

But what is really sent to and from the server by invoking the web service this way? A little bit farther down the test page you will see what is going on behind the scenes (see Listing 6-4).

Listing 6-4. *The SOAP Message Sent Between the Client and the Server*

```
POST /EconomyWS/Account.asmx HTTP/1.1
Host: localhost
Content-Type: text/XML; charset=utf-8
Content-Length: length
SOAPAction: "http://localhost/WebServices/GetSalaryOnAccount"

<?XML version="1.0" encoding="utf-8"?>
<soap:Envelope xmlns:xsi="http://www.w3.org/2001/XMLSchema-instance"
    xmlns:xsd="http://www.w3.org/2001/XMLSchema"
    xmlns:soap="http://schemas.xmlsoap.org/soap/envelope/">  <soap:Body>
    <GetSalaryOnAccount xmlns="http://localhost/WebServices">
      <AccountID>1</AccountID>
      <StrUserID>Rickard</StrUserID>
    </GetSalaryOnAccount>
  </soap:Body>
</soap:Envelope>
```

```
HTTP/1.1 200 OK
Content-Type: text/XML; charset=utf-8
Content-Length: length

<?XML version="1.0" encoding="utf-8"?>
<soap:Envelope xmlns:xsi="http://www.w3.org/2001/XMLSchema-instance"
xmlns:xsd="http://www.w3.org/2001/XMLSchema"
xmlns:soap="http://schemas.xmlsoap.org/soap/envelope/">
  <soap:Body>
    <GetSalaryOnAccountResponse xmlns="http://localhost/WebServices">
      <GetSalaryOnAccountResult>3000</GetSalaryOnAccountResult>
    </GetSalaryOnAccountResponse>
  </soap:Body>
</soap:Envelope>
```

First, you can see an ordinary post to the web services containing a SOAP message. The body contains a method declaration and its parameters.

The second part shows the response from the server. It contains the SOAP envelope and a body that has a GetSalaryOnAccountResponse (named after the requested method and a suffix of Response). The return value shows a suffix of Result added to the method name.

Normally you will not invoke web services this way. In .NET it is very easy to consume web services and use them as objects, as you will see in Chapter 10.

Soap Faults

Normally, when an error occurs and you want to pass it back to the caller, all you need to do is throw an exception. By doing this, the server creates a SOAP exception message and throws it to the caller application. The proxy on the server will serialize the error in the returning SOAP message sent to the caller. Normally you would want to add some extra information to the fault message so that the caller can get a clue as to why the request failed. To return a more complex fault message, you'll need to use one of the other constructors of the SoapException class. The following constructors suit this purpose:

```
Public Sub New(ByVal message As String, _
ByVal code As System.XML.XmlQualifiedName, _
ByVal actor As String, _
ByVal detail As System.XML.XmlNode)
```

This code takes a fourth parameter, an xmlNode. What this lets you do is populate your own XML document and put it in the returning fault message!

Let us look at an example. Add a validate function named ValidateWithdraw to the code in Listing 6-3. The function will take two parameters. The first will identify the user, and the second is the account number that should be used. Of course, the last parameter will be the amount that should be withdrawn from the specified account number. If the action is allowed (that is, if there is enough money in the account), the function will return true. If not, a specific fault message will be filled with information about the error. (The function could have returned false to tell the user that the withdrawal was not allowed, but we are returning a specific fault message for the purpose of this example.) Listing 6-5 shows the complete code for the ValidateWithdraw function.

Listing 6-5. *The ValidateWithdraw Function*

```
Private Function ValidateWithdraw(ByVal UserID As String,_
                                  ByVal Account As Long, _
                                  ByVal Amount As Decimal) As Boolean
'Verify that there is enough money in the account for the current action.
Const MAXWITHDRAWVALUE As Integer = 1000
If UserID.Equals("Bandit") Then
'This guy shouldn't be allowed to do anything.
ThrowComplexException("ValidateWithdraw", _
"We're not allowed to do anything here.", "", UserID, _
Account, Amount)
Else
'A withdraw > MAXWITHDRAWVALUE not allowed.
    If Amount > MAXWITHDRAWVALUE Then
    ThrowComplexException("ValidateWithdraw", _
    "We're not allowed to withdraw more than " & _
            MAXWITHDRAWVALUE, "", UserID, Account, Amount)     End If
End If
End Function
```

The ThrowComplexException function in Listing 6-6 is a little bit more complicated.

Listing 6-6. *The ThrowComplexException Method*

```
Private Sub ThrowComplexException(ByVal ProcedureName As String, _
ByVal Message As String, _
ByVal stacktrace As String, _
Optional ByVal UserID As String = vbNullString, _
Optional ByVal Account As Long = Long.MinValue, _
Optional ByVal Withdraw As Decimal = Decimal.Zero)
        Dim doc As New System.XML.XmlDocument()
        Dim detail As System.XML.XmlNode = _
        doc.CreateNode(XmlNodeType.Element, _
        SoapException.DetailElementName.Name, _
        SoapException.DetailElementName.Namespace)
        'The procedure name

        Dim procNode As System.XML.XmlNode = _
            doc.CreateNode(XmlNodeType.Element, _
          "Procedure", SoapException.DetailElementName.Namespace)
        procNode.InnerText = ProcedureName

        Dim StackNode As System.XML.XmlNode = _
            doc.CreateNode(XmlNodeType.Element, _
        "StackTrace", SoapException.DetailElementName.Namespace)
        StackNode.InnerText = stacktrace
        detail.AppendChild(procNode)
        detail.AppendChild(StackNode)
```

```
      If UserID.Length > 0 Then
          'There exists user information - add it.
          Dim newAttr As XmlAttribute = doc.CreateAttribute("ID")
          newAttr.Value = UserID
          Dim UserNode As System.XML.XmlNode = _
              doc.CreateNode(XmlNodeType.Element, _
          "User", SoapException.DetailElementName.Namespace)
          UserNode.Attributes.Append(newAttr) 'Adds the userid as an attribute.

          Dim AccountNode As System.XML.XmlNode = _
              doc.CreateNode(XmlNodeType.Element, _
          "Account", SoapException.DetailElementName.Namespace)
          AccountNode.InnerText = Account
          Dim WithdrawNode As System.XML.XmlNode = _
              doc.CreateNode(XmlNodeType.Element, _
          "Amount", SoapException.DetailElementName.Namespace)
          WithdrawNode.InnerText = Withdraw
          'Add Account node and Withdraw node as children to the usernode
          UserNode.AppendChild(AccountNode)
          UserNode.AppendChild(WithdrawNode)
          'Add the usernode to the detail node.
          detail.AppendChild(UserNode)
      End If

      'Throw the new exception

      Dim ex As New SoapException(Message, _
          SoapException.ClientFaultCode, _
          "", detail)
      Throw ex
  End Sub
```

Since the SOAP body is made of pure XML, you can add any kind of structure to the fault part, including a complete XML document, if you like. In Listing 6-6, notice that some new nodes were created below the detail node.

As this listing demonstrates, you start by creating the doc object, which is the XML document you want to include. The next object is the detail object, which will act as a root node to all other nodes you add later in the subroutine.

You use the XML document as a root node, and by creating new nodes and adding them together, you finally have a complete detail message in the XML document.

Extending SOAP

From our discussions about web services and SOAP, it should now be quite clear to you that SOAP is only the backbone for a message-based communication or an RPC/encoded communication, leaving it up to the implementation to fulfill the requirements from the application.

Web services and SOAP are being changed rapidly, much faster than traditional applications, as new protocols and extensions continuously influence the market.

The ability to easily apply security and functionality to your web services is very important, if you want to create cost-effective solutions through which web services and SOAP really add value to your business. To this end, we will discuss ways to extend SOAP in the following sections.

SOAP Headers

SOAP header elements are meant to extend SOAP communication with information that is not necessarily part of the message data, but is nevertheless required for processing the message, such as a transaction ID and user information and credentials.

The soapenv:Header element is an optional child element of soapenv:Envelope that can be used to convey such information in the form of application-defined child elements. Headers can be sent with the response/request messages to communicate information back and forth between the client and the service. One use of the SOAP header might be to put credentials in it, which will verify on the server side that the requester is allowed to use the server's resources:

```
<soapenv:Envelope
xmlns:xsi='http://www.w3.org/2001/XMLSchema-instance'
xmlns:xsd='http://www.w3.org/2001/XMLSchema'
xmlns:soapenv='http://schemas.xmlsoap.org/soap/envelope/'>
<soapenv:Header>
 <authInfo
  xmlns="http://schemas.mycomp.com/WSHeader">
   <uid>bond</uid>
 <pwd>james007</pwd>
 </authInfo>
</soapenv:Header>
...
</soapenv:Envelope>
```

Since this header information is defined by the application, a problem might arise when a client sends a header the service does not understand. In many cases, the sender must be certain that the application-defined SOAP headers added to a request really are understood by the receiver. To meet this requirement, SOAP defines a soapenv:mustUnderstand attribute that can be placed on a header element; if set to 1, the recipient must understand this header or send back a Soap fault element, indicating that it does not understand the header. The following code snippet shows you how to apply this attribute to the envelope with the application-defined headers shown previously, in order to ensure that the server understands the authInfo element:

```
<soapenv:Envelope
xmlns:xsi='http://www.w3.org/2001/XMLSchema-instance'
xmlns:xsd='http://www.w3.org/2001/XMLSchema'
xmlns:soapenv='http://schemas.xmlsoap.org/soap/envelope/'>
<soapenv:Header>
 <authInfo
  xmlns=http://schemas.mycomp.com/WSHeader soapenv:mustUndertand="1">
   <uid>bond</uid>
 <pwd>james007</pwd>
 </authInfo>
</soapenv:Header>
```

```
...
</soapenv:Envelope>
```

The attribute soapenv:mustUnderstand="1" tells the receiver it must understand this header. The receiver should send a fault message back to the caller if it does not understand the tag.

SOAP Extensions

Another way to extend the web services is to use the .NET feature called *SOAP extension functionality*. To get an idea of how this feature works, consider Figure 6-12.

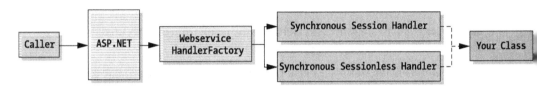

Figure 6-12. *The flow for a web request to your web service*

The ASP.NET engine handles the web service request from a caller. The ASP.NET engine instantiates the web service HandlerFactory and calls the getHandler method. This method will return an object (called handler in this example) that has implemented either the sync session handler or the sync sessionless handler interface, depending on the configuration of the chosen method of the web service. If the requested method uses sessions (for example, the attribute session =False is not set), the object returned from the web service handler factory is an object implementing the sync session handler interface. If the web method does not use sessions, the object returned would of course implement the sync sessionless handler interface.

This returned object is responsible for handling the incoming request, and may be the one that invokes your class, executes the method, and returns the result to the caller serialized in a SOAP message. We say that the Httphandler object *may* be the one that invokes your class, because at the point where this would happen, other possibilities could occur, as evidenced by the dotted arrows in Figure 6-12. This is the place where the SOAP extension will do its job. Here it is possible to plug in customized classes that process the web services request in any way you like. All you need to do in a class is to inherit System.Web.Services.Protocols.SoapExtension, and insert it along the request processing path between the HTTP handler and your web service. These classes make it possible to do pre- and post-processing of web service requests, such as authentications, usage counts, and the like. Since this occurs outside the real web service, this is a good place to implement infrastructure functions that seldom change over time (or at least less often than the content in the web service itself).

Let us dig into the structure of the SOAP extension and look at some examples showing what you can do with it. All SOAP Extension classes inherit system.Web.Services.Protocols.SoapExtension and override the base class's methods.

There are plenty of methods for the Extension class, but one of the most important (in our opinion the *most* important) is the ProcessMessage, shown in the following code:

```
Public MustOverride Sub ProcessMessage(ByVal message As _
System.Web.Services.Protocols.SoapMessage)
```

It is quite clear by its name what this method is intended to do, and that it is used frequently in processing web service messages. It is used four times in the normal processing of a message: twice for the request and twice for the response. You'll probably want to optimize this code as much as possible to keep the overhead down when using the Extension classes. So how do you know what you are processing at any given time, the request or the response? The parameter message has a property called Stage, which tells you at what stage the processing is occurring: BeforeDeserialize, AfterDeserialize, BeforeSerialize, and AfterSerialize.

- *BeforeDeserialize*. This stage occurs just before the request is deserialized from the message into the corresponding data types on the system.

- *AfterDeserialize*. AfterDeserialize is called directly after BeforeDeserialize. This is when the object is instantiated on the server and the requested method is executed.

- *BeforeSerialize*. This stage occurs just before the result from the executed method is serialized and sent back to the caller.

- *AfterSerialize*. Finally, this stage occurs when the result has been serialized into the return format.

Note One thing to remember is that for each web services request there is one instance of the Httphandler object created earlier. This means that the same object handles all the stages for one web service request.

Using SOAP Extensions to Implement Authorization for a Web Service

Now that you have the big picture of web service flow, the next step is to see what you can do with this information. The SOAP Extension class example in this section will demonstrate how to implement simple authorization functionality. You can dictate who should be able to access your valuable web service. In the "WSE and Security" section later in this chapter, we will take a look at WS-Security, WSE SDK, and how to implement authorization and authentication in web services. But until then, let us implement some security via the SOAP extension.

The first thing you'll want to know is when the request for a particular web service occurs so that you can later store this request somewhere that allows you to see when people have used your web service, as well as how many have tried to use it without permission. To achieve this we override the Initialize method and store the desired information in a local variable in the class. Remember, since all the stages are handled by one instance of this HTTP handler, all stages will be able to access this information:

```
Public Overrides Sub Initialize(ByVal initializer As Object)
    mstrTimeInitialized= System.Guid.NewGuid().ToString()
End Sub
```

When you need to do per-instance initialization, this is the place to put the code. Starting here, you insert the new Extension class into the web service stream between your class and the HTTP handler. There are two ways to use the new SOAP extension in your web services. To apply a SOAP extension to all web methods on all web services in a particular virtual root on the web server, you simply edit the virtual root's web.config file and add a reference to the SOAP extension by inserting the following into the web services section:

```
<soapExtensionTypes>
    <add type="WebExtensionTypeName,WebExtensionAssemblyName"
    priority="1" group="0"/>
</soapExtensionTypes>
```

The preceding type reference should be the fully qualified name of your SOAP Extension class, including the namespace. If your class is named MyNameSpace.SecurityExtension and located in an assembly called InfraSecurity.dll, then the type reference would be

```
Type=" MyNameSpace.SecurityExtension, InfraSecurity"
```

The priority attribute here specifies the priority used by the HTTP handler to decide in which order the Extension classes should be processed on the incoming request. If you have a security Extension class, you should process that one before any other extensions. The priority value is from 0 on up; the Extension class with a priority of 0 is processed first, and subsequent Extension classes are processed in ascending order. The group attribute gathers the types together, and the priority is applied on a per-group basis.

The second approach is to apply this SOAP extension to specified methods of the web service. To do this, you first need to create an attribute for the Extension class, and then set this attribute on the methods in the web service that you would like to monitor.

To create a custom attribute, you create a class that inherits from System.Web.Services.Protocols.SoapExtensionAttribute and override its two properties: ExtensionType and Priority.

ExtensionType is a read-only property that tells ASP.NET the SOAP extension's class type. Priority is a read-write property used to tell ASP.NET the extension's priority and, because it is writable, lets the developer using your SOAP extension specify the extension's priority. In Listing 6-7, the property is empty so as not to allow the user to change the priority order for this very important security extension.

Listing 6-7. *SOAP Extension Attribute Class*

```
<AttributeUsage(AttributeTargets.Method)> _
Public Class SecurityExtensionAttribute
    Inherits SoapExtensionAttribute

    Private Priority As Integer
    Private Permissions As String

    Public Sub New(ByVal RequestedPermissions As String)
        Permissions = RequestedPermissions
        Priority = 1
    End Sub
     Public Property Permissions() As String
        Get
            Return _Permissions
        End Get
        Set(ByVal Value As String)
```

```
            Permissions = Value
        End Set
    End Property
    Public Overrides Property Priority() As Integer
        Get
            Return Priority
        End Get
        Set(ByVal Value As Integer)
            'It is not possible to change the priority for this class.
        End Set
    End Property
    Public Overrides ReadOnly Property ExtensionType() As System.Type
        Get
            Return GetType(SecurityExtension)
        End Get
    End Property
End Class
```

Reading the Streams

The last thing we'll discuss here is how you can read the incoming stream in your Extension class, and how you can write to the outgoing stream. Access to the streams, both incoming and outgoing, is available in the function ChainStream located in your SOAP Extension class. This function includes the incoming stream as a parameter, and the return value of the function indicates the outgoing stream. Streams are chained: The output stream from the first SOAP extension becomes the input stream to the second SOAP extension. It is, however, important not to use the Stream object passed as parameter to the ChainStream directly. Instead, you should create an instance of the Stream object. Save the instance in a private member variable, copy the contents for the SOAP message to this private Stream object, and finally return the private instance to the calling program from the ChainStream method.

To summarize, the application should read from the incoming Stream object passed as a parameter and write to the outgoing Stream object, which is the return value from the function.

We will not dive deeper into SOAP extensions here, since we recommend in most cases that you instead use WS-Security, WS-Attachment, WS-Transaction, and WS-Routing, which will make it easier for you to create more sophisticated and flexible web services.

Handling Binary Data

Sending binary data via SOAP messages requires some special handling, since your message may contain only legal characters. In other words, you can't just put binary data in the body of a SOAP message and send it to the receiver. You can choose between several different methods for handling binary data, based on the size of the data and the nature of the application.

For binary content of relatively small size, you can encode the bits into a legal character representation using any encoding/decoding scheme that is convenient for your service and its clients. Base64, one such encoding scheme, is fairly widespread and available in many implementations. Both the .NET Framework and the SOAP Toolkit support Base64 encoding/decoding of data.

We recommend the use of Base64 instead of a homemade encoding scheme if you cannot use WS-Attachment. Because Base64 is so well known, it makes it easy for others to integrate your web services into their business. Despite the simplicity of Base64 encoding, we would like to encourage you to use the new WS-Attachment, which has the benefit of reducing overhead because the attachment does not need to be serialized/deserialized (and it is not harder to use, as you will see in section "WSE and Binary Attachments in DIME Format" later in this chapter).

■ **Note** Although Base64 encoding works well for content that is small (approximately less than 20KB), it becomes impractical for large content, such as images and files, because of the processing required to encode and decode content, and the significant increase in size of the encoded content compared to the original size. For instance, encrypting a SOAP response with WSE SDK (which uses Base64 encoding) increases the size by approximately 30 percent. As a rule, if the binary data that you would like to send together with the SOAP message is larger than approximately 20KB, use the WSE and binary attachment in DIME format instead.

Handling Attachments

The SOAP with Direct Internet Message Encapsulation (DIME) attachments specification defines how a SOAP message can be transmitted along with arbitrary binary content, such as images and files in their original format, all combined into one document. This document, called a *Multipurpose Internet Mail Extensions (MIME)* document, contains several parts. One part contains the SOAP message, and each binary content item has a unique content ID. MIME, on the market for several years, has some drawbacks. You need to traverse through the data stream to be able to find the headers for each binary message. This makes it slower compared to the DIME specification discussed later in this chapter. DIME takes the best of MIME and tries to simplify it. For instance, the header of a DIME message contains the encoding type, the length of the header, and the payload. This makes it possible to jump between the different headers in the binary message without reading the actual data. In .NET, it's easy to handle attachments by using the WSE SDK and its support for DIME, as you will soon see in the section "WSE and Binary Attachments in DIME Format."

WS-I Specifications and Support for Security

Many new specifications are being developed that will help you solve many of the problems that have existed in the past in the traditional client server environment.

Problems involving transaction and security issues will be easier to handle with a collection of new specifications named WS-I. Some of the specifications this collection includes are as follows:

- *WS-Attachment*. Represents a framework for sending binary attachments.

- *WS-Coordination*. Helps you coordinate distributed transactions.

- *WS-Inspection*. Defines how to find web services and determine their functions.

- *WS-Referral*. Provides support to find alternative paths for messages.

- *WS-Routing*. Defines a message path, and is, together with WS-Referral, very powerful for the next generation of web services.

- *WS-Security*. Makes it easier for you to use secure calls and add authentication and authorization to your web services.

- *WS-Transaction*. Serves as a definition of how to support transactions via web services and distributed applications.

Previously we gave a hint on how to use the SOAP extension to add security and authorization functionality to web services. Soon we will explore WS-Security and see how it lets you handle security issues in an even easier way—but first we want to give you a short overview of what WS-Security is.

WS-Security functions as a dependable framework for message authentication, integrity, and confidentiality by relying on the XML Encryption, XML Signature, and Security Assertion Markup Language (SAML) specifications. Although these specifications on their own provide security to a service when being accessed by a requestor, WS-Security groups them together in a more convenient and useful way.

When using only the specifications just mentioned to include a combination of signatures, encryption information, and authentication information in a SOAP message, no information about the sequence of processing these steps is included. In other words, the lack of an indicator for the order in which the message was processed makes it possible for the corresponding functions to fail on the server side. WS-Security addresses this and includes security headers for storing all the preceding information, and it specifies the order in which the security information needs to be processed.

WS-Security headers can also be used to specify information intended for a specific node or destination in a multi-sequence situation, where the caller and the service need to separate encryption, signing, and authentication on different services.

Until WS-Security appeared, no standardized mechanism for passing authentication information in web service messages existed. Some web services have solved the security issues by using SSL with client authentication, HTTP Basic/Digest, and NTLM for authenticating messages—for example, transport authentications. Others have added SOAP parameters for passing login data in the SOAP header, or in the body itself, with an implicit contract between the client and the server for understanding of these parameters. We previously showed how to use the SOAP extensions to add authorization to web services. We hardly need to say that this is inconvenient from an administrative point of view, because it requires managing the specification of the extra parameters and broadcasting these specifications to all new users of the web service.

The downside of using SSL and Transport Layer Security is that you do not know if forthcoming nodes in the routing chain will handle the SOAP message over secure connections. Therefore, you are dependent on all nodes to handle the message in a secure way. This is irrelevant when you have a single start point and endpoint where you have control over the transport layer; but as soon as your web services are rerouted by other servers or third parties, you can't be sure that they all are using SSL to secure your data. As we said before, using the WS-I specification can help you to secure the information in the message, and this does not occur on the transport protocol level.

By moving security from the transport layer into the SOAP message, security is guaranteed to follow the message from its source to its destination, no matter what kind of transport layer is used.

Standard security tokens such as Binary tokens (X509 certificates, Kerberos tickets) and XML tokens (SAML) are being introduced by WS-Security for passing information.

One component of WS-Security, XML Signatures, gives you the ability to sign your messages using enveloping signatures, enveloped signatures, or detached signatures.

When you sign a message, you decide the algorithms, key and certification passing mechanisms, and transformation algorithms for determining the target of the signatures to use, according to the WS-Security specification recommendations. When signing multiple SOAP parts using the same key, we encourage you to define the public key for verifying the message only once within the message. To do so, you would reference a Binary token for an X509 certificate. This reduces the overhead of using security in the SOAP message.

Another component of the WS-Security framework gives you the ability to keep the message you are sending confidential. Keeping SOAP messages private is important for an application though when such messages, which could contain confidential information, are sent over the Internet. To prevent people from reading the information when it travels down the line, SOAP messages can be encrypted. The encryption in use is specified in security headers in the SOAP message.

This specification allows for the encryption of any combination of body blocks, headers, and attachments, either by symmetric keys, asymmetric keys, or keys placed in messages in encrypted form. In order to handle this flexibility, you use the XML Encryption standard. (What you're really doing is adding a security part to your SOAP header.)

Finally, when the message has arrived at its destination, you should find some way to ensure that the content is valid at the time of arrival. This capability is supported in WS-Security by letting SOAP security information be valid for a specific time, through Kerberos service tickets or SAML assertions. WS-Security also provides standard timestamp headers that can be used for determining the validity of the message. It is thereby possible to specify a date for the message when it is no longer valid to use its content. An order or an offer, for instance, may not be valid after a specific date due to changes in currencies. Another issue is that replay attacks may be detected by using a signed timestamp.

Even security functions can fail. Therefore WS-Security provides standardized error fault codes that can be used to propagate error information while processing security headers—for example, authentication failures or missing security information. As noted, WS-Security leverages and enhances many existing specifications, so security information can be created and processed in a more standardized manner. This is useful in providing the next level of web services interoperability.

Web Services Enhancements (WSE) SDK

The standards of web services—XML, SOAP, XSL, XSD, WSDL, and UDDI—provide enough features to build simple solutions. But when you want to build more complex solutions, the standard web services functionality is not enough to handle the complex integrations that exist in many applications today. For instance, there are no standard approaches (until now) for building secure web services besides using the transport layer support of security, such as SSL.

Security is only one of many issues that standard web services do not address fully. Another issue is the lack of architecture structure for handling the routing of messages, such as ensuring reliable delivery, coordinating in distributed networks, or using compensation transactions. Until now, it hasn't been a standard solution.

To achieve this, IBM, Microsoft, and others have started to write architecture protocols that describe ways to implement these needs. Microsoft has released an implementation of a subset of these architecture protocols. The first version of this WSE SDK focuses on the basic message-level protocols: WS-Security, WS-Routing, and finally DIME and WS-Attachment.

Since the first version of WSE, Microsoft has released two more of them. The first version was mainly to show how to implement some of the specifications into practical classes, the later ones tied the different specifications together in an efficient way.

WSE 2.0 added support for WS-Policy, WS-Trust and role-based security.

WSE 3.0 made the policy handling even easier. Microsoft also added support for using the WSE 3.0 kit from Visual Studio 2005. The main goal for web services is to handle the security issues outside the code by using policies. By doing so we don't need to recompile the code (which can introduce new bugs) when we want to release our intranet web services for internet access. All we need to do is to deploy our dll:s to the internet web server and change the policy files.

The support for WS-SecureConversation, that WSE 2.0 implemented, has now in version 3.0 been improved to even work in web farms (which is necessary since today most of our enterprise solutions are implemented in web farms and NLB).

If a session in WSE 2.0 was broken, the application needed to initialize a new connection. In WSE 3.0, the session can simply be reestablished. In WSE 3.0 we can also cancel a session, which makes the handling of web service sessions more manageable.

We also have an option of support for sending large amount of binary data by supporting the SOAP Message Transmission Optimization Mechanism (MTOM) specification.

Finally, like the .NET Framework 2.0, WSE 3.0 allows a developer to choose between the SOAP 1.1 and SOAP 1.2 protocols.

WSE is very powerful because it is closely wrapped around the message model and manipulates the protocol headers directly. WSE gives you the ability to use the specifications in an easy and object-oriented way through various classes.

WSE is an engine that applies advanced web service protocols to SOAP messages. This can be simple things, like timestamps, or more complex operations, like encrypting or decrypting the body of the SOAP message.

WSE functionality is encapsulated into two types of filters: filters for incoming messages and filters for outgoing messages. As shown in Figure 6-13, all messages leaving a process are dealt with using the outbound message filters. The inbound message filters deal with all messages that are entering a process.

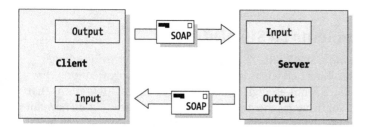

Figure 6-13. *The input and output filters used for applying the WS-Security implementation*

The filters in Figure 6-13 are classes (SOAP extensions) attached to the incoming and outgoing pipes for SOAP messages on the server and client. They are accessible through a new proxy class called Microsoft.Web.Services.WebServicesClientProtocol and are an extension of the default base class for web service proxies, System.Web._Services.SoapHttpClientProtocol. This new proxy class makes it possible for the WSE extension to process the incoming and outgoing SOAP messages whenever a client invokes one of the proxy's methods. In order to use WSE, you must change the base class of each of your proxies to use WebServicesClientProtocol. This is necessary regardless of whether you generate your proxy code using the wsdl.exe command-line tool, Visual Studio .NET Add Web Reference, or Update Web Reference commands.

The WebServicesClientProtocol proxy base class uses two new communication classes named Microsoft.Web.Services.SoapWebRequest and Microsoft.Web._Services.SoapWebResponse. These classes are in turn derived from the standard WebRequest and WebResponse classes.

All input filters and output filters are chained together. The result from the first input filter is the next input filter's input. The same goes for the output filters.

The behavior of an input filter (a SoapWebRequest) is very simple. It parses the outgoing SOAP message stream with a standard XML DOM API into an instance of the SoapEnvelope class. Then, it passes it to the next output filter in the chain. Normally an output or input filter modifies or reads the header of the SOAP envelope. Sometimes though, the content in the body is also altered—for instance, when you are working with security issues and encrypting or decrypting the body content.

A SoapContext class controls the behavior of the input and output filters. Each instance of the SoapContext class records a specific protocol option. This can be usernames, digital certificates, signatures, and creation and/or expiration timestamps using a simple object model. It is possible to access SoapContext for a particular SoapResponse via its property SoapContext. The process of a SoapResponse instance is specified in its SoapContext instance. Figure 6-14 illustrates the complete flow for an incoming SOAP message and the SoapResponse and SoapContext positions in the SOAP chain.

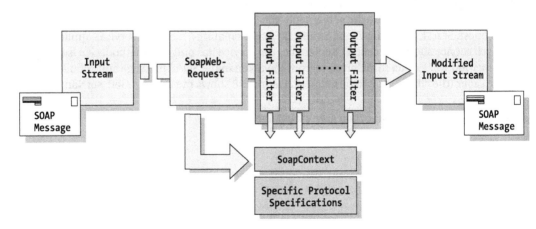

Figure 6-14. *The complete flow for SoapWebRequest processing*

However, you seldom need to tap into the pipe and manipulate the output and input filters directly. As shown in Figure 6-15, the WebServicesClientProtocol encapsulates these and exposes them as the properties RequestSoapContext and ResponseSoapContext, both of type SoapContext.

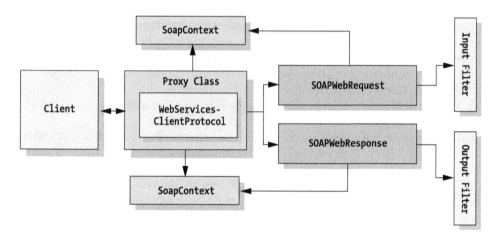

Figure 6-15. *The complete client architecture with the new web services client protocol*

It is time to show you how to use the WebServicesClientProtocol to hook into the process pipeline of incoming and outgoing SOAP messages. Because our example will be a simple one, it doesn't represent the best approach for sending username and passwords, due to the lack of encryption for the information. What we demonstrate here is the simplicity of using the WebServicesClientProtocol to add a username and a password in a security token to the header of the SOAP message. We will then show you how to extract the username and password from the server side and echo the username back to the client.

The first step is to create the server-side web service that will extract the username from the request. Start by opening Visual Studio .NET and creating a new web services application. The web service should be called UserService. The service has only one method: GetUserName. This method will extract the username from the token in the SOAP message and echo it back to the caller (the client, soon to be created). Listing 6-8 shows the method GetUserName.

Listing 6-8. *The GetUserName Function: <WebMethod()> _*

```
Public Function GetUserName() As String
    Dim userName As String
    Dim reqCtx As SoapContext = HttpSoapContext.RequestContext
    Dim token As Security.SecurityToken
    For Each token In reqCtx.Security.Tokens
        If TypeOf token Is Security.UsernameToken Then
            userName = CType(token, Security.UsernameToken).Username
            Exit For
        End If
```

```
        Next
        If userName.Length = 0 Then
            'Not a valid username
            Throw New Exception("No username found.")
        Else
            'Return username to caller
            Return userName
        End If
    End Function
```

The first thing that is done here is to retrieve a reference to the request context. The request context is the incoming pipe on the server and is actually a static lookup in the HttpContextItems collection, with the key RequestSoapContext and ResponseSoapContext. Then all security tokens (in the incoming request) are iterated over, and the current token is checked to see if it is of type UsernameToken (in the client, a username token is added to the security tokens with a username and password). When the username token is found, the application extracts the username from the token. Finally, the function checks whether the username is empty or not. The console application that will use the web service needs a web reference to it.

WSE and Security

One of the main goals of the WSE SDK is to make using the more secure web services easier. In the previous example, you saw that it is quite easy to tap into the SOAP pipelines to read and write information. This is just what the web Service Enhancements does when it adds security information to your web services. You are not restricted to using only the underlying transport protocol support for security. Instead, you can now easily code security into your SOAP messages. The WSE SDK sits on top of the .NET Framework. The heart of WSE is the Microsoft.Web.Services .SoapContext class that provides you with an interface for reading the WS-Security header and other headers for incoming SOAP messages, and adding or modifying WS-Security and other headers for outgoing SOAP messages.

The first thing you need to do is to configure WSE to work correctly with your web services— this involves configuring your ASP.NET application to use the WSE SOAP extension. As with all .NET applications and .NET security, it is possible to apply security settings at different levels, including the machine level, application level, and user level. We strongly advise you to apply the WSE SDK at application level, since other applications on the server may not benefit from the WSE SDK, but remember that there is a performance hit when you include WSE in the SOAP chain. To use WSE SDK from an existing web application, you need to add the /configuration/ system.Web/WebServices/soapExtensionTypes/Add element to the web.config file. This element will look similar to this example:

```
<webServices>
  <soapExtensionTypes>
    <add type="Microsoft.Web.Services.WebServicesExtension,
        Microsoft.Web.Services, Version=1.0.0.0, Culture=neutral,
        PublicKeyToken=31bf3656ad464e55" priority="1" group="0" />
  </soapExtensionTypes>
</webServices>
```

This is the minimum effort you need to make to be able to use the WSE SDK from your web service. What you're actually doing through this code is adding a WebServicesExtension to the web application (the virtual directory). This acts as an ISAPI filter in IIS. ISAPI filters can have different priorities. By setting the attribute priority to 1, you ensure that the ISAPI filter has the highest priority and will be processed first when a request comes into the web application.

Before you can continue, you'll need to know some security basics—in particular, you must have an understanding of digital signatures. Validating the integrity of a digitally-signed message from Dr. Evil when you expected it to come from Miss Nice doesn't give you much protection. Therefore we will introduce you to username tokens and how you can use them from WSE.

A username token is defined in WS-Security to allow simple username/_password valida-tions. The username token and its use is similar to the basic authentication found in HTTP traffic. The different forms of username tokens are displayed in Listing 6-9.

Listing 6-9. *The Different Username Tokens*

```
<!-- No Password -->
<UsernameToken>
  <Username>Steve</Username>
</UsernameToken>
<!-- Clear Text Password -->
<UsernameToken>
  <Username>Steve</Username>
  <Password Type="wsse:PasswordText">Opensezme</Password>
</UsernameToken>
<!-- Digest: SHA1 hash of base64-encoded Password -->
<UsernameToken>
  <Username>Steve</Username>
  <Password Type="wsse:PasswordDigest">
    QSMAKo67+vzYnU9TcMSqOFXy14U=
  </Password>
</UsernameToken>
```

The first form of username token does not include any password and is used only for simple identification. The second one sends the password in clear text, which is not a wise solution in a real application. The last one sends a digest (hashed version) of the password. The good thing about the last solution is that the password is never sent over the wire—the bad is that Dr. Evil can take this hashed password and resend it.

To avoid this problem, you can specify that the hashed password should be sent together with a unique string that identifies this request. The digest sent is a combination of this *number used once*, or *nonce*, and the password:

```
<!-- Revised UsernameToken -->
<wsse:UsernameToken
    xmlns:wsu="http://schemas.mycomp.com/ws/2003/01"
    wsu:Id="SecurityToken-13564463-5bdc-4a6b-a7fb-94a0d7357a20">
  <wsse:Username>Steve</wsse:Username>
  <wsse:Password Type="wsse:PasswordDigest">
    gpBDXjx79eutcXdtlULIlcrSiRs=
  </wsse:Password>
```

```
<wsse:Nonce>
  h56sI9pKVOBVRPUolQC8Sg==
</wsse:Nonce>
<wsu:Created>2003-02-04T19:13:30Z</wsu:Created>
</wsse:UsernameToken>
```

Even if you now have a nonce unique for each request, Dr. Evil may still take the whole username token and put it into his own request. This can be avoided by setting the timestamp expiration (another feature in WSE) to a short duration that is just enough time for the message to be handled on the server. The server will then refuse requests older than the expiration time. This is not the optimal solution, however, as clock differences between the sender and the server may cause some trouble. To be even safer, the server can keep a list of recently used nonces and reject requests if the same nonce is used again. Since you do not know if the first request or the second one is the original, you need to ignore both requests. The use of username tokens with a hashed password requires that the sender and the server know the user's password. On the sender side, the user has probably entered his or her password, but on the server side you use the password provider found in WSE. The password provider has an interface, Microsoft.Web.Services.Security.IpasswordProvider, which a class should implement in order to register as a password provider. The interface has only one function—GetPassword—and takes UsernameToken as an input parameter. The GetPassword function returns the password for the user in UsernameToken. The idea is that you should be able to store passwords and usernames in any way you like, and then create a class used by WSE to retrieve passwords. In order to let WSE take advantage of your new password provider class, you need to add some configuration to your config file on the application level, as in this example:

```
<configSections>
  <section name="microsoft.web.services"
    type="Microsoft.Web.Services.Configuration.WebServicesConfiguration,
    Microsoft.Web.Services, Version=1.0.0.0, Culture=neutral,
    PublicKeyToken=32bf3856ad364e344" />
</configSections>
```

Remember that the type attribute should be on one line, but we have broken it into several lines here for readability. Then you should add something similar to the following in your web.config file code for enabling your password provider class for WSE:

```
<microsoft.web.services>
  <security>
    <!-- This is the class that will provide
         the password hashes for the UsernameToken signatures. -->
    <passwordProvider
        type=" WS-NameSpace.PasswordProvider, My_WS_Security" />
  </security>
</microsoft.web.services>
```

The type attribute contains the class (PasswordProvider) that you have written in your namespace WS-NameSpace. The namespace is found in My_WS_Security.dll.

The code for your password provider class is very simple:

```
Namespace WS-NameSpace
    public class PasswordProvider
    inherits IPasswordProvider

        public Function GetPassword(token as UsernameToken) as String
                return "mypassword"
        end sub
    End class
End Namespace
```

Well, the previous solution may work in many cases—but here you are dealing with Dr. Evil. He is able to tap your line for incoming requests, take a username token, and use it in his own requests—hence there will only be one nonce with a valid timestamp! To avoid this security problem, you need to digitally sign your requests.

It is quite easy to digitally sign a SOAP message with WSE. To be able to digitally sign a SOAP request, you must have a certificate. In a traditional Windows environment, the certificates are stored in a certificate store. Each user has a private certificate store where the user's public certificate, the public key, and the private key are stored. A user signs a SOAP request with its private key, and then the server can use the public key in the certificate for verification. In WSE, you can use Microsoft.Web.Services.Security.X509 to access the installed certificate in a user's certificate store. The function CurrentUserStore is used to retrieve an object of type X509CertificateStore that contains the current user's certificate store. The X509CertificateStore object has a collection (Certificates) containing all certificates for the current user.

Now that you know how to retrieve the available certificate, you can use it in your SOAP request. The following code takes the first certificate and adds it to the request context:

```
X509Certificate cert = (X509Certificate)store.Certificates[0];
proxy.RequestSoapContext.Security.Tokens.Add(new X509SecurityToken(cert));
```

Listing 6-10 presents the server-side code to retrieve the added certificate from the SOAP request.

Listing 6-10. *The Server-Side Code to Retrieve Certificates from the SOAP Request*

```
[WebMethod]
public string PersonalHello()
{
    // Only accept SOAP requests
    SoapContext requestContext = HttpSoapContext.RequestContext;
    if (requestContext == null)
    {
        throw new ApplicationException("Non-SOAP request.");
    }
    // We only allow requests with one security token
    if (requestContext.Security.Tokens.Count == 1)
    {
        foreach (SecurityToken tok in requestContext.Security.Tokens)
        {
            // Only accept X.509 Certificates
```

```
            if (tok is X509SecurityToken)
            {
                X509SecurityToken certToken = (X509SecurityToken)tok;
                return "Hello " + certToken.Certificate.GetName();
            }
            else
            {
                throw new SoapException(
                    "X.509 security token required.",
                    SoapException.ClientFaultCode);
            }
        }
    }
    else
    {
        throw new SoapException(
            "Request must have exactly one security token.",
            SoapException.ClientFaultCode);
    }
    return null;
}
```

Only adding a certificate to a request doesn't automatically sign the request. Anyone can add a certificate to your request. What you need to do is use the certificate to digitally sign your request (or part of it) with your private key, and then let the server side validate your request with the certificate you have brought with the request. Normally, you would not include the certificate in all requests to the server because it is a performance hit to send it with every request. More likely you will store the public certificate on the server to be able to retrieve it when a request arrives. Here, however, we will show you how to send it with the request to complete our example. To digitally sign a SOAP request, you need to take advantage of another collection, SoapContext.Security.Elements, in which you put a Signature element. Building from the previous client code that included a digital certificate, you can now use that same certificate to sign the request. The code to do this is shown here:

```
X509Certificate cert = (X509Certificate)store.Certificates[listBox1.SelectedIndex];
X509SecurityToken certToken = new X509SecurityToken(cert);
proxy.RequestSoapContext.Security.Tokens.Add(certToken);
proxy.RequestSoapContext.Security.Elements.Add(new Signature(certToken));
```

When you have applied the digitally-signed information and the certificate to a SOAP message, the result looks something like Listing 6-11 (the message is cleaned up to show only the parts we are going to discuss later).

Listing 6-11. *A Digitally Signed SOAP Message*

```
<?XML version="1.0" encoding="utf-8"?>
<soap:Envelope
    xmlns:soap="http://schemas.xmlsoap.org/soap/envelope/"
    xmlns:xsi="http://www.w3.org/2001/XMLSchema-instance"
```

```
     xmlns:xsd="http://www.w3.org/2001/XMLSchema">
 <soap:Header>
   <wsrp:path
        soap:actor="http://schemas.xmlsoap.org/soap/actor/next"
        soap:mustUnderstand="1"
        xmlns:wsrp="http://schemas.xmlsoap.org/rp">
     <wsrp:action
         wsu:Id=" Id-c126ad70-7a1b-4895-a05c-5f6596ca1421"
             ...
   </wsrp:path>
             ...
   <wsse:Security
        soap:mustUnderstand="1"
        xmlns:wsse="http://schemas.xmlsoap.org/ws/2002/07/secext">
     <wsse:BinarySecurityToken
         ValueType="wsse:X509v3"
         EncodingType="wsse:Base64Binary"
         xmlns:wsu="http://schemas.xmlsoap.org/ws/2002/07/utility"
         wsu:Id="SecurityToken-f6f96b4b-23c5-421e-92ff-f1050d531e82">
       MIIFezCDBXugAwIBAgID  . . .  29Vmjd10Lw==
     </wsse:BinarySecurityToken>
     <Signature xmlns="http://www.w3.org/2000/09/xmldsig#">
       <SignedInfo>
         <CanonicalizationMethod
             Algorithm="http://www.w3.org/2001/10/XML-exc-c14n#" />
         <SignatureMethod
             Algorithm="http://www.w3.org/2000/09/xmldsig#rsa-sha1" />
         <Reference URI="#Id-14cc3130-6f1a-23fe-a949-51d7ed9fc111">
           <Transforms>
             <Transform
                 Algorithm="http://www.w3.org/2001/10/XML-exc-c14n#" />
           </Transforms>
           <DigestMethod
               Algorithm="http://www.w3.org/2000/09/xmldsig#sha1" />
           <DigestValue>
             /8iL3OP9mfzuixI/ilkhHMbatVO=
           </DigestValue>
         </Reference>
         <Reference URI="#Id-c126ad70-7a1b-4895-a05c-5f6596ca1421">
           <Transforms>
                ...
       </SignedInfo>
       <SignatureValue>
       ZX4MgHzCYz+CCdAz1LhAFjy6QxQoKKoA7l2eC45QVOhDI
       JrmXwLEGrPnpX+uPan5+MS6hm+oL/sGTbKJ/DJMp/t5Zy
       qY1qvngGQLcYXRy538zemwFfeGN5R2wmOoUSeCBUqprQV
       Ubnkz+qlVp/5f7t7VGD3Ee55Q3ol+ApFoGQD=
       </SignatureValue>
```

```
        <KeyInfo>
          <wsse:SecurityTokenReference>
            <wsse:Reference
    URI="#SecurityToken-f6f96b4b-23c5-421e-92ff-f1050d531e82" />
          </wsse:SecurityTokenReference>
        </KeyInfo>
      </Signature>
    </wsse:Security>
  </soap:Header>
  <soap:Body
      wsu:Id="Id-14cc3130-6f1a-23fe-a949-51d7ed9fc111"
      xmlns:wsu="http://schemas.xmlsoap.org/ws/2002/07/utility">
    <PersonalHello xmlns="http://tempuri.org/" />
  </soap:Body>
</soap:Envelope>
```

Yes, it's a big message, but we will help you to figure out what the different parts do.

The first interesting part is in the security header, which contains a Base64-encoded element. This is the X509SecurityToken that was added to the Tokens collection in the last example. You do not actually need to include it in the request (and you certainly shouldn't when the number of SOAP messages sent is high, since it makes the request larger than necessary), but we have provided it here to smooth out the verification.

The second interesting thing in the security part is the Signature element in the security header. There are three different child elements within the Signature element: SignedInfo, SignatureValue, and KeyInfo. The SignedInfo element describes the parts of the SOAP message that are digitally signed, how it is being encoded, and what algorithm is being used for computing the signature. The reference elements are the elements in the request that are signed. The first one has the URI that is later found in the body—the body is thereby digitally signed. The URIs found in the reference list are the signed ones. These can be any kind of element. The second reference you have is to the action part in the path header. WSE automatically includes the path and the timestamp headers in the digitally-signed part. The following is a list of the elements that WSE will reference in the SignedInfo header and thus will be included in the digital signature:

/soap:Envelope/soap:Header/wsrp:path/wsrp:action

/soap:Envelope/soap:Header/wsrp:path/wsrp:to

/soap:Envelope/soap:Header/wsrp:path/wsrp:from

/soap:Envelope/soap:Header/wsrp:path/wsrp:id

/soap:Envelope/soap:Header/wsu:Timestamp/wsu:Created

/soap:Envelope/soap:Header/wsu:Timestamp/wsu:Expires

/soap:Envelope/soap:Body

The complete path and timestamp headers are signed because they are used in the WS-Routing definition and need to be "protected" to be sure that messages are routed the correct way (so that no one hijacks a message and reroutes it to another destination).

The last thing in the Signature element is the KeyInfo part, which has a reference back to the BinarySecurityToken that contains your certificate. The public key for your certificate can then be used to verify that your message comes from a person who knows the certificate's private key (probably the owner).

The final step is to verify that the message actually comes from the person who owns the certificate that is used to digitally sign the incoming SOAP message to the server. Obviously you need to verify that the body part is digitally signed with the certificate—it's not enough to verify that the message is digitally signed. It may only be the path and timestamp headers that are digitally signed—the rest of the message might be altered. To verify that the body of the message is digitally signed by the right certificate, you need to add the code shown in Listing 6-12 to your web service.

Listing 6-12. *The Code to Verify the Digitally Signed SOAP Body*

```
[WebMethod]
public string PersonalHello()
{
    // Only accept SOAP requests
    SoapContext requestContext = HttpSoapContext.RequestContext;
    if (requestContext == null)
    {
        throw new ApplicationException("Non-SOAP request.");
    }
    // Look for Signatures in the Elements collection
    foreach (Object elem in requestContext.Security.Elements)
    {
        if (elem is Signature)
        {
            Signature sign = (Signature)elem;
            // Verify that signature signs the body of the request
            if (sign != null
                && (sign.SignatureOptions &
                    SignatureOptions.IncludeSoapBody) != 0)
            {
                // Determine what kind of token is used
                // with the signature.
                if (sign.SecurityToken is UsernameToken)
                {
                    return "Hello " +
                        ((UsernameToken)sign.SecurityToken).Username;
                }
                else if (sign.SecurityToken is X509SecurityToken)
                {
                    return "Hello " +
                        ((X509SecurityToken)sign.SecurityToken)
                        .Certificate.GetName();
                }
            }
        }
```

```
        }
    }
    // No approriate signature found
    throw new SoapException("No valid signature found",
        SoapException.ClientFaultCode);
}
```

To protect yourself from different kinds of attacks from Dr. Evil, we recommend you use WS-Security. To sum up: Reply attacks are handled by using expiration timestamps in the SOAP messages together with tracking of the requests. The man-in-the-middle attack is mitigated by using X509 certificates with a digital signature that the receiver verifies via a Certification Authority (CA), which in turn is trusted by both sides to verify the public key that is in use. You should also encrypt the content of the message to make it difficult for Dr. Evil to read your message.

We recommend that you sign and encrypt all your data in any SOAP message that needs to be protected from alteration.

In the previous example, the complete body was signed, but sometimes you may only want to sign specific parts of information in the body. This can be done by using SignatureOptions in the Signature element. SignatureOptions tells WSE what parts of the message should be digitally signed. The different values for SignatureOptions are as follows:

- IncludeNone

- IncludePath

- IncludePathAction

- IncludePathFrom

- IncludePathId

- IncludePathTo

- IncludeSoapBody

- IncludeTimestamp

- IncludeTimestampCreated

- IncludeTimestampExpires

You can combine these to get the parts you want signed. IncludeNone gives you the ability to sign only the parts of the body (or anything else) that you want to be signed in the message. WS-Security specifies that there are two ways to define what should be signed in the message. The first one is to define a transformation of the message and then create a signature of the result. This is not implemented in the WSE SDK from Microsoft. The second way is to mark all elements that should be signed with their own ID and put these IDs in the reference part of the SignedInfo portion of the Signature element. This is how WSE has implemented support for partially signed messages. We are going to look at an example in which only a portion of the SOAP body is signed by adding an ID to the part to be signed. To follow this example, you first create a web service that will return some account information.

It is very important that you use the right namespace for the property of the class that will be serialized to an XML attribute that matches the namespace in the WS-Security specification; use the Namespace parameter of the XmlAttribute attribute to set it to http://schemas.xmlsoap.org/ws/2002/07/utility:

```
public class AccountNum
{
    [XmlAttribute("Id",
    Namespace="http://schemas.xmlsoap.org/ws/2002/07/utility")]
    //Line above is very important!!!!
    public string ID;
    [XmlText]
    public string AccountNumber;
}
```

This class will be used in the following code, which serializes an instance of the class, generates a GUID for the ID, puts the ID in the SignedInfo portion, signs the message (for example, the ID attribute), and finally returns the message to the client.

You need to be able to access the local certificate store from ASP.NET where your web service is hosted. To be able to do this, permit the ASP.NET user (normally the one under which the ISAPI filter for ASP.NET is running) to access the local certificate store. In real-world applications, this isn't so good from a security point of view, however. Other applications may then be able to read your certificates! But we'll include this process here, since the main purpose of this example is to show how you can partially sign a SOAP response. Now when you have a security token, you can create an instance of the signature passing in your token in the constructor. The first thing you should do is set SignatureOptions to IncludeNone to define the parts of the message that should be signed by you. Finally, add a reference to your ID, shown previously, and send in the generated GUID by using the function AddReference on the Signature object, as demonstrated in Listing 6-13. The # indicates that it is a local reference in the same message.

Listing 6-13. *Adding a Certificate to Your SOAP Message*

```
[WebMethod]
public AccountNum Get AccountNum ()
{
    SoapContext responseContext = HttpSoapContext.ResponseContext;
    AccountNum Acc = new AccountNum ();
    Guid referenceID = Guid.NewGuid();
    Acc.ID = "Id:" + referenceID.ToString();
    Acc.PONumber = "Acc123";
    X509CertificateStore store =
        X509CertificateStore.LocalMachineStore(
            X509CertificateStore.MyStore);
    store.OpenRead();
    X509Certificate cert
        = store.FindCertificateBySubjectName(
```

```
            "CN = bill.summerland.corp.msdotnet.nu")[0];
    X509SecurityToken token = new X509SecurityToken(cert);
    responseContext.Security.Tokens.Add(token);
    Signature sig = new Signature(token);
    sig.SignatureOptions = SignatureOptions.IncludeNone;
    // The # indicates a local reference.
    sig.AddReference(new Reference("#" + Acc.ID));
    responseContext.Security.Elements.Add(sig);
    return Acc;
}
```

The client code used to verify that it is the right certificate, and that the right person has signed the account ID in the returned message, appears in Listing 6-14.

Listing 6-14. *The Client Code to Retrieve the X509 Certificate from the SOAP Message*

```
localhost.Service1Wse proxy = new localhost.Service1Wse();
localhost. AccountNum Acc = proxy.GetAccountNum();
foreach (Object element in proxy.ResponseSoapContext.Security.Elements)
{
    if (element is Signature)
    {
        Signature sig = (Signature)element;
        foreach (Reference reference in sig.SignedInfo.References)
        {
            if (reference.Uri == "#" + Acc.Id)
            {
                X509Certificate signatureCert
                    = ((X509SecurityToken) sig.SecurityToken).Certificate;
                if (signatureCert.Equals(poCert))
                    MessageBox.Show("Whow - It's signed!");
            }
        }
    }
}
```

WSE and Binary Attachments in DIME Format

When you want to send large attachments to SOAP messages, it's often inconvenient to encode them in standard Base64 encoding. Instead, you likely want to send them as binary attachments. There are still some problems involved, though, such as how to handle these binary packages and tell the receiver the total number of packages included in such a request, so that you can enable the receiver to know when all data has been retrieved successfully. The solution to this problem is to use the DIME format and pack the information into data packets (see Figure 6-16).

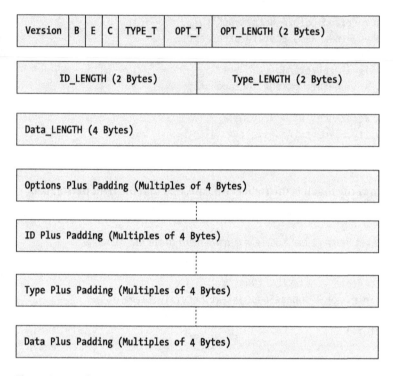

Figure 6-16. *The DIME structure*

The first five bits contain the DIME version number. This number is used by DIME to determine whether it can parse the DIME message successfully or not. If the parser does not support the DIME version, the DIME message is deleted. The SOAP Toolkit supports DIME version 1. The B (Beginning) flag indicates the start of the DIME record. The first DIME record in a DIME message has this bit set to one, while the rest of the records in the DIME message have this bit set to zero. The E (End) flag indicates the last DIME record in the DIME message. This is zero for every DIME record in the DIME message, except for the last one. Since a binary stream can be chunked over several DIME records, the C (Chunky) flag specifies whether the current DIME record is part of a chunky block. This is set to one if the current DIME record is part of a chunky block. The TYPE_T block is a 4-bit field that indicates the structure of the value of the type field. This field can contain the following values:

- 0x00 indicates that the type is unchanged from the previous record (used for chunking DIME records).

- 0x01 indicates the type is specified as a MIME media type.

- 0x02 indicates the type is specified as an absolute URI.

- 0x03 indicates the type is not specified.

- 0x04 indicates the record has no payload.

Additional fields in the DIME record include the following:

- OPT_T is a 4-bit field that indicates the format of the option bytes. A value of zero indicates that there is no option present. The current version of SOAP does not support any DIME record options.

- OPT_LENGTH is a 16-bit field that indicates the length of the options in octets, without any padding.

- ID_LENGTH is a 16-bit field that specifies the length (in bytes) of the ID field in the DIME record. The ID field stores the unique ID of the payload and the ID_LENGTH field is always a multiple of 4 bytes.

- TYPE_LENGTH is a 16-bit field that provides the length (in bytes) of the TYPE field of the DIME record.

- DATA_LENGTH is a 32-bit field that specifies the length of the DATA field in the DIME record.

- OPTIONS carries the actual value of the options. The length of this field must be a multiple of 4 bytes. If the OPTIONS value is not a multiple of 4 bytes, padding is used. The OPT_LENGTH field provides the length of the OPTIONS value, but does not include the padding used.

- The ID field provides the unique ID value (a URI) of the attachment in the record. The ID_LENGTH field of the DIME record specifies the length of this field. The same rules regarding padding are applied to this field as to the OPT_LENGTH field.

- The TYPE part of the DIME records describes the type of the payload (attachment type). The TNF (Type Name Format) field describes the structure of the value in this field.

- DATA carries the actual payload (a SOAP message or an attachment). The length of this field is always a multiple of 4 bytes. Padding is used if the actual value is not a multiple of 4 bytes. The padding is not included in the DATA_LENGTH field.

Through this technical description of the DIME records, you can see that the size of the record and thus the start for the next DIME record header can be calculated from the DIME record information. This removes the need to traverse the data to find the next header. Let's present some examples of how this works. We'll show you how to create a simple web service that will return images as a binary attachment. We will then demonstrate the creation of a client that can consume the binary attachments and include them in the application.

Start by creating an ASP.NET web service project with the name DIMEImages. Next, add references to the Microsoft.Web.Services and System.Web.Services assemblies. You then need to modify the web.config file as follows so that support of WSE is available to the web service:

```
<!--This element adds WSE functionality to the Web Service -->
<configuration>
    <system.web>
        <webServices>
            <soapExtensionTypes>
                <add type="Microsoft.Web.Services.WebServicesExtension,
                Microsoft.Web.Services, Version=1.0.0.0,
                Culture=neutral,
                PublicKeyToken=31bf3866ad364e36"
                priority="1" group="0" />
            </soapExtensionTypes>
```

```
        </webServices>
    <system.web>
<configuration>
```

What we are showing you here is how to configure this web service to use
WebServicesExtension when it is invoked. Note that the type attribute in the preceding
configuration file is split into several lines. In code, the type should be on one line.

Import the following namespaces into the web service:

```
Imports Microsoft.Web.Services.Dime
Imports Microsoft.Web.Services
Imports System.Net
```

The last step is to add a web method that will return a DIME attachment to the SOAP
response. The final code for the web service is shown in Listing 6-15.

Listing 6-15. *The Complete Web Service Code*

```
Imports System.Web.Services
Imports Microsoft.Web.Services.Dime
Imports Microsoft.Web.Services
Imports System.Net
<WebService(Namespace:="http://tempuri.org/")> _
Public Class DIMEImages
    Inherits System.Web.Services.WebService
    <WebMethod(Description:= _
"This method returns an image as a dime attachment.", CacheDuration:=20)> _
    Public Sub GetDimedImage(ByVal ImageName As String)
        Dim respContext As SoapContext
        respContext = HttpSoapContext.ResponseContext
        'This will fail if we are using the ordinary Web service proxy.
        Dim dimeAttach As DimeAttachment
        If ImageName.Length > 0 Then
            dimeAttach = New DimeAttachment( _
            "image/jpg", TypeFormatEnum.MediaType, _
            ImageName)
        Else
            dimeAttach = New DimeAttachment( _
            "image/jpg", TypeFormatEnum.MediaType, _
            "C:\images\sunset.jpg")
        End If
        respContext.Attachments.Add(dimeAttach)
    End Sub
End Class
```

Well, so far there is nothing tricky. The method has to get a reference to the response context
and be able to add an attachment to the response. This attachment is a DIME attachment, and
the source is a file you put on the server. Now you have a server—but how will the client be able
to unpack the DIME attachment? You deal with this by adding a Windows application to your
Visual Studio solution. Name this application DIMEClient, as shown in Figure 6-17.

Solution 'DIMEImages' (2 projects)
- DIMEClient
  - References
    - AssemblyInfo.vb
    - frmMain.vb
- **DIMEImages**
  - References
    - Microsoft.Web.Services
    - System
    - System.Data
    - System.Web
    - System.Web.Services
    - System.XML
  - AssemblyInfo.vb
  - DIMEImages.asmx
  - DIMEImages.vsdisco
  - Global.asax
  - Web.config

Figure 6-17. *The DIMEClient added to the solution file*

Add a text box, a button, and a picture box to the application as shown in Figure 6-18.

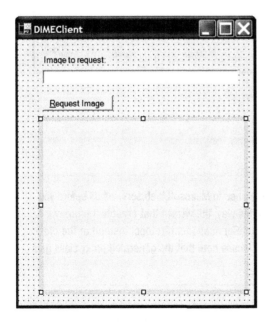

Figure 6-18. *The user interface of the DIMEClient application*

Simply add a web reference to the DIMEImages web service you recently created (see Figure 6-19).

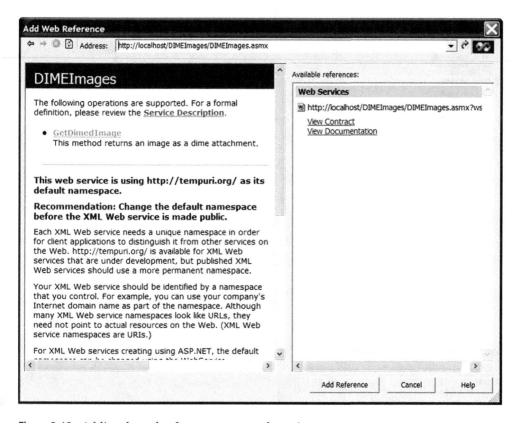

Figure 6-19. *Adding the web reference to your web service*

Now you've told the Visual Studio to create a proxy for you.

Tip A faster way to solve this problem is to add the reference to Microsoft.Web.services dll before you add the web reference to your web service. By doing it this way, the wizard that creates the proxy is deriving the proxy from the Microsoft.Web.Services._WebServicesClientProtocol instead of the old System.Web.Services._Protocols.SoapHttpClientProtocol. Please note that the generated proxy class gets the suffix WSE added to the original class name.

If you still want to add a proxy the hard way (you may have existing proxies that you do not want to regenerate for some reason), you need to go into the reference file and manually change the implementation for the proxy from the old System.Web.Services to the new Microsoft.Web.Services. The proxy class is found beneath the References folder, as shown in Figure 6-20.

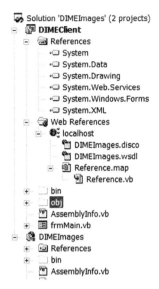

Figure 6-20. *Changing the proxy class*

If the proxy class is not visible, click the "show all files" icon (the second from the left) in the Solution Explorer and expand the References folder. Beneath it you should see the Reference.vb file. Open this proxy class and change the inheritance from System.Web.Services.Protocols. SoapHttpClientProtocol to Microsoft.Web.Services.WebServicesClientProtocol.

Now you only have some small code parts left to include before you can run the attachment example. Add the code in Listing 6-16 to the button in the client application.

Listing 6-16. *The Code to Read the Attachment from the SOAP Message*

```
Public Class frmMain
    Inherits System.Windows.Forms.Form
Private Sub btnRequest_Click(ByVal sender As System.Object, _
                            ByVal e As System.EventArgs) _
                            Handles btnRequest.Click
    Dim objDimeServer As New localhost.DIMEImages()
    Try
    Cursor.Current = Cursors.WaitCursor
    objDimeServer.GetDimedImage(txtImageToRequest.Text)
  If objDimeServer.ResponseSoapContext.Attachments.Count = 1 And _
  objDimeServer.ResponseSoapContext.Attachments(0).Type = "image/jpg" Then
                'We have something there...
                pbxRequestedImage.Image = New _
Bitmap(objDimeServer.ResponseSoapContext.Attachments(0).Stream)
            End If
        Catch ex As Exception
            'Oops this wasn't good. Show an error message.
            MsgBox("An error occured. - Please verify that" & _
```

```
            " the Web Service is running correctly.", _
            MsgBoxStyle.Critical Or MsgBoxStyle.OKOnly, _
            "An error occured.")
        Finally
            Cursor.Current = Cursors.Default
            objDimeServer.Dispose() 'Clean up when we have finished.
        End Try
    End Sub
End Class
```

Now you've created a web service that adds a DIME attachment and returns this SOAP request to the caller. The caller (your DIMEClient) simply retrieves the binary stream from the first attachment and puts it into a picture box.

One drawback with using the WSE SDK enhancement for web services is that not too many WS tools have support for its specifications. It will be all right when you have total control over the client and the server environment and can choose tools that support WS-Security and WS-Attachment on both sides. If you can't guarantee that both sides support WS-Security, you can choose a middle way—accepting security by the transport layer from the client to the web service facade, and from there using WSE internally on the server when you need to do more jumps.

WSE and Binary Attachments with MTOM

Prior to version 3 of WSE , sending binary data was done by using DIME. However, the MTOM has some benefits over DIME.

1. MTOM conforms to WS-Security witch DIME doesn't. This means that we can encrypt the attachment.

2. MTOM has a new encoding algorithm, which does not suffer from the Base64 encoding algorithms 33 percent increase of the size.

3. The new MTOM is easier to use than DIME attachments. DIME attachments were put in separate collections, while with MTOM we can indicate in the configuration file that the service is using MTOM and WSE automatically takes care of MTOM encode Byte[] return values.

A simple example of a web service that uses MTOM to return an image looks like this:

```
[WebService(Namespace = "http://tempuri.org")]
public class ImageMTOMService : System.Web.Services.WebService
{
    //This WebMethod returns MTOM encoded binary data for the requested image.
    [WebMethod]
    public GetImageResponse GetImage(string fileName)
    {
        GetImageResponse.response = new GetImageResponse ();
        response.FileName = fileName;
        String filePath = AppDomain.CurrentDomain.BaseDirectory +
  @"App_Data\" + fileName;
        response.FileContents = File.ReadAllBytes(filePath);
        return response;
```

```
    }
}

// Web Method return type
[XmlRoot("GetImageResponse ",
Namespace = "http://tempuri.org")]
public class GetFileResponse
{
    [XmlElement("fileName", IsNullable = false)]
    public string FileName;

    [XmlElement("fileData", IsNullable = false)]
    public byte[] FileContents;
}
```

The code has no special tweaks in the web service itself, except for the return type of the method. The return type is actually a byte array that is automatically returned to the caller as a MTOM attachment.

To archive this, you must turn on the MTOM Settings on the Messaging tab in the WSE configuration tool.

To call this web service from a client and write the image to disc, we simply do the following:

```
//Get mypic.jpg file as a binary file
BinaryDataMTOMServiceWse serviceproxy = new BinaryDataMTOMServiceWse();
localhost.GetFileResponse response = serviceproxy.GetFile("mypic.jpg");
Console.WriteLine("Retrieved File with name: {0}", response.fileName);
Console.WriteLine("Unsecured Bytes Received (at Client): {0}",
response.fileData.Length);
File.WriteAllBytes(response.fileName, response.fileData);
```

For large data files the previous solution is impractical since all the data is loaded into the server's memory before it is returned to the caller. When dealing with large data files, you can instead stream the bytes back to the caller without the need to read the complete file into memory first. For more information on this, see the specification for WSE 3.0.

Web Services and Transactions

The intersection of transactions and web services is interesting because of the disconnected nature of web services and the controlled, connected nature of traditional transactions. Transactions are a fundamental functionality in a business-critical system, and the four main components in transactions are the well-known ACID properties:

- *Atomicity.* If successful, then all the operations happen; and if unsuccessful, none of the operations happen.

- *Consistency.* The application performs valid state transitions at completion.

- *Isolation.* The effects of the operations are not shared outside the transaction until it completes successfully.

- *Durability.* Once a transaction successfully completes, the changes survive failure.

A web service requires the same coordination performance as a traditional transaction mechanism, for controlling the operations and the results from applications, but with some changes. Web services need to be able to handle transactions in a more flexible way than the ACID specifications provide. Instead, what's required is a method of coordination, rather than complete ACID transaction functionality. The WS-Coordination and WS-Transaction specifications provide a WSDL definition for such coordinated behavior.

The Coordination Framework is defined in the WS-Coordination specification (`http://msdn.microsoft.com/library/en-us/dnglobspec/html/ws-coordination.asp?frame=true`). In a nutshell, the Coordination Framework supports the Activation service, which creates activities; the Registration service, which coordinates protocol selection and registers participants; and the Coordination service, which performs activity completion processing.

The Coordination Protocols, as defined in the WS-Transaction specifications (`http://msdn.microsoft.com/library/en-us/dnglobspec/html/ws-transaction.asp?frame=true`), can separated into two categories: protocols for atomic transactions, and protocols for business transactions. You can use both types of protocols in your transactions, depending on the length of time for various activities.

Atomic transaction protocols are used for short-lived activities, and they serve as two-phase commitment protocols. The transaction scope specifies that all work is completed in its entirety; as you can see by the definition of atomicity we provided earlier, a successful activity results in all operations being performed. With an unsuccessful activity, no operations are performed. Upon completion, the results of successful activity become available to other users.

Unlike atomic transaction protocols, business transactions protocols support long-lived activities. Release of the results of operations at various intervals before an activity has been fully completed allows other potential users to readily access the resources engaged by the activity. Inclusion of mechanisms for fault- and compensation-handling allows the effects of previously completed business activities to be reversed.

Next we will go through the different services that the WS-Coordination specification supports.

Activation Service

The first service is the Activation service. You can use this service to create a message, to begin a new activity, or to specify the protocols for a specific activity. You can also use it to connect two different activities—for example, specifying a relationship between a new and a previously created activity—and thereby create hierarchical relationships.

Registration Service

With the Registration service, a web service registers and selects a protocol to coordinate an activity. By using the Registration service, it's possible for a web service to participate in a transaction, either in the role of a coordinator or as a general participant. The registration process identifies the specific protocol that should be used for activity coordination between the different roles. You can register for unlimited number of Coordination Protocols by adding multiple registration operations.

The writers of this specification predict that there will eventually be other ways of getting WS-Transaction to set its Coordination Protocol definitions. This would likely involve a specification of the transaction protocols that a web service would support. The actual method for getting information passed from the coordinator to the participant is not yet defined, however.

Coordination Service

The Coordination service is the last service we will discuss. It contains an Activation service, a Registration service, and at least one Coordination Protocol. The Coordination service controls the completion process for a web service using the attached Coordination Protocols. A Coordination Protocol defines the behavior requirements for a web service. The protocol also defines the operations that are supported to complete the process and in which order they should be conducted. The operations are grouped around roles. For instance, a role can consist of a consultant submitting a reservation for buying a new computer. The consultant provides an interface for the coordinator to control the direct agreement of the reservation (preparing it in this case). The boss in turn provides an interface for the Coordination service that has functions for completing the submission (commit and roll back of the submitted reservation).

The message format between the different services is called a context. For instance, the Activation service returns a CoordinationContext containing the following fields:

- *Identifier*. A unique name to identify the coordination context.

- *Expires*. An expiration date for the activity.

- *CoordinationType*. Coordination Protocols that define the supported, completed processing behaviors.

- *Registration service*. A service that contains the address of the Registration service. This service is used to register interest and participation in a Coordination Protocol for determining the overall outcome of the activity.

The last element in the context is the extensibility element provided for optional implementation-specific extensions. The example that follows comes from the WS-Coordination specification (http://msdn.microsoft.com/library/_en-us/dnglobspec/html/ws-coordination.asp?frame=true) and shows an implementation of the WS-Coordination extensions we have talked about so far:

```
<soapenv>
    <soapbody>
        <wscord:CoordinationContext
        xmlns: wscord=http://www.w3.org/2002/06/Coordination>
            <Identifier> ... </Identifier>
            <Expires> ... </Expires>
            <wscord:CoordinationType> ... </wscord:CoordinationType>
            <wscord:RegistrationService>
                <Address/>
            </wscord:RegistrationService>
            <!--extensibility element ->
        </wscord:CoordinationContext>
    </soapbody>
</soapenv>
```

We will leave the WS-Coordination specification here, and talk about how you can scale your web services to support many concurrent users.

Scaling Web Services

So far we haven't talked about scalability in relation to web services. Why? Because you need to know what kind of functionality to use before we can show you the problems involved in scaling web services.

Web services are run on web servers. These web servers are scaled out or scaled up, or even both, to be able to serve more requests.

When scaling out, we normally talk about web farms, As you may recall, a web farm consists of two or more web servers tied together that look like one big machine on the outside.

Note For more information about scalability issues, see Chapter 3.

Web Services in Web Farms

When designing and using web services in web farms, you need to keep a couple of issues in mind.

As with all performance issues involving web servers, keep the session-required services down to a minimum. If you need session-based web services, you must keep the session handling in a central place, since you never know if the next request will be redirected to the same instance of the web service handler or not.

Caching Web Services Results and Other Performance Tips and Issues

When using .NET, you get a lot of functionality for free. It's possible for you to use the caching functionality implemented in ASP.NET for caching requests to your web services. By caching a request for a web service for a limited time, the load on the back-end servers will be reduced, along with the response time from the web service. (We have previously shown how to use DIME attachments from a web service.) For the DIME web service example, a cache of the response for five minutes will reduce disk access on the server, thereby also reducing the load.

However, you don't want to cache everything you have on your server. Let's show you some rules that can help you to decide what to cache.

How much of your data is dynamic and how often is the data changed? For instance, NASDAQ information cannot be cached for 30 minutes, but your images in the DIMEImages project are possible to cache, because they will rarely change.

What's the scope of the data—is it public or private? If it is private, is the data different between different users, or is it only protected behind authentication routines? In many cases web services deal with user-specific data, and in such instances it is ineffective to cache the result, because you will end up with a cache for each user.

Does your web service rely on resources that you can reuse between different requests? Many times expensive resources, such as reading files from disc and reading the same data from a database, are used for each request. By caching this information, the response time for the web service will be reduced dramatically.

If you know the resources you are using today, can you predict the resources your web service might use tomorrow? This may be tricky, but take a look at your use cases and try to figure out new combinations, maybe totally new ones that could change the usage of resources in the future.

If you are going to cache data, where will you do that? Today, your data is probably cached "everywhere" in the application, but where is the best place from a security, performance, maintenance, and user point of view? See Figure 6-21 for a common data flow between a client and several servers.

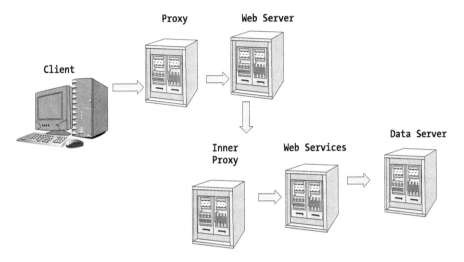

Figure 6-21. *A common dataflow between client and servers*

In every server in Figure 6-21, response data can be cached to boost the performance of web services.

When will the data expire? Is the data valid a constant amount of time, or will it change at random intervals? You have to find an optimal time interval for updating the cache, or else watch for the action that makes your cached data invalid.

How do you notify your web services customers that the data has expired? The answer to this depends on where and how you are caching your data. If you are caching data as an XML data island at the client's computer, you could include an expiration date in the XML data that you return to the client. If you are using a web-based client, you can set an expiration date on a data page that you have embedded in the client.

If you try to apply the preceding questions to the DIMEImages project, you can see that it helps to use cached information because the data is nearly static. It is public for everyone, and it does not have any kind of personalization that is user-specific. The data will be cached on the web server where the web service resides.

OK, now we'll demonstrate how to add caching functionality to the DIMEImages web service. First you need to open the .asmx file for the web service. In the DIMEImages example the page is called DIMEImages.asmx. The easiest way to add cache functionality to a web service is to add the CacheDuration attribute to the web method you would like to cache. For this example, you want to cache the response from GetDimedImage for 50 seconds, and add the following attribute to the method:

```
<WebMethod(Description:="This method returns an image as a dime attachment.",
CacheDuration:=50)> _
```

Done! The power of .NET has once again been made visible to you!

.NET Remoting vs. Web Services

So far in this chapter we have mostly discussed web services and how you can use them to tie different applications together. There is, however, another solution for letting remote objects talk with each other: .NET Remoting. .NET Remoting provides an infrastructure for distributed objects, similar to DCOM in old Windows DNA. .NET Remoting exposes the complete .NET Framework to remote objects, using plumbing that is both flexible and extensible for the future. Simply speaking, the main differences between web services a la SOAP and .NET Remoting are that the latter offers access to the complete .NET Framework, whereas web services do not. By using .NET Remoting, you can pass objects by value or by reference, easily do callbacks, manage multiple object activation and life-cycle policies, and more. We will explore .NET Remoting in more detail to make the differences clearer between .NET Remoting and web services.

.NET Remoting is a way to allow objects to talk to each other from different processes. All kinds of distributed communication have two things in general: the marshalling of data and objects to allow their distribution, and a description of what those messages look like. The former is achieved by using a marshaller, while the latter is often achieved by using some kind of metadata. The serialization engine for DCOM interfaces is normally the type-library marshaller, and the type library itself provides the metadata. The two areas where the web services and .NET Remoting differ are how they serialize data into messages and the format they use for the metadata.

.NET Remoting Serializer and Metadata Description

.NET Remoting relies on the .NET Framework. The .NET Framework contains an interface, IFormatter, that is used by System.Runtime.Serialization to marshal data to and from messages. You can use two formatters found in .NET Framework for serialization: System.Runtime.Serialization.Formatters.Binary.BinaryFormatter and System.Runtime.Serialization.Formatters.Soap.SoapFormatter. .NET Remoting normally uses the BinaryFormatter to format objects and so on into a binary stream, but .NET Remoting can also use the SOAPFormatter and protocols like HTTP.

But where is the metadata stored—and how? .NET Remoting relies on the common language runtime (CLR) assemblies, which contain all relevant information about the objects and data types found in the .NET Framework. By relying on these assemblies, .NET Remoting marshalling can include all of a class's private and public members, handle graphs correctly, and support all kinds of container types like hash tables and sorted lists. This is both the strength and weakness of .NET Remoting. By relying on the .NET Framework, the client using the .NET Remoting object also needs to have the .NET Framework installed to be able to marshal the object and its types back. In a homogenous internal network where you have total control of the configuration of remote clients, this may not be a huge problem. In situations where you do not have complete control (which is the more normal case), this can be a real problem.

■**Note** By using .NET Remoting, the client needs to understand the complete .NET Framework, since .NET Remoting is using the complete scope of data types and the like found in the .NET Framework. You will also have more administration of firewalls when using .NET Remoting than with web services, since port 80 is normally open in a firewall.

Web Services Serializer

The web services used in .NET rely on the System.XML.Serialization.XmlSerializer class to marshal data to and from SOAP messages at runtime. For metadata, web services employ WSDL and XSD. Both of these rely on XML, which makes web services better suited for situations where clients and servers are in different environments and where .NET Remoting can't be used (for example, either the client-side or the server-side system does not have the .NET Framework installed). Since the metadata describes the content in a simpler way, in order to allow web service toolkits on different platforms and with different programming models to interact with each other, the type definition is not as rich as for .NET Remoting. In other words, the only data types that can be exposed via web services are those that can be expressed in XSD. For instance, XMLSerializer will not marshal graphs, and it has limited support for container types such as sorted lists and so on.

Choosing .NET Remoting or Web Services

Now that you have seen the main differences between .NET Remoting and web services, the question is when to use .NET Remoting and when to use web services. ASP.NET web services favor the XML Schema type system and provides a simple programming model with broad cross-platform reach. .NET Remoting, on the other hand, favors the runtime type system and provides a more complex programming model with much more limited reach. Today you need to have the .NET Framework installed or use Intrinsyc's Ja.NET for Java. These differences are the primary factors in determining which technology to use; however, there are many more factors to consider that may force you to choose one of the technologies over the other. Next we'll discuss the five main factors that are based on Microsoft's recommendations, which can be found at http://msdn.microsoft.com/library/default._asp?url=/library/en-us/dnbda/html/bdadotnetarch16.asp.

Transportation of the Data and Hosting of the Process

The transportation of data back and forth between the client and the server can be done in several ways. The SOAP specification used in your web services does not explicitly say that the only transport protocol that can be used is HTTP or HTTPS. In real world it is, however, more or less a standard to use HTTP for transporting the information, because web services are hosted by IIS, which only supports HTTP/HTTPS. Another great benefit of using HTTP as a transport protocol is that most firewalls are already configured to allow HTTP traffic on port 80 (the same port you use when surfing the web). In a large enterprise, a lot of firewalls exist, and it would be a tremendous task for administrators to open up specific ports and set up security for a transport protocol that needs other ports.

You have two choices of transport protocols when using .NET Remoting: TCP or HTTP. The use of HTTP gives you the same benefits as it does for web Services—there is no need to reconfigure existing firewalls. When using TCP, the firewall needs to be configured to allow traffic on the desired port. The benefit of using TCP over HTTP is that the former is slightly faster.

Hosting .NET Remoting objects in IIS and the ASP.NET worker process (aspnet_wp.exe, which is an ISAPI filter that executes ASP.NET requests) can be done by using the .NET Remoting HTTPChannel and integrating the .NET Remoting object into it. By hosting the .NET Remoting object in IIS, you can automatically start the object by simply requesting it via HTTPChannel. This is actually the only way to automatically start a .NET Remoting object remotely, because you don't have the Service Control Manager (SCM) that DCOM provides. When hosting your .NET Remoting object, you also automatically take advantage of the fact that the ASP.NET worker process is thread-safe, and that you can use the secure support found in IIS for cross-process .NET Remoting calls. This is much easier than coding your own security handling, formatters, and channels.

Web services have the advantage, because administration of firewalls likely does not need to be performed. Normally you already allow HTTP traffic on port 80. .NET Remoting does have more flexibility in giving you a choice between TCP and HTTP, but the client needs to have the .NET Framework installed. When you would like to have security support, the use of IIS is a good choice, regardless of whether you use web services or .NET Remoting objects. We advise you to use IIS to avoid having to develop your own security handlers, formatters, and channels for your .NET Remoting object because it normally introduces too much complexity.

Security Support

When you use IIS as host for your web services and your .NET Remoting objects, you get full support for secure transport (in the form of HTTPS) and authentication. When a request comes into a web service, the authentication is done before your actual web service code is called. This means you do not have to make code changes when switching between different authentication methods. When you need to secure the content of your web Service calls, you can use the WS-Security, which has functionality to encrypt the content.

.NET Remoting objects hosted by IIS will also be able to leverage full security functionality, but when you have .NET Remoting objects outside IIS and use the TCPChannel or HTTPChannel, you need to handle all the security by yourself.

Web Services have the advantage, for the ease of its security functionality and because it is applied outside your web services.

State Management

As you know, HTTP is stateless by default. Most of the web applications created today are stateless (or at least, developers try to keep them stateless), in order to reduce the resources bound on the server between each call from the user. Web services are therefore stateless by default. State management and its attendant problems are the same as for traditional web applications. The state can be stored in a state server (which is preferred if you are going to use a web farm) or directly in cookies.

With .NET Remoting, it is possible to choose what kind of state you want to have. Single call objects are stateless (just like your web services are, by default). Referring back to the Singleton pattern discussion in the section "Design Patterns and Layers" in Chapter 5, remember that Singleton objects share their state between all created Singleton objects and client-activated objects that manage state for the client (the same result as using a state server or storing the state in some other way for a web service).

.NET Remoting has the advantage, because it takes care of handling the state for you automatically.

Performance Issues

If you are looking at raw performance, using .NET Remoting with binary formatting over TCPChannel is the faster option. However, in tests carried out to compare the relative performance of web services and .NET Remoting, web services outperformed .NET Remoting endpoints that used the SOAPFormatter with either HTTPChannel or TCPChannel. The performance of web services and .NET Remoting using binary formatting and the HTTPChannel were very similar. Please note that if you are using .NET Remoting with marshal-by-reference objects, a web service solution may outperform .NET Remoting! Why? Because a marshal-by-reference object in .NET Remoting calls the remote object for almost every call to the proxy object, and can give you long response times if the transport communication is slow. web services, on the other hand, are more of a service provider, with one chunky call to get the requested data back. Always strive for chunky interfaces instead of chatty interfaces.

.NET Remoting has the advantage, if TCPChannel with binary formatting is used—otherwise the advantage goes to web services, because of the improved performance and the option to scale out easily. For us, web services has been our choice even if performance has been a customer criteria, because the small performance boost we gain by using .NET Remoting with TCPChannel and BinaryFormatter has not been worth the loss of simplicity and security support that we get using web services. We must also make sure the client(s) has the .NET Framework installed to use .NET Remoting over TCPChannel, and this is not always possible.

.NET Enterprise Services

Traditional two-phase commits are not supported by web services by default because distributed transactions are expensive due to the communication for all involved transaction objects. However, the new WS-Transaction and WS-Coordination specifications give web services support for some kinds of transactions (see the section "Web Services and Transactions" earlier in this chapter). When working with a single transaction towards one database, web services can take advantage of local transaction support found in .NET Enterprise Services.

Interoperability/Reusability

If you build your solution based on web services, all systems (.NET based or otherwise—does not matter as long as they can use SOAP) can access your business logic. This way you have the opportunity to reuse business logic anywhere in a large enterprise, without a recompile or rewrite of the code. This saves you both money and time.

Summary

The use of web services is very important in the next generation of integration between different applications. In this chapter, we have briefly looked at web services. These services consist of many vendor- and platform-neutral parts, such as XML, SOAP, WSDL, and UDDI, which all make web services powerful for cross-platform interoperability. But, even if web services are really powerful for cross-platform communications and exposing functionality in existing legacy systems in a controlled and programmatic model, web services should not be used everywhere. You must be aware that in certain scenarios web services will cost you performance without giving you any benefits. As we mentioned, if you have an application on a single machine, web services will not benefit the application. But even if the application is running on a single machine today, you should use an application framework that allows you to later change the application's objects to also act as web services. By using the .NET Framework, the single-machine application can be converted easily into an application exposing web services for other clients as well.

In this chapter, we have also discussed how to use the new WSE SDK from Microsoft. This is an implementation of the WS-Security, WS-Routing, and WS-Attachment specifications that the WS-I group has written.

Finally, we delved into .NET Remoting and compared .NET Remoting to web services. Based on our experience, we suggest you use ASP.NET web services by default. They are easier to implement because they are hosted by IIS and therefore include the security support of IIS. If you need a more traditionally distributed application and are certain that you will only use .NET everywhere, and no other system or user will ever try to access your application from any other platform not supporting the complete .NET Framework, then use .NET Remoting— it offers a more complete object model and more functionality around objects. If you are using a .NET Remoting client, opt for binary formatting, since it is the fastest choice. However, use the HTTPChannel integrated with ASP.NET/IIS to achieve the benefits of security and authentication; otherwise you have to code for those benefits by yourself.

So far, we have followed these guidelines ourselves, and have never had to create an application based totally on .NET Remoting. Instead, we have been even more inclined to stick to web services, which we think is the first choice for most of the applications being created today—and will remain so tomorrow.

■ ■ ■

CHAPTER 7

Service Oriented Architecture (SOA)

Over the years, new technologies and architectures have popped up in the IT world. Some of them have been heavily promoted by only a few advocates, while others have become widely accepted. Quite a few of them have been hyped by developers and, to some extent, decision-makers alike, but these solutions still haven't managed to get a real breakthrough and become used in the way they were intended. Some argue that this has happened to Component-based Development (CBD), as you will see shortly, and that this has paved the way for Service Oriented Architecture (SOA).

Overview

We have seen an evolution: from procedural programming to functional development to object orientation to component-based development. These techniques have all had their benefits, and object orientation, for example, is probably something that won't ever be unnecessary, no matter which architecture you design your applications with.

It's been a long winding road to reach the latest stop on the architecture tour—Service Oriented Architecture. However, SOA seems to have been one of the architectures that have been widely accepted. How can this have happened so soon? Well, Component-based Development, or CBD, promised all kinds of benefits, such as reuse and an open market in components. These benefits would (purportedly) drastically reduce the time it takes to develop new applications and systems, according to Lawrence Wilkes and Richard Veryard, in their paper "Service-Oriented Architecture: Considerations for Agile Systems." Many companies used, and still use, techniques like CORBA or COM, but they never got the breakthrough and the results that were promised to them. You may wonder why this has happened and we wouldn't be surprised. But if we look back, we really can't say that the component market has blossomed as it was promised or that companies reuse components to a great extent.

According to Wilkes and Veryard, many companies saw other benefits instead. Some of these were improved scalability and the possibility to replace components as needed for instance.

But, we think that the reason that companies have failed to reuse components lies more with us: the developers and architects. How much effort did we really put into reusing components? Think about it for awhile, how many times have you reused components compared to the number of times you have reused code snippets? We can honestly say that for us, code reuse has been greater than components reuse. It's been easier to build a new component reusing code snippets than it has been to adapt old components to new requirements. We do make sure that we build systems using components and object orientation, but we don't build them after the principles of CBD.

In 2003, Don Box, speaking at the XML Web Services One conference, likened objects to software-based integrated circuits and said that programmers would do better to focus on services instead (Vincent Shek, *Microsoft Architect Touts SOAs*, http://www.eweek.com/article2/0,1759,1655790,00.asp). We agree with Don Box, and we tried to push for this in the first edition of our book.

When web services emerged a few years ago, new ideas for architecture came to the surface. Web services provided us with benefits in several areas:

- *Platform independence.* We can use web services built on any platform, as long as they use standard protocols for communication (that is SOAP, XML, and WSDL). We really don't care how they've been implemented, so long as we know how to contact them and what their interface is.

- *Loose coupling.* Components hold a connection: clients using web services simply make a call.

- *Discovery.* We can look up a specific service using a directory service like UDDI.

These features of web services fit nicely into the more and more connected world of today. But, if we're going to build systems in large enterprises in the future, we need to change the way we look at architecture. This is where the Service Orientation (SO) comes into Service Oriented Architecture (SOA).

What Is a Service?

What is a service? Many people have a hard time understanding what to think when they are discussing services. At one of my recent .NET courses, the students and I were involved in a long process until a revelation occurred among the participants. At first, they couldn't stop thinking in a traditional, component-based way, but after several discussions, the coin finally dropped down. After that first barrier was removed, all our architecture discussions went very smoothly, and suddenly there wasn't any problem at all. The students now had lots of ideas and thoughts about how to implement services in their own projects.

Let's start with a real life example. I recently applied for a renewal of my driving license from the Swedish Road Administration (SRA). The SRA's whole procedure for handling this can be said to be a service. The service, in this case, being to process my application and then, based on various (and for me, hidden) facts and procedures, they either issue me a new license or reject my application. I don't need to bother about how the SRA processed my information or which routines they followed internally to process my application. In this case, my application is a request to a service which SRA expose and their answer (whether a new license or a rejection) is the response to my request.

So, a service doesn't have to be a mystery or something hard to understand. Think of it as something that encapsulates a business process or an information area in your business. A common scenario could be the management of customer information, something that most companies have to deal with. The service CustomerManagment can expose extensive functionality, based on the input parameters. For instance we can find functions that let us add new customers, update customer information, delete customers, return customer information and lots of other things concerning customer management. One of the keys is that the user of the service, the consumer, does not have to know what goes on behind the hood. All the processing is hidden from the consumer, who should only need to know how to call the service.

One common problem is confusion as to where to draw the line between the depth of our services during the design phase. We need to make sure that the service we are about to develop is valid and does not cover too much or to little. We will get back to this a little further down.

What Is This Thing Called SOA?

If we have built some cool web service that our company uses does this mean we have implemented an SOA? Definitely not, we say. Web services are only parts of a service-oriented architecture. What web services really are, to be honest, is just a set of protocols by which services can be published, according to Sprott and Wilkes, at http://www.cbdi.com. Web services are programmatic interfaces to capabilities which conform to the WSnn specifications (WSnn is just an acronym for all the parts of web services available to us like SOAP, WS-Security, WS-Federation, and so on).

But who are Sprott and Wilkes? Why should you listen to them? These two guys are perhaps not as well known as Don Box, but they have been in this business a long time, and they are considered to be experts. They both work for CBDI Forum, which is an independent analyst firm and thinktank, and David Sprott is one of its founders. They both give plenty of lectures and write numerous articles on various aspects of business software creation, including, to a large extent, web services and SOA.

But web services aren't a must in SOA either. We can expose our services by other means as well (using message queues, among other things), although web services will probably be the way we implement SOA in the foreseeable future.

If you look around on the Internet, you can find different definitions for SOA. The World Wide Web Consortium (W3C) defines SOA as "a set of components which can be invoked, and whose interface descriptions can be published and discovered." This sounds like web services doesn't it? This view might perhaps be a tad too technical and probably not entirely correct either.

Sprott and Wilkes of CBDi Forum (http://www.cbdiforum.com) define SOA as "the policies, practices, and frameworks that enable application functionality to be provided and consumed as sets of services published at a granularity relevant to the service consumer. Services can be invoked, published and discovered, and are abstracted away from the implementation using a simple, standards-based form of interface." As we can see, this definition is both wider and more correct, if you ask us.

Why Use SOA?

There are several implications to consider when implementing an SOA in an organization. SOA is much more than simply developing a few web services and thinking you're finished. If you're going to successfully make the move to service orientation, you'll need to have the whole company management on the wagon as well. So how do we do that?

Let's start with considering EAI or Enterprise Application Integration. This topic was discussed earlier, in Chapter 1. One major problem that many large organizations struggle with is the integration of their existing applications into their new infrastructure. The problem is that many times they only succeed in exposing functionality in a proprietary way, shutting out everybody who doesn't speak this language.

The solution, in many cases, has been developing interfaces sitting on top of these systems. This way, a lot of legacy applications have had their functionality exposed to new applications in a convenient and standards-based way. The problem with this is that we have to develop the interfaces that enable this integration, and this obviously costs a lot of money. Imagine if the architects implementing the legacy applications had a way of making sure that the applications could easily be accessible by the new systems without new development being necessary!

With SOA, this isn't just a dream anymore. Since the whole idea is to expose services through a standards-based interface, not proprietary to anyone, we can make sure that their functionality can be accessed by new systems easily. This way we don't have to build special interfaces to give access to their functionality.

We think this might be the strongest argument of all. By using TCP, XML, SOAP, web services, and any other standards-based technology, today we can build systems that are still accessible to all new applications fulfilling these standards in the future. And, since they are standards, we have a whole lot more certainty that they will be around in 10 or 20 years time.

This will save companies a lot of future development costs. And let's face it. It won't have to be 10 or 20 years before we can start calculating savings from this approach. Enterprises have new systems coming out all the time, and using SOA we make sure that we can reuse functionality in a far better way than we could with component-based development.

Remember though, it's no walk in the park to implement SOA in an organization. It will take a whole lot of consideration before it can be rolled out properly. SOA is not intended for single applications either, but for organizations as a whole. This means that if we're going to be successful we need to incorporate SOA in the enterprise IT plan from day one. If SOA isn't considered for all new development or all the future enhancements for the existing systems, we will fail in implementing service orientation.

But once we start letting SOA influence all IT issues in our organization, we make certain that the ROI (Return On Investment) will be great.

Services and SOA

Now we'll start looking at the characteristics of services and examine what some very influential people think about them. We'll then take a look at how architecture in SOA should be considered. Let's start with some more of Don Box's thoughts and take it from there.

The Four Tenets of Don Box

To better understand what a service is and why we must think of architecture in a slightly different way than we did with object-oriented programming and components, we'll now look at the four important tenets that Don Box, of Microsoft's Windows Communication Foundation team, identifies as crucial. For the complete coverage of this, please see "A Guide to Developing and Running Connected Systems with Windows Communication Foundation" by Don Box. This document is available on the Microsoft web site and is well worth its time.

Don Box's first tenet is that *boundaries are explicit*. When services that build up an application or system are spread across large geographical areas, things get more complex. We might run into large geographical distances, multiple trust authorities, and perhaps, different execution environments. Communication in such an environment, whether between applications or even between developers, gets potentially costly, as complexity is great and performance may suffer. An SO solution to this is to keep the surface area as small as possible, by reducing the number and complexity of abstractions that must be shared across service boundaries. Service Orientation, according to Box, is based on a model of explicit message-passing, rather than implicit method invocation, as it is in component-based development.

Don Box then states that *services are autonomous*. Services must always assume that nobody is in control of the entire system. Having total control of a system would be impossible in a service-oriented architecture. Components or object-oriented programs are often deployed as a unit, even though many efforts have been made to change this over the last decade. In SO this isn't always the case, if it ever can be. Service-oriented systems are often deployed across a large area instead. The individual services, are often deployed as a unit, but the whole system is dispersed. A SO system never actually stands still, because new services may be added all the time and old services given new interfaces. This increased ubiquity of service interaction makes it necessary for us to reduce the complexity of this interaction.

When a service calls another service it can't expect a return value because messages are only passed one way. We can get a return message of course but this can disappear on the way and we can never be certain it arrives in the end. This means that the service and the consumer are independent of each other. They are autonomous, or sovereign as Bruce Johnson puts it on Bruce Johnson's SOA(P) Box (http://objectsharp.com/Blogs/bruce/). So in a scenario where a service calls another service and gets no expected return message, the service must be self healing so that there isn't a noticeable impact. The caller must not have to depend on anybody else to complete the invoked method.

In a connected world, many things can go wrong with communication, and our services must take this into account. When a service accepts an incoming message that is malformed, or even sent for a malicious purpose, it must be able to deal with it. The way to do this is to require the caller to prove that he has all the rights and privileges necessary to get the job done. This burden is never placed on the service itself. One way to solve this is to set up trust relationships instead of per-service authentication mechanisms.

The third tenet is one of the most important ones: *services share schema and contract, not class*. In OO programming, abstractions are developed in the form of classes. They are very convenient, as they share both structure and behavior in a single named unit. This is not the case in SO, as services interact only based on schemas (for structure) and contract (for behavior). Every service we build must advertise a contract that describes the messages it can send or receive. Even though this simplifies things we must still be aware that these schemas and contracts remain stable over time. We can't change these when they are implemented. To increase future flexibility, we can use XML element wild cards and/or optional SOAP header blocks, so that we don't break already deployed code. We might even have to build a new service function instead, and make that available.

The last tenet that Don Box mentions is that *service compatibility is determined based on policy*. Every service must advertise its capabilities and requirements in the form of machine-readable policies, or operational requirements, in other words. One example is a service that requires the caller to have a valid account with the service provider. Another could be a situation where all communications with the service should be encrypted.

These four tenets seem pretty straightforward to us and we strongly agree with them. But, let's look at how others characterize SOA.

Sprott and Wilkes SOA Characteristics

Sprott and Wilkes also show some principles of good service design enabled by service-oriented architecture characteristics.

- *Abstracted.* A service is abstracted from its implementation. This means a consumer of a service shouldn't have to worry about how the service is implemented, only how to invoke it.

- *Published.* The implementation should be hidden by a precise, published specification of the service functionality. This is something we recognize from Don Box's tenets, when he talks about policies.

- *Formal.* There must be a formal contract between the provider and the consumer, which is also something Box stresses.

- *Relevant.* Functionality should be presented at a level of granularity that the recognized by the user as a meaningful service.

- *Reusable.* We should reuse services, not copy and paste code.

Web services enable good service design because they are

- *Technology neutral.* We do not care about their platform as long as they are:

- *Standardized.* This means that they should use standards-based protocols (SOAP, XML, and WSDL).

- *Consumable.* Web services enable automated discovery and usage.

There is nothing here that contradicts what Don Box says and we agree with what Sprott and Wilkes have come up with.

Sundblad and Sundblad

Let's now take a look at what Sundblad and Sundblad say in Sten Sundblad's Swedish document "Service Oriented Architecture—An Overview," or as its called in Swedish "Serviceorienterad arkitektur—En översikt."

Sundblad starts by pointing out that the idea of SOA is to organize IT systems as a set of services that can be reached through a message-based interface. It builds on the same foundation as SOAP and XML, but is not dependent on either. The idea itself is nothing new—it's been around for over ten years and was started in the CORBA community in the 1990s. But now, thanks to XML, SOAP, and web services, the idea has been getting the attention it deserves. Sunblad continues that the reason for this is obviously because these building blocks have made it possible for a service to be both language- and platform-independent.

Sundblad also states five characteristics that are usually mentioned when talking about services. We'll now take a closer look at each one of these.

- A service should be autonomous.

- A service should have a message-based interface.

- A service should have its own logic that encapsulates and protects its own data.

- A service should be clearly separated from and loosely coupled to the surrounding world.

- A service should share schema—not class.

Autonomy

You'll recognize this characteristic from Don Box's four tenets. Autonomy means that the service should be possible to develop, maintain, and evolve independently of its consumers. The service must take full responsibility for its own security and be suspicious of anything and anybody who tries to use it. Don Box also stresses that these features are important for a service to possess.

Message-Based Interface

No consumer should ever be in contact with the inner logic of a service. You must develop the services so that they are only accessible when you send a message to them with a wish to get the service performed. It's the logic of the service that handles the message and determines whether to process the request or not.

Let's take a little example from real life. When I recently applied for a renewal of my driving license I got a form sent to me via snail mail. This form was preprinted with text, leaving spaces for me to insert information about myself and attach a photo showing my best side. I also had to sign it, so that my signature could be printed on the license. The form's instructions explained how I should fill it out and how to return it to the authorities. After a few weeks, I would either get a new license or an answer as to why my application would not be approved. (And yes, I was approved.) Nowhere in this process did I have to know how the authorities handled my application or how they would process my information. The only thing I needed to care about was filling my form out correctly and making sure I sent it back to the correct address.

If we translate this experience into our examination of services, we can say that the form I filled out was a message that was being sent to the service. I also got a message in return, in this case either a new license or a rejection. But these messages are totally asynchronous. They don't depend on each other in any way, except for the fact that my application must come in before the agency's reply. But otherwise, there is no connection between me and the authorities, during the waiting period. So, this example shows not only a message-based interface, but also the autonomy of this service. Keep this example in mind, because we will return to it in a little while.

Even though we often talk about web services when SOA is discussed, Sundblad firmly points out that this does not have to be the case. There are other ways to display a message-based service, including by using a message queue. But, to be realistic, we could probably assume that most service-oriented solutions will use web services.

One thing worth noticing here is that using a message-based interface means that we should send all parameters encapsulated in the message. This goes for both the consumer and the service. We don't build service, for instance, that take integers as parameters—instead we embed the integers in an XML document and send this to the service. In return, we'll get an

XML document with the result of our request. A benefit of this procedure is that it's easy to add new parameters for future needs without changing the signature. The only thing that has changed is that the content of the message and both old and new messages will now work.

Encapsulation of Data

One of the important aspects of a service is that it should be autonomous, as we have learned from all of the previously mentioned authors. According to Sundblad, this also means that a service should encapsulate its data. No other service or application should be allowed to touch the data (see Figure 7-1).

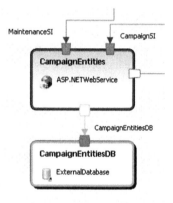

Figure 7-1. *A service should encapsulate its own data*

The only way that your service's data should be reached is when a user sends a message requesting that some modification of the data is to be performed. If the consumer is validated and has the correct credentials, and has sent a well-formed message according to the service specifications, its request will be performed. It's the logic of the service that it touches the data, never the message itself.

■**Note** A service's data can be both persistent and non-persistent. The objects in a service often have non-persistent data in their RAM, just like any other object, but instead of relying on another component to save persistent data, in this case the service itself saves this to the database.

Clearly Separated From and Loosely Coupled to the World

As you may already understand, a service must be clearly separated from its surrounding world—just like the driving license renewal process, where the service (renewal) was separated from the message sender. The driving license example also showed that the process of determining whether or not the application for a new license was approved (or not) was loosely coupled to the renewer. The same goes for services in service orientation. The renewer, in the case of the driving license, sent a message to the authorities, waited, and finally got the reply. No persistent connection between the two existed at any time. When a consumer sends a message to a service, no persistent connection should exist either. If a new message needs to be sent, a new non-persistent connection has to be made. The only thing that consumer and the service share is the structure of the message and the contract that controls the communication between the two.

Share Schema—Not Class

For SOA to work, the consumer and the service have to agree on the schema that determines the structure of the message.

Since the object model of consumer and service might be completely different, the service doesn't need to, (and shouldn't) share its object model. It should only share the schema of the message structure. In our driving license example, the schema would be the form and its instructions. When we are talking about web services, the schema would be the WSDL file.

Sundblad continues that when you first start designing your services you should always start by defining the message-based interface that your service will expose. After you do this, it's time to think about how to design the logic. This is so that you can create all of the XML schemas and contracts before you even think about the objects that implement the interfaces.

Four Types of Services

What most people agree upon is that the concept of services encapsulates a whole business process or business information area. All businesses have somewhere between 10 and 20 higher level services according to Sten Sundblad in the Swedish paper "Service Oriented Architecture and processes" (unfortunately only available in Swedish). Higher level services could include the Purchasing process or the Sales process, for example.

Sundblad pushes for doing a process-oriented analysis of the business in question, when you're implementing your SOA. As you do this, you'll find that there are at least four kinds of services that should implement the functional requirements as follows:

- Entity Services

- Activity Services

- Process Services

- Presentation Services

The *entity services* are services that are rather persistent or stable over time. A business is not likely to change these processes, because they supply and protect the information that the business is depending on. If you think of these different kinds of services as four layers, they would be the foundation at the bottom level of Figure 7-2.

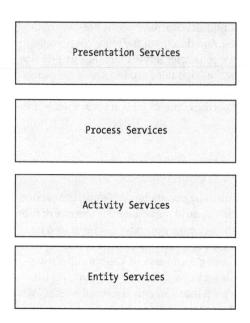

Figure 7-2. *Four kinds of services in a business*

Activity services are slightly less stable than entity services. In other words, they may be changed over time. Activity services are placed one layer up from entity services, and are the services that perform the actual work in one or more processes.

High-level *process services* are in the next layer. It's very probable that these kinds of services will change over time, since they often reflect the changes in a company's way of doing business and are often trimmed away to give competitive benefits when the company needs them. When we change these no lower level services should have to change.

Presentation services comprise the top layer. These are the user interface services and they provide users with a way or of accessing other services. As you probably recognize from your own company, these kinds of services are very likely to be changed as times goes by.

Architecture of a Service

Now you know what services are and what they do. You also have a pretty good idea about how they interact with the outside world. As we mentioned, though SOA is a way of structuring a whole business IT support, it's not intended for single applications. So, if a company wants to implement SOA, they'll first have to get a grip of the total IT structure within the company.

How should you structure your services on the inside? Well, when we design services we often use Sundblad & Sundblad's reference architectures.

Note We can also choose to design individual services using standard Object Orientation techniques. There is nothing contradictory in this and this will probably be a common way of developing services.

We will give the following two examples of these reference architectures here:

- Entity Services Architecture

- Presentation Services Architecture

Entity Services

Figure 7-3 shows an overview of the architecture of an entity service, according to Sundblad & Sundblad.

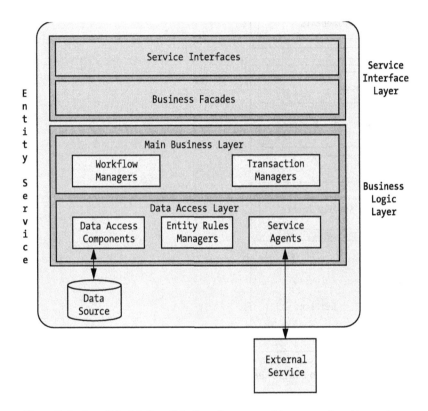

Figure 7-3. *Sundblad & Sundblad's reference architecture of entity services*

Compare this to the architecture of a component-based application, as shown in Figure 7-4, and you see several similarities.

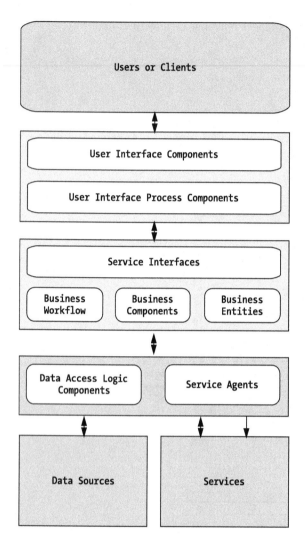

Figure 7-4. *The standard architecture of a component-based application*

We find that this architecture is layered and can be executed in one process, and, since it's layered, that we have the opportunity to scale the service on several servers or server farms. In the business interface layer we find the Service Interfaces (SI) that our service will expose. They will be implemented as web services, which will communicate with the business facades, which in their turn will handle the communication with the business logic.

Figure 7-3 also clearly shows that the data source is kept within the boundaries of the service, so that no one other than the developer can access the data except by sending a message request to the service. It's only the data access layer that handles communication with the database. Service agents manage communication with external services, if this is needed.

Presentation Services

Figure 7-5 shows the reference architecture for presentation services. These are interfaces for users, which are built as Windows or web forms. But, in a true SOA, they are also services with clear boundaries and autonomy.

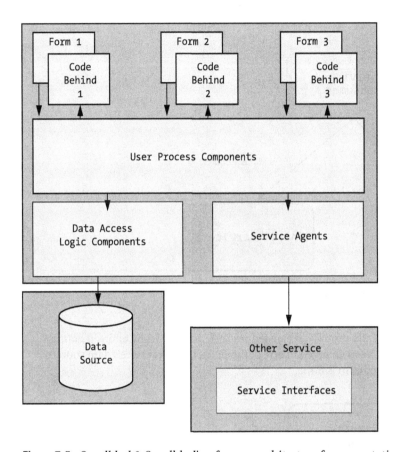

Figure 7-5. *Sundblad & Sundblad's reference architecture for presentation services*

The user process components do the same as user interface components which, as you may recall, is to avoid redundancy in our forms.

You can also see that you should have service agents handling your communication with external services, such as process services or entity services. This communication is based on SOAP, XML, and WSDL just like any other service would be. In the Figure 7-5 you can also see that a presentation service has a data source of its own, where it stores session data or cached data, such as product catalogs, or any other data that isn't likely to change often. The contents of a customer's shopping cart before checkout would be excellent information to store here.

Transactions in SOA

You learned earlier that services should be self-healing. Nothing but the service itself should be responsible for making sure its requests are carried out. In order for a service to keep an atomic transaction going that spans over several services, we need to make sure it's certain that the whole transaction is performed. In Figure 7-6 you can see an example of a service sending update requests to two other services in one transaction.

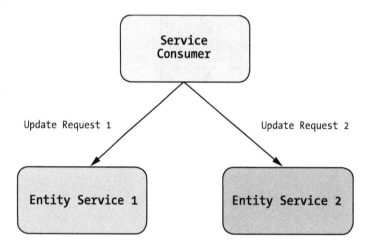

Figure 7-6. *An atomic transaction spanning two services*

If both of these service calls should fail (see Figure 7-7), nothing really bad will happen. This is because nothing has been changed in any of the participating service's data sources during the transaction, so no harm is done.

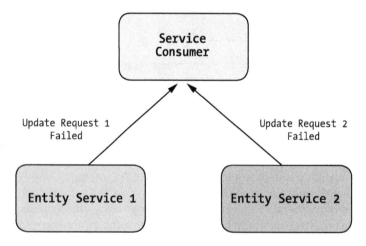

Figure 7-7. *If both requests fail no harm is done*

But if one request fails and the other succeeds, things can be much worse. In Figure 7-8, you see that the update request to Entity Service 1 fails while the other request is OK. Now you have a problem, because the state of the services is out of balance.

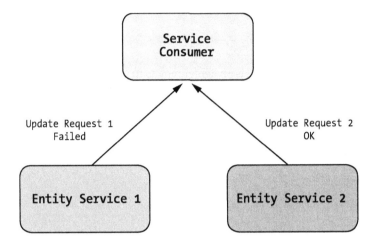

Figure 7-8. *One request fails*

How can you solve this? You can do this by building logic into your services that send a compensating request (as in Figure 7-9) to the service, whenever the update was OK. In other words, you must write logic of your own that will perform a rollback when you have services that need to use transactions. Then your services must try the transaction again (since it needs to get it done) until it is successful.

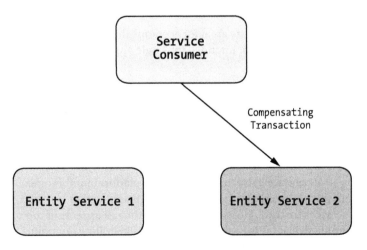

Figure 7-9. *Sending a compensating request after the failure of an atomic transaction*

So, we've just given you an example of how a service must always be prepared for the unexpected and be able to handle situations like this. In other words, a service needs to be self-healing, as we mentioned earlier.

Note that the responsibility always is placed on the service that is keeping the transaction together and not on the services that are part of the actual transaction.

Summary So Far

So, what have you learned so far? It seems like there is an agreement as to what the most important parts of services and SOA are among various industry people. You now know that there are several characteristics a service must have:

- Be autonomous.

- Share schema and contract—not class.

- A message-based interface.

- Provide its own security.

- Clear boundaries.

- Be loosely coupled to the world.

- Encapsulate its own data.

There are also at least four types of services that we can use:

- Entity Services

- Activity Services

- Process Services

- Presentation Services

You have also learned that while web services are great for accomplishing an SOA, they are *not* mandatory. You're also aware that SOA is not intended for single applications either, but rather for a whole business IT infrastructure.

Component-Based Application Design vs. Service Design

Now we'll give you an example of how to implement Service Orientation. In Chapter 1 we showed you an example of using UML, and we'll use that example as a platform for this one. First, you'll see how to implement this as an ordinary component-based application and then you'll see how it could look as services instead. Please keep in mind that all aspects of the application have been overly simplified, just for the sake of more easily illustrating our points. As they say about stunts in the movies; don't try this at home.

In the Chapter 1 example, you might recall that we used several actors, including Sales_Clerk, Supply_System, Sales_Manager, and Customer. We'll only consider Sales_Clerk and Customer for this example.

We found that a Sales_Clerk had a use case called Maintain Campaign and that Customer had one called Request Campaign Email, as shown in Figure 7-10.

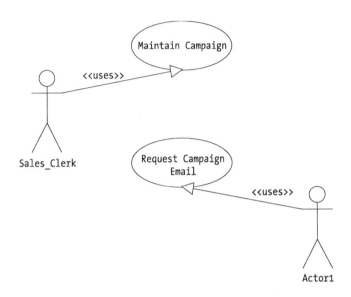

Figure 7-10. *The use cases from Chapter 1*

For this example, we will develop one User Interface (UI) for each of the two actors that we're working with, as you can see in Figure 7-11.

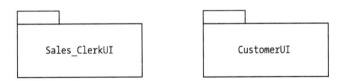

Figure 7-11. *The User Interfaces for our actors*

These UIs will be implemented as one web application that encompasses both the customer and the sales clerk. In almost all applications, you'll find that several functions are similar or even the same for many user interfaces. Therefore we'll avoid such redundancy in our example by implementing these functions in a User Interface Process (UIP), as we see in Figure 7-12.

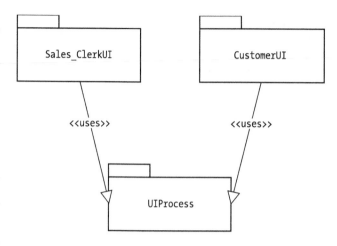

Figure 7-12. *User Interfaces and User Interface Process*

We'll connect all the user interface objects with the business logic. This way we isolate the UI objects from all contact with business objects (see Figure 7-13).

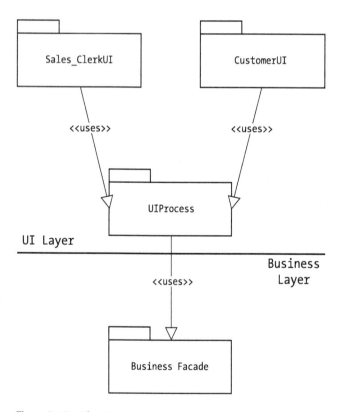

Figure 7-13. *The UI processes are isolated from the business objects.*

As you know already, the reason for having facade objects is that they delegate work to the real logic, implemented as business objects. Inside the business logic, there are three kinds of business objects that you can delegate to (see Figure 7-14).

- *Business Rules Managers*. Evaluates new and changed information against a predefined set of rules.

- *Workflow Managers*. Handles workflows.

- *Transaction Managers*. Responsible for keeping transactions and transaction integrity together.

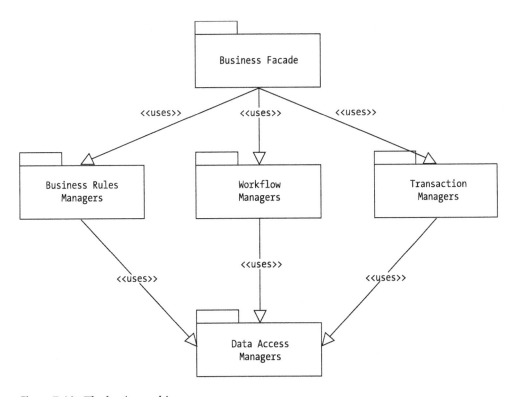

Figure 7-14. *The business objects*

The data access managers will then help our application to access its data.

So now we have the structure of our application. When we deploy it, it will be very much like in Figure 7-15, and we can see that it probably will be implemented on three servers or server farms. These include the following:

- Web farm

- Application server (farm)

- Database server (not shown in Figure 7-15)

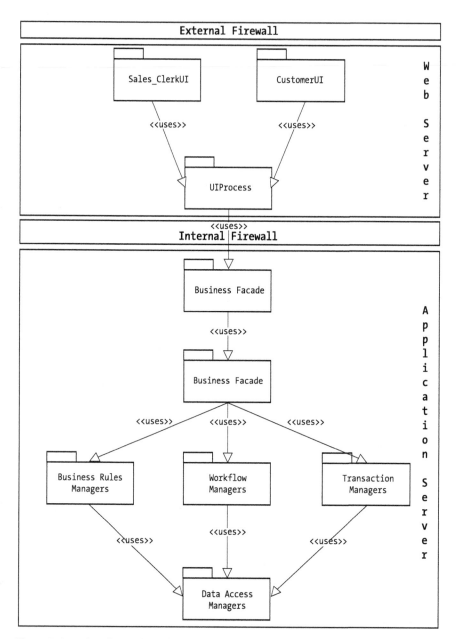

Figure 7-15. *The physical implementation*

This is pretty much a standard way of developing applications and you'll notice that we also employed our recommended way of doing things, as outlined in previous chapters.

So, let's think about this for a while. What are the potential problems with this architecture? Well, a major one you should consider is that of future development. Let's say we need a new application in our enterprise, which also needs to access the same data as the one just described (see Figure 7-16). What happens then?

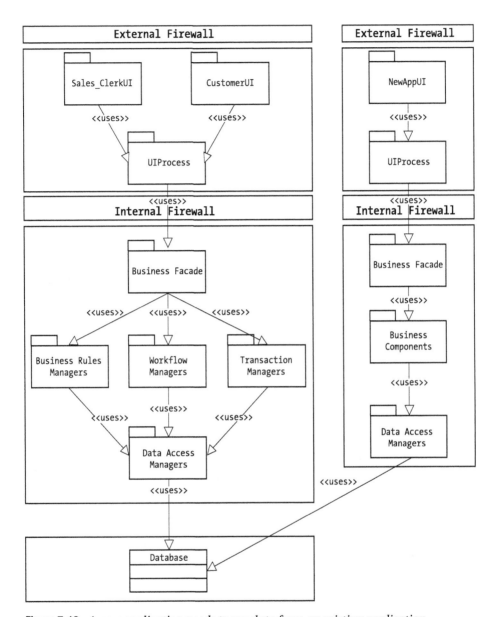

Figure 7-16. *A new application needs to use data from an existing application*

One thing that certainly will happen is that the database will have to change to reflect the needs of the new application. And as Sundblad writes, the more you let additional applications extend the original requirements, the more complex your maintenance and new development will be.

Sundblad also stresses the fact that the original rules will become dispersed. If both appli-cations need to access the same data, both applications will also have to implement the rules for access control and for deciding which data is valid. This will complicate things even more.

One possible solution to this problem is to reuse the business components of the original application by letting the business layer of the new application connect to the business facade of the old one. We could also create a new, separate, database for the new application (see Figure 7-17).

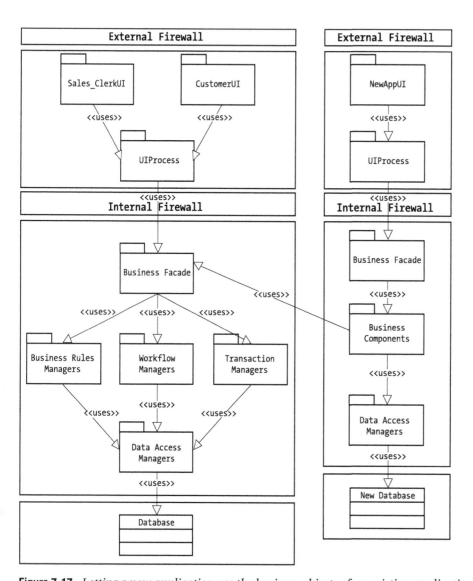

Figure 7-17. *Letting a new application use the business objects of an existing application*

This would work fine for just one additional application, but what if several others are added? Then the situation would soon be unbearable. That's why services are such a great idea. If we had built our application with SO in mind from the start, we'd have autonomous services ready to be used by anybody we authorized. Figure 7-18 shows what such a scenario could look like.

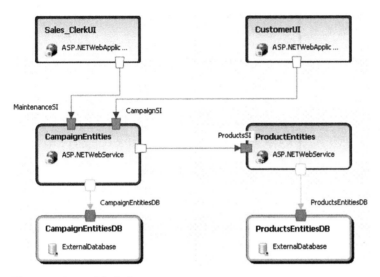

Figure 7-18. *An SO design*

In this scenario, we've built our UI as presentation services and the business logic as entity services, using Sundblad & Sundblad's recommended architectures. We can also see that each entity service is responsible for its own data. Nobody else touches it without sending a message to the service (see Figure 7-19).

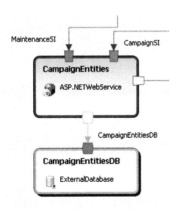

Figure 7-19. *The entity services protect their own data*

If we wanted to add a new application (or service as it would be called here), there's an easier and more flexible way we can do this. In this technique, a new service quite simply connects to the Service Interfaces (SI) of the existing service that it needs to use functions from, as shown in Figure 7-20. We've have created a new service that uses the CampaignEntities service.

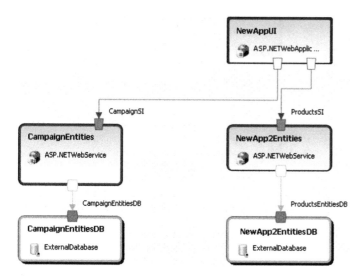

Figure 7-20. *Adding new services to our SOA*

There is no need for splitting the rules across several applications here, because all the services are responsible for their own data and security. This gives us the benefit of being able to add any new services we want in the future, and in a much easier way.

You can see our deployment of this scenario in Figure 7-21. Here, the UI services would be in the DMZ, while the rest of the services are implemented behind our Intranet firewall.

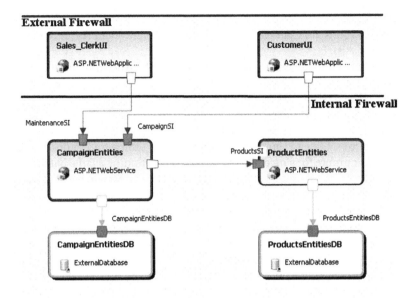

Figure 7-21. *Deploying services*

Scalability Issues in an SOA

When systems are built up of independent and autonomous services, you no longer have control over all parts of the system. This also means that you no longer have control of performance and scalability. This is most likely OK, since maximum performance is not always the most important thing.

What you can do is to make sure that all of the parts of the service or services you're responsible for are optimized as much as possible. You can use the same techniques we covered in earlier chapters to accomplish this.

If you have a layered service, like the reference architectures we saw previously, you can scale the presentation services (as long as they are web forms) on a web server farm. Web Services Interfaces in our entity services can also be scaled this way. You can optimize performance internally as well, since the service is a single unit. This does mean that it might be great to use .NET Remoting for communication between components.

There are a lot of tricks you can use. Consider your services carefully and choose performance enhancers where they fit. Try to find and adjust the bottlenecks you can and have control over.

Other Issues to Consider

Making the choice of an SOA for a given domain is a delicate task. It's not uncommon for an architect to focus on the online transactions between one or more services, but then forget (or at least postpone) to think about the architecture of offline transactions (also known as *batches*).

Once the architects realize that they've made this kind of mistake they, at best, *try* to run batches in the same manner as the online transactions (for example, one transaction at a time). But in medium to large systems though, this is devastating for the performance.

Consider a 7x24 system that is very transaction-oriented and that has a lot of online registrations as well as batch registrations (for example, large files whose content should be imported into the system on a regular basis).

In this case, the system must be available to the online users, with an acceptable level of performance 24 hours a day and the system must also be able to run the batches in a reasonable amount of time. These two requirements can be difficult to fulfil and most likely impossible to satisfy, if these things aren't carefully considered in the architecture.

The most common mistake is for an architect to handle all objects one at a time, which works fine for online transactions, but can cause huge problems with offline transactions. This can result in a thousand calls or more for single objects, when you're running a large batch for verifying a single object's correctness, for example. This has a devastating impact on performance for the batches—in particular if the objects are returned by another service master over the network—and it means that the batches are at risk of not ending in time.

Instead, the architect should design the architecture considering the offline transactions first, and then use the same routine for single, online transactions—*not* the other way around.

Also, the architect must carefully choose the scope of each offline transaction. In this case the architect has to decide how many objects that are affected by a single transaction before committing it. This has to be done in order to prevent poor performance for online transactions when they run simultaneously (i.e. increasing serializability).

It is also important for the architect to keep the traffic between service masters to a minimum; hence he or she should consider using cached data. Cached data can be stored very well in a database controlled by the consuming service master: and it doesn't have to be stored in-memory.

So what are we really saying here? Well, sometimes you need to think batch first and online processing second. This conclusion is not unique for the SOA architect though— it's applicable for any architecture that must consider both online and offline transactions, in medium to large 7x24 systems. Since many services will communicate over the internet this issue is even more important in such cases than when the services communicate solely inside the company network boundaries. Network performance will probably be better inside the company than across the internet which obviously increases performance.

Windows Communication Foundation

Finally, we'll mention some quick things about Windows Communication Foundation, formerly known as Indigo. According to Don Box, Windows Communication Foundation is "a unified programming model and infrastructure for developing connected systems." Windows Communication Foundation will ship with the next version of Windows (so far code-named Longhorn). The goal of Windows Communication Foundation is to simplify service-oriented development where autonomous applications are built using asynchronous message-passing. Windows Communication Foundation implements SOAP and other web services technologies (like the WS-* Specifications) that allow us to create better services. This new programming model will make it possible for us to add security, reliability, and transactions to SOAP-based applications.

Windows Communication Foundation will ship with Longhorn, but we'll also be able to download it for Windows XP and Windows Server 2003 as well. There will be small differences between these versions, as Windows Communication Foundation will be optimized to use all aspects of Longhorn. But Don Box contends that Windows Communication Foundation will provide the developer with a consistent service-oriented programming model, no matter which operating system you develop on.

Since Windows Communication Foundation uses SOAP as a communications mechanism, we can let our Windows Communication Foundation applications interact with other services on any platform as long as they also use SOAP (see Figure 7-22).

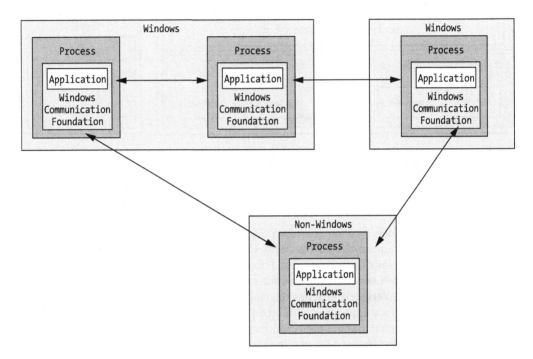

Figure 7-22. *Windows Communication Foundation will interact with any platform as long as SOAP is used*

What Is Windows Communication Foundation?

Windows Communication Foundation takes a bunch of existing technologies, including COM, COM+, MSMQ, .NET Remoting, ASMX, System.Messaging, and .NET Enterprise Services and offers their features as a single unified programming model for any CLR-compliant language (see Figure 7-23 for more information).

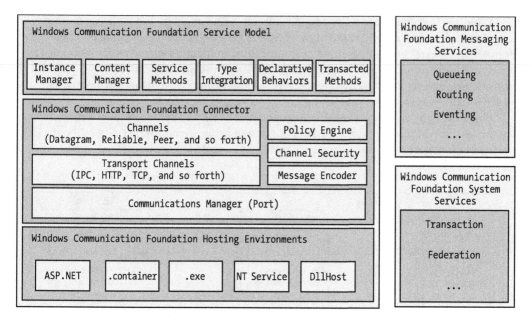

Figure 7-23. *The internals of Windows Communication Foundation, formerly code-named Indigo*

There are five major subsystems in Windows Communication Foundation.

- *The Windows Communication Foundation Service Model* has one major function and that is to associate incoming messages with user-defined code. When incoming messages are detected, Windows Communication Foundation routes them to an instance of user-defined service types. Windows Communication Foundation provides instance and context management for a service and allows developers to use declarative attributes to control the way instances are associated with incoming messages. Windows Communication Foundation's session management routes multiple messages to a common session object. By using declarative behavior, the service model can automate security and reliability as well.

- *The Windows Communication Foundation Connector* is a managed framework that provides both secure and reliable message-based connectivity. By using the SOAP data and the processing model, the connector allows us to let our services be independent of the target platform or transport.

- *The Windows Communication Foundation Hosting Environment* hosts systems like dllhost.exe, svchost.exe, ASP.NET and IIS, to mention a few.

- *System and Messaging Services* provide support for transactions, among other things. A service-based transaction manager, which developers can access via System.Transactions or the WS-AtomicTransactions protocol, is available. You can also find the WS-Federation implementation here, which allows you to securely broker authentication between the service and its corresponding trust authorities. You'll also find queuing and other stuff here.

At the time that we wrote this chapter, Windows Communication Foundation was available for download in beta versions. So, you have a chance of trying it out for yourself before Longhorn arrives, at least if you have a MSDN subscription. We as authors will be sure to do this as it looks promising and seems like it could make life easier for .NET developers.

Summary

This chapter has focused on Service Oriented Architecture and how this might differ from component-based applications. You have seen examples of services and how to use them. Implementing Service Orientation affects the whole company, not just the development of single applications. This means that it's quite an effort to implement SOA in your business. But, we believe that the future benefits are so great that you should definitely take a closer look at this area.

CHAPTER 8

■■■

Internet Information Services

Internet Information Services (IIS) is Microsoft's web server suite, which includes a web server, FTP server, NNTP server, and a few other things. Originally called Internet Information Server, Microsoft partly changed the name in version 5.0. "Server" became "Services" to reflect a shift in Microsoft's view of what IIS really is. Earlier, IIS was more or less an add-on product to Windows NT, but now it's an application running like a service, closely integrated with the operating system.

As mentioned in Chapter 2, IIS 5.0 was introduced with Windows 2000. This edition represented a giant step forward compared to its predecessors. Reliability and performance were greatly increased with this version, and the need for restarting an entire web server when an application error occurred almost vanished. (Well, not entirely, but this version was a great improvement.)

IIS 6.0 was delivered with Windows Server 2003 and is a giant leap forward. Even though the administrational tools may look similar to earlier versions, not much of the same functionality remains. Microsoft has rewritten and re-architected IIS and even further enhanced reliability, performance, and, not least of all, security.

In this chapter, we will take a deeper look at the architecture of the two versions of IIS. We will also look at performance, scalability, and security so that you can implement a web server that fulfills your demands when you're building web applications and sites.

Toward the end of the chapter, we will also give you an overview of the ASP.NET architecture.

Internet Information Services 5.0

In this chapter we'll show you the architecture of IIS. We will start with IIS 5.0 and then continue with IIS 6.0. We will examine some of the exciting features in the latest version that let you build scalable web applications and web services, and show you how you can use IIS 5.0 in a scalable environment.

Architecture

Let us start with an exploration of IIS 5.0. IIS includes more than just the web server, as mentioned earlier, but because these other features fall outside of the scope of this book, we won't discuss them here. However, if you would like to learn more about these, please see
`http://www.microsoft.com/WindowsServer2003/iis/default.mspx`.

As a service, IIS is running closely integrated with the operating system. This way it can use many of the other services running on Windows 2000. For example, security can be used in conjunction with Active Directory, and scalability can be improved with Network Load Balancing (NLB). Because it's close to the Windows 2000 security model, dedicated user account administration is unnecessary. Even if the server is not running Active Directory, IIS employs its user account handling (see Figure 8-1).

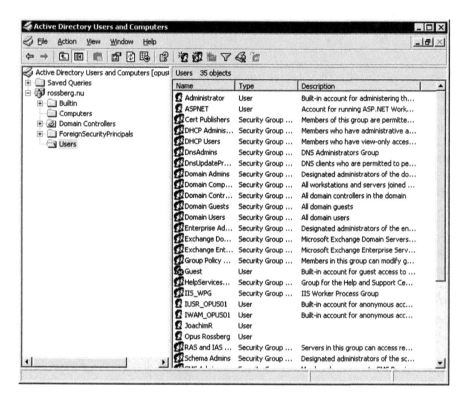

Figure 8-1. *The Windows 2000 user-management feature*

When it comes to administration and monitoring, IIS 5.0 also takes advantage of operating system tools like the System Monitor, Event Viewer, and MMC. A benefit of this is that administrators get tools that are similar to all other tools in Windows 2000, and therefore they don't have to learn a completely new user interface just to manage the web server.

Figure 8-2 presents an architectural overview of IIS 5.0.

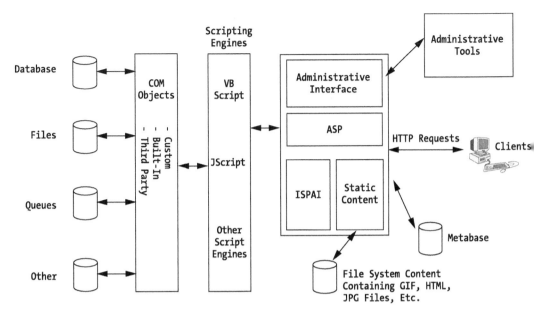

Figure 8-2. *An overview of the IIS 5.0 architecture*

All Windows-based services and applications are run in memory areas called *processes*. The Internet services in IIS 5.0 reside in the Inetinfo process (inetinfo.exe). This process also contains the shared thread pool, cache, and logging services of IIS.

■**Note** The Inetinfo process is *pageable*. This means the system can remove all or part of this process from RAM and write it to disk if not enough RAM is left (which negatively affects IIS performance). The remedy is to provide enough RAM to your web servers so you can avoid paging and keep the Inetinfo process in RAM at all times. But as you will see, there is a limit to how much RAM IIS can handle, which you also have to consider.

One of the problems of versions of IIS prior to version 5.0 was that a single application error could bring down the entire server, due to all Internet Server API (ISAPI) applications (like ASP) sharing the resources and memory of the Inetinfo process. When an application is run like this, it is said to run *in-process*. Another problem with such applications was that they could not be unloaded without a restart of the entire physical server. This provided some problems naturally, since all web sites hosted on the server became affected by this. You might think such an approach to running applications had too many drawbacks, but it had its benefits, too. Performance for one thing was high, but honestly the disadvantages were so great that this was not enough to promote this technology in the long run.

IIS 5.0 provides three ways to run your applications, as listed here (and illustrated in Figure 8-3):

- Running applications in-process in the Inetinfo process

- Running applications isolated from web services in a process called dllhost.exe, which is called *out-of-process*

- Running applications in a pooled process separate from web services. This is also an out-of-process procedure handled by the dllhost.exe

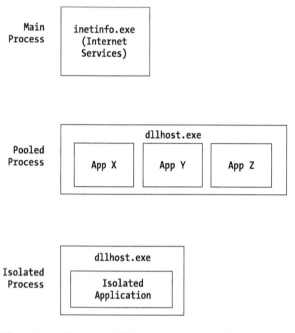

Figure 8-3. *The three different ways an application can be run in IIS 5.0*

This solution is called *application protection* and provides for a much more stable and reliable application architecture than was possible before. If you run applications in a pooled process, an error will not take the whole server down. All applications in the pool will fail, but the web server will still be up and running. If you have a very important application, you can run it as an isolated process. This application will then be run in a separate instance of dllhost.exe, making it harder for other applications to bring it down with them if they encounter an error.

But all good things usually come with a price tag. In this case, performance is negatively affected by running pooled or isolated applications. Microsoft has tried to overcome this performance drop by looking over the IIS 5.0 code, but our recommendation is not to run more than ten isolated applications on a server.

Figure 8-4 shows how to set the application protection level for a specific site. You can only set this on the Home Directory or Virtual Directory properties sheet of a web site. You can select High (Isolated), Low (IIS Process), or Medium (Pooled) from the Application Protection drop-down list.

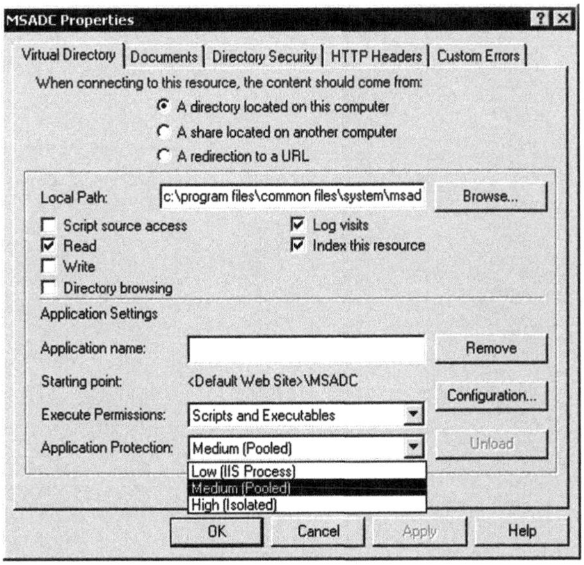

Figure 8-4. *Setting the application protection for a web application or site*

The default setting for application protection specifies that web services in inetinfo.exe will run in their own processes. All other applications will be run in a single, pooled process using dllhost.exe, unless you manually change the settings. We recommend keeping the default setting, and only letting applications with the highest priority run as isolated processes.

If an error occurs, the best way to solve the problem is *not* by rebooting the server. This behavior was what gave Microsoft's operating systems a bad reputation in the first place. Nonetheless, in the past this was necessary to reboot the server in order to unload troublesome applications from memory and restart the web server. Imagine if you had to do the same if a CD player in your car started misbehaving: "Sorry, a CD player error has occurred. Please turn off the engine and restart the car." You would probably not buy that car. To overcome errors, Windows 2000 includes *IIS Reliable Restart*, which provides a faster, easier, and more flexible one-step restart, as shown in Figure 8-5. The administrator can restart IIS by right-clicking an item in the MMC.

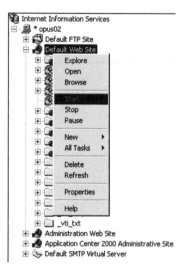

Figure 8-5. *The new IIS Reliable Restart*

You can also restart the IIS by issuing the iisreset command at the command prompt as you can see in Figure 8-6.

```
C:\WINNT\System32\cmd.exe                                              _ □ X
Microsoft Windows 2000 [Version 5.00.2195]
(C) Copyright 1985-2000 Microsoft Corp.

C:\>iisreset /?

IISRESET.EXE (c) Microsoft Corp. 1998-1999

Usage:
iisreset [computername]

        /RESTART            Stop and then restart all Internet services.
        /START              Start all Internet services.
        /STOP               Stop all Internet services.
        /REBOOT             Reboot the computer.
        /REBOOTONERROR      Reboot the computer if an error occurs when starting,
                            stopping, or restarting Internet services.
        /NOFORCE            Do not forcefully terminate Internet services if
                            attempting to stop them gracefully fails.
        /TIMEOUT:val        Specify the timeout value ( in seconds ) to wait for
                            a successful stop of Internet services. On expiration
                            of this timeout the computer can be rebooted if
                            the /REBOOTONERROR parameter is specified.
                            The default value is 20s for restart, 60s for stop,
                            and 0s for reboot.
        /STATUS             Display the status of all Internet services.
        /ENABLE             Enable restarting of Internet Services
                            on the local system.
        /DISABLE            Disable restarting of Internet Services
                            on the local system.

C:\>
```

Figure 8-6. *The command-line tool to restart IIS if an error takes down the Inetinfo process*

IIS uses the Windows Service Manager to automatically restart IIS. By doing this it lessens some of the tasks an administrator otherwise has to do.

To increase performance, it is important to optimize access to your web site. Clients access your site by an IP address and a port number. On a web server the default port is port 80. This unique identifier (IP address:port number) is called a *socket*. In IIS 4.0, sockets were allocated on a per-web-site basis. You could bind various web sites to different IP addresses. Each site on an IP address had several sockets, but the sites didn't share sockets. Since each socket consumed a good deal of RAM, performance would suffer if too many sites were hosted on a server.

In IIS 5.0, a technique called *socket pooling* enables the possibility of allocating sockets on a per-port basis. All connections are pooled on 0.0.0.0:X, where X is the port that the web sites are set up to listen on. This is usually port 80. Socket pooling is done regardless of the actual IP address of the target virtual host. So, when IIS starts up, it sets up a shared socket pool across all of the available IP addresses, and starts for IIS traffic on all of the IP addresses, on the assigned port. This means that sites on different IP addresses, using the same port, also share the same sockets. No matter how many sites you place on a port, they all share the same sockets. This reduces resource consumption dramatically. But there are also some problems with this. IIS 5.0 locks out other applications from setting up sockets on all IP addresses. So, if you success-fully create a socket using a port that IIS wants to use before IIS is started, IIS will fail to start and return an error.

Socket pooling is enabled by default. If you have a mission-critical web site, it might be a good choice to disable this feature for that specific site. Although resource consumption is decreased with socket pooling, performance can still be affected if too many sites share the same port. Also, if you have another application that needs port 80 on an IIS server, or you want to finely tune the performance of one of your virtual hosts and not another, you will need to disable socket pooling. Read more about disabling socket pooling at the following URL: http://support.microsoft.com/default.aspx?scid=kb;EN-US;813368. Otherwise, we recommend not changing the default values. You must use a script to disable socket pooling because there is no GUI way of altering this setting. To change it, open a command prompt and enter

```
x:\inetpub\adminscripts\cscript adsutil.vbs set w3svc/disablesocketpooling true
```

which will return

```
"disablesocketpooling : (BOOLEAN) True"
```

when the command has executed.

As you understand from the preceding reasoning, IIS 5.0 can help you host several sites on one server. This is hardly anything new, though. IIS 5.0 offers three ways to distinguish between multiple sites:

- Port numbers

- IP addresses

- Host header names

This is quite logical, since each web site has a unique identity consisting of three parts: IP address, port number, and host header name. Host header names are simply either the NET-BIOS or the Fully Qualified Domain Name (FQDN) associated with a web site in IIS. By varying these parts, you can create unique identities for your main sites. You could, for instance, have your main site at address 192.168.0.1:8 and another site at 192.168.0.1:9, where the first site uses port 8 and the second port 9. They still share the same IP address. The problem here is that you always need to include the port number after the IP address or DNS name. Therefore, it might be better to use multiple IP addresses or perhaps different host header names.

Two more things in IIS 5.0 can help you increase performance on your sites. The first is *process throttling*, which helps you control how much processor time a web site and its applications can use. This is something you can use only for out-of-process applications, so it isn't possible to use with the Inetinfo process. The other, called *bandwidth throttling*, is similar to process throttling. The difference is that bandwidth throttling allows you to control the amount of bandwidth a site can use on the network interface card (NIC). Keep in mind that this solution, as well as process throttling, only affects static content like HTML files or graphics files. It does not affect dynamic ASP files or other dynamic content, so you can't use this to trim your ASP sites. Please also note that if you use socket pooling, bandwidth throttling affects all applications in the pool on that port number.

Apart from the IIS architecture itself, a lot of improvements were made to enhance the application environment. With the help of *flow control capabilities* in ASP, you can write more efficient web applications by cutting down on round-trips to the server. Figure 8-7 shows the benefits of using server.transfer instead of server.redirect, when a redirect to another ASP page on the same server is necessary.

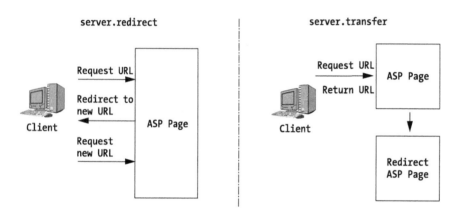

Figure 8-7. *Server.transfer cuts the number of round-trips to the server, which increases performance*

Many of the web-based components were also improved to increase performance and to make them scale well. Most of them were in large part rewritten to accomplish this. An example of one of these components is browscap.dll, which determines browser capabilities.

IIS 5.0 creates up to four threads per CPU in its default settings. The number of threads is continuously changed by IIS, depending on the activity on the server. For most systems this setting is OK, but in some cases it might be necessary to change this value. If you monitor your system and find that the CPU is not always active, but almost all threads seem to be busy, it might be a good thing to increase this value. But you must make sure you have enough processor capacity left: otherwise this change will lead to less processor time per thread. If you need to change this value, you must use a registry editor and add the MaxPoolThreads entry to the following registry string:

```
HKEY_LOCAL_MACHINE\SYSTEM\CurrentControlSet\Services\Inetinfo\Parameters
```

This entry sets the units of threads per processor and should be a value between 2 and 20. After this is added, it's important to monitor the system so that this change accomplishes what you wanted it to do. One tip is to try this in the lab before implementing it on a production server.

Caution As always, be careful when modifying the registry.

ASP thread-gating is a part of the *ASP self-tuning* features. This feature monitors the CPU(s) and starts restricting the number of threads when a set threshold is reached. This is done by IIS to dynamically control the number of concurrent threads that are allowed to execute. By default, thread gating is disabled because the settings are appropriate for most applications anyway. If you change this setting when you really don't need to, performance can deteriorate. And IIS actually increases or decreases the number of threads anyway, even if thread gating is disabled.

IIS 5.0, being tightly integrated with Windows 2000, also works together with COM+ to enable developers to write and build web applications. IIS uses COM+ for mostly three purposes:

- Handling transaction coordination

- Managing communication between COM components

- Isolating applications into distinct processes

Performance and Scalability

Now that you have seen a little of the architecture of IIS 5.0, it might be a good idea to have a closer look at how to achieve good performance and scalability in an IIS 5.0 application. A lot of things need to be considered when you're designing the infrastructure for a scalable application. Both hardware and software work together to achieve this. What good is it to you if you design the best application possible, but you run it on low-budget, nonperforming hardware? And to turn that around: What use do you have for a top-of-the-line server park if your application designers don't know the benefits of good design and thorough testing?

This part of the chapter will focus on the IIS, but we cannot avoid consideration of other aspects as well, such as operating system tuning and solutions to hardware issues in general.

So, let's start with performance. How do you really know whether performance is good or bad on your web server? And if you really suspect performance is bad, how do you know what is causing this? To answer these questions, you need to develop a plan for evaluating performance. This plan might look different from web site to web site, but the main thing is that you sit down and consider this matter. There are, however, a few rules of thumb to follow when carrying out the plan:

- Use a test lab where you have a controlled environment

- Monitor the test lab servers under different workloads

- Test applications and solutions before deployment

- Apply changes one at a time

- Monitor the production servers

- Have a backup plan

The plan, as well as the tuning itself, will help you remove bottlenecks from your system. This can be beneficial to you in several ways. First of all, the user experience will improve because response times will be better. Secondly, your friends in the accounting department will be happy because you might not need to add as many servers to the cluster as you calculated in the first place. The period before the next upgrade might be longer because you can make better use of the resources you already have. But in our opinion, the most important reason is that by tuning your system to take advantage of your hardware in the best way, your applications can have more, and probably better, features that improve your business.

To be able to determine what to tune in your system, it is important to have a baseline for your system. To collect this baseline, you'll need to monitor your system for a period of time, and under different loads, before you start experimenting. That's right, *experimenting*, because most of the tuning is done by trial and error. This is why it is so important to only change one setting at a time.

To gather a baseline, you use the Performance Monitor in Windows 2000, shown in Figure 8-8, and the built-in performance counters that are provided by the operating system and IIS.

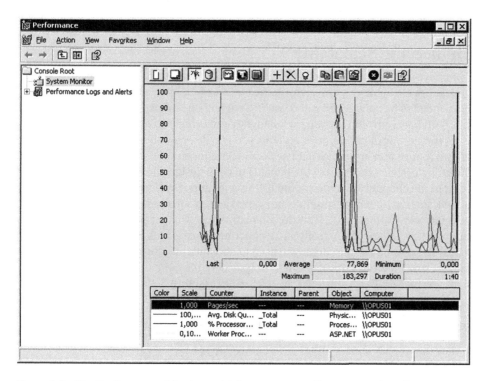

Figure 8-8. *The Performance Monitor, which you use to collect a server baseline.*

Once you have a baseline, you can start comparing your changes to it and see whether the performance was affected the way you wanted. You can do this by running a new monitoring period after a change has been implemented and seeing what effect it has.

One important thing that we can't stress enough is testing. Many developers don't take testing as seriously as they should. This is a dangerous attitude that often will punish these developers in the long run. Before implementing anything, you need to be certain that everything has been tested and that it all works as planned. You must be sure that your hardware is up to the task. You must be confident that the application design and your code have been thoroughly tested as well. You also must be certain any changes to your system have been tested before you implement them. To do this, you need to have a test plan and a test environment. In this test lab, you'll deploy your applications and test all aspects of them. To have a quality test, it might be a smart choice to have a test leader who is separate from the project. This way the test leader is more objective, which almost always leads to better testing.

Note In the lab you should also stress test your applications. This is done with a stress test tool like Web Application Stress Tool, from Microsoft, or Application Center Test, included with Visual Studio .NET Enterprise Architect version. These tools fake client requests based on values you have provided before the test and give you a summary report so you can evaluate performance afterwards.

When you've finally accepted the results of lab testing, you can start deploying the application, or changes, in your production environment. The monitoring does not stop here, however. Once you have deployed the application, you need to continue surveying it so that you can catch possible misbehavior before it happens.

Next, we will discuss just what you should monitor and the problems that might be solved by this.

Hardware

If your hardware platform is under-dimensioned, you have a problem. No matter how well you have designed your application, performance will suffer anyway. You must first make sure your system has enough RAM to avoid problems. The absolute minimum amount of RAM to run Windows 2000 with IIS 5.0 is 128MB. But no one in his or her right mind would try to run a server with this configuration. Our recommendation is starting with at least 512MB or more, preferably 1GB of RAM, depending on the type of applications you are going to run on the system. By default the IIS file cache is set to use half of the RAM available, so the more the merrier, at least to a certain degree. If you have too much RAM, the IIS file cache can't use it fully and excessive paging might occur. Therefore, it might be good not to exceed 2GB to 3GB of RAM for a standard web server.

Note The static file cache lives in the Inetinfo process and can store up to 1.5GB of content. But in reality the ObjectCacheTTL value is set to a default of 30 seconds, which is too small for the file cache to grow to this size. ObjectCacheTTL determines the amount of time that objects (like files) are held in cached memory before they are discarded. This is a registry value not added by default, so if you want to change the default setting for this, you must use a registry editor to add MemCacheSize and ObjectCacheTTL to HKEY_LOCAL_ MACHINE_SYSTEM\CurrentControlSet\Services\Inetinfo\Parameters. Please note that if the MemCacheSize is set to a too large value excessive paging can occur so again, test in your lab first before deploying in production. For more information about this, please refer to http://www.microsoft.com/technet/ or the Windows 2000 Resource Kit.

To determine if memory provides a bottleneck, you should monitor and log the following performance counters on your system:

- *Memory: Available bytes.* Try to have at least 10 percent available for times with heavy loads.

- *Memory: Page faults/sec.* When a process requests a page in memory, and the system can't find it at the requested location, we say that a page fault has occurred. There are two kinds of page faults: soft page faults and hard page faults. Soft page faults can be measured with Memory: Transition faults/sec and occur when a page is found somewhere else in memory. This is not very serious, since most operating systems handle these faults and minimize the impact they could have. Hard page faults, on the other hand, are more severe and can result in unnecessary delays. You measure this type of fault with Memory: Pages input/sec to determine how many pages were read from disk to resolve this. It might also be a good idea to monitor Memory: Page read/sec to find out how many times the disk was read to correct hard page faults. If these numbers are high, the rest of your system does not have enough memory because too much is reserved for the caches. To resolve this, you might have to lower the cache sizes or add more RAM.

- *Memory: Cache bytes.* You should monitor this counter to see if your system cache is running out of memory. Remember that the IIS file cache by default is set to use a maximum of 50 percent of available memory.

- *Internet Information Services Global: File cache hits %.* This counter tells you whether the requests find their target in the cache or not. The higher the value, the better performance you have. For static content, a good value might be as high as 80 percent.

- *Process (Inetinfo): Virtual bytes, Process (dllhost#n): Virtual bytes, Process (Inetinfo): Working set, and Process (dllhost#n): Working set.* These monitor the amount of virtual space available to IIS 5.0 and the number of memory pages used by each process.

Another important thing to monitor is the capacity of the processor(s). You must be certain that one or more processes do not consume too much processor time. If they do, other processes must wait in queue to be executed. Even though memory issues are the biggest problems on a Windows 2000/IIS 5.0 system, you should not forget the processor(s). Before you add more CPUs to your system, however, you must rule out memory problems, because solving such problems often results in the biggest performance gains. IIS 5.0 scales very well on a two-four CPU system. If you have a system with more CPUs, you must do a little tuning to get it to work properly. Remember, you can't get it to scale on more than eight CPUs without partitioning the system.

■**Note** To learn more about this, please visit http://www.microsoft.com/technet/ or refer to the Windows 2000 Resource Kit.

Here are a couple performance counters to help you determine if the CPUs are a problem in your system:

- *Processor: % Processor time.* If you have a constant high value here, you might begin to assume something is eating processor time. But before you take any action, you must check to see if the disk I/O and NIC usage are below capacity. If they are, you might assume you have a processor problem.

- *System: Processor queue length.* This value indicates the number of threads waiting to be executed in the processor queue. If the value is two or higher, for a longer period of time, you have a processor bottleneck.

If you have added CPUs to your system and still have problems, you'll have to turn to other methods to solve this issue. A good idea at that point is to scale out on more servers by using Network Load Balancing. This issue is dissected in Chapter 2.

There are more hardware issues to consider if you are to optimize your system. Network capacity and disk optimization are important too, but we will not go into these areas here. Some of these will pop up in the next chapter, and the rest we'll leave to the system administrators. This does not mean they are not important; they just do not have that much to do with IIS.

Security

Even security has an impact on performance. This means you have a delicate situation to handle, because you must make your users feel secure when accessing your site and still give them a good user experience without bad performance. Let us consider when you use Secure Sockets Layer (SSL), for example. SSL connections are cached in the SSL session cache. The default setting for sessions to live in this cache is five minutes in Windows 2000. If a request needs to reconnect to a session that has expired, this comes with a penalty five times as expensive as finding the connection in the cache.

■**Note** If you want to support longer SSL sessions, you must increase the time-out period by setting the ServerCacheTime value in the registry. Please refer to the Windows 2000 Resource Kit for how to change this value.

Since most security issues are tightly integrated with the operating system, it can be hard to monitor them separately. Therefore security overhead must often be measured by running tests. Run the tests with and without the security feature(s) and compare the results.

Web Applications

You are in a good spot if you have made sure your hardware is working smoothly. But does this really matter if your applications misbehave? Of course it doesn't. You must also make sure the applications work properly, as we have stressed before. A badly written application can degrade performance terribly. This is the reason you must spend a good deal of time on designing and testing your applications.

■**Note** If your applications retrieve information from legacy systems, like AS/400 and UNIX, or from other web sites, you might not have control over the performance of these sources. You might also experience problems if remote SQL Servers behave poorly. If you can, you should try to monitor these applications as well, but this might not be possible in many cases. If you suspect an application bottleneck, you need to determine whether the problems are caused by your own server, or whether the problems occur on systems out of your control. If they occur on your server, you still have a chance of taking care of them. If they appear on remote databases, you must begin to consider whether it's worth the trouble of setting up a database to cache the information from the remote system on the same subnet as your system and then configuring the replication between this database and the remote system.

If you have a lot of ASP pages, the following performance counters are good to keep an eye on:

- *Active Server Pages: Requests/Sec.* This counter will give you a hint whether your applications are causing the bottleneck. If values are low during peak traffic, you might have a troublesome application.

- *Active Server Pages: Requests executing.* This shows how many requests are executing at the moment.

- *Active Server Pages: Requests wait time, Active Server Pages: Executing time, and Active Server Pages: Requests queued.* These three counters should be close to zero if everything is OK. Otherwise, requests take too long to execute and others are waiting in the queue. The queue's maximum length is determined by the value ASPRequestQueueMax in the metabase. If these values are constantly high, you need to go over your code and try to rewrite to optimize performance where you can. It is a bit tricky to know the correct value for this, and you must consider many factors to calculate it. When trying to determine the value, please consider the number of CPUs, the setting for ASPProcessorThreadMax, and the number of processes hosting ASP.

- *Web Service: CGI requests/sec, Web Service: ISAPI extension, Web Service: Get requests/sec, and Web Service: Post requests/sec.* The latter two counters show how many get and post requests are made to your system. This can give you a good estimate of the load on your system. If these values are constantly high, it might be a good solution to scale out on more servers. The first two counters should not drop under a heavy load. If the latter two are high and the first two are low, you need to do something about the design of your application or about the code itself.

We have so far mostly talked about scaling up—that is, adding more hardware and doing application rewrites to solve performance problems. There is, however, another way to increase performance, and we mentioned it briefly earlier. What we're talking about is scaling out—that is, spreading the load on several servers in a cluster (or web farm, as it is also called). Keep in mind, though, that scaling out in no way replaces scaling up or monitoring an individual server. In order to get as much performance as possible from your solution, you have to work on a broad front. Scaling out helps you in more ways than just enhancing your performance. It is a great way of increasing both scalability and reliability, as we showed you Chapter 2. In a web cluster, one of the most common ways to enable load balancing is by using NLB, at least on a Microsoft solution. NLB is relatively easy to enable. The next chapter will show you how to enable it on a Windows 2000 Server and Windows Server 2003 solution.

Now you have seen a few of the monitoring possibilities for tuning a separate web server running IIS 5.0. A lot of these tricks are also valid on IIS 6.0. There are several other important things to think about when you plan your web application infrastructure as well. We will now take a look at some best practices when it comes to securing IIS 5.0. These can be a great help in preventing attacks against the web server itself.

Security

While we were writing this book, a new attack on Internet servers had just occurred. The virus this time, called Slammer, infected SQL Servers and degraded performance on many servers all over the world. The irony in this is that Microsoft provided a fix for this potential problem some six months before someone actually exploited the vulnerability. This fix had been available for download all the time. But IT professionals all over the world hadn't updated their servers because the fix was a bit complicated to apply. Even Microsoft had several servers unpatched and experienced some problems due to the virus, which is the real irony. (Yes, we must admit, one of us missed a server as well.) Even though Microsoft should have made the patch easier to install, that isn't what we would like to point out here. No, our point is that the importance of keeping up to date with the latest security patches and service packs. This is important since outages of your systems cost a lot, and put in perspective to the cost of applying patches, there really is no discussion. You must keep your servers up to date on this issue.

There are a few ways to do this:

- *Windows Update.* This is included with most Windows versions nowadays.

- *Windows 2000 IIS 5.0 Hotfix Checking Tool.* This tool helps you distribute patches to all your web servers (http://www.microsoft.com/Downloads/_Release.asp?ReleaseID=24168).

- *Microsoft Product Security Notification.* Subscribe to this e-mail list to get information about security issues (http://www.microsoft.com/technet/security).

You should also change the default web site location on your disk from c:\inetpub to some other volume. This is worthwhile because it would cause a hacker some problems when he tried navigating the directory tree. In this case, the command "..\" would not give access to the C drive, but hopefully we have taken steps to further hinder a hacker from doing this. This means you should disable the Enable parent paths option that allows you to use ".." in calls to functions such as MapPath. To disable it, follow these procedures:

1. Right-click the root of the web site.

2. Choose Properties.

3. Click the Home Directory tab.

4. Click Configuration.

5. Click the Apps options tab.

6. Uncheck the Enable parent paths checkbox, shown in Figure 8-9.

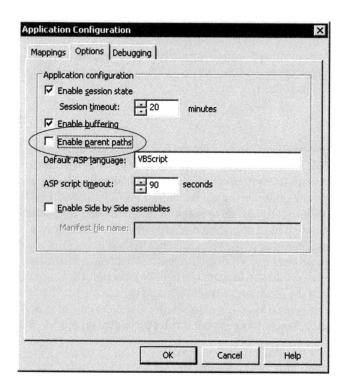

Figure 8-9. *The Enable parent paths option*

While we are talking about the directory structure, we may as well continue with removing the samples directories included with IIS 5.0. These are not necessary on a production server and could be a threat to your system. Remove the following (if they exist):

- `\inetpub\iissamples`

- `%systemroot%\help\iishelp`

- `\program files\common files\system\msadc`

You should also consider removing unnecessary virtual directories in the inetpub directory. IISADMPWD is not needed unless you have an absolute demand for this management feature. If this is present, consider removing it.

The *IIS Lockdown Tool*, a handy helper, is available for free from Microsoft (`http://www.microsoft.com/technet/treeview/default.asp?url=/technet/security/_tools/tools/locktool.asp`). This tool enables you to lock down IIS 5.0 without specifying individual registry settings and security policies. Use this to reduce the area exposed to potential hackers.

Remove all unused script or application mappings. IIS is preconfigured to support common filename extensions such as .asp and .shtm. If you install the .NET Framework, even more mappings are added. Remove any that aren't needed and then rebind them to the 404.dll extension available with the IIS Lockdown Tool.

Make sure that all the accounts you use only have the minimum privileges they require. The ASPNET account used for running ASP.NET code, for example, should not be given more privileges than it needs. This is created as a local service account when installing the .NET Framework redistributable code and belongs to the users group on the machine. Add this account to the web application group created by the IIS Lockdown Tool. This will prevent the account from running any unauthorized command-line executables if an attack occurs.

Another great tool included with IIS Lockdown Tool is *URLScan*. This is an ISAPI filter that can help you control which set of extensions can be used in the application, and also block long requests. Long requests are exploited when an attacker tries to insert malicious code by user input, and by using URLScan you can block that.

Another way to enhance security is by controlling access to the web content directories. You should, as always, apply the rule of not letting anyone have more privileges than is absolutely necessary. The ASP.NET process often only needs read access to content files, for instance. Anonymous users should only have read-only permissions to the content according to what is appropriate for the situation. It is vital to look over the Access Control Lists (ACLs) so you don't miss anything.

You should also consider restricting access to the log files. This way you can prevent a hacker from covering up his or her tracks by altering the log files. But for this to be of any use, you obviously must enable logging on your server. Follow these steps to enable W3C extended logging format:

1. Start the Internet Information Services Tool.

2. Right-click the web site.

3. Choose Properties.

4. Click the web site tab.

5. Check the Enable logging checkbox.

6. Choose W3C extended log file format from the active log format drop-down list.

7. Click Properties and click the Advanced tab.

8. Click the Extended properties tab and select the following (see Figure 8-10):

   - Client IP Address

   - User Name

- Service Name

- Server Name

- Server IP Address (if this applies to multiple sites)

- Server Port

- Method

- URI Stem

- URI Query

- Protocol Status

- Protocol Substatus

- Win32 Status (for debugging)

- User Agent

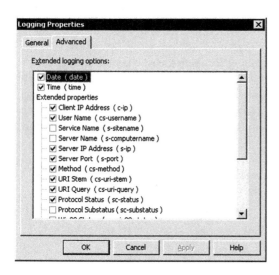

Figure 8-10. *The extended logging options of the W3C extended log file format*

These logs can help you determine what a hacker has tried to do to your system. It might be a good idea to let a developer write an application that scans these log files regularly and looks for, amongst other things, error 5 in Win32 status, which means that access has been denied.

Another thing worth considering is setting an IPSec packet filtering policy on all web servers, in order to provide extra security if someone gets past your firewalls. Try to block all TCP/IP protocols and ports that you don't need to support.

By executing the NetBIOS adapter status command, a hacker could get access to the name of the currently logged-on user. To avoid this, you should consider disabling NetBIOS over TCP on public connections of the server. But before you do this on any of your connections though, you must be sure none of your administrational applications, tools, or other applications depend on this. So our advice is to try this in the test lab before implementing it in the production environment.

Now you have seen various ways of enhancing performance, scalability, and security on systems running Windows 2000 and IIS 5.0. These are some of the best practices we have found relevant in many cases. But as always, they are not all applicable to every situation. Try them in the test lab first to avoid unexpected problems in your production environment later.

Next we will move on to Internet Information Services 6.0 and show you what is new in this latest version of IIS.

Internet Information Services 6.0

Although IIS 5.0 was a giant leap forward from previous versions, IIS 6.0 is even better. Under the hood almost everything has been rewritten to improve all aspects of its components and services. A significant change has been made to the IIS architecture that enhances scalability, reliability, manageability, security, performance, and application development. The next part of this chapter will try to show why this is not marketing hype.

The following five services are the cornerstones of IIS 6.0:

- *World Wide Web Publishing Service (WWW Service)*. This service is provided by iisw3adm.dll and is hosted by the svchost.exe.

- *File Transfer Protocol Service (FTP Service)*. ftpsvc.dll provides this service, which is hosted by the inetinfo.exe.

- *Simple Mail Transfer Protocol Service (SMTP Service)*. smtpsvc.dll is also hosted by inetinfo.exe.

- *Network News Transfer Protocol Service (NNTP Service)*. nntpsvc.dll, which provides the NNTP Service, is also hosted by the inetinfo.exe.

- *IIS Admin Service*. This last service, provided by iisadmin.dll, is hosted by the inetinfo.exe as well.

In the rest of this chapter, we will focus primarily on the WWW Service and its architecture. There will also be a walkthrough of the improvements for performance, scalability, and security in this latest version of IIS. First we will start with the new architecture.

Architecture

As you have seen, applications can contain code that sometimes generates errors such as memory leaks, access violations, and many others. An error generated in one web application can bring a whole web server down, and thereby affect more sites than the one the error occurred in. The processes hosting the applications need to be active managers of the runtime environment to catch these errors in time to take actions that minimize the effect they have on other applications. If the hosting process also is fault tolerant, and has the ability to restart processes and queue requests in the meantime, users of the application might not even notice the error. To provide all this, IIS 6.0 includes a new application isolation environment with active process management. This is named *worker process isolation mode*, but before we take a closer look at this, we'll show you how the IIS 6.0 request processing architecture works.

The Inetinfo process was the main web server process in IIS 5.0 that let dllhost.exe handle requests to out-of-process applications. In IIS 6.0, the architecture presents a new kernel mode driver that two components, also new, use. These new components are *HTTP.SYS*, which is a kernel-mode HTTP listener, and the *WWW Service Administration and Monitoring Component*, which is a user-mode configuration and process manager.

Note All web application processing done by the lisw3adm.dll, which is the WWW Service, is loaded into one or more host processes called worker processes. The worker process executable is w3wp.exe. An application pool corresponds to one request queue within HTTP.SYS and one or more worker processes. The application pool is a collection of one or more web applications or sites.

HTTP.SYS listens for requests and sends them to the appropriate application pool queue. No third-party code runs in HTTP.SYS, which provides for high fault tolerance, since failures in user-mode code cannot affect it. If an error occurs that terminates the user-mode request processing, HTTP.SYS continues to accept and queue requests because the only thing being affected is the worker process. This means that the WWW Service is still running. When WWW Service notices the failed worker process, it automatically starts a new one as long as there are requests left in the queue. Since the requests are still accepted, an end user should experience minimum disruption to the service. However, HTTP.SYS can't queue requests forever. Three conditions stop it from accepting requests:

- No queues are available.

- No space is left on the queue.

- The web service has been shut down.

The WWW Service Administration and Monitoring Component is responsible for configuration and process management. When initialization of the service occurs, metabase information is read, and the HTTP.SYS namespace routing table is initialized with one entry for each application. The routing table maps a URL to a specific application pool. This way HTTP.SYS knows that there is an application pool that will respond to requests for a specific namespace. First, after this mapping, it can request the start of a worker process for an application pool when there is demand for it.

The WWW Service Administration and Monitoring Component is also responsible for controlling the lifetime of the worker processes. In this role it determines the following:

- When to start a worker process

- When to recycle a worker process

- When to restart a worker process

Let us now take a closer look at the worker process isolation mode. As you saw earlier in the chapter, a performance penalty is incurred for running applications in isolation mode with IIS 5.0 and earlier versions. This is no longer true with IIS 6.0.

After an HTTP request has been routed to the correct application pool queue, the worker process pulls the request from HTTP.SYS. This eliminates the overhead of sending a request to an out-of-process DLL host and back again.

Figure 8-11 presents an overview of IIS 6.0 running in worker process isolation mode.

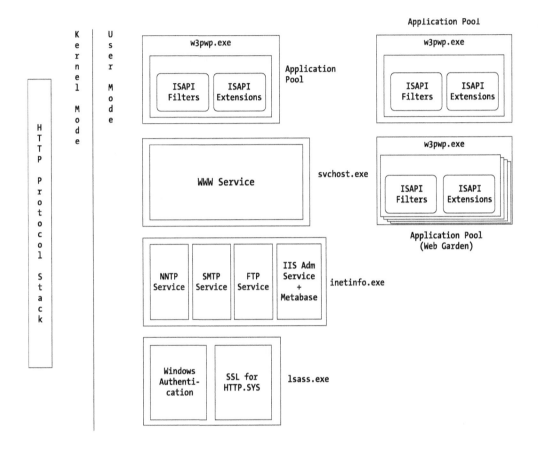

Figure 8-11. *An overview of IIS 6.0 when running in worker process isolation mode*

Here is what really happens when a new request arrives at HTTP.SYS:

1. The new request arrives at HTTP.SYS.

2. HTTP.SYS decides if the request is valid.

3. If the request is invalid, code for the invalid request is sent back to the client.

4. If it is valid, a check is made by HTTP.SYS to find out if the request can be located in the kernel-mode cache.

5. If it is found in the cache, a response is immediately returned.

6. If not in the cache, HTTP.SYS places the request in the correct queue.

7. If no worker processes are assigned to the queue, WWW Service starts one.

8. The worker process pulls the request from the queue and processes it.

9. The response is sent back to HTTP.SYS by the worker process.

10. HTTP.SYS sends the response back to the client.

11. If logging is enabled, HTTP.SYS writes the request to the log.

In IIS 6.0, all HTTP application runtime services, like ISAPI support, are available to every application pool. There is no longer any notion of in-process applications, which means an application error in one specific web application or web site can't affect other web applications or sites.

Next we will examine the application pools. As an administrator, you can collect one or more web applications or web sites into a separate group, called an *application pool*. The applications or sites in a pool share one or more worker processes. Application pools are separated from each other by process boundaries, which prevents one pool from affecting others and also makes sure an application can't be routed to another pool as long as the current pool is servicing it. However, you can quite easily assign applications to other pools if you want, even when the server is running. Each of these application pools is represented in HTTP.SYS by a request queue. The user-mode worker process(es) serving a pool fetches requests from this queue.

Note By default, each application pool has only one worker process, but you can configure it to have n worker processes sharing the work. HTTP.SYS distributes among the worker processes in the pool. This configuration is known as a web garden. The difference between a web garden and a web farm is that the former resides on one server and the latter on many. One benefit of this is that if one worker process fails, there are others to take its place immediately.

Here is how you create a new application pool (see also Figure 8-12):

1. Open IIS Manager.

2. Expand Application Pools.

3. Right-click Application Pools.

4. Choose New\Application Pool.

5. Enter an ID for the pool (for example, MyNewPool).

6. Click OK to create the new application pool.

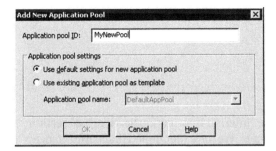

Figure 8-12. *Adding a new application pool*

By providing the worker process isolation mode, IIS 6.0 makes sure you can prevent one application or site from stopping the others.

To be compatible with IIS 5.0, IIS 6.0 includes something called *IIS 5.0 isolation mode.* This is an isolation mode that works very similarly to the corresponding mode in IIS 5.0 and lets you more easily move your existing applications without upgrading them immediately. In this mode, you can isolate applications as you did in IIS 5.0. You have Low isolation (in-process), Medium isolation (pooled out-of-process), or High isolation (out-of-process). You still can benefit from many of the new features in IIS 6.0 in this mode. We will not, however, cover this feature in more detail here, but if you have troubles with an IIS 5.0 application on a IIS 6 system try switching to IIS 5.0 isolation mode as this might solve your problems.

Table 8-1 shows the isolation modes that IIS is set to after installation.

Table 8-1. *Overview of the Isolation Modes of IIS 6.0 After Installation*

Installation Method	Isolation Mode
New installation of IIS 6.0	Worker process isolation mode
Upgrade from previous installation of IIS 6.0	Same as new installation of IIS 6.0
Upgrade from IIS 5.0	IIS 5.0 isolation mode
Upgrade from IIS 4.0	IIS 5.0 isolation mode

If you want to change the isolation mode, follow these steps:

1. Open the IIS Manager.

2. Right-click the web site's folder.

3. Choose Properties.

4. Click the Services tab.

5. Note the Isolation Mode checkbox. If the checkbox is checked, IIS 5.0 isolation mode is active.

6. Check/uncheck the checkbox as required.

7. Click Apply.

8. Click Yes to restart the web services.

9. Click OK.

Performance and Scalability

Many of the performance issues discussed in the "Internet Information Services 5.0" section are still valid in IIS 6.0, so we won't cover them again. We have mentioned that performance has been improved in IIS 6.0. Now we'll examine some of the features responsible for this improvement, and the benefits they confer on reliability as well.

First of all, you have a clean separation between user code and the server. This is provided by letting the worker processes handle all the user code. Since the worker processes are completely separated from the server, an error in user code will not affect the server, only the worker process in which it occurred. The WWW Service creates a new worker process to replace the failed one, which prevents the user from noticing the error. By providing the worker process isolation mode, IIS 6.0 makes sure you can prevent one application or site from stopping the others, thereby greatly improving reliability.

By cutting down most of the overhead, IIS 6.0 improves performance when isolating applications or sites. This way you can host many more sites and applications on your server and still get great performance and reliability.

If an error occurs in a specific application, IIS 6.0 can fire events and commands when the WWW Service detects the problem. By providing this *extensibility model*, IIS 6.0 also allows load balancers and switches to be configured to automatically stop routing traffic to a faulty application, while not affecting routing to the healthy ones. If you have two applications and one of them fails so often that IIS automatically shuts it down, you will still want the healthy one to receive requests. This is when the extensibility model comes in handy.

As you just saw, IIS now can shut down an ill-behaving application. This feature, called *rapid-fail protection*, occurs when a specific application pool encounters many failures in a row. When this happens, the application pool is placed in "out-of-service" mode and HTTP.SYS returns the error message "503—Service unavailable" to anyone making a request to the pool or requests in the queue for the pool. This feature is configurable, so you can decide if and when rapid-fail protection should occur.

To free unused resources, you can configure an application pool to shut down its worker processes if they are idle for a specified time. When there is demand for additional worker processes, they are automatically started again.

The HTTP.SYS is a new kernel driver. It is a single point of control for all incoming HTTP requests, and as such it provides high performance in regard to connectivity for HTTP server applications. According to Microsoft, this new architecture provides performance gains of up to 200 percent with static content, and up to 165 percent higher throughput for cached responses—compared to IIS 5.0, that is.

Sometimes it is not desirable to cache an item just for the sake of caching. It might be too costly in terms of memory and management to keep it cached. To prevent this, IIS 6.0 includes a new advanced heuristic to determine what to cache. The decision is based on the distribution of requests to a specific application. This better use of server resources increases scalability, while still keeping the performance high on frequently requested services.

In IIS 5.0, all ASP code is converted to an *ASP template* by the ASP engine. This template is then stored in the process memory. The cache is cleared based on the age of the templates, so older templates make room for newer ones. In IIS 6.0, these templates are saved and persisted to disk. The advantage of this is that you do not have to spend CPU time on compiling them again. Instead, you load the templates from disk.

Security

Microsoft has been criticized over the years for the lack of security in its products. But with Windows Server 2003, a lot has changed. Earlier versions of IIS were installed by default with many of its features already enabled. The downside of this was that many administrators actually were not aware they had a web server and did not take any actions to secure it. It was left open for intruders to exploit. This is no longer the case. IIS 6.0 is not installed if you do not specifically select it for installation during Windows Server 2003 setup (see Figure 8-13).

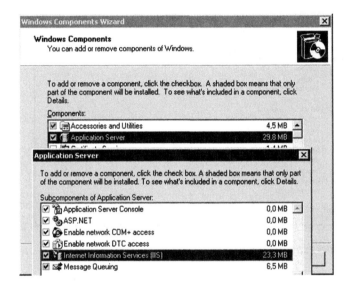

Figure 8-13. *IIS 6.0 has to be installed separately*

You must open Windows Setup through Add or Remove programs in the Control Panel to install IIS 6.0. This way you won't unknowingly expose the web server.

If you perform an upgrade of the operating system to Windows Server 2003, IIS is disabled. The reason for this is to prevent accidentally installed IIS from earlier Windows versions from being active after the upgrade. The first time this feature was introduced in the beta of Windows Server 2003, it took us quite some time before we figured it out. After that, we performed no upgrades without first reading the readme file.

To prevent users from installing IIS on their machines without the administrator knowing about it, you can restrict installation by group policy. This is a great way of keeping track of web servers in the company, so you know which servers to patch when new security updates are available. The only thing you have to worry about now is ducking when the users find this out.

Even after you have installed IIS, only static content, like HTML files, JPEGs, and so on, is served. An administrator must enable ISAPI and ASP/ASP.NET support manually for the server to handle such requests (see Figure 8-14). This feature enhances security further.

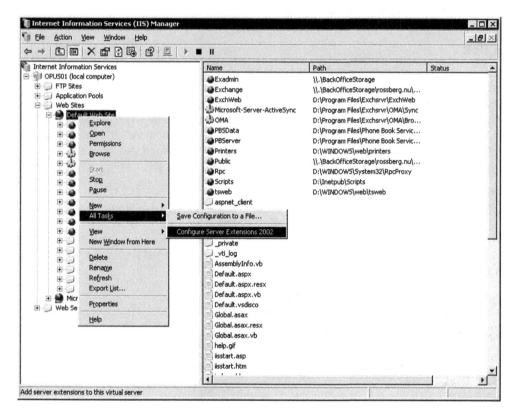

Figure 8-14. *Enabling FrontPage Server extensions*

It is also important to disable the web service extensions—for instance, .asp, asp.net, or server-side includes—that are not necessary for your solution. To manually enable or disable web service extensions, follow these steps:

1. Open Internet Information Services Manager and expand the local computer.

2. Click Web Services Extensions.

3. Click the Web Service Extension to enable/disable it in the details pane.

4. Click Allow to enable web service extensions, or Prohibit to disable them (see Figure 8-15).

5. Click OK.

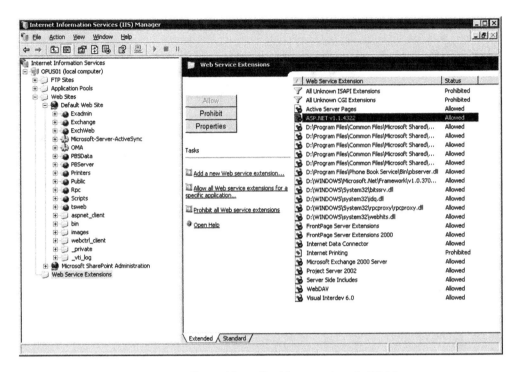

Figure 8-15. *Here you can manually enable or disable extensions in IIS Manager*

To be really flexible, you can even add a new web service extension if you want to, as Figure 8-16 shows, by following these steps:

1. Open Internet Information Services Manager and expand the local computer.

2. Click Web Services Extensions.

3. Click Add a new web service extension.

4. Enter the name of the new extension in the Extension name box.

5. In the Path to file text box, you can supply a path to any files necessary for the new extension. Click OK to close.

6. Click Add.

7. Select the Set extension status option to Allowed to automatically enable the extension (optional).

8. Click OK.

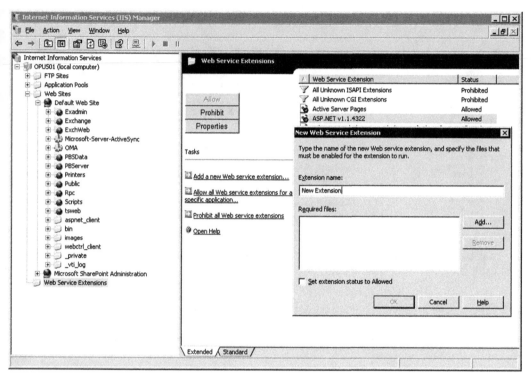

Figure 8-16. *Adding a new web service extension*

One of the most important security principals, which we can't stress enough, is not letting anyone have more privileges than absolutely necessary. This makes it harder for anybody trying to exploit a security vulnerability. In IIS 6.0, the worker process runs as NetworkService, a new, built-in account with few privileges on the underlying system.

One popular way of trying to hack a web server is by executing command-line tools via the web server. This is no longer possible because IIS 6.0 will not allow command-line tools to be executed by the web server. When examining one of the logs on one of our own web sites, we realized the extent of this behavior. So this is a welcome addition to our servers.

There have also been some improvements to Secure Sockets Layer in IIS 6.0. According to Microsoft, IIS 5.0 was the fastest software-based SSL implementation on the market. The result has been that approximately half of all SSL servers use IIS. The new IIS in Windows Server 2003 is said to be even faster. Microsoft has put a lot of effort into tuning SSL, but unfortunately we have not been able to test this yet, so we really do not know if it stands up to real-life testing.

One problem with having many IIS servers with SSL certificates is how to manage them. In IIS 5.0 this was not possible, but IIS 6.0 provides the CertObject to allow you to do this.

To speed up cryptographic computations when using SSL, a separate accelerator card is often used. This offloads the CPU on the server, so performance will remain high during SSL connections. In IIS 6.0, you can easily plug in your own Crypto API (CAPI) provider and let the web server use this.

To further enhance security, Microsoft has done a lot when it comes to authentication and authorization in IIS 6.0. Table 8-2 shows an overview of the different authentication methods you can use with IIS 6.0.

Table 8-2. *Overview of the Authentication Methods in IIS 6.0*

Method	Security	How to Send Passwords	Can Be Used with Proxy Servers and Firewalls	Client Requirements
.NET Passport	High	Encrypted	Yes, by using an SSL connection	IE and Netscape
Certificate	High	N/A	Yes, by using an SSL connection	IE and Netscape
Integrated Windows	High	When using NTLM, hashed; when using Kerberos, Kerberos ticket	Not unless PPTP is used	IE 2.0 and later for NTLM W2K; IE 5.0 or higher with Kerberos
Advanced Digest	Medium	Hashed	Yes	IE 5.0 or later
Digest	Medium	Hashed	Yes	IE 5.0 or later
Basic	Low	Base64-encoded clear text	Yes	Almost all browsers
Anonymous	None	N/A	Yes	All browsers

Figure 8-17 also shows where in IIS Manager you handle authentication.

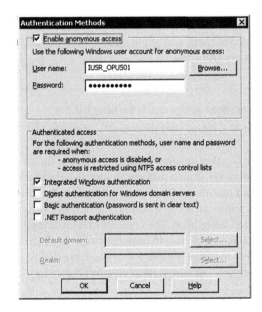

Figure 8-17. *The Authentication Methods dialog box in IIS Manager*

Let us take a closer look at some of these methods, starting with *Passport authentication*. IIS 6.0 employs Passport version 2 and can be used with standard Passport components, enabling you to take advantage of the enormous Passport user base. As of this writing, the number of Passport users was way past 150,000,000 and counting. By using Passport, you do not have to bother with password expiration or other issues related to account management. But you really need to give some thought to this matter before you use it. Is it really a good idea to let another company (Microsoft) handle the accounts? Can you trust the security provided? We say it depends on your application. If the web site or application provides sensitive information, you would probably be better off without it. But you can map a Passport account to an Active Directory account if you want to. If you do, once the authentication with Passport is made, and the mapping to the AD account is done, the Local Security Authority (LSA) creates a token for the user, which IIS uses for the request.

When using *Advanced Digest authentication*, the user credentials are stored as an MD5 hash in Active Directory on the domain controller. Since it is stored in AD, user passwords can't be discovered easily by anyone with access to the domain controller. This is the preferred authentication method of the two digest modes available.

After a user is authenticated, you must control what and how much the user is allowed to do. This is called *authorization*. To restrict an authenticated user from gaining too many privileges, we have often used Access Control Lists to make authorization decisions. The problem with this method is that it is too focused on the NTFS and its requirements. Windows Server 2003 includes a new *authorization framework* that lets you extend authorization to operations or tasks. Most of today's business applications have a tendency to be more operation or task dependent than object (file system) oriented, and ACLs do not solve this problem. Windows Server 2003 provides, for example, a gatekeeper authorization to URLs to solve this.

Web applications can use this *URL authentication* in combination with the Authorization Manager to control access. This can be done from the same policy store to control application-specific tasks and operations and also URLs that perhaps are compromising a web application. This provides you with a single point of administration for URLs and application features, which clearly eases the job of administering your applications and sites.

Note To open Authorization Manager, select Start I Run and enter azman.msc in the Open text box.

Another feature in IIS 6.0 is *constrained, delegated authentication*. Imagine a site that shows information about a customer and his or her purchasing history. To provide all such information to the user, the web site might need to gather data from many sources on your network. To handle all authentications to these sources, the server application can act as a user on the network with sufficient privileges to access information. This is called *delegation*. The concept of constrained delegation was introduced with Windows Server 2003 to enable you to have control over which computers and services you delegate control to. This method is great when you have RPCs (Remote Procedure Calls) and DCOM calls in your network, because it simplifies authentication across the network.

To avoid problems, you should allow servers to connect to only the specific services, like a SQL Server, necessary for the applications to run. The concept of assigning the least privileges necessary is valid here as well. You should also make sure the client does not need to share its credentials with the server either. Otherwise someone with bad intent might try to use this to gain access to the whole domain.

When it comes to security, a lot of the best practices in IIS 5.0 are valid with IIS 6.0. Here is an overview of some of these.

Log On with the Least Credentials Necessary

When logging on to your servers and computers, you should do so with an account that has no administrative privileges. When you need to use an administrative feature or make a change through such a feature, you can use the "run as" command. This way you minimize the possibility of making an irreparable error by mistake, just because you had too many privileges.

Patch the Servers

Use Windows Update or Auto-Update to keep the servers up to date. The new process model makes it possible to apply patches without restarting the web server.

Read the security bulletins Microsoft provides to keep up to date. If a security vulnerability is discovered, some people are likely to try and exploit it. If you have not patched your servers, you have no excuse when someone takes advantage of this weakness.

Reduce the Attack Surface

Disable all services you do not use. You do not need to worry about the security of a disabled service. If you do not need Internet Printing, FTP, NNTP, SMTP, or any other service, disable it.

The best way to make sure you do not need a service is by testing the solution in your lab. There you will quickly find out whether the service is needed or not.

Beware of the Domain Controllers

Think twice before using a domain controller as an application server. If someone compromised security on a domain controller, the whole network might be in danger. You definitely don't want this.

Restrict Access to Files and Directories

The IUSR_computername account should have restricted write permissions, for instance. By restricting access to the file system, you prevent users from changing the system, whether on purpose or accidentally.

To more easily set access to executables, you should gather them in a specific directory. You can then conveniently control access permissions to them. Also deny execute permissions for anonymous users to this directory.

Use the Most Restrictive Permissions Possible

This can't be said too often. It is easy to forget an account that you do not use regularly, and this could lead to unhappy events if someone uses it. Don't give anyone more privileges than they actually need.

Place All Anonymous User Accounts in a Separate Group

If you do this, you can set permissions to the group itself and not the separate users. This eases administration.

Now you have seen most of the security features provided with IIS 6.0. As you can see, many old best practices still apply, but you now have available some nice tools and concepts that help you further enhance security. Our best advice is to try them in the test lab before implementing them in the production environment. This way you know their impact on performance so you can take the correct actions to enhance both security and scalability.

Integrating ASP.NET with IIS

Before we leave this chapter, we will briefly look at ASP.NET. When you use ASP.NET, all clients communicate with ASP.NET through IIS, as shown in Figure 8-18.

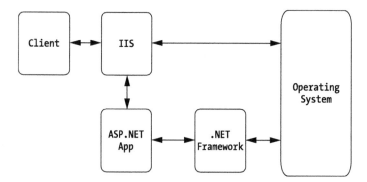

Figure 8-18. *Communication between IIS, ASP.NET, and the operating system*

ASP.NET hosts the runtime environment to provide for a scalable server-side operation of managed code. It provides the opportunity to use both web forms and web services on your web servers by working directly with the .NET runtime. ASP.NET is, however, more than just a host for the runtime. It offers a complete architecture for developing both web sites as well as distributed objects. IIS and ASP.NET are the publishing mechanisms for applications, and both have supporting classes in the .NET Framework.

An ASP.NET application is simply all the files, folders, and content in a virtual directory in IIS. ASP.NET applications are processed in a single instance of aspnet_wp.exe, which is the ASP.NET worker process. When a request for an ASP.NET file type is made, the ISAPI extension aspnet_isapi.dll handles them. This DLL file runs in the inetinfo.exe process address space. It is actually IIS that maps the file requests to aspnet_isapi.dll (see Figure 8-19), even though ASP.NET has its own object model, session state scheme, and process isolation scheme.

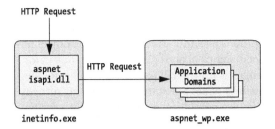

Figure 8-19. *How aspnet_isapi.dll maps file requests to aspnet_wp.exe*

The request is then forwarded by aspnet_isapi.dll to aspnet_wp.exe. Figure 8-20 shows how the ASP.NET worker process handles the request internally.

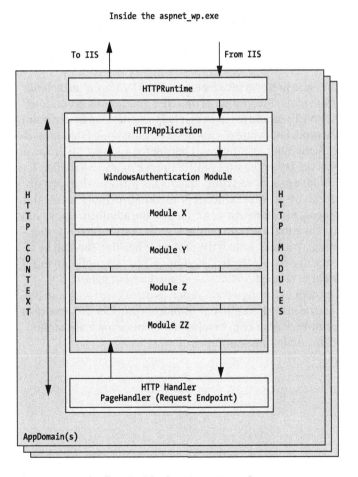

Figure 8-20. *The flow inside the ASP.NET worker process*

The HTTPRuntime object starts the processing chain, and the HTTPContext object conveys details about the request and the response generated throughout the lifetime of the request. Some of these details are exposed to external actors as properties. After the HTTPRuntime object has examined the request, it passes it on to the correct instance of an HTTPApplication object for further processing. When the HTTPApplication object is finished, it passes the request to one or more HTTPModule objects. These objects provide services like state management, authentication, and output caching. You can also create your own module objects to provide for a flexible request processing architecture. Finally the HTTPHandler object processes the request before the response is sent back to the caller. There is one HTTPHandler for *.aspx files, another for *.asmx files, and so on.

Note Each virtual directory in the IIS represents one application domain (AppDomain(s) in Figure 8-20). You can say that ASP.NET treats individual virtual directories as individual applications, if you like. Each application domain contains a pool of HTTPApplication objects, and there is a separate HTTPApplication object created to handle each simultaneous request. They are pooled for performance reasons.

Many of the scalability, reliability, and performance features of ASP.NET are already built into IIS 6.0. This is, of course, the result of the integration of the .NET Framework in Windows Server 2003. On an IIS 5.0 system, ASP.NET will add features that help you develop better, more reliable applications. For instance, it provides an out-of-process execution model that protects the server process from user code. Remember, this makes it harder for application errors in user code to bring down the entire server. Other features ASP.NET provides are two models for process recycling. The first, called *reactive process recycling*, restarts the process when certain symptoms occur. These symptoms can be deadlocks, access violations, memory leaks, and more. The conditions to trigger a process restart can be controlled by the administrator to suit a certain application environment. The other recycling model, *proactive process recycling*, simply works by periodically restarting a process, even if the process is healthy. This can be of great use to minimize denial of service due to undetected conditions. You can configure this restart to occur after a specific number of requests or after a certain time-out period.

With ASP.NET you also get the benefit of having a web garden as mentioned earlier in the chapter. If using this configuration, you need to choose an out-of-process provider (NT Service or SQL) for maintaining session state, however. Also keep in mind that application state, statics, and caching is per application domain and not per computer.

ASP.NET 2.0

Let us take a closer look at how requests are handled in the ASP.NET runtime (see Figure 8-21).

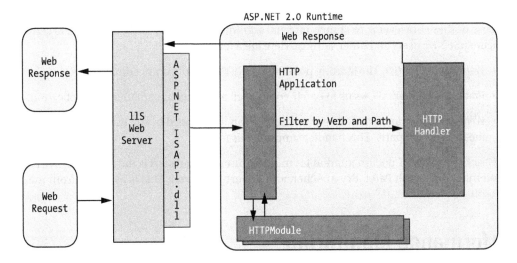

Figure 8-21. *Request handling inside the ASP.NET runtime*

All requests are passed from IIS to the aspnet_isapi.dll. From there they are forwarded to the ASP.NET Runtime. Once a request comes into theASP.NET runtime it starts a HTTPApplication object. This object is the host for the ASP.NET web application. There are three main tasks for the object:

- It checks the configuration files (machine and application level) for the web application.

- It forwards requests to one or more HTTPModules. These provide different services for the application (like session maintenance, authentication, profile maintenance and so on) before it gives the request back to the HTTPApplication.

- It forwards the request to an HTTPHandler. This in its turn gives the response back to IIS after its processing is done.

The correct HTTPHandler is chosen depending on whether the request is a GET, POST, FTP, or other (Figure 8-21) and which path, or URL, within the application, is used. All ASP.NET requests are for instance processed by a handler implementing the IHTTPHandler.

This model stays as it is in ASP.NET 2.0. The major difference is that a lot of new handlers and modules have been added. This is a result of all the new features in ASP.NET 2.0.

Some of the new modules are created to support *Role management* and *Profiles*. We also have a new *SessionID* process which has been separated from the ASP.NET 1.x session module so we can have greater control over session ID generation (using cookies, URL rewriting, and so on).

If you have looked into ASP.NET 2.0 you know there are personalization features which support anonymous users, so a new module helps keep track of the features this user can access. Web site statistics have also been enhanced with the new *Page Counters* module as well.

Apart from the new modules a few of the old have been changed, so read the ASP.NET 2.0 documentation carefully. Even though Microsoft says they will have backwards compatibility this is not always the way it works, so make sure to test your applications as well.

The new application configuration tools in ASP.NET 2.0 have got new handlers to support them. We will only mention a few here as this might change when ASP.NET 2.0 goes RTM. The main use of these however is to launch internal administrative tools so that developers can configure ASP.NET users and other settings. Here are a few:

- *WebAdminHandler.* The starting point of ASP.NET 2.0 application administration.

- *PreCompHandler.* Allows us to batch-compile all aspx pages in an ASP.NET application.

- *WebPartExportHandler.* The layout of a page can be changed by the user himself with the help of web parts. This handler supports this feature.

Check the ASP.NET documentation for more features. A good start is the paper "ASP.NET 2.0 Internals" by Jayesh Patel, Bryan Acher, and Robert McGoven. This is available from the Microsoft web site.

Performance Monitoring

The following performance counters are good to keep an eye on:

- *ASP.NET: Requests/Sec.* This counter will give you a hint if your applications are causing the bottleneck. If values are low during peak traffic, you might have a troublesome application.

- *ASP.NET: Requests executing.* This shows how many requests are executing at the moment.

- ASP.NET. Requests wait time, ASP.NET:Executing time, and ASP.NET:Requests queued: These three counters should be close to zero if everything is okay.

- *ASP.NET: Worker processes running.* This displays the number of aspnet_wp worker processes.

- *ASP.NET: Worker processes restarts.* Restarts are expensive, so you do not want them. Different process model configuration settings, memory leaks, and access violations affect this, so keep an eye on what is causing the restarts if you suspect anything out of the ordinary.

- *ASP.NET Applications.* The *Cache* counters are worth looking at here. Examine them carefully and take action if anything seems wrong. But many of the others are worth watching too. Note that these are reset to zero when a process restarts.

- *.NET CLR Exceptions: #Excepts thrown/sec.* This counter indicates how many exceptions are thrown per second. If you have an excessive number of exceptions, performance degrades. Exceptions should normally not be a part of processing.

- *.NET CLR Loading: Bytes in loader heap.* If this counter shows a continuously increasing value, you should watch the *.NET CLR Loading: Current assemblies* counter to examine if too many assemblies are loaded per application domain.

Summary

Both IIS 5.0 and IIS 6.0 offer great possibilities to help you build a scalable and secure web site with high performance. When it comes to choosing the correct platform to build your applications and web sites on, we hope this chapter has been a help. We argue heavily in favor of the use of Windows Server 2003 and IIS 6.0 with ASP.NET. But unfortunately, it is not always up to us to decide. As we see it, though, with the stability of Windows Server 2003 and IIS 6.0, combined with the scalability, security and performance boost they both offer, there really is no choice when deciding which platform to use for your new applications. We hope that after reading this book you will agree, and have good arguments for this approach so that you can implement it in your company.

In Chapter 9, we will compare the same .NET application running on Windows 2000 with IIS 5.0 and on Windows Server 2003 with IIS 6.0. The difference in performance will hopefully be of help when convincing a decision maker to taking the next step forward to the .NET platform.

But no matter which platform you use, there are similar rules of thumb to follow:

- Test in a test lab before going live.

- Monitor your servers both in the lab and in production.

- Carefully consider your security choice.

If you follow the guidelines presented here, you can build the best solution on the hardware and software platform you have chosen.

CHAPTER 9

■ ■ ■

Data Storage Design and SQL Server

All the applications that you build store data in some way or another. It has become vital for enterprises to increase efficiency and reduce Total Cost of Ownership (TCO) for data storage as well as all other infrastructure components.

Many factors must be considered when planning storage: Do you need your data to be available 24 hours a day? What recovery times can you expect if your data is compromised in any way? How much will your data grow with time? Are you using your data storage architecture effectively as it is?

It's not only your applications that need to be designed carefully. When it comes to storing data, you need to weigh an increasing number of issues, not only for the application you are currently building, but also for the entire enterprise data storage design. Considering how much important data is actually stored at a given company, it is surprising that many do not take it as seriously as they should.

Many enterprises create new database servers for almost every new application. This has resulted in data being scattered all over such companies and storage areas not being fully utilized. The scattered data has made manageability harder and more costly than it should be. By not using data storage effectively, a lot of investment is wasted, costing money in the long run.

Availability, scalability, and security have been emphasized throughout this book. These topics are important not only when building applications, but also when it comes to designing storage architecture. You can use various technologies to increase these aspects of an application, but they have some trade-offs that you need to consider. Availability always costs money. Redundant technology comes with a rather hefty price tag, and this is true in development and in data storage alike. When you try to increase scalability, availability can suffer. This requires you to purchase even more hardware to avoid problems.

Security most often affects performance and manageability due to the added overhead and complexity of secure solutions. The more you tighten security, the more performance and manageability suffers as a direct result.

You need to design your storage solution to meet goals of lowered TCO, high availability, great scalability, tight security, and, of course, simplified management. That is quite a lot to live up to, as you can see. When you design your storage solution, you must plan for enabling your organization to quickly create new business applications, and at the same time provide security and minimize the potential of data loss. You must also make sure new applications can be implemented with minimum disruption to your existing business. The decisions you make for the data storage architecture have an impact on how you design your future business projects.

The tasks facing a data storage team are not easy ones, so first we will take a look at some of the technologies for storing data and see how they can ease the burden. Then we will move on to choosing and implementing a logical design for a storage system, before diving into SQL Server.

This chapter will explore the most common storage technologies available to you. It will also present some benefits and concerns about different storage designs so that you can more easily choose what suits your solution. We will finish the chapter with a presentation of SQL Server—examining both its architecture and how it fits into your storage policy.

Three Storage Technologies

There are basically three different storage technologies you can use: Storage Area Networks (SANs), Network-Attached Storage (NAS), and Direct-Attached Storage (DAS). They each have their advantages and disadvantages, naturally, but by combining them, you can perhaps overcome their individual shortcomings. We will look at these in more detail in the following sections.

Storage Area Networks (SANs)

A SAN is a specialized network, the sole purpose of which is to provide access to high-performance and highly available storage subsystems. This solution is quite interesting. The SAN is constructed of several devices, all interconnected by fiber or copper wiring. The subsystem is available to multiple applications at the same time, just like a network-attached storage appliance. The major difference is that it provides higher scalability and performance. Even though a DAS is still faster than a SAN, this performance gap is diminishing constantly with the evolution of SAN technology. (For more on DAS, see the section "Direct-Attached Storage.")

The SAN concept is quite simple. An external RAID (short for *redundant array of independent disks*, and sometimes called *redundant array of inexpensive disks*) cabinet has a connection that goes directly from the Host Bus Adapter (HBA) to the external RAID subsystem. The SAN, on the other hand, connects the HBA to a switch instead, providing other servers access to the data storage that way (see Figure 9-1).

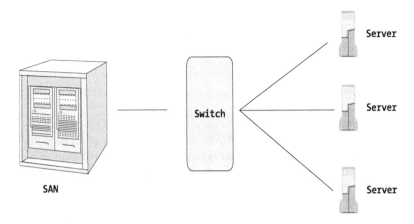

Figure 9-1. *A SAN connects the HBA to a switch.*

Next, we will take a closer look at NAS and DAS, after which we will introduce you to some of the logical designs for storage solutions.

Network-Attached Storage (NAS)

A network-attached storage system is a file server, to put it simply. This solution is built on an operating system, often designed for the sole purpose of providing file services. It thereby provides a flexible and scalable solution for most enterprises. Many applications can access a NAS appliance over the LAN by using protocols like TCP/IP. But, since this solution is accessed across a LAN, performance might be slow. When compared to a DAS system, performance is lower, but with the help of Gigabit Ethernet you can decrease this performance hit.

WINDOWS STORAGE SERVER 2003

Microsoft has developed a dedicated file server based on Windows Server 2003. This edition of the Windows Server family is called *Windows Storage Server 2003* and is only available through OEMs. The Storage Server is enhanced to offer a scalable, available, and quickly recoverable solution for enterprise file servers.

Besides being a file server, the Windows Storage Server 2003 also acts as a gateway to SANs, so that you aren't limited to the features offered in the server itself. To learn more about this server, direct your web browser to http://www.microsoft.com/storage.

Direct-Attached Storage (DAS)

As the name implies, *direct-attached storage* refers to a storage device that is directly attached to a server—specifically storage devices such as local hard drives and RAID systems that are attached with an IDE or SCSI interface to a computer.

This solution is fast, allows great performance on the server it's attached to, and is often only the attached server that can access it. This could be a great solution for a small SQL Server perhaps, but if you're planning a larger enterprise application with clustering, this isn't a good choice, because many servers might need to access it to provide redundancy.

Logical Design

We feel that it is better for an enterprise to develop a storage architecture that all their projects can comply with, rather than letting every project develop its own strategy. With a well thought-out plan for storage, the teams working on new projects can spend time on designing and building applications without bothering with planning how to store data. Furthermore, the more you centralize your storage, the more you can simplify management and decrease complexity.

One of the buzzwords these days is *consolidation*. Everything should be consolidated: databases, servers, applications, and so on. This isn't a bad idea if you look behind the hype. Take storage, for example: Many companies have little control over where all of their data is located, because there are a lot of smaller databases distributed around their networks. If you want a strategy or a policy that dictates that all your data be located at the same place, you could utilize your storage space better, as you will see later in this chapter. SANs and NASs are great for accomplishing this.

To illustrate this, we will now show you some examples of how you can develop your logical design for storage purposes.

Distributed Model

In a distributed model solution, such as the one shown in Figure 9-2, all servers have their own data stored on a DAS. An example that fits this model is a SQL Server that has its data files and log files on local RAID systems.

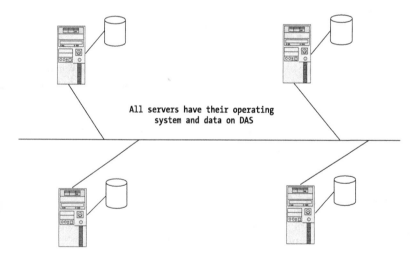

All servers have their operating system and data on DAS

Figure 9-2. *A distributed storage design*

Although there are several benefits to this design, such as flexibility, the disadvantages can outnumber these benefits. If you deploy this kind of solution, all your projects will need to have expertise in data storage applied by somebody during the design phase. The same storage decisions have to be made again and again, and this process is costly, since many man-hours are spent discussing which storage solution to choose and where to deploy it physically—every time a new project is started.

Because data is scattered in data islands all over the network, manageability will suffer. As you saw earlier, this situation can also lead to underutilization of the total storage capacity in the enterprise. This will inevitably lead to greater TCO than is necessary, making it an expensive solution in the end. Although this might seem like a cost-effective path to follow for a single project, the total cost for your company will only be greater as time goes by.

Centralized Model

The opposite of a distributed solution is a completely centralized one, where all data is located on the SAN (see Figure 9-3). In this model, the operating system and application files are the only things placed on local hard disks. By using a powerful SAN, you can supply a solution that can fulfill the business requirements of an enterprise.

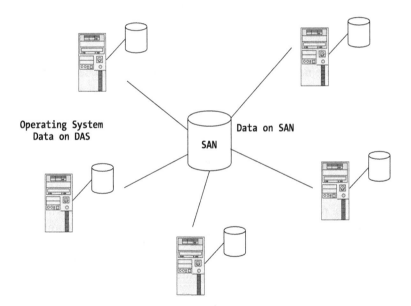

Figure 9-3. *A centralized storage design*

The advantages of this solution are numerous. Since you keep all data in a central place you can also manage it easier. This lowers the TCO and makes it less expensive in the long run. You must be aware that the startup costs are high when you implement this design, but over time it's worth it. This is why it is important for an enterprise to have a clear view of how data should be stored from the start. If no guidelines exist, many projects will continue to invent their own solution every time. In the end, this will be more expensive than if a clear policy exists, even if the chosen policy might have a high initial implementation cost.

Another benefit is that you can provide high security for the enterprise data, since you have it all in one place. This security does not come without manual labor, but is easier to set up with a centralized solution.

A disadvantage with this solution, besides initial costs, is that you can't distribute your data store to separate geographic locations. So, if you are unlucky, you can lose a lot of data if the geographic placement of the SAN is destroyed. Without a doubt, this is sure to change in the near future; in the meantime you do have opportunities available to back up data to a separate geographic location, so you can overcome this problem.

A Middle-Way Design

The last example is a middle-way data storage design. Here you use various technologies to store your data. Some of it is stored on DAS, some on SAN, and the rest on NAS appliances. This solution is very flexible, and offers several possibilities for your projects. This way you can let the team leads on each project decide what best serves their purposes.

This could be a more complex design to implement, however. Many design considerations have to be made, and, just as with the distributed model, making the process long and complicated before it can be implemented. Without proper guidelines, it will also be costly. Since this solution involves a lot of storage technologies from different vendors, TCO risks being higher than a centralized solution.

Choosing Your Storage Solution

Once you have determined the requirements for your storage solution, you must decide how you want to go about meeting those requirements.

Reasons for Choosing a DAS

A DAS is a popular choice for storing data. It is a solution with a low-entry cost, because hard drives are cheap these days. It is tempting for a department or a workgroup to choose this technique, because it is easy to implement. A small organization or an individual; department in a larger organization often doesn't want to spend time and money on shared storage or on the enhanced availability and higher performance that comes with it. Our view is that this might harm the organization in the end. A large number of DAS solutions might very well be complex and expensive to manage. The hardware often comes from different vendors, so standardization might suffer. This could lead to isolated data islands that might not be accessible to any server other than the one that the hardware is attached to. From an enterprise view, such a solution is probably not what you should aim for.

On the other hand, a DAS solution is easy to launch and most administrators feel at home with this kind of technology. Another issue is performance—because DAS is directly attached to the server, performance is great. Depending on the data, it can also be hard to get more than one server to access it at the same time, so a SAN or NAS appliance might be a better choice if you need the data to be available for many servers or applications. And, in a large enterprise, you can bet that this is the case. It's true that a database with database files stored on a DAS can be accessed by many applications, but then you will have the resultant manageability issues to deal with. You should also be aware, however, that access to the data is limited to the number of physical network connections the server can handle at the same time.

We would recommend using DAS when you need to have a database close to your web server, and for use as a caching server—that is, a server that you only use for data immediately needed for your web solution. All your user data, customer data, product data, and so on should be stored on a more permanent basis in a centralized data store like a SAN. The contents of your user sessions information, shopping baskets, and the like, should be stored in your DAS caching database. This way you can provide fast access to such info for your web solution.

Reasons for Choosing a NAS

Network-attached storage is a scalable and flexible way to fulfill your enterprise file-sharing needs. This technology, like DAS, offers great simplicity, and furthermore most administrators know about it. You can easily administer security and access control for this solution. Access to a network-attached storage system is limited to the LAN, however, and if you do not want to use Gigabit Ethernet, this can be a potential bottleneck.

Compared to a SAN, a NAS system is simpler and less expensive. SANs require additional hardware and cables, and a lot more effort has to go into the design of it. The fact that you attach it directly to the LAN infrastructure also makes it more complex to implement.

In addition, you may run into problems with your database applications, because not all of them support the storing of database or log files on network-attached storage appliances.

Your backup solution is something you also have to consider. It must allow you to back up over the LAN; otherwise, you might run into trouble. Even if it allows you to back up over a LAN connection, you must plan your backup schedule carefully. You do not want to run your backups when network traffic mostly consists of business-critical operations.

Reasons for Choosing a SAN

SANs make it possible to implement highly available storage subsystems to multiple hosts. *SAN fabrics* are networks that connect hosts to storage devices. By using fabric switches, you can connect separate SAN fabrics (or *SAN islands* as they are sometimes called), so that they can teach each other.

One of the benefits of SAN is that you can expand it quite easily. You can add new storage devices to your SAN when you need to, without interrupting the existing structure in the meantime. This means you can scale the SAN when the need for it arises.

Another benefit is that backup and restore operations are done over the SAN fabric. This way you get high speed on these actions, while at the same time minimizing the impact on the LAN. If you want to implement a server-free backup, you can do so by using the appropriate hardware, but you should be aware that this takes a few extra configurations to maintain the integrity of your application data.

It's also possible to manage the SAN from one place, which makes overall manageability easier. This way you can pool your storage together and allocate it to those servers that need it.

One of the problems with a distributed model has been that it often has a lot of excess storage, and thus doesn't utilize resources as well as it could. With a SAN, the excess storage can be fully used, and nothing is wasted.

All this might sound great, but there are, of course, disadvantages. A SAN is very expensive to implement, as you have seen. Luckily, most of the expense occurs at the initial implementation, and the centralized management as well as the reduction of wasted storage and greater flexibility makes the TCO decrease over time.

Note One of our customers implemented a SAN over the last year. Although it has cost a lot of money, it seems that both administrators and users alike are satisfied with the solution. This customer implemented SharePoint Portal Server at the same time, and now has a truly centralized solution in place.

A SAN also demands a lot more from your administrators, since they might need to learn a new technology. If a SAN is not already implemented in the company, once you start planning for it, you soon find that it is a complex solution. A SAN requires specialized knowledge to design, administer, and maintain.

If you could choose it, a SAN could be perfect for your applications, but unfortunately the choice isn't always yours to make. Implementing a SAN requires an enterprise to develop a new storage architecture and policy. Since the initial costs are high, many might hesitate at this, especially since the long-term perspective is often forgotten in the cost-aware times in which we are living.

Consider Combinations

Rather than choosing just one the preceding technologies, you could use various combinations of these technologies. Many new NAS devices also handle access to SANs (see Figure 9-4). This increases their scalability, while still offering the benefits of network-attached storage. You can also improve backups and restores, because this setup lets you perform these operations to backup devices on the SAN. This way, you get server-free backup of your network-attached storage devices as well.

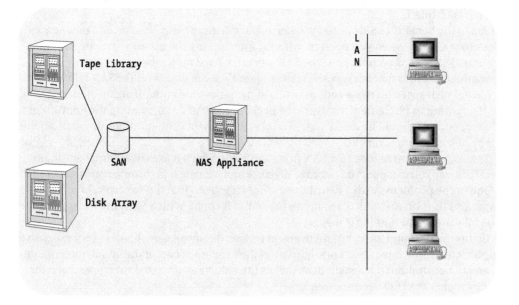

Figure 9-4. *A NAS appliance that also provides access to SANs*

By using this combination design, you can take advantage of the best features from the different storage technologies. At the same time, you get a great deal of flexibility and high performance. This combination is not perfect, however. The price tag is not something everybody can afford. You must also be aware of the increasing complexity in your solution, since you mix hardware from different vendors. Naturally, this affects operability and manageability.

You have to consider what kind of storage solution you actually need and the requirements that your business for your storage before you run out and purchase anything. Design is something you should never take lightly, and it is often worthwhile to take a little extra time to think about it early on.

Next, we'll move on to our discussion of SQL Server. SQL Server is a powerful database manager, and it is important to know how it works and how it can be used in a storage policy. We will show you the different versions you can use, examine the architecture of SQL Server, and share some tips for working with SQL Server that we have learned over the years.

Introduction to SQL Server

We have been working with SQL Server since version 6.5 or so. Back then, we would never have suggested to a customer that they should use SQL Server in a business-critical application. Fortunately, SQL Server has grown since then, and with the 2000 edition, it has become one of our most commonly-suggested applications to customers these days. We can't wait for the next version, SQL Server 2005, to come out, as it looks very promising—both on paper, and in the evaluations we have made. We will only quickly cover it here since it was only in beta when writing this and hence not many real solutions have been created using it as a storage solution. That makes it hard to evaluate if it really offers better performance and scalability even though we strongly suspect it will.

SQL Server still has a reputation to fight against, however. A lot of people think it can't perform as well as many of its competitors. That isn't true if it's configured correctly, and if it's deployed on a good platform.

■ **Tip** For those interested in SQL Server performance, check out `http://www.tpc.org` to see the latest test results and database system configurations.

SQL Server's ease of use has also been an issue over time. The general misconception has been that something that is as easy to use with a graphical user interface is as worthless as a Steven Seagal movie. This in effect has led many companies to give someone like a department secretary the responsibility of setting up and managing a SQL Server, while the database administrator handles an Oracle database or the like. Now we don't intend any disrespect to the secretary, but this isn't a good solution, since getting great performance out of SQL Server requires the skills of a trained and experienced database administrator.

Many database administrators haven't had an interest in working with SQL Server because it is so easy to use and there isn't much configuration to be done once it's set up. Setting up a new SQL Server takes a good deal of planning, however, and some knowledge about how to do it the right way.

Fortunately, much of this attitude has changed, and nowadays trained IT staff people handle most SQL Servers in enterprises.

Several versions of SQL Server are available. To help you choose the most suitable for your solution, we'll present an overview of the different versions and their intended use in the following sections.

SQL Server Editions

SQL Server 2000, like Windows Server, comes in various editions to suit a large number of uses:

- SQL Server 2000 Enterprise Edition

- SQL Server 2000 Enterprise Edition (64-bit)

- SQL Server 2000 Standard Edition

- SQL Server 2000 Developer Edition

- SQL Server 2000 Personal Edition

- SQL Server 2000 Desktop Engine (MSDE)

- SQL Server 2000 Windows CE Edition (SQL Server CE)

SQL Server 2005 will ship in the following version (we haven't seen any news about a Developer Edition, but we suspect it will exist as well):

- SQL Server 2005 Workgroup Edition

- SQL Server 2005 Standard Edition

- SQL Server 2005 Enterprise Edition

- SQL Server Express Edition

- SQL Server Mobile Edition

We will explore each edition and look at its intended use. As you learn about each edition, you will see that you now actually do have one version for your department secretary, another for your developers, and still others for your database administrators. Now you don't have to compromise—you can have the database you need for every occasion. Let us start with a look at the Enterprise Edition.

SQL Server 2000 Enterprise Edition

SQL Server 2000 Enterprise Edition is the top-of-the-line for SQL Server. It includes all the features that SQL Server offers. The Enterprise Edition comes in both 32-bit and 64-bit versions, so you can use it on most hardware available. This edition includes tools that let you store data, and also extract and analyze it as well.

SQL Server 2000 Enterprise Edition is a suitable solution for large web sites, Online Transaction Processing (OLTP) systems, and data warehouses. Good platforms for running the Enterprise Edition are Windows Server 2003 Datacenter and Windows 2000 Server Data-center. You should definitely let an experienced database administrator handle this edition.

SQL Server 2000 Standard Edition

SQL Server 2000 Standard Edition includes the core functionality of SQL Server. It doesn't include all of the advanced tools that the Enterprise Edition does, but it does have some great tools that let you analyze data, too.

The Standard Edition is intended for small and medium-sized organizations. Recommended platforms include Windows Server 2003 Enterprise Edition and Windows Server 2003 Standard Edition, as well as the equivalent Windows 2000 Server Editions. We still recommend an experienced database administrator for handling this edition, however.

SQL Server 2000 Developer Edition

Basically, SQL Server 2000 Developer Edition is the Enterprise Edition in disguise. It's intended for developers to use when new applications and solutions are developed—it is not intended or licensed for any production databases. By offering all the features of SQL Server, a developer can use it to develop all kinds of applications. The Enterprise Edition also includes licenses and download rights for the CE Edition, just to make sure that everything SQL Server has to offer is available at a reasonable price.

■**Note** Microsoft had cut the price down to $49 at the time of this writing, so this edition should be affordable. One of the major reasons for this price-cut is the threat posed by free database tools, such as mySQL.

SQL Server 2000 Personal Edition

Most companies have mobile users, such as salespeople, who need to have large sets of data available on their business trips. SQL Server 2000 Personal Edition is the ideal choice to install on a laptop, because it lets users sync data with the company database when they are at the office.

■**Note** The Personal Edition is only available with the Enterprise and Standard Editions. It is not available separately.

The Personal Edition can also be of use for the department secretary (you knew this was coming) when he or she requires an application that needs to store data on a local database. It doesn't offer the scalability and flexibility of the previously mentioned editions, but it is nevertheless a great tool in some cases.

SQL Server 2000 Desktop Engine

The Desktop Engine is a redistributable version of the SQL Server Database Engine (MSDE). It isn't available separately, but you'll find it included in the MSDE catalog in the root directory of the Enterprise, Standard, and Developer Edition CD-ROMs. Developers can include it with their applications when local data is needed and requiring a stand-alone database would be overkill.

The limitations, other than the hardware issues, are that it only supports up to 25 concurrent users. Or to be clearer, this limitation isn't fixed, but is the number of connections that Microsoft recommends as the limit. This is what Microsoft says on the Web (http://msdn.microsoft.com/library/?url=/library/en-us/architec/8_ar_sa2_0ciq.asp?frame=true): "Like all versions of SQL Server 2000, SQL Server 2000 Personal Edition and MSDE 2000 allow 32,767 connections to an instance of the database engine. There is no limit for the number of connections that can be executing operations at the same time. The only effect of the workload governor is that it starts slowing down the database engine when more than eight operations are actively running at the same time."

Tip Check http://www.microsoft.com/sql/ for more information about obtaining MSDE, and the licensing issues that may come with it. You'll find all the information you need about the various SQL Server editions there.

If you need to, you can use SQL Server Enterprise Manager to access the Desktop edition, giving yourself a graphical user interface for it. Otherwise, this edition doesn't include any GUI, which can be a clear drawback in some cases, since your system doesn't show much evidence that MSDE is installed on it. Only the "traffic light" beside the clock gives the user any indication that it's there, which could lead to trouble when new patches need to be applied. It's easy to miss applying a patch to a machine and the recent SQL Server worms clearly show that this can be disastrous.

SQL Server 2000 Windows CE Edition

SQL Server 2000 CE Edition is intended for use on PDAs and other Windows CE devices. It has a small footprint, which enables it to run smoothly on these devices, but it still provides tools that let you store data on a small device, such as a Pocket PC, for instance. It also includes APIs, so that you can develop applications for your Windows CE devices that use a full-fledged SQL Server as a data store, instead of flat files, or any other solution.

Table 9-1 shows the system requirements of the various SQL Server Editions.

Table 9-1. *SQL Server 2000 Editions Overview*

Edition	Operating System	Scalability
Enterprise Edition (64-bit)	Windows Server 2003 Enterprise Edition; Windows Server 2003 Datacenter Edition	Max 64 CPUs, max 512GB RAM, max 1,048,516TB database size
Enterprise Edition (32-bit)	Windows Server 2003 Standard Edition, Enterprise Edition, Datacenter Edition; Windows 2000 Server, Advanced Server, Datacenter Server; Windows NT 4.0 Server, Enterprise Edition	Max 32 CPUs, max 64GB RAM, max 1,048,516TB database size

Edition	Operating System	Scalability
Standard Edition	Windows Server 2003 Standard Edition, Enterprise Edition, Datacenter Edition; Windows 2000 Server, Advanced Server, Datacenter Server; Windows NT 4.0 Server, Enterprise Edition	Max 4 CPUs, max 2GB RAM, max 1,048,516TB database size
Developer Edition	Windows Server 2003 Standard Edition, Enterprise Edition, Datacenter Edition; Windows XP Professional; Windows 2000 Professional; Windows 2000 Server, Advanced Server, Datacenter Server; Windows NT 4.0 Server, Enterprise Edition	Max 32 CPUs, max 64GB RAM, max 1,048,516TB database size
Personal Edition	Windows Server 2003 Standard Edition, Enterprise Edition, Datacenter Edition; Windows XP Professional; Windows 2000 Professional; Windows 2000 Server, Advanced Server, Datacenter Server; Windows NT 4.0 Server, Enterprise Edition	Max 2 CPUs, max 2GB RAM, max 1,048,516TB database size
Desktop Edition (MSDE)	Windows Server 2003 Standard Edition, Enterprise Edition, Datacenter Edition; Windows XP Professional; Windows 2000 Professional; Windows 2000 Server, Advanced Server, Datacenter Server; Windows NT 4.0 Server, Enterprise Edition	Max 2 CPUs, max 2GB RAM, max 2GB database size
Windows CE Edition	Windows CE 2.11 or later, Handheld PC Pro (H/PC Pro), Palm-size PC (P/PC), Pocket PC	Max 1 CPU, max 2GB database size

SQL Server 2005 Workgroup Edition

This edition is the newest member of the SQL Server family. It's intended for use in small workgroups, as the name implies. The closest we thing we can find to compare with it is the SQL Server 2000 Personal Edition, but this edition has more features.

SQL Server 2005 Standard Edition (32- and 64-bit)

Compare this with SQL Server 2000 Standard Edition.

SQL Server 2005 Express

This is an updated version of the old MSDE database. It has some cool features that we recommend that you look into. And guess what? Now there is a SQL Server 2005 Express Manager which lets us manage the Express edition. And it's free of charge as well.

SQL Server Mobile Edition

The previous version was called SQL Server 2000 Windows CE Edition and is intended for the same use. Naturally, some new features have been added.

Table 9-2 shows the system requirements of the various SQL Server Editions.

Table 9-2. *SQL Server 2005 Editions Overview*

Edition	Operating System	Scalability
Enterprise Edition	Windows Server 2003 Enterprise Edition, Windows Server 2003 Datacenter Edition; Windows 2000 Server, Advanced Server, Datacenter Server	Unlimited no. of CPUs, Unlimited RAM, Unlimited database size
Standard Edition	Windows Server 2003 Standard Edition, Enterprise Edition, Datacenter Edition; Windows 2000 Server, Advanced Server, Datacenter Server	Max 4 CPUs, max Unlimited RAM, Unlimited database size
Workgroup Edition	Windows Server 2003 Standard Edition, Enterprise Edition, Datacenter Edition; Windows XP Professional, Windows XP Media Edition, Windows XP Tablet Edition; Windows 2000 Professional; Windows 2000 Server, Advanced Server, Datacenter Server	Max 2 CPUs, max 3GB RAM, max Unlimited database size
Express Edition	Windows Server 2003 Standard Edition, Web Edition, Enterprise Edition, Datacenter Edition; Windows XP Professional, Windows XP Media Edition, Windows XP Tablet Edition, Windows XP Home Edition; Windows 2000 Professional; Windows 2000 Server, Advanced Server, Datacenter Server	Max 1 CPU, max 2GB RAM, max 4GB database size

Edition	Operating System	Scalability
Developer Edition	Windows Server 2003 Standard Edition, Web Edition, Enterprise Edition, Datacenter Edition; Windows XP Professional, Windows XP Media Edition, Windows XP Tablet Edition, Windows XP Home Edition; Windows 2000 Professional; Windows 2000 Server, Advanced Server, Datacenter Server	N/A at the time of writing

SQL Server 2000 Architecture

We have already mentioned that SQL Server is quite easy to use, but this can also be one of its drawbacks when it comes to people's perceptions of this product. As long as you understand what it does and can tell when it behaves the wrong way, we argue that there is no value in having to tune a database server manually—especially when you can let the built-in logic do it. You want your database administrators and IT staff spending time on other stuff, like designing, planning, and deploying applications. Obviously such staff would still need to provide maintenance and surveillance of your existing SQL Server system, because if it behaves strangely they must have the knowledge to troubleshoot it. This shouldn't be their main occupation, however.

To give you a better understanding of SQL Server, we will outline its architecture in the following sections. Please note that we are speaking of SQL Server 2000, unless otherwise noted.

Memory Management and Memory Architecture

Memory management requires little or no manual work in SQL Server, at least not in most cases. SQL Server dynamically allocates and de-allocates memory as needed and by default. This way, SQL Server optimizes its memory for best performance, based on the amount of physical memory it has to work with.

SQL Server uses the virtual memory in Windows for two main components (see Figure 9-5) as follows:

- The memory pool

- Executable code

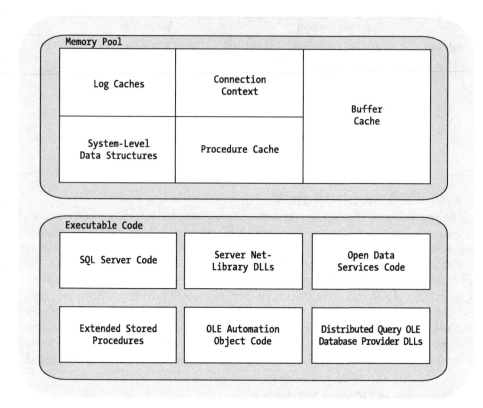

Figure 9-5. *SQL Servers' two main components in the SQL Server address space*

The *memory pool* is an area of memory from which some objects allocate their memory. These components are as follows:

- *System-level data structures*. These hold data that is global to the SQL Server instance, such as database descriptors and the lock table.

- *Buffer cache*. This cache stores data and index pages read from a database. If these items need to be accessed again, they can be found in the cache, which speeds up processing.

- *Procedure cache*. This holds the execution plans so that they can be reused for stored procedures and Transact-SQL statements.

- *Log cache*. The log cache is used to hold pages that are both read from and written to the log. Each database has one log cache.

- *Connection context*. This constitutes a set of data structures that keeps a record of the current state of a connection.

Determined by the number of user requests, the size of the memory pool varies, simply because the objects within it vary in size. When a new database is defined, the different data structures are allocated. The same goes for when a table or view is referenced.

The buffer cache, log cache, and procedure cache are constantly managed and adjusted by SQL Server to optimize performance so it fits the current workload. So, if the procedure cache needs to have more memory, SQL Server dynamically increases the whole memory pool size. It does this by allocating more memory from the physical memory. If no more physical memory exists, it tries to resize the other objects in the memory pool.

You can control the size of the memory pool by setting minimum and maximum values for it. You don't need to control the size of the objects within the memory pool, as SQL Server handles this best by itself.

The executable code is more or less the SQL Server engine. It includes the code for the engine itself, as well as the DLLs the executables for Open Data Services and Net-Libraries.

Let's take a closer look at the buffer cache, since this is an important part of SQL Server. The buffer cache consists of a number of memory pages that are initially free when SQL Server starts up. When SQL Server starts reading a page from disk, this page is stored in the first page of the buffer cache's free list. When this page is read or modified by the same process (or another), it's read from the cache instead of from disk. This reduces the amount of physical I/O required for the operation, and performance increases.

A page that has been modified in the buffer cache but not yet written to disk is called a *dirty page*. Whether a page is dirty or not is written into each buffer page's header information. A reference counter also resides in the header, which is incremented and decremented with each reference to the page. The buffer cache is scanned periodically, and if a page has been referenced less than three times since the last scan and is not dirty, the page is considered to be free. It is then added to the free list, which we talked about in Chapter 4. If the page is dirty, the modifications are written to disk first. This work is done by the worker processes of SQL Server.

To prevent the free list from being too small, a worker process called the *lazywriter* periodically checks to see that the free list doesn't fall below a certain size. The size depends on the size of the buffer cache. If the free list is becoming too small, the lazywriter scans the cache and reclaims both unused pages and pages that have a reference counter set to zero.

■**Note** The lazywriter is mostly used in very I/O-intense systems, because the other threads can handle these tasks on less heavily used systems.

To allow the buffer cache to have as much memory as possible, you should see to it that your system has enough physical memory (RAM) for the task it performs. Memory is cheap these days, so this does not have to be too expensive, even for small companies.

Memory Configuration in SQL Server

As we have mentioned, SQL Server dynamically adjusts the memory for the memory pool. It not only allocates memory for its parts, but it also de-allocates memory if other applications need it. But, it only de-allocates memory if another process asks for it; otherwise it maintains its memory at the current size.

The virtual memory SQL Server uses is maintained at 5MB less than the available physical memory. This stops excessive memory-swapping to disk, while still giving SQL Server the largest memory pool possible. SQL Server always tries to keep 5MB of free physical memory on the system by de-allocating memory from its pool, if another process tries to access these megabytes.

To make sure SQL Server always has a certain minimum memory pool, you can set the *min server memory* option so SQL Server does not release memory less than this value. The min server memory option is always set in megabytes.

You can also set the *max server memory* option so that SQL Server doesn't steal too much memory from other applications running on the server.

Carefully use these options so that none of your applications (including SQL Server) starts any excessive swapping. You can keep an eye on this by using the Performance MMC (see Figure 9-6) and the Pages/sec counter for the memory object. This counter shows the paging on the system. A value between 0 and 100 is considered normal.

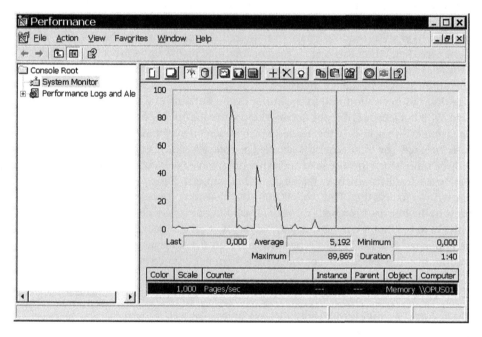

Figure 9-6. *The Memory: Pages/sec counter in the Performance MMC*

The best approach is to let SQL Server handle memory usage and not set the manual options yourself. This is especially true when you only have SQL Server running on the machine. When you have other applications running, you might need to manually configure these settings, however. With all the consolidation going on these days, it is not unlikely that SQL Server has to share room with other applications, so it could be nice to know that these options are available. The following code shows how to set these values from Transact-SQL:

```
sp_configure 'show advanced options', 1
go
sp_configure 'min server memory', 256
go
RECONFIGURE WITHOUT OVERRIDE
go
```

You can also set minimum and maximum memory values from Enterprise Manager if you want to, as shown in Figure 9-7.

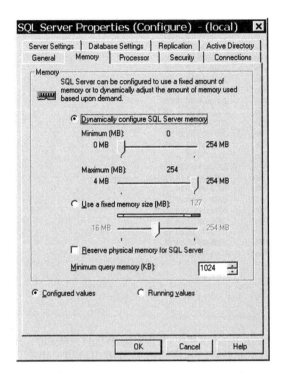

Figure 9-7. *Setting the memory pool size from SQL Server Enterprise Manager*

Data Files and Log Files

No database manager would be of any value if you didn't store your data somewhere. SQL Server stores its data in a set of operating system files. Each file is made up of smaller parts called *pages*. The following are the three kinds of files that SQL Server uses (see Figure 9-8):

- Primary data files

- Secondary data files

- Log files

Name ▲	Size	Type	Date Modified
distmdl.ldf	768 KB	Database File	2002-12-17 15:55
distmdl.mdf	2 304 KB	Database File	2002-12-17 15:55
InterchangeBTM.mdf	2 688 KB	Database File	2003-04-03 14:55
InterchangeBTM_log.LDF	768 KB	Database File	2003-04-03 14:55
InterchangeDTA.mdf	1 408 KB	Database File	2003-04-03 14:55
InterchangeDTA_log.LDF	768 KB	Database File	2003-04-03 14:55
InterchangeSQ.mdf	896 KB	Database File	2003-04-03 14:55
InterchangeSQ_log.LDF	768 KB	Database File	2003-04-03 14:55
master.mdf	17 344 KB	Database File	2003-01-27 10:06
mastlog.ldf	3 840 KB	Database File	2003-01-27 10:06
model.mdf	768 KB	Database File	2003-04-03 14:55
modellog.ldf	512 KB	Database File	2003-04-03 14:55
MSCNT_Data.MDF	2 432 KB	Database File	2003-04-03 14:55
MSCNT_Log.LDF	1 024 KB	Database File	2003-04-03 14:55
msdbdata.mdf	12 032 KB	Database File	2003-04-03 14:55
msdblog.ldf	2 304 KB	Database File	2003-04-03 14:55
northwnd.ldf	1 024 KB	Database File	2003-04-03 14:55
northwnd.mdf	3 328 KB	Database File	2003-04-03 14:55
pubs.mdf	1 792 KB	Database File	2003-04-03 14:55
pubs_log.ldf	768 KB	Database File	2003-04-03 14:55
rossberg_Data.MDF	1 024 KB	Database File	2003-04-03 14:55
rossberg_Data_Secondary_Data.NDF	1 024 KB	NDF File	2003-08-20 17:53
rossberg_Log.LDF	1 536 KB	Database File	2003-04-03 14:55
tempdb.mdf	8 192 KB	Database File	2003-04-12 14:32
templog.ldf	1 024 KB	Database File	2003-07-26 10:55
XLANG.mdf	768 KB	Database File	2003-04-03 14:55
XLANG_log.LDF	504 KB	Database File	2003-04-03 14:55

Figure 9-8. *The different files in SQL Server*

Primary data files contain different kinds of database information, such as startup information for the database, pointers to the other files for the database, system tables, and objects. These files can also contain database data and objects. There is one primary data file for every database, and you can identify this file through the file extension .mdf.

Secondary data files, which sport the extension .ndf, are an option for every database. You don't need to have one of these, and you can use the primary data file instead, if you want. Secondary data files hold data and objects that are not in the primary file. Here we find tables and indexes. The reason you might want to use secondary files is that you can spread the data on separate disks, thereby improving I/O performance.

Log files are files that hold all the information about the transactions in the database, and they can't be used to hold any other data. You can have one or more log files (like the ones shown in Figure 9-8, with an extension of .ldf), but our recommendation is to use one only. This is because the log file is written to sequentially, and hence doesn't benefit from being separated on several physical disks. To enhance performance, you should try to use RAID 1+0 instead, and place the log file on such hardware.

One important thing to understand about the log file is that it actually consists of several files, regardless of whether you use only one or not. These files are called *virtual log files* (VLFs) and are created by SQL Server (see Figure 9-9). Of these virtual log files, only one is active at a time. When a backup of the log is performed, all inactive VLFs are cleared. The active VLF is never cleared, so contrary to what you might have been told, a log backup does not clear the whole log. But don't worry, this isn't a problem.

Inactive VLF	Inactive VLF	Inactive VLF	Inactive VLF	Active VLF	Inactive/ Unused VLF

Figure 9-9. *The virtual log files in a log file*

If you have too many VLFs, the overhead of maintaining them can degrade your performance. To see how many VLFs you have in your databases, you could use an undocumented DBCC command, which returns as many rows as there are VLFs in the database. To do this, execute DBCC LOGINFO and have a look at how your database appears. Figure 9-10 shows our results after we ran DBCC LOGINFO against the Northwind database on our system. As you can see, a total of four VLFs exist in our database.

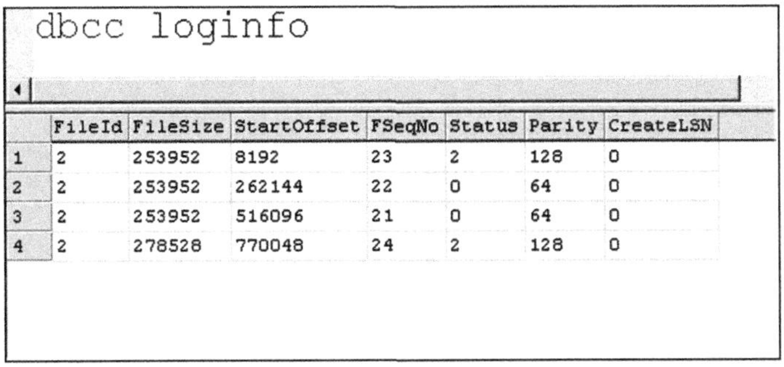

```
dbcc loginfo
```

	FileId	FileSize	StartOffset	FSeqNo	Status	Parity	CreateLSN
1	2	253952	8192	23	2	128	0
2	2	253952	262144	22	0	64	0
3	2	253952	516096	21	0	64	0
4	2	278528	770048	24	2	128	0

Figure 9-10. *Executing DBCC LOGINFO against the Northwind database*

To reduce the number of VLFs, you should perform frequent log backups. You also don't want to forget to shrink the log file through the command DBCC SHRINKFILE (logfilename, truncateonly), otherwise the number of VLFs will not be reduced.

When designing a log file, you should make a good estimate for the size of the log file and create it with that size. If auto-growth is enabled on a small log file, new VLFs are created every time the log is increased. So it's important to make it as close to the size you will need as possible.

Filegroups

A simple database might only hold a primary data file and a log file. A more complex and larger database, on the other hand, often consists of secondary files and more log files as well.

By building *filegroups*, you can create your secondary data files in these groups for data placement purposes. When you create your database, you specify the filegroup that you want to place your database objects in. This way, you can have control of where you place your objects, since you also know which disk the filegroups are placed on. You can even create a table or other object across multiple filegroups to increase performance. (This is obviously only true when the filegroups are created on separate disks.)

To better understand this, imagine a database that has two tables: Table_A and Table_B. The database also has two RAID disk arrays, as you can see in Figure 9-11. Table_A is constantly accessed sequentially, with read-only requests, whereas Table_B is accessed only occasionally with write requests (perhaps only once every minute or so).

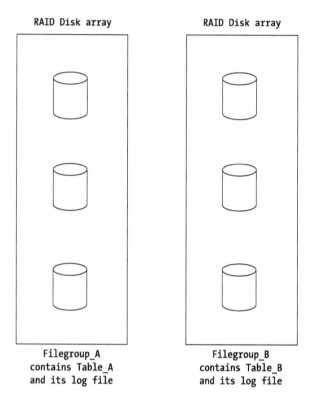

Figure 9-11. *Two tables are separated on two different filegroups and then placed on different disk arrays.*

In this scenario, it would be great for performance to place a filegroup on each disk array and then place each table in separate filegroups. This way you could separate the heavily accessed table from the less accessed one, which improves performance. If one of the disk arrays had more disks than the other, you should also place the read-only table on that array, because doing so also improves read performance.

If some of your disks are too heavily accessed, despite this, you could create only one filegroup and place it on both disk arrays. You could then place both tables on this filegroup, which spreads out I/O on both arrays. Table data will be written to both disk arrays, because the filegroup spans the two.

Since the best way to optimize disk I/O is to distribute your data on as many disks as possible, you should consider this during the *physical design phase* (as you will see later in the section "Physical Design"). By using filegroups, we can even further distribute I/O evenly, because when the data is written to a table on a filegroup that spans many disks, the data is spread in proportion across all the files in the filegroup.

You can use the following three kinds of filegroups:

- Primary filegroups

- User-defined filegroups

- Default filegroups

The *primary filegroup* contains the primary data file. It also contains all the files not specifically put into another filegroup. All system tables are always placed on the primary filegroup. The primary data file must also always be placed in the primary filegroup.

User-defined filegroups are the filegroups that you create yourself.

The *default filegroup* is where all tables and indexes are placed if they're not specifically put in another filegroup. The primary filegroup is the default filegroup—if you do not specify otherwise. You can, if you want, switch the default filegroup with the ALTER DATABASE command in Transact-SQL.

Another benefit of using filegroups is that you can perform backups on separate filegroups independently of each other. You can also restore them separately. This can speed up backup and restore operations considerably.

Automatic File Growth

A cool feature of SQL Server is that you don't have to expand the files manually when they run out of space. SQL Server handles this by itself, if you specify this when creating the file (see Figure 9-12).

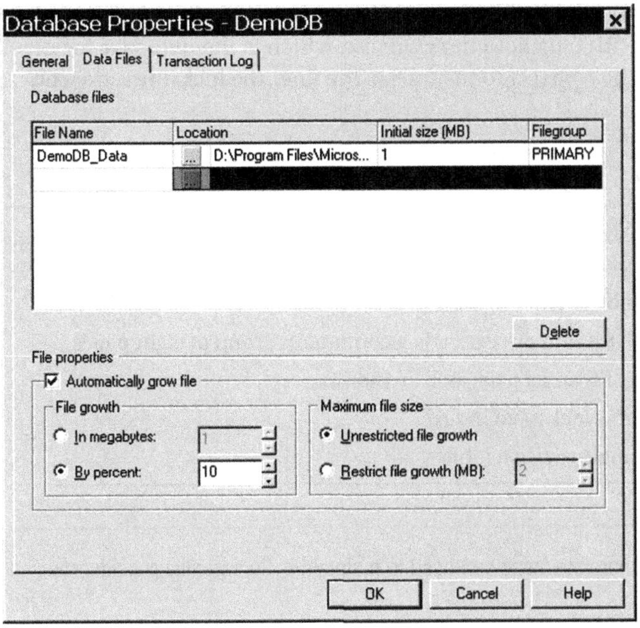

Figure 9-12. *Specifying automatic file growth and maximum file size in Enterprise Manager*

■ **Tip** If you use this option, you should probably also remember to specify the maximum size of the file. You do not want to run out of space on a disk, which could happen if you forget to set this option.

As you can see, you need to do some planning before you set these options, but with a little careful thinking, it will prove to be a great help for you.

Lock Management

If you have a database that is accessed by many users or applications, you'll need an option to prevent the same data from being modified by two or more processes at the same time. By using locks, you can make sure a process has a dependency on a resource, and as a result has access rights to it. This means that other processes can't modify the resource until the first process releases the lock. Locking ensures that multiple users can read and write to the same database without getting inconsistent data and without overwriting each other's modifications by accident. All locks are managed on a per–SQL Server connection basis.

■ **Tip** If you want to learn more about SQL Server and the way it handles locks, please see the document "Understanding Locking in SQL Server" at the following URL: http://msdn.microsoft.com/_library/ default.asp?url=/library/en-us/acdata/_ac_8_con_7a_7xde.asp.

Different levels of locks can be used with SQL Server. They vary in granularity from the finest, which is the Row Identifier (RID) lock, to the coarsest, which is the database lock. Table 9-3 describes the locks from the coarsest to the finest. The finer the lock, the more concurrency among users you have.

Table 9-3. *Lock Levels in SQL Server*

Lock Type	Description
Database	Simply locks the entire database. No other user is allowed in the database.
Table	Locks a table, including indexes.
Extent	Locks a 64KB unit. An extent is a contiguous group of eight pages.
Page	A page is 8KB and a page lock locks 8KB.
Key	This is a row lock in an index.
RID (Row Identifier)	Locks a single row in a table.

■ **Note** The finer the lock you use, the more overhead you need to maintain it. So carefully consider the kind of lock to use.

There are also different kinds of locks you can use. SQL Server uses six different kinds of modes, as you see in Table 9-4.

Table 9-4. *The Six Modes of SQL Server Locks*

Mode	Description
Shared	Used for read-only operations
Exclusive	Used when modifying data
Update	Used on updatable resources
Intent	Used to establish a locking hierarchy
Schema	Used for instance when modifying tables or the schema
Bulk update	Used for bulk-copying data into a table

Luckily, you do not have to consider which mode to use since SQL Server does this for you. It chooses the most cost-effective lock for the current operation.

Threads in SQL Server

Now we've come to the final part of the SQL Server architecture—threads. SQL Server 2000 uses Windows threads and fibers to execute tasks. We have covered threads earlier (in the section "Threads" in Chapter 4), but the fiber concept is new. Before we take a look at fibers, you'll need to understand the concept of context switching and why this occurs. When SQL Server doesn't use fibers, it uses threads. These are distributed evenly across the available CPUs on the system. If you want, you can specify which CPUs SQL Server should use, but in most cases SQL Server handles this better than you can. When one thread is moved off a CPU and another is moved on, a context switch occurs. This is a very performance-costly operation, because the switch is between user mode and kernel mode (we covered this switching process in more detail in the early part of Chapter 4). To get the most out of your system, you should minimize context switching—and using fibers is one way of doing this.

A fiber is a subcomponent of a thread, and is something you must enable for your SQL Server to use. Fibers are handled by code running in user mode. This means that switching fibers, and thereby switching tasks, is not as costly as switching threads. The reason for this is that the switch doesn't occur from user to kernel mode, but instead takes place in only one mode.

As opposed to threads, fibers are handled by SQL Server and not by the operating system. One thread is allocated per CPU available to SQL Server, and one fiber is allocated per concurrent user command. There can be many fibers on one thread, and fibers can also be switched on the thread. During the switch, the thread still remains on the same CPU, so no context switch occurs. By reducing the number of context switches, performance is increased.

■**Note** Use fibers only if the server has four or more CPUs, and only use them when the system has more than 5000 context switches per second. We would suggest you do not enable fibers unless someone from Microsoft tells you to. Read more about the perils of fibers at http://msdn.microsoft.com/library/default.asp?url=/library/en-us/dnsqldev/html/sqldev_02152005.asp?frame=true.

You can use SQL Server Enterprise Manager to enable fiber mode (see Figure 9-13), or you can run sp_configure to set the lightweight pooling option to 1.

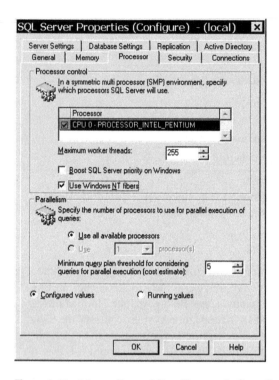

Figure 9-13. *Manually enabling fiber mode from Enterprise Manager*

Worker Processes

SQL Server keeps a pool of threads or fibers for all user connections. These threads or fibers are called worker processes. You can limit the number of worker processes by setting a maximum value for this. When this value is reached, SQL Server begins thread-pooling. As long as the maximum worker process value has not been reached, SQL Server starts a new thread for the user commands, but as soon as the limit is reached and thread-pooling has begun, each new request has to wait for a thread to be available. You should not set the maximum value too high (default is 255) because the more worker processes you have, the more resources are consumed. This eventually affects performance. Experiment with it in the lab, and find the best setting for your system.

Database Design

Designing a database means more than just jotting down some objects on a piece of paper and trying to create tables from them. It requires an understanding of the business functions you want to model, as well as how you can implement them, by using database concepts and features. As you saw in Chapter 1, Object Role Modeling (ORM) can be a great way of achieving your database design.

When you are beginning to design your database, you should consider performance issues. Even though you can change the database design once it is implemented, this is not a desirable way of doing things. It costs both time and money to go back and redesign a database at a later stage.

During database design, you should consider the purpose of the database. An Online Transaction Processing (OLTP) database will not be normalized in the same way that you would normalize a decision support database, for instance. The more update-intensive processing of the transactions in an OLTP database might often require a more normalized design than a decision support database, since the latter often has less redundant updates. The decision support database might actually be more efficient, if you do not normalize it too much. This is because by having fewer joins, performance is better and data will be easier to understand.

You must always create a database plan that will fit your purpose. You should also get an overview of the security requirements for the database. Do you need to set up Active Directory Application Mode, or ADAM (as discussed in more detail in the section "Windows Authentication"), or can you manage with your existing Active Directory? If you aren't going to have many users, you may be able to use SQL Server authentication and skip a directory altogether.

Another aspect you should consider is how much data you will store, and how much you believe this data will grow over time. This affects how you plan your hardware. You also need to address scalability and reliability when designing your database. Do you need to cluster the database, or can you live with some outages of your SQL Server? You should also start planning a disaster recovery plan as early as possible.

■ **Tip** A good rule of thumb, as always, is to dedicate enough time in the beginning for the design, so that later on the project won't have any performance or security issues. The time you need should be estimated based on the kind of application you are going to build, so it is hard to give exact advice here.

In the best-case scenario, your company has a policy for data storage, so you don't have to make these decisions for every new project, since they take some time to work through.

Database design involves the following two things:

- Logical design

- Physical design

We will explore these in more detail in the following sections.

Logical Design

During the logical design phase, you should model your business requirements and data using tables, constraints, and other database components (see Figure 9-14). Preferably you should do this by using ORM. (At this stage, you don't have to think about how you will store data physically yet.)

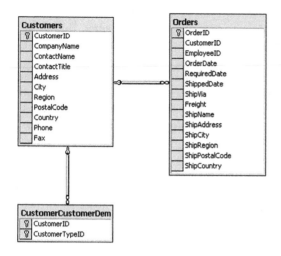

Figure 9-14. *A logical database design*

One of the first things you should do during logical design is to remove as much redundancy as you can from the database. The primary function of this process, called normalization, is to make sure that redundant data is stored in a separate table, with a foreign key pointing to the right row in the table. Normalization is also used to break down the data into smaller parts; for example, the name of an employee can be broken down into first name and last name and then placed in separate columns.

You also need to consider the integrity of your data during this phase. By using primary keys, check constraints, foreign keys, default values, and other database features, you can make sure that your data is not compromised. These features also help you maintain your business requirements.

Tip Use fixed-size columns when you only need to store small values in such columns. If you have fewer than five characters per cell in a column, you should use a fixed column size like char(4). This enhances the way a data row is read and hence increases performance.

If a column will include more than 20 characters in each cell, you should use a variable size like varchar(100).

Anything in between is difficult to advise you about here, so try different sizes in a test lab before deciding.

Please remember that a bad logical design most often results in a bad physical design, which in the end negatively affects performance.

Physical Design

The physical database design phase involves mapping the logical design to your physical hardware. You do this by taking advantage of the hardware and software features available to you. In other words, this is where you allow the data to be physically accessed and maintained as quickly as possible.

Note Indexing your data is also part of this design phase. We will cover indexing later on in this chapter in the section "Index Tuning."

When you do your physical design, you often benefit if your company already has a data storage policy. Otherwise, you must decide where to store your data: on a DAS, a NAS appliance, or a SAN. Depending on the business requirements for your solution, you may need to deviate from corporate standards, and the design stage is the time to determine these things.

Optimizing Performance

Now that you know how the internals of SQL Server work and how database design affects performance, we are going to introduce you to some performance tuning topics of interest.

Database Performance and I/O Configuration Options

Here we will discuss some of the performance counters you might want to keep an eye on, in order to ensure your SQL Server is working like it should.

When SQL Server reads data from tables, it uses Windows system I/O calls to do it. SQL Server then decides when and how this access is performed, but it's the operating system that actually performs the work.

Disk I/O is the most frequent reason for performance bottlenecks, so you should not forget to monitor this activity on your server. As always, use System Monitor (or Performance MMC, as it is called in Windows XP/Windows Server 2003) to monitor your system.

Figure 9-15 shows two performance counters:

- *PhysicalDisk*. % Disk Time, which is the percentage of time that the disk is busy with read/write operations.

- *PhysicalDisk*. Current Disk Queue Length, which shows the number of system requests waiting for disk access.

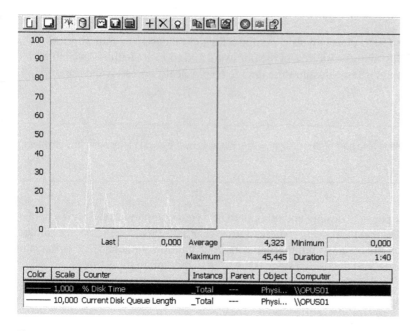

Figure 9-15. *Two performance counters that are used to monitor disk access*

If the PhysicalDisk: % Disk Time value is above 90 percent, you should monitor PhysicalDisk: Current Disk Queue Length to see how many system requests are waiting in line for disk access. This value should be no more than 1.5 or 2.0 times the spindles making up the physical disk, so check out the hardware before counting. If both of these counters are consistently high, you probably have a bottleneck in your system. To solve this problem, consider using a faster disk drive or moving some of the files to an additional disk or even a different server. You could also add additional disks to your RAID system if you use this storage technology.

You should only use these counters if you have just one disk partition on your hard drives. If you have partitioned your disks, you should monitor the LogicalDisk counters instead of the PhysicalDisk counters (the names of the corresponding LogicalDisk counters are similar to those just mentioned for PhysicalDisk).

As you saw in Chapter 4, you should avoid paging on your server. To monitor this, use the Memory: Page faults/sec counter.

If you want to isolate the disk writes/reads that SQL Server is responsible for, monitor the following two counters (see Figure 9-16):

- SQLServer: Buffer manager page reads/sec

- SQLServer: Buffer manager page writes/sec

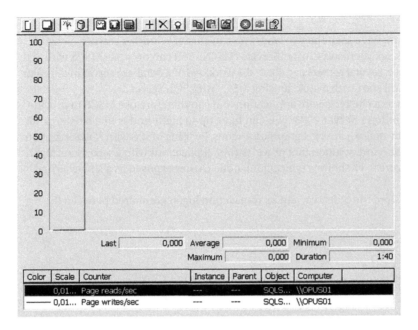

Figure 9-16. *Two performance counters are used to separate SQL Server disk I/O from other I/O.*

If the values for these two counters are near the capacity of the hardware, you should try to reduce them by tuning your databases or applications. You can do this by reducing I/O operations. Do this by checking your indexes to make sure they are accurate or try normalizing your databases even more. If this still does not help, try increasing the I/O capacity of your hardware or adding more memory.

■**Tip** If you find your bottleneck involves inserts and updates, you could try to normalize your data more. If you find instead that queries cause the bottleneck, you could try to denormalize the database. The problem with such a solution is that you might need to rewrite your applications in order to handle a new database structure. This might not be a problem if you discover this early in development, but in production this can be costly. Sometimes this might be the only way to correct the problem, however, and then you just have to deal with it. But please make sure you have tried optimizing the SQL Server first: that is you've tuned all indexes, polished your stored procedures and basically done all that you can do with your database before you start denormalizing. This most often does the trick.

You could monitor how much memory SQL Server is using by checking the value for SQL Server: Memory Manager Total Server Memory (KB). Compare this to how much memory the operating system has available by checking the counter Available Kbytes from the Memory object. This could give you a clue to making a decision as to whether there is a need to restrict how much memory SQL Server is allowed to use.

Next, we will move on to clustering SQL Server.

Clustering

In previous chapters, you have seen the two ways you can cluster Windows servers: Network
Load Balancing (NLB) and Microsoft Cluster Service (MSCS). You can only use MSCS with SQL
Server, but as you will see, several servers can share the workload of a database server in a similar
way as NLB. First, we will start with a look at using MSCS with SQL Server.

SQL Server is built as a cluster-aware application and can therefore use MSCS to provide
high availability. In Windows Server 2003, you can have up to eight nodes in a cluster, and
you can also disperse the nodes across geographic locations. By using MSCS with SQL Server, you
can build a back-end data store solution that provides your applications with a secure and highly
available data feed. Figure 9-17 shows a typical four-node cluster exposed as a single virtual
server to the clients.

The disks used to store the database and its transaction log(s) are shared between the
nodes in the cluster.

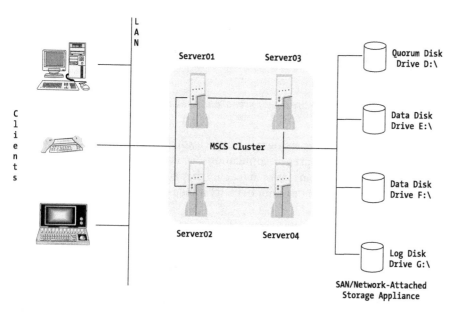

Figure 9-17. *A MSCS cluster with four nodes*

■**Note** To avoid a single point of failure, duplicate all fiber channels and other communications hardware
that your cluster uses.

Remember that only one instance of SQL Server can access the database at a time, and when
a node fails, it takes a little time before the failover node is online and processing requests. If
the failure depends on a corrupt database, obviously the failover node will not work either.
Database corruption, whether it's the kind a user can make, called logical corruption, or the

type that occurs within a database, called internal corruption, is not prevented by clustering. This means you must always provide a disaster recovery plan, and also make certain that it works when you need it.

This sounds so logical and easy, but this is not always the case. One time, a client of ours experienced an erroneous update in their sales batches during the night, which corrupted 25 customer databases. All of the customers had regular database backups scheduled, but only 15 of them were able to perform a restore operation. We ended up writing scripts and doing tricks so that the databases were rolled back to an earlier date, and all batches were then inserted again, this time with correct data. That took us close to a week. Don't put yourself in this situation—we can guarantee it is not pleasant.

Index Tuning

Indexes are one of a database designer's best friends. Efficient index design is a crucial part of achieving good performance. An index reduces the amount of I/O necessary to retrieve requested data by helping SQL Server to quickly determine where data is stored, hence making retrieval quicker.

If you do not have an index in your table, all the data must be read and compared to what you are looking for. Compare this to how hard and slow it would be to find a certain topic in a book without a table of contents or index, and you soon understand the importance of good indexing. By using indexes, you speed up the process of finding what you are looking for.

The following are the two kinds of indexes that SQL Server uses:

- Clustered indexes

- Nonclustered indexes

A clustered index can be compared to a phone directory. All data is sorted alphabetically, in the phone directory by last name and first name, and in a database depending on what column(s) the index is created on. Only one clustered index can exist in a table, because the clustered index dictates the physical storage order of the data.

A nonclustered index can be compared to an index in a book. The data is stored in one place and the index, with pointers to the data, is stored in another. The index and the items it consists of are stored in the order of the index key values. The data in the table can be stored in a different order. You can, for instance, store it in the order of a clustered index, but if you do not have a clustered index in your table, it can be stored in any possible way. SQL Server searches the index to find the location of the data, and then retrieves it from that location. You can have multiple nonclustered indexes in a table, and use different ones depending on your queries.

When to Use Which Index

If you have a column in a table where the data is unique for every row, you should consider having a clustered index on that column. An example of this is a column with Social Security numbers or employee numbers. Clustered indexes are very good at finding a specific row in this case. This can be effective for an OLTP application, where you look for a single row and need access to it quickly.

Another great opportunity for using clustered indexes is when you search a table for a range of values in a column(s). When SQL Server has found the first value in the range, all others are sure to follow after it. This improves performance of data retrieval.

If you have columns often used in queries that have a GROUP BY or ORDER BY clause, you can also consider using a clustered index. This eliminates the need for SQL Server to sort the data itself, since it is already sorted by the index.

Tip We have learned from experience that it isn't a good idea to have a clustered index on a GUID (or any other random value). The clustered index works well for columns that you know will be sorted a particular way (according to last name, for example), because you do not need to perform a sort after retrieval. You will rarely (if ever) sort or seek data according to their GUIDs (or random values for that matter)—that would only increase the overhead during and after data retrieval, since you then would have to re-sort the data to be able to use it properly.

Nonclustered indexes are used to great advantage if a column or columns contain a large number of distinct values. (Refer to a combination of last name and first name here to get the picture. There can be many John Smiths in a table, for example.)

You can also use the nonclustered indexes when queries do not return large data sets. The opposite is, of course, true for clustered indexes.

If you have queries that use search conditions (WHERE clauses) to return an exact match, you can also consider using nonclustered indexes on the columns in the WHERE clause.

Note SQL Server comes with a tool called the Index Tuning Wizard, which can be used to analyze your queries and suggest the indexes that you should create. Check it out on a few queries and tables, and do some testing. We will cover this feature some more, later in this chapter.

Query Optimizer

SQL Server 2000 comes with a built-in query optimizer that in most cases chooses the most effective index to use. When you design your indexes, you should provide the query optimizer with a carefully thought-out selection of indexes to choose from. It will in most cases select the best index from these.

The task of the query optimizer is to select an index when it attempts to optimize performance. It will not use an index that will degrade performance. The truth is that having an index does not necessarily mean you get the best performance, especially if an index is designed poorly. So you should be grateful that there is logic built into the query optimizer to help you out. The rule is to test your indexes, just as you test all other solutions, in order to find the most effective ones.

Index Tuning Wizard

As you saw in the previous section, in SQL Server does provide a tool that helps you analyze your queries and that suggests indexes for your tables. If you were going to do this manually, you would have quite a task in front of you. First of all, you would need to have an expert understanding of the database. If you are the database designer, this would not be a problem, but that is not always the case. You would also need to have deep knowledge of how SQL

Server works internally. If you are like most developers, you just don't want to dig that deep into the tools you use, and you shouldn't need to either. That is why it's good to have tools that make your life easier.

To use the Index Tuning Wizard, you need a sample of the normal workload your SQL Server has to deal with. You can use this as input for how you should design your indexes, so you know they will be effective. Only this time it will be the Index Tuning Wizard that makes the recommendations for you.

To create the sample, use another tool that ships with SQL Server: the SQL Profiler. Once you are satisfied with the trace SQL Profiler creates, you can let the Index Tuning Wizard analyze the workload and provide a sample Transact-SQL statement. When done, the wizard will recommend an index configuration that will improve the performance of the database. At this moment, you can choose to let it implement the suggested changes immediately, schedule the implementation for later, or save it to a SQL script that you can run at any time.

■**Note** Run the Index Tuning Wizard against a test SQL Server. It consumes quite a lot of CPU from the server, which could create problems in a production environment. Also, try to use a separate computer to run the wizard from, so it is not running on the same server where the SQL Server instance is installed.

Partitioned Views

You can't use Network Load Balancing to distribute the workload for a SQL Server. Another method lets you accomplish the same thing, however, or at least something similar.

Take a look at an example. If you have a customer database that only stores information about your customers A–Z, you can partition the data. One partition could hold all customers in the range from A–E, another F–I, and so on. Once you have decided which way to partition the data, you must select one out of the two following choices of storing it (keeping best performance in mind):

- Local partitioned view
- Distributed partitioned view

Local Partitioned Views

A *local partitioned view* stores all partitions in the same instance of your SQL Server. (See the section "Separating Read Data from Write Data" later in this chapter for a discussion on when this is a good solution.)

Distributed Partitioned Views

A *distributed partitioned view* uses a federation of servers to store data. Although this sounds like something out of Star Wars, it is really quite simple. A federation of servers consists of two or more servers, each holding one partition of the data (see Figure 9-18).

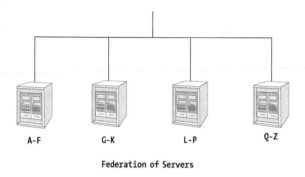

Federation of Servers

Figure 9-18. *A federation of SQL Servers*

Every server runs a separate instance of SQL Server. The servers are administered independently of each other, but they cooperate to share the processing load of the data. The horizontally partitioned table is exposed as a single table through the use of partitioned views.

On every server, the other SQL Servers are added as linked servers so that you can execute distributed queries on them. You can then create a distributed partitioned view on each of the servers, as the following code listing shows, so that clients can access this view on any of the servers and still get the view of the full table. As you'll see, the view is a set of SQL statements whose individual result sets are combined into one, using the UNION ALL statement in Transact-SQL:

```
create view CustomerView as
    select * from server01.MyDatabase.dbo.Customers_01
union all
    select * from server02.MyDatabase.dbo.Customers_02
union all
    select * from server03.MyDatabase.dbo.Customers_03
union all
    select * from server04.MyDatabase.dbo.Customers_04
```

You can also make the view updatable if you want to, which further adds to the flexibility of this solution.

Remember that you can use the servers for storing other data at the same time as they store a partition. The servers are not dedicated to this partition in any way. You might only need to partition one large table, in which case it would be a pity not to use the servers' capacity to their full extent.

By using this method, you can let several servers share the burden of handling a large table. Clients can access any of the servers and get results from all of them by using one single view, allowing this solution to scale even though you do not use NLB. Since you can use a MSCS cluster behind each of the participating servers, you can also achieve high availability with this technique.

■ **Note** The most common way of implementing distributed partitioned views is by letting the client appli-cations access the member server that has most of the data required by the SQL statement. This is called collocating the SQL statement with the data it requires.

Separating Read Data from Write Data

There is a way to reduce the impact that locking has on your database. As you may recall, locking can reduce performance, and if you have a lot of read activity, you shouldn't let a write command lock these reads. By defining vertical partitions, you can separate read columns from write columns and place them in different tables. This can improve performance in your applications.

You could also use horizontal partitioning to separate read data from write data. Say you have a table that stores sales data for your company. Data is written on a daily basis, and all other data is maintained for reporting purposes. This kind of table could grow extremely large and unmanageable. By partitioning the data horizontally, you can enhance performance on write and read operations. You could create a table for the current month, another for the cur-rent year, and a third for the rest of the data. How you do the partitioning is determined by the way the table is used. After that, you create a view that lets you display data from all the tables.

By partitioning this way, you also enhance backup performance, since you don't need to back up all historical data every day.

During the design phase, you should carefully consider how your data is going to be accessed so you minimize locking.

Query Tuning

Even if you have top-of-the-line hardware and it is tuned extremely well, you might still experience performance troubles. It is as important to optimize your queries as it is to optimize your hardware. Although writing queries is quite easy, if you have no knowledge of query design issues, your queries could degrade performance. Resources are used intensively, especially in two particular cases: queries returning large result sets and highly non-unique WHERE clauses. We have seen some horrible queries in our time (not to mention the embarrassing queries we ourselves have produced over the years), despite the fact that the developers who wrote them should have known better.

Sometimes you can't avoid using very complex and resource-intensive queries; however, you could try to move the processing of these to a stored procedure, where such a query would probably execute better than if the application issued it. This would also reduce network traf-fic if the query returned a large result set, as you can see in the Stored Procedure section that follows.

If this still doesn't help, you could also add more CPUs to your server if your hardware allows this possibility. This way SQL Server can execute queries in parallel, and performance will increase.

What you should do first of all is to go over the design of the query one more time. Is there really no way you can rewrite it to make it perform better? If you use cursors in your query, you should definitely see if you can make them more effective. It might also be possible to exchange the cursor for a GROUP BY or CASE statement instead.

If your application uses a loop that executes a parameterized stored procedure, every time you travel down the loop, a round-trip is made to the SQL Server. This slows down performance. Instead, you should try to rewrite the application and the stored procedure to create a single, more complex query using a temporary table. This way the SQL Server query optimizer can better optimize the execution of the query. A temporary table causes a recompile of the stored procedure, however, which negatively affects performance. So if you find it causing problems, you could use a table variable instead. Try to avoid getting too large of a result set back, since this also degrades performance. These issues can be like walking on the edge of a blade, so test, test, and test.

■**Note** Not all stored procedures are good, unfortunately. See the section "Stored Procedures" later in this chapter for specifics.

A long-running query costs a lot, since it might prevent others from getting their queries executed. It also consumes a lot of resources. You can stop these queries by setting the query governor configuration option. The default is that the query governor allows all queries to execute. You can set the query governor to not allow queries that will take more than a specified number of seconds to execute. It also allows you to control this type of query execution on each separate connection, or on all of them if you wish. The query governor estimates the cost of the queries and stops long-running queries before they have even started executing. Since it does not allow them to run, the overhead of this process is quite low.

Connecting to the Database

There are several ways you can connect to a SQL Server, named pipes and TCP/IP being the most common. In certain situations, one of these may be preferable to the other if you want to get the best performance out of your solution.

If you have a fast LAN, not much differs between these two approaches. On a slower network, like a WAN or dial-up network, the difference becomes apparent. A named pipe is a very interactive protocol—it sends a lot of messages before it actually begins reading any data. Named pipes communication starts when one peer requests data from another, using the read command. After they have exchanged pleasantries, data is read. On a fast network, this communication won't be noticed much, but on a slower connection this costs performance because the network traffic consists of many messages. Obviously, this affects clients on the network negatively.

TCP/IP sockets have more streamlined data transmissions with less overhead than named pipes. Windowing, delayed acknowledgements, and other features of TCP/IP sockets help you improve performance. This is very useful on a slow network for providing significant performance benefits for your client applications.

Our suggestion is to use TCP/IP on WANs and dial-up connections, because it will save a lot of complaints about slow data retrieval.

If the application using the SQL Server is located on the SQL Server itself, you can use local named pipes, which can result in great performance. Local named pipes run in kernel mode, making them extremely fast. Use this option if you are planning to implement the data access component on the same server as the SQL Server database.

To summarize what we have just covered is as follows:

- Use TCP/IP on slower network connections.

- Use local named pipes when data access components are running on the SQL Server itself.

- Use either TCP/IP or named pipes on a fast connection.

Stored Procedures

A good way of optimizing the ways that your data access components talk to SQL Server is through stored procedures. Because they are compiled on the server, they execute much faster than if you had used a Transact-SQL statement to retrieve data. You don't want to move business logic to the database in most cases; you only want to use the enhanced performance you get from including parameterized stored procedures.

Note All database interaction can benefit from using stored procedures. Your insert, select, and delete operations could, and should in most cases, be implemented as stored procedures.

However, even stored procedures can negatively affect performance. Try to avoid stored procedure recompiles because they cost performance. One good thing to remember is to be careful with the use of temporary tables in stored procedures, since they cause a recompile of the stored procedure every time it is executed. In the case of temporary tables, you could try using a table variable instead.

If you want to learn more about troubleshooting stored procedure recompilations, you can find a good document on this topic at http://support.microsoft.com/default.aspx?scid=kb;en-us;243586.

Another benefit is that stored procedures utilize the network more efficiently than an ordinary SQL statement does. For example, say you have an INSERT statement that inserts a large binary data value into an Image data column. If you do not use a stored procedure, the application issuing the Insert statement must convert the value to a character string. This doubles the statement's size. Only after this conversion can it send the data to the server. The server in turn converts the statement back to binary format and stores it in the image column. If you use a stored procedure instead, the image would stay in binary format all the way to the server. This would greatly reduce overhead on the server and the client, as well as cutting down on network traffic.

Sometimes it can be of great use to move the business rules from the business logic into the database server. You must carefully consider your use of this, however, so you don't lose control of your application. The benefits of moving processing to a stored procedure are purely performance-related. Instead of moving a large set of data to where the processing usually occurs, you bring the processing functionality to the data, which increases performance. The complexity of your application increases, however, so you should think twice before using this technique. The best way to see if the performance gains outweigh the increased complexity is to test the solution in the lab.

SQL Server Security

So far we have covered some important topics when it comes to data storage and SQL Server. The last topic we will cover before taking you through our demo application in the next chapter is SQL Server security.

In Chapter 4, we discussed authentication and authorization. Authentication occurs when a user or application tries to log on to your SQL Server. Authorization determines what the user is allowed to do in the database server and its tables. In the following section, we will take a look at how authentication works in SQL Server.

Choosing Your Authentication

There are two ways SQL Server can authenticate a user or group. Early in the design process, you should decide which method you are going to use, because each affects the way you set up your user accounts for your application. The two methods are

- SQL Server authentication

- Windows authentication

SQL Server Authentication

If you use SQL Server authentication, SQL Server matches the account and password the user supplies to a list that is stored in the sysxlogins system table. This table is found in the master database (see Figure 9-19). SQL Server authentication is quite easy to implement, and you can use SQL Server Enterprise Manager to add, remove, or modify these logins (see Figure 9-20).

Column Name	Data Type	Length	Allow Nulls
srvid	smallint	2	✓
sid	varbinary	85	✓
xstatus	smallint	2	
xdate1	datetime	8	
xdate2	datetime	8	
name	sysname	128	✓
password	varbinary	256	✓
dbid	smallint	2	
[language]	sysname	128	✓
isrpcinmap	smallint	2	✓
ishqoutmap	smallint	2	✓
selfoutmap	smallint	2	✓

Figure 9-19. *The sysxlogins table from the master database*

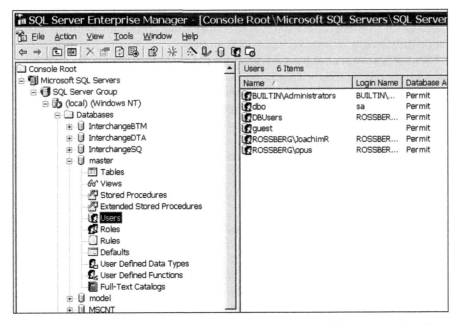

Figure 9-20. *The Enterprise Manager gives you an overview of the users in a database.*

The logins you created are local to the server on which the SQL Server resides, which is not a good solution if you have a multiserver environment. In that case, you can't manage them very easily, and you would have to implement the accounts on several servers. This solution could work, however, if the number of users does not exceed 20 to 25. With more users, you will soon discover how impractical this is, and how much administrative overhead this will cost. Imagine implementing a change to only one user on several servers.

Windows Authentication

What you should have used in the preceding scenario is Windows authentication. When SQL Server authenticates using this method, it asks a domain controller to validate a user's credentials. A domain controller must be accessible for this to work, so you need to make sure one is available. When SQL Server authenticates a user or group against a domain controller, it receives an access token containing the user's SID and the SIDs of every group the user has membership in. SQL Server will then assign access to the database server based on these SIDs.

You can use Active Directory (AD) to store your users and groups for your applications, but in many cases you do not want to mix your internal corporate users with your application users. The SQL Server will perhaps be used only for a web solution and not needed by anyone but those accessing the web site. In that case, it could present a security risk to use the same AD as for your enterprise. To solve this, you could implement a separate AD infrastructure and set up a new server and domain, but this is not something you can do just like that. Luckily, Microsoft recently released a "light" version of Active Directory, called Active Directory Application Mode, or ADAM. ADAM is a stand-alone version of AD, intended for the use as a directory for web-based applications and other types of applications. ADAM is deployed separately from the standard AD, and its directory data is not replicated throughout the enterprise core NOS directory. It also gives administrators the flexibility to deploy a directory without having to set up an entire Windows Server operating system environment on a domain controller. Nor do they have to activate Kerberos, DNS, or PKI.

ADAM is Microsoft's answer to web-based directories from competitors like Sun's ONE Directory Server and Novell's eDirectory. (Given Microsoft's aggressive marketing in the past, ADAM will probably be seen on a server near you rather soon.)

Windows authentication gives you central management control regardless of whether you use AD or ADAM, which will give you lower TCO over time.

There are also ways of accessing SQL Server over the Internet using IIS, but this solution is not especially relevant when it comes to building an enterprise application, so we will not cover it here.

Determining Permissions

After you have decided which authentication method you should use, you must plan what permissions you will give to your users and groups. (We will only consider Windows authentication in this discussion.) You should strive to give the permissions to your database server only to groups. If you do, you'll find that you can more easily manage who has access to the server. Say you have a group of users belonging to the accounting department. Often these users will need the same permissions in the SQL Server. You do not want to add every user from this department to the database server and give them each the same permissions. What you do want to do is create a domain global group, add the accounting users to this group, and give only the domain global group database access. So instead of granting 30 people access and permissions on the server, you only do this for the domain global group they belong to, which cuts down on administrative overhead.

When you want to give permissions in a database on your SQL Server, you can use something called *roles*. There are some built-in roles you can use (see Figure 9-21), but you can also create your own. You give permissions only to roles, and then make the domain global groups members of those roles.

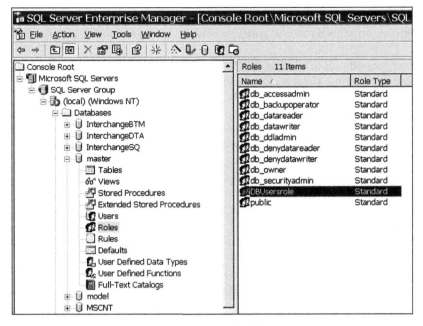

Figure 9-21. *The roles in SQL Server*

You create the roles you need, name them so you understand what they are, and then add the correct domain global group to the role. After that, you assign database permissions to it.

■**Note** A good practice is to name roles after the domain global groups, so as not to cause confusion.

This procedure is the same one that is often used to give both users and groups the access they need to data on a server. The global groups are members of local groups, and it is only the local groups that are given permissions to the data.

SQL Server 2005

We are in the middle of evaluating SQL Server 2005 at this time. Since a company's database servers aren't usually something that people want to experiment with, only few, if any, of our customers have gone further than test lab evaluations either. Therefore, it is hard to know how this edition really stands up to the competition. As of this writing, SQL Server 2005 has not reached it's RTM status yet, which means features might still be changed, added, or even removed. What we can say is that the changes are more evolutionary and less revolutionary than we might have expected them to be. Don't get me wrong. The features are powerful and many will be most appreciated by administrators and developers alike. Its beta status does mean that it is hard to come up with recommendations for its use, so we'll settle for highlighting some features instead.

Availability and Scalability

Some cool enhancements have been made to enhance availability and scalability. Let's focus on availability first.

Failover clustering now extends to all parts of SQL Server. That means that even SQL Server Agent is now covered by clustering. There is also clustering support for Analysis Services, Notification Services, and replication as well. This all adds up to a greater availability on all aspects of SQL Server database management.

Database mirroring might sound like something ordinary. Microsoft's version is an enhancement of the log-shipping possibilities. It works by continuously streaming transaction logs from the source server, or the principal server as Microsoft calls it, to the mirror server. All transaction logs are then replayed on the mirror so that it will be as up-to-date as possible. If a failure occurs in the principal server, the mirror server detects this within seconds and quickly sets itself in a state so it can accept the client connections instead. This way the risk of loosing important data has been minimized.

There is also a third server present in this kind of setup. We need a witness, someone objective, who can determine which server is the principal and which is the mirror. If two servers out of these three agree on this their opinions win out.

So, if we have a failover to the mirror it becomes the principal and accepts incoming connections. When the failed server is brought back online it becomes the mirror and starts getting all transaction logs so it can be up to date again. It remains the mirror until somebody changes it (or a new failure in the principal occurs).

The need for *restarting the database* has been minimized. Many administrative tasks, such as changing the database server affinities for RAM or CPU, needed a restart of the database server in previous versions. Microsoft seems to have been determined to minimize downtime of the database due to such tasks and it looks like they have been working hard to reduce the need for restarts. This is a really welcome change, since it is annoying if simple tasks must be made during strange hours just so we do not disrupt database availability to users.

If we needed to *restore a database*, we used to have to take the database down, making it unavailable for a period of time, even if only a filegroup needed to be restored. Now we don't have to take the database offline. We can do a restore wherein only the data being restored is unavailable. This means that the rest is still there for the users.

We can also recover a database more quickly with SQL Server 2005. We haven't tried this feature ourselves yet but it does look promising.

The last thing we will mention when it comes to availability is the *Online Index Operations* feature. This feature is only available with the Enterprise Edition so it does not work on all versions. In SQL Server 2000 index operations like rebuilding or building an index held a lock on the data making it unavailable until the indexes had been built. Not anymore; now the data will be available for queries and updates even if the indexes are being rebuilt or added.

When it comes to scalability there has been some improvements as well. Especially when it comes to Very Large Databases (VLDB) improvements have been made. This is an area where Microsoft has had a bad reputation before. Many companies have not dared to put their large, important databases on a SQL Server, even though this changed quite noticeably with SQL Server 2000. Now Microsoft has put even more effort into those scenarios and we will definitely see a lot of SQL Servers in this field in the feature.

Let's look at two improvements. First there is the *snapshot isolation level*, which gives us better possibilities for increasing data availability for read-only applications. We also get non-blocking read operations in an OLTP environment, and conflict detection (mandatory) for write transactions. This is all made possible because snapshot isolation allows us to access the previously committed value of the row. This will prevent the scenario where a reader can't read a row because a change is locking the data.

Table partitioning has been improved so that we can partition tables across filegroups. Remember we speak of horizontal partitioning here. This is a great way of increasing scalability.

Other Improvements

There have been improvements all over SQL Server which will help developers and database administrators alike. The administrative interfaces have been changed, giving a more flexible view of the database management tasks.

For example, there is now .NET Framework hosting in SQL Server which allows developers to use VB.NET or C# in the database and also allows for a greater possibility of debugging.

We will leave this version here but wants to finish with saying that the features look interesting so take every possibility to try it out.

Summary

In this chapter we've covered some important issues when it comes to data storage and how SQL Server fits into a storage policy. You have also seen some tricks you can use to improve performance in your SQL Server systems.

The focus of the chapter has been SQL Server 2000 since that is the database server most of our customers use right now. We also shortly covered SQL Server 2005 just to show a few of the cool features coming, buts since it has not even reached Release Candidate status when writing this we will not get deeply into it here.

Now it is time to put everything you have seen in this book to work. The next chapter will cover the development of a new application, following the guidelines we have discussed so far.

CHAPTER 10

■ ■ ■

An Example Application

Now that you have reached the last chapter, it is time for us to tie it all together. During the book we have tried to set a course for how to bring an enterprise application safely to shore. We have shown you a lot of tips and tricks for how you should design your products. As we walk through our demo application, you'll see that we won't be able to apply all of the techniques to the application. And we wouldn't be able to in a real-world application either. It all varies depending on the circumstances for each project, so you should carefully consider what best suits your application and apply those principles as needed. In this chapter, we are going to design and build an enterprise time reporting application. It will be used for employees to report the amount of time they have spent on projects and tasks during the week. Let's begin by looking at some assumptions about this application.

Application Assumptions

We have made some assumptions regarding the fictional company that we are creating this example application for and put them in Table 10-1.

Table 10-1. *The R & R Enterprise*

Company name	R & R Corporation
Number of employees	35,000
Number of countries with branch offices	15

Every Friday by 5:00 p.m., the R & R staff must report the time that they have spent at work during the week. This means that from around 4:00 to 5:30 p.m. the time-reporting application will be heavily used. Luckily, all 35,000 employees do not report to the same application; they report to one application in each country that R & R has offices in. The load can still be considerably high though, especially in a country like the U.S., where more than 9000 R & R employees work. The design of the application must be able to handle this load.

Application Requirements

Management has a number of requirements for the new application as follows:

- Employees must be able to create and save a weekly report. They should then be able to reopen it and continue adding hours and projects to it, until they submit it for approval to their immediate manager.

- Once submitted, employees cannot recall the report in order to make changes. In a case where something needs to be changed, an employee needs to contact his or her manager. The manager can then reject the report, and the employee can make the necessary changes after that.

- A time report can be rejected on the row level. That is, a manager can reject only a part of the time report so the employee does not have to go through the whole report to find the error.

- A root project can have any number of subprojects.

- There are no limits to how many levels of subprojects can exist under one root project.

- Different employees, who have access to the same root project, can be shown different subsets of the subprojects. (A salesperson does not have the same subprojects as a project manager, for example.)

- Each employee should only have access to the specific root projects and subprojects that are relevant to them.

- An administrator can tie projects to an employee.

- The normal working hours for an employee are 40 hours per week. The system must check a report so that exactly 40 hours are reported as normal time each week.

- Time above 40 hours must have another time type.

- An administrator can add new time types (such as overtime normal hours, flex time, and so on) for specific projects.

- The application must handle at least 2000 simultaneous users.

- Users should be placed in Active Directory (AD) or Active Directory Application Mode (ADAM). The choice depends on whether ADAM has been released or not when we start development.

- R & R Enterprise has no current SOA strategy, but wants the application to be open so that its logic can be used for future applications.

How the Application Will Work

Here is a little background on what will happen in our application. The user accesses the time-reporting system through a web browser. Access can be made over the Internet (via VPN) or from the intranet. After logging on, the user sees the main page, from which all reporting is done. The user then clicks the link Create time report and is redirected to a page that displays the weeks that are available to create new reports on. This page also shows all submitted reports and saved reports. This way the user can view old reports and also continue reporting time on a saved report.

The user then selects a week, and the system displays the page for this week in editing mode. After that, the employee selects a project and the correct subproject from the form. A new row is added to the report. The user fills in all information for the row (including time type, number of hours on the specific project during all days of the week, and so on). He or she then continues adding projects to the report until all hours during the week have been reported.

Before submitting or saving the report, the user can modify or delete any row by first clicking on it.

When the user is satisfied with the report, he or she can choose to save the report for further editing, or submit it for approval by a manager. After that, the user can log out or continue reporting on a new report.

This is the basic flow of what happens when a user registers a time report. We can now move on to UML modeling.

UML Modeling

Once we have agreement on the application requirements with our customer, it is time to start generating our UML models. We can't show all the models and use cases for the application in this book, however, so we have chosen to follow one specific use case. Here we'll concentrate on how a project member registers a time report. We can now move on to our activity diagrams.

Activity Diagrams

Before we start with the use case, we will spend a few moments on some activity diagrams that we need to make early in the process. These diagrams will give us a good picture of what we are attempting to build. We will then follow these diagrams through our examples and see how they evolve.

You can create activity diagrams whenever you want during the modeling stage, in order to explain a flow simply, when something needs to be clarified. We often use them to show a customer or decision maker what will happen in the application.

Figure 10-1 shows an activity diagram that explains what is happening when a user selects a project to report his or her time on.

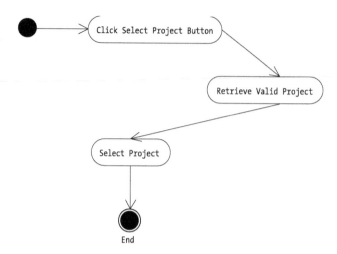

Figure 10-1. *Activity diagram for selecting a project*

The user clicks Select project on the screen. The system then checks for valid projects and subprojects for the user and displays them on the form. The user selects the correct project, and the flow ends.

The next activity diagram, shown in Figure 10-2, maps out what happens when a user wants to remove a project row from the week report.

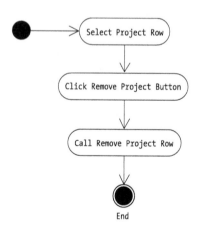

Figure 10-2. *Activity diagram for removing a project row*

This is a very simple example. The user selects the correct row for deletion and clicks the remove button. A call is then made to the remove project row function and the flow ends. What the Remove project row function will do in real life is check to see whether the report has been saved previously. It does this because if it has, we need to update the information in the database as well.

Now you will see a more complex activity diagram. The diagram in Figure 10-3 shows what happens when a user submits the report.

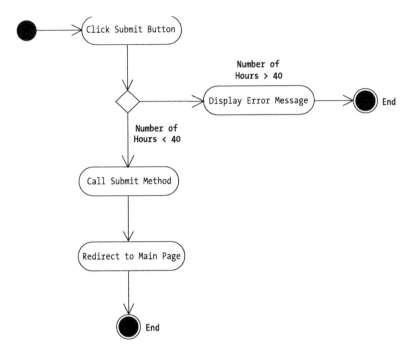

Figure 10-3. *Activity diagram for submitting a report*

When a user is finished with the time report, the report must then be submitted for approval by a manager. The user clicks the submit button, and the application checks the number of normal hours that the user has reported during the week. If the amount is not 40, an error message will be displayed and the flow ends. (Remember that 40 hours is a normal week, but if a week has a holiday in it, the amount can vary.)

If the user has reported 40 normal hours, the Submit method is called, and information about the report is saved to the database. An e-mail is sent at the same time to the manager, who can then open the report for approval. After submission, the user is redirected to the main page again.

SAVING TO THE MSMQ QUEUE

The report is not saved to the database immediately, however. We first save it to a MSMQ queue so that we can speed up the user experience. If many users save reports at the same time, they will have to wait for the system to complete. This could take some time during peak hours. The only thing we update is the status flag, so the user will be unable to edit this report further. This way we just do an update in a single table with a stored procedure, instead of having a more complex update on several tables. The only opportunity to change this report will be if the manager rejects it.

We will have a component that checks the queue and retrieves the information for insertion into the database. This component also e-mails the manager that the report has been submitted.

Saving reports for future editing is not done by the same function that saves to the queue, however. This is because saving reports often occurs during non-peak hours when the load on the server is moderate, and the reports can be directly inserted into the database.

As you can see, this is pretty straightforward, and if we use this kind of simplicity, it is easier to reach consensus with the customer so that no disagreements will occur at the end of the project.

Actors

Now we are going to find our actors. To simplify things, we will only show one actor here: the project member (see Figure 10-4). Other actors in our system might be administrators, project managers, and so on. After we have identified our actors, we can start finding our use cases.

Project Member

Figure 10-4. *The only actor in our simple example*

Use Cases

To determine the use cases, we need to ask ourselves why our actor(s) want to use the system. What is it that the system can do for our users? In our case, the whole idea behind the system is for our users (project members) to report their time in the application. In order to do this, they must register a time report. When a user enters information about the report and clicks the submit button, the system registers the report via one of its functions. In other words, a project member uses the register time report function that the system offers. This means we have found a use case to follow, as shown in Figure 10-5.

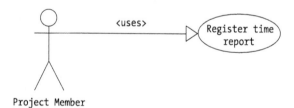

Project Member

Figure 10-5. *The use case we are going to follow*

Once we have a use case to work with, it is time to start documenting it. What is it that really happens when a user registers a time report? We need to find the flow of events for the process.

Sequence Diagrams

Sequence diagrams are used to illustrate the interaction between the objects in a model in a chronological order. They also show the messages sent between objects. This gives you a dynamic view of a system so you can see (and show others) what is going on.

We're going to examine three sequence diagrams here, which are all parts of the flow described earlier. The first one is shown in Figure 10-6, and depicts what happens when a user selects a subproject for the time report he or she is working on.

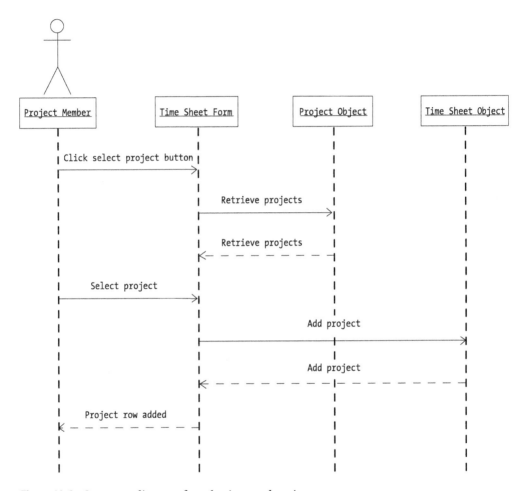

Figure 10-6. *Sequence diagram for selecting a subproject*

The objects that participate in this sequence diagram are

- The project member.

- The time sheet form, which is the input form for the user. It displays the time report in editing mode, amongst other things.

- The project object handles all functions associated with the project.

- The time sheet object exposes functions to update the time sheet form.

So what happens in this scenario? Say the user wants to add a new project to the time sheet. He or she clicks the select project button, which then makes the time sheet form call a function in the project object that retrieves all projects and subprojects for the current user. The user then selects a project and clicks the add project button. The time sheet form calls a function on the time sheet object that updates the form by adding a new row to the week report. The user can then add information to the row.

The next sequence diagram, shown in Figure 10-7, illustrates the flow when a user wants to remove a row from the weekly report.

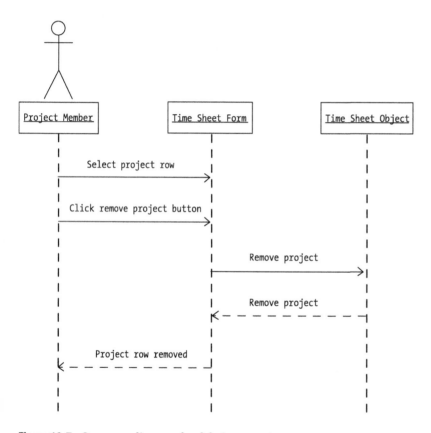

Figure 10-7. *Sequence diagram for deleting a project row*

The objects that participate in this sequence diagram are

- The project member

- The time sheet form

- The time sheet object

This sequence occurs when a user wants to remove a row from the weekly report. The user selects the row to be deleted and clicks the remove project button. The time sheet form tells the time sheet object to remove the project row. The time sheet object removes the row and updates the form. The user then sees the updated form in his or her browser.

The last sequence diagram that we are going to show you here demonstrates what happens when a user submits a report (see Figure 10-8).

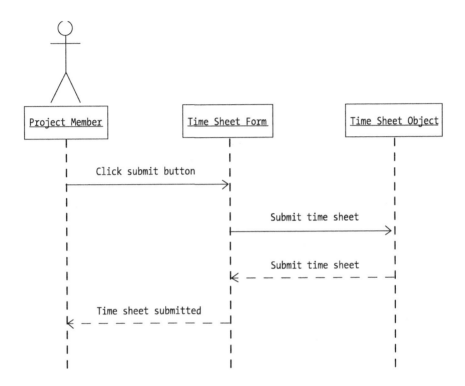

Figure 10-8. *Sequence diagram for submitting a report*

The objects that participate in this sequence diagram are

- The project member
- The time sheet form
- The time sheet object

When a user has finished editing a time report, he or she can submit it for approval by a manager. After editing the report, the user clicks the submit button on the time sheet form. The form then calls the time sheet object and asks it to submit the report. The time sheet object saves the report to an MSMQ queue and updates the form. The user is then redirected to the main page and is notified that the report has been saved.

Class Diagrams

As you saw in the UML discussion in Chapter 1, a class is a collection of objects with a common structure, behavior, and semantics. If you look at our example here, you can quite easily see that the reports have all these things in common, no matter which user submits them. So we can make a class to represent our weekly reports called WeekReport. Our users would probably have common characteristics, so we'll make User the second class. A third class is Projects, since they also have a lot of common denominators. We'll keep doing this until we are finished and can't come up with any more classes.

To exemplify how we work with classes, we will focus on the three we just mentioned and see where they lead. Unfortunately, we do not have enough room in this book to look at all the classes for our application. However, our examination of the User, Project, and WeekReport classes should give you an idea of how to approach class diagrams.

Determining the Attributes We Need

The first thing to do in designing class diagrams is to go over the business requirements and see which attributes are needed for each of them. So in our case, which attributes might we desire for the user? UserID is probably one we want (we could also call it EmployeeID). First-name and Lastname are two more. To keep it simple, let's add only these two other attributes: Department and Jobtitle. Then we continue doing this with the other two classes. Figure 10-9 shows the ones we have come up with.

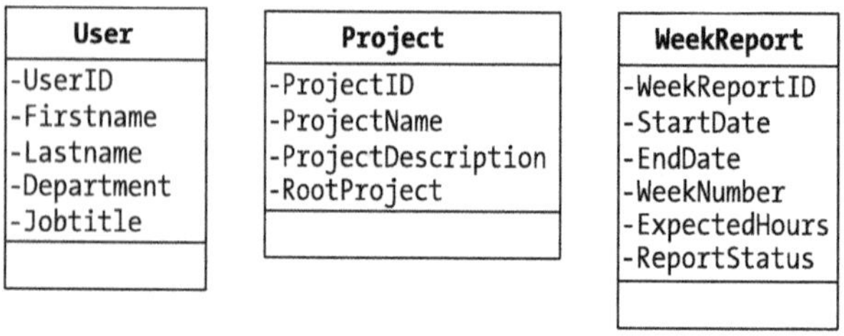

User	Project	WeekReport
-UserID	-ProjectID	-WeekReportID
-Firstname	-ProjectName	-StartDate
-Lastname	-ProjectDescription	-EndDate
-Department	-RootProject	-WeekNumber
-Jobtitle		-ExpectedHours
		-ReportStatus

Figure 10-9. *The attributes of our three classes*

■**Note** The RootProject attribute of the Project class is only filled if the project is a subproject to another project.

Determining the Operations of Our Classes

When we are satisfied with the attributes that we have found, we continue with the operations, or behavior, of each class. All of these three classes will probably have at least three operations in common: add, delete, and modify. These three operations cover most of what we want to do, so we will stop here and add them to our model (see Figure 10-10). We could, of course, find many more, but that is not necessary for our example.

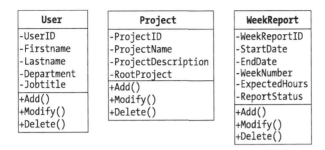

Figure 10-10. *The three classes updated with operations*

Determining Relationships Between Classes

So now that we have attributes and operations for our classes, it is time to find the relationships between them.

A user can work on many projects. There is nothing stopping this in our business rules, and in fact it is quite common in R & R Corporation. We also know that projects rarely have only one project member; instead, many members participate in a project. This is what would be described as a many-to-many relationship, and Figure 10-11 shows how this would be depicted in UML.

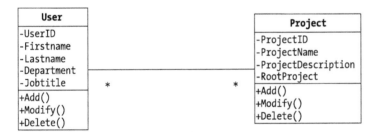

Figure 10-11. *A many-to-many relationship*

We want to split up a many-to-many relationship, since they are harder to implement. We do this by adding a middle class between the two so that we get two one-to-many relationships instead. In this case, we would create a new class called UserProject (see Figure 10-12). We would then add the attributes and operations we need for this new class.

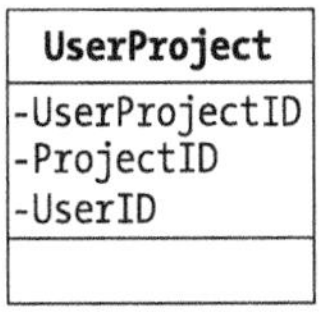

UserProject
-UserProjectID
-ProjectID
-UserID

Figure 10-12. *Our new class*

After the introduction of this class, we have new relationships between the classes (see Figure 10-13). One UserProject can only have one User and one UserProject can only belong to one Project. But a User can have many UserProjects, since he or she can participate in many projects. A Project can also belong to many UserProjects, since a project can have many members.

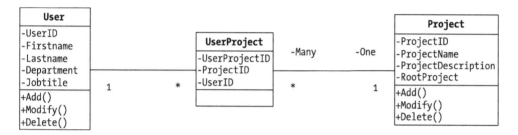

Figure 10-13. *The new relationships*

■**Note** You can also see that the same UserProject cannot belong to several Users, and the same UserProject cannot have more than one Project.

Let's continue with the relationship between User and WeekReport. A user can submit many WeekReports, since they report every week. Many Users can submit reports for the same week. As you can see, we have a many-to-many relationship here as well, and we need to split that up. This means we add a new class between the User and WeekReport classes. Hence we create a class called UserReport and add the relationships between the new class and the two old ones (see Figure 10-14).

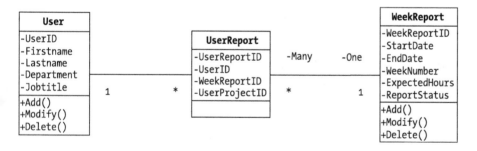

Figure 10-14. *A new class between User and WeekReport*

Now one User can have many UserReports and one WeekReport can be part of many UserReports. We can never have a situation where one UserReport relates to many Users or where one UserReport is related to many WeekReports.

What you also can see in these classes that we have added is that we need a relationship between UserReport and UserProject. This is because all UserReports need to have an association to a Project, and it is UserProject we relate it to. In Figure 10-15 you see the total picture.

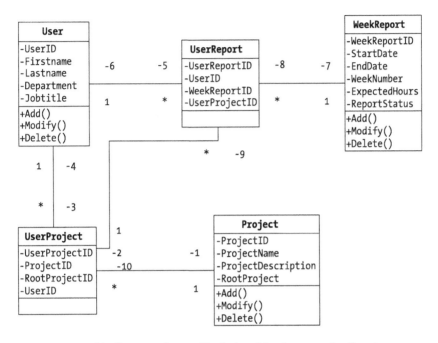

Figure 10-15. *This diagram shows all relationships between the five classes.*

This procedure shows that mapping out relationships can be quite complex when we determine our classes. We started with three classes in this simple example but ended up with five due to the many-to-many relationships we found. Here we did not include any inheritance or aggregation either, so it could be more complicated.

When we are finished with defining our classes and the relationships between them, it is time to start designing the database.

Designing the Database

Now that we have found our use cases and actors, it is time to start tackling the logical database design. We are going to use Object Role Modeling (ORM) to come up with our design. We will not show how we constructed all of this design, but we are going to show parts of it so that you understand how you approach this process in real life.

Our users are placed in AD or ADAM as we stated earlier, so we do not have to consider them in our model. Instead, we are going to take a closer look at the report lines that belong to a user's weekly report. A line has information about the time type and number of hours worked on a project that the employee has spent time on during the week.

Object Role Modeling (ORM)

What we need to do first is find the objects that are going to be participating in our model. The User is the first object we find. We know that users create user reports every week, so UserReport represents another object in our model. (We have also found a predicate here that we will need for our ORM model, but let's come back to this a bit later.) What else do we know? Well, every UserReport has one or more report lines. Hence we can make ReportLine another object. The objects are shown as ovals in the model as you can see by the example object in Figure 10-16.

Figure 10-16. *An object in the ORM model*

As we discussed in Chapter 1, objects are connected by predicates. These are portrayed as sequence boxes in an ORM model (see Figure 10-17). As we mentioned, we have already found a predicate for our example earlier.

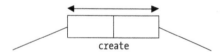

Figure 10-17. *A predicate sequence box in the ORM model*

Referring back to "users create UserReport," you can see that the sequence box in this case is *create*. The predicate is the whole phrase "users create UserReport," and the box is only a role that exists within the predicate, as demonstrated in Figure 10-18.

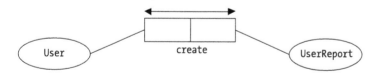

Figure 10-18. *A predicate with a role and sequence box in the ORM model*

The next predicate we find is UserReport has ReportLine. This is pretty obvious too, since we know a report is built up by one or more report lines. If we continue looking at objects and how they function, we can find many more predicates. The most relevant for this example are the following:

- ReportLine has ReportLineID

- ReportLine has Description

- ReportLine has ReportedHours

- ReportLine is of TimeType

- ReportLine has ReportLineStatus

The number of predicates all depends on the business requirements we have. The ones just listed serve our purposes, however, so we stop with these.

Some of the objects involved with ReportLine are unique. For example, a report line has only one ID and it can also only be of one time type and so on. We show this uniqueness with an arrow-tipped bar over the sequence box, as you can see in Figure 10-19.

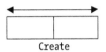

Create

Figure 10-19. *Uniqueness is shown with an arrow-tipped bar in the ORM model.*

Next we see if we have any mandatory roles in our model. We show this as a dot on the connector. In our case, the report line ID is mandatory, as shown in Figure 10-20. We must have an identifier for the report line. We also find that reported hours, time type, and user report ID are mandatory.

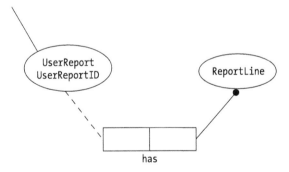

Figure 10-20. *Mandatory roles are shown with a dot on the connector.*

We do not find any constraints in our model, however.

When we combine all of our findings to form a complete model, we end up with something similar to Figure 10-21.

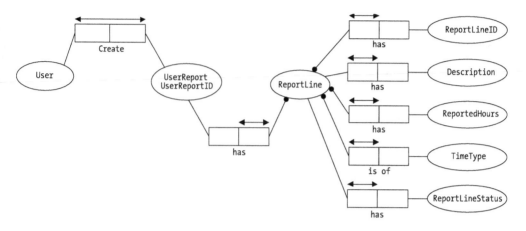

Figure 10-21. *The completed ORM model*

The Logical Database Design

Now we are going to transform the ORM model into a logical database model. In it, we are going to describe the ORM model in tables and columns instead of in sentences. Figure 10-22 shows how we have transformed our ORM model into a database schema.

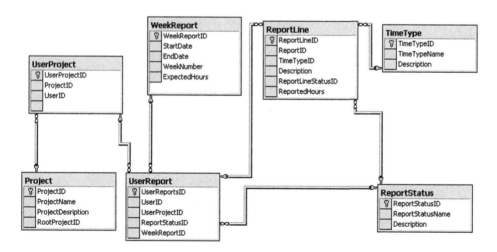

Figure 10-22. *The database schema*

■**Note** We do not show that we have taken the decision to horizontally divide the data. For performance and maintenance purposes, we will separate the data into three sets of identical tables. One set will hold the current week and any saved weeks to come. The next set will hold all data for the current year. The last set will hold all historical data. We will create views to display this data for reports so it looks like they all belong to the same tables. By doing this, we make sure that read and write data gets locked as little as possible. We do not have to back up all historical data as often as we back up the current data. This speeds up backups.

As our database schema shows, we end up with the following tables:

- *Project*. Here all projects in the company will be stored. To allow any number of subprojects, we have a column called RootProjectID, which references ProjectID in the same table.

  To simplify, you can think of this concept as illustrated in Figure 10-23. Recursive references will make a project like Project01 the root to Project02, which in turn will be the root project for Project03, and so on. This way we eliminate the need for a separate reference table.

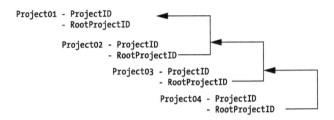

Figure 10-23. *Recursive projects by ProjectID references*

- *UserProject*. This table contains all the projects that are tied to a specific user. We keep track of them by the UserID.

- *WeekReport*. This table simply keeps track of the weeks during a year. Each week's start and end date is entered as well as the expected number of hours an employee should work that week.

- *UserReport*. This table holds all reports for a user. Even if a report has been rejected, the ReportStatus holds an ID for that report.

- *ReportLine*. Here is where all the individual report lines for a UserReport are kept. The StatusID is filled only if the line has been rejected.

- *ReportStatus*. A table that contains all status values that a report can have, such as submitted, rejected, saved, and so on.

- *TimeType*. This table keeps track of the time types available to our users. Examples of this are normal hours, overtime, vacation, and so on.

- *Users*. Although users are not stored in a table, as evidenced in Figure 10-22, we will remind you of them here anyway. As we said earlier, they will be fetched from AD or ADAM. All their information will be maintained in the directory.

Figure 10-22 also shows the relations between the tables. We have created one ID column for each table as well.

Before we start looking at how to index our database, we are going to consider the physical database design.

The Physical Database Design

Our database server has four mapped drives from the SAN (Storage Area Network): E, F, G, and H. They all offer RAID 10 so that we get both good read and write performance from these drives.

The log will be maintained in a single log file. It is always written to sequentially, so we do not benefit from splitting it up. We'll create it on drive E with a size of 100 megabytes. We'll also enable auto-growth in case our estimate is incorrect and the file needs to be expanded, as well as set a maximum value for the log file.

We will maintain the tables as follows:

- The tables for the current and future weeks will be maintained in filegroup1 on drive F.

- The tables for the current year will be maintained in filegroup2 on drive G.

- The tables for the historical data will be maintained in filegroup3 on drive H.

All data files have auto-growth enabled and a maximum file size specified so they will not grow beyond control. As we stated earlier, we will partition the data horizontally. Since the current week is the only one being written to, we can place it on a separate mapped drive. Managers will probably generate reports from the current year mostly, so we'll also place these on a separate drive. All other historical data will be maintained on yet another drive. The benefits of this setup are as follows:

- Write operations are fast.

- Read operations lock write operations as little as possible.

- Backups can be taken off of the filegroups separately, enabling us to implement a different backup strategy for each group. This way we do not need to back up the historical data as often as we back up the rest of the data. This will increase performance on backups.

- A restoration of the database can be done on separate filegroups, which increases restoration performance.

Indexing the Database

At this point we can start planning our indexes. We do this by looking at each table and then estimating how it will be accessed. For example, which columns will be used most frequently in the WHERE clauses of SELECT statements must be considered, and so on. Table 10-2 shows our first estimates. After that we will have to monitor the application and see if we need to change anything, first in the lab, and then in production.

Table 10-2. *The First Estimate of the Indexes for Our Application*

Table	Indexes
Project	Clustered on ProjectID, nonclustered on ProjectName and RootProjectID
ReportLine	Clustered on ReportID and ReportLineID
ReportStatus	Clustered on ReportStatusID

Table	Indexes
UserProject	Clustered on UserID and ProjectID, nonclustered on UseProjectID
UserReport	Clustered on UserID and WeekReportID
WeekReport	Clustered on WeekNumber

Choosing the Application Platform

For our time reporting application, there are mainly two tracks to follow regarding platform: either Windows 2000 Server or Windows Server 2003. Figure 10-24 shows the two in a side-by-side comparison.

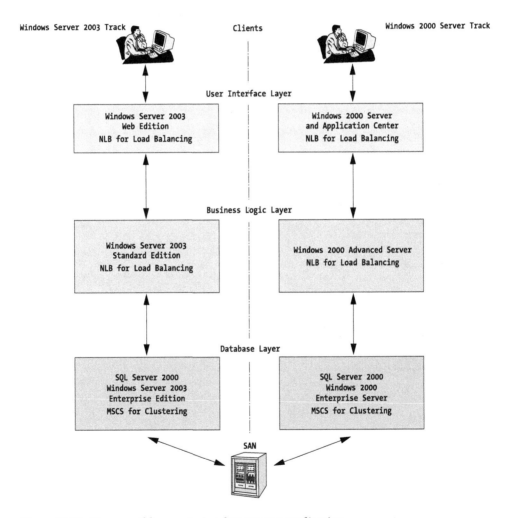

Figure 10-24. *Two possible ways to implement our application*

The performance test we showed in Chapter 4 makes us confident that Windows Server 2003 is the right choice for us. This platform has worked out very well for all of our customers and proven itself to be stable and reliable ever since the time of its release.

The Chosen Platform

Figure 10-25 shows how we will design the platform, and as you can see, we have decided to use different versions of Windows Server 2003 in different layers of the architecture.

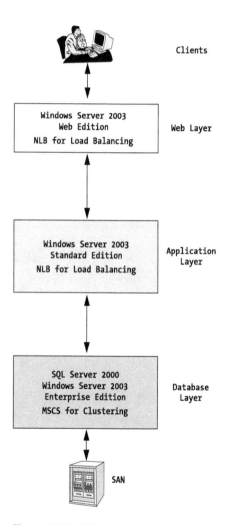

Figure 10-25. *The chosen platform*

Our web servers, which provide the ASP.NET pages that the users access, will all run Windows Server 2003 Web Edition. They will be load balanced with Network Load Balancing. At first we will start with five servers, but during our stress testing we will evaluate how many we actually need, so this figure is a bit uncertain at this point.

The application layer will run Windows Server 2003 Standard Edition, and we will use NLB to load balance these, too. We can use NLB because it exposes the business logic as Web services, and hence use the IIS to host the logic.

The database servers will run Windows Server 2003 Enterprise Edition. We did not choose the Datacenter Edition because our application does not need the kind of power that edition provides. We will build a two-node cluster with the help of Microsoft Cluster Service, and have one active and one passive node. They will each have at least four CPUs and 4GB of RAM. We will examine during testing if this is a good setup or if we need to change the hardware. The data and the log files will be stored on the SAN, where we can provide good performance, a reliable environment, and also great back-up capabilities. The SAN will be accessed through Windows Storage Server 2003.

The Test Environment

We do not own all the equipment to build this solution on the hardware we would like, so we decided to use VMware for development. This is actually something we would do for a real-life solution as well. If we configure VMware with the servers we need, we can easily develop the solution and test it so we know it works. When that is done, we take the application and install it in a physical test environment, which should be a replica of the production environment. We then perform all the stress testing and other testing against this environment before real deployment.

■**Note** There can be some performance issues with VMware, since all virtual servers run on the same machine. Our recommendation is to always test your solutions on replicas of the production environment. VMware is great for developing the application, but not so great when it comes to performance and performance testing.

If we need to correct something, we can do so in our virtual test lab before updating the physical test environment. To us, this has proven to be a good solution for developing our applications. The only thing to consider is having lots of RAM on the machine VMware is running on. We recommend at least 1GB if all tiers need to be running on the same VMware machine.

■**Note** Microsoft's Virtual Server is Microsoft's own solution to building virtual servers. Since we are more familiar with WMWare, so far we have chosen this instead of Virtual Server. But if you have other preferences or experiences go with that solution instead.

Since some performance issues can arise when you're running VMware (and all virtual server solutions for that matter), all tests in this environment should be considered carefully. Running several virtual machines always has a performance penalty when they are running on the same server, so we will see how it works out in our example.

Another benefit with VMware or Virtual Server is that we can have the whole application on a laptop, ready to be displayed at any meeting. This is great for decision makers to see how the work is going.

For this example, we will only develop our time-reporting application on VMware. That is enough for the purposes of this book. We will create the following three primary virtual servers:

- One web server running Windows Server 2003 Web Edition

- One application server running Windows Server 2003 Standard Edition

- One database server running Windows Server 2003 Enterprise Edition

We will also create the following servers so we can test load balancing:

- One web server running Windows Server 2003 Web Edition

- One application server running Windows Server 2003 Standard Edition

These are not necessary to use for more than testing the code in a cluster. The point of our solution is that we could start with only one server in each tier, and then expand it if necessary.

We will also use two physical domain controllers in our environment. These machines run Windows Server 2003 Standard Edition with Active Directory and DNS.

Next, we will show you how we set up the web server clusters for our application.

Web Server Clusters

In our test lab, with our servers built on VMware 4, we start creating the Web server cluster for our user interface (which consists of ASP.NET pages). We decide to use only two virtual machines, on which we install Windows Server 2003 Web Edition. We then run Windows Update on each machine to get all the latest patches.

What We Did to Secure and Tune Our System

This section will cover a little bit of what we do to secure and tune our system. Remember that processes like these should be done in close cooperation with your local IT staff. They know their hardware better than anybody else.

User Accounts

When the servers are installed, we disable the IUSR_MACHINE user account and create another account named AnonymousWebAccess (see Figure 10-26). This way we prevent anyone from trying to use the default anonymous account for attacks.

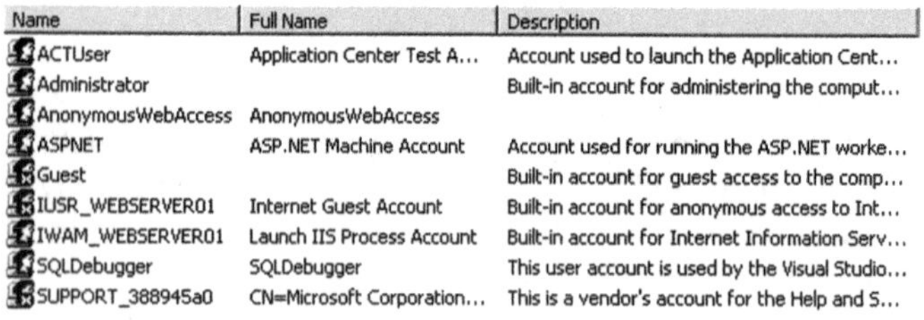

Name	Full Name	Description
ACTUser	Application Center Test A...	Account used to launch the Application Cent...
Administrator		Built-in account for administering the comput...
AnonymousWebAccess	AnonymousWebAccess	
ASPNET	ASP.NET Machine Account	Account used for running the ASP.NET worke...
Guest		Built-in account for guest access to the comp...
IUSR_WEBSERVER01	Internet Guest Account	Built-in account for anonymous access to Int...
IWAM_WEBSERVER01	Launch IIS Process Account	Built-in account for Internet Information Serv...
SQLDebugger	SQLDebugger	This user account is used by the Visual Studio...
SUPPORT_388945a0	CN=Microsoft Corporation...	This is a vendor's account for the Help and S...

Figure 10-26. *Disabling the IUSR_MACHINE account*

After we create the new account, we tell IIS to use the new account for anonymous access, as you can see in Figure 10-27. This account has minimum privileges in our system. Creating this account is only necessary if we are going to use anonymous access, of course; so if we have an application that we are planning to use forms with, authentication it is necessary.

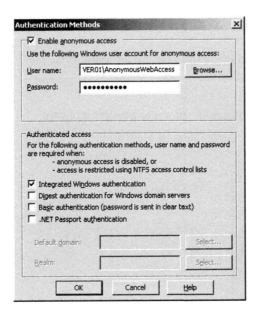

Figure 10-27. *Telling IIS to use the new account*

We then disable the Guest account and create a new Administrator account. We add this to the local Administrators group. After that, we disable the original Administrator account so no one can try to exploit it (see Figure 10-28).

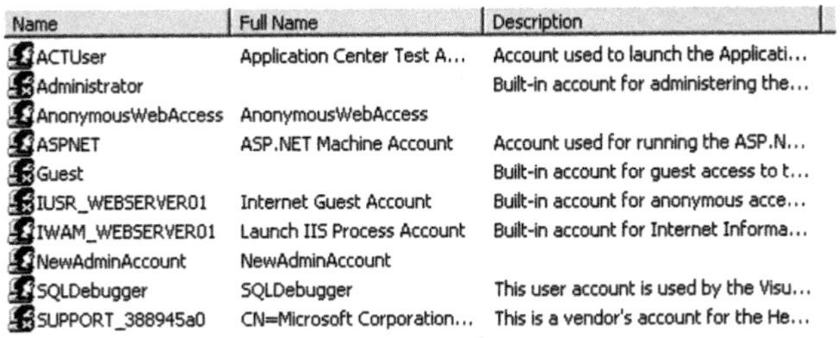

Name	Full Name	Description
ACTUser	Application Center Test A...	Account used to launch the Applicati...
Administrator		Built-in account for administering the...
AnonymousWebAccess	AnonymousWebAccess	
ASPNET	ASP.NET Machine Account	Account used for running the ASP.N...
Guest		Built-in account for guest access to t...
IUSR_WEBSERVER01	Internet Guest Account	Built-in account for anonymous acce...
IWAM_WEBSERVER01	Launch IIS Process Account	Built-in account for Internet Informa...
NewAdminAccount	NewAdminAccount	
SQLDebugger	SQLDebugger	This user account is used by the Visu...
SUPPORT_388945a0	CN=Microsoft Corporation...	This is a vendor's account for the He...

Figure 10-28. *Disabling the Administrator and Guest accounts*

System Services

The next thing we do is make sure no unnecessary services are running. This could vary from system to system, depending on the needs of a particular application. We make sure that the FTP Service, NNTP Service, SMTP Service, and so on, aren't installed (see Figure 10-29). We also disable the DHCP Server and Client, for example.

Tip Always make sure to go through the services list and ensure only those that are necessary will run.

This way we can be certain that as much CPU processing power as possible is always available to service Web requests.

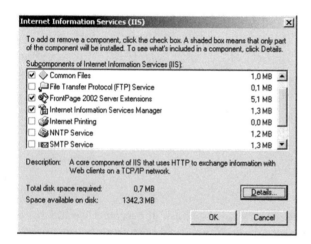

Figure 10-29. *Making sure no unnecessary services are installed or disabled*

Then we prohibit WebDAV, Internet Data Connector, RPC Proxy Server Extensions, and all unknown CGI and ISAPI extensions (see Figure 10-30).

Web Service Extension	Status
All Unknown ISAPI Extensions	Prohibited
All Unknown CGI Extensions	Prohibited
Active Server Pages	Allowed
ASP.NET v1.1.4322	Allowed
FrontPage Server Extensions 2002	Allowed
Internet Data Connector	Prohibited
Phone Book Service	Allowed
RPC Proxy Server Extension	Prohibited
Server Side Includes	Allowed
WebDAV	Prohibited

Figure 10-30. *Prohibiting unwanted Web Service extensions*

The Directory Structure and Permissions

To confuse a malicious attacker, at least a little, we move the default Web site root directory for IIS, and place it on another disk. We make sure only a minimum number of user accounts have access to this directory (see Figure 10-31).

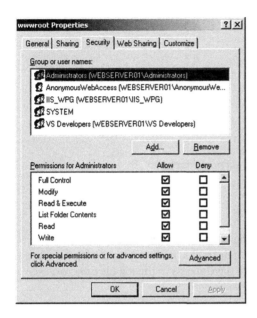

Figure 10-31. *Limiting who has access to our web server root directory*

As we are already changing NTFS permissions, we continue to remove the Everyone account from the following directories:

- System directory (windows\system32)

- NET Framework tools directory (windows\Microsoft.NET\Framework\{version})

- Root (\)

- The new Web site root directory

We also make sure our new anonymous user account has no write access to any of the Web content directories. Since this is the only directory this account has any privileges to, we do not have to check for it in any other directory.

The next step is to make sure we have no unwanted virtual directories in our Web site root directory (see Figure 10-32).

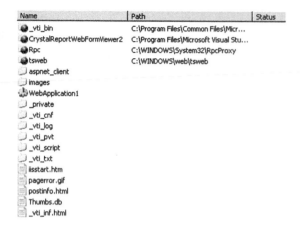

Name	Path	Status
_vti_bin	C:\Program Files\Common Files\Micr...	
CrystalReportWebFormViewer2	C:\Program Files\Microsoft Visual Stu...	
Rpc	C:\WINDOWS\System32\RpcProxy	
tsweb	C:\WINDOWS\web\tsweb	
aspnet_client		
images		
WebApplication1		
_private		
_vti_cnf		
_vti_log		
_vti_pvt		
_vti_script		
_vti_txt		
iisstart.htm		
pagerror.gif		
postinfo.html		
Thumbs.db		
_vti_inf.html		

Figure 10-32. *Minimizing the number of unnecessary virtual directories*

Logging

We need to make sure we have W3C extended logging enabled and also change the directory for the log files. To prevent anyone from covering their tracks by changing the log files, we ensure only administrators and the SYSTEM account have access to the log file directory (see Figure 10-33).

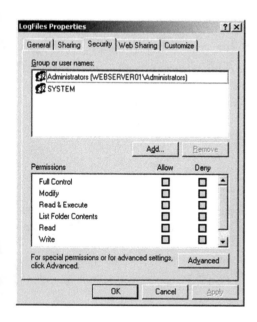

Figure 10-33. *Restricting access to the log files*

Security

Microsoft has two tools that you can use to harden security on IIS servers: the IIS Lockdown Tool and URLScan. These are most useful to you on a Windows 2000 system with IIS 5.0, since most of their security fixes have been implemented in IIS 6.0 on Windows Server 2003 from the start. The IIS Lockdown Tool won't even be installed on an IIS 6.0 system, for instance.

URLScan 2.5 can be installed, however; but if you carefully read the document "URLScan Security Tool" (http://www.microsoft.com/technet/treeview/default.asp?url=/technet/security/tools/tools/URLScan.asp), you can see that it does not really offer much for a Windows Server 2003 system. One thing you could use, perhaps, is the ability to disable or change the server header. By doing this, you could confuse an inexperienced hacker for a while when he or she tries to hack your Windows system with tools for hacking a Linux machine. But tools are available to the more experienced hacker to get around this obstacle, so your hacker could soon find out that you have a Windows system anyway. But it could be fun to create a header for a new operating system and see the newsgroups being posted with requests for this system.

The document has a good comparison of the differences in features between URLScan 2.5 and IIS 6.0 that you should read to determine for yourself if you need to install it or not for your own applications. For our example application, we chose not to.

Since our servers will use SSL, we need to implement a server certificate. For our purposes, we request a trial certificate from VeriSign (https://www.verisign.com/cgi-bin/go.cgi?a=w29710122100110000). This certificate is valid for 14 days, giving us enough time to evaluate it in the context of the demo application.

Installation is pretty simple. We follow the instructions provided by VeriSign, and within minutes have our server configured.

Certificates are managed from the Internet Information Services Manager. From the MMC console, right-click Default Web Server (or the server you are going to use) and click the Directory Security tab (see Figure 10-34). On this tab are three buttons used for certificate management: Server Certificate, View Certificate, and Edit.

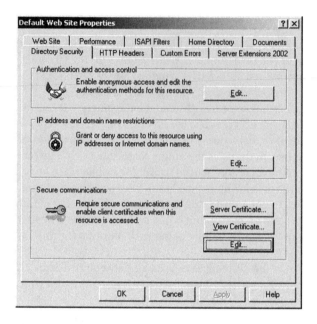

Figure 10-34. *The Directory Security tab*

- *Server Certificate.* This button opens a wizard that lets you manage your certificates (see Figure 10-35). You can add new certificates, remove old ones, export certificates, and so on.

Figure 10-35. *The Web Server Certificate Wizard*

- *View Certificate*. This button allows you to view installed certificates. Figure 10-36 shows our trial certificate from VeriSign.

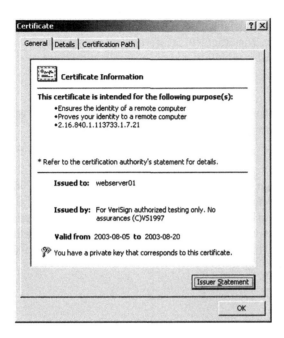

Figure 10-36. *The trial certificate from VeriSign*

- *Edit*. The Edit button is used when you want to edit the communications settings for your site. As you can see in Figure 10-37, for our purposes we can configure the site to require SSL, and so on.

Figure 10-37. *The communications setting for SSL on our site*

Clustering

Our virtual machines have two Network Interface Cards (NICs), which is perfect, because we can separate the internal and the external networks. One of them has a connection to the outside world (the Internet). This also has a default gateway configured. It will be through this gateway our clients will access the cluster. The other NIC is internal and will be used for cluster administration tasks and also for our cluster servers to access the application layer.

■ **Note** We are not going to go through the whole configuration process in detail here; instead we will highlight the simplicity of creating a NLB cluster using the Network Load Balancing Manager.

The Network Load Balancing Manager is a tool that comes with Windows Server 2003 and is found under administrative tools. It is not our intention to cover the network infrastructure design here, since it is complex and has to be considered with the input of enterprise administrators and security experts. As you saw in Chapter 4, however, we can choose to have a firewall both in front of the Web cluster (external firewall) and behind it (internal firewall) to create a perimeter network (see Figure 10-38).

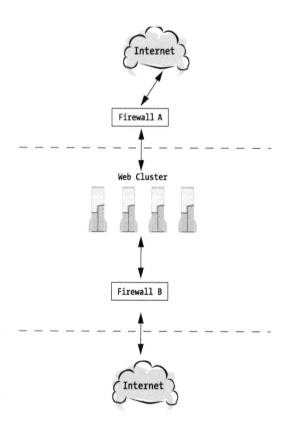

Figure 10-38. *Firewalls protecting the system from both the external world and the internal*

This approach is a good way to increase security, but we can also choose to only have the external firewall. As long as security is high we are okay; with your own applications, discuss this setup with the security experts at your company to be sure.

Note Keep in mind that building a perimeter network does not mean you do not have to spend time on your external firewall. You still need to put as much effort into that firewall as you would if no internal firewall existed.

So let's start by walking through the creation of our NLB cluster. From Administrative Tools we open the Network Load Balancing Manager (see Figure 10-39).

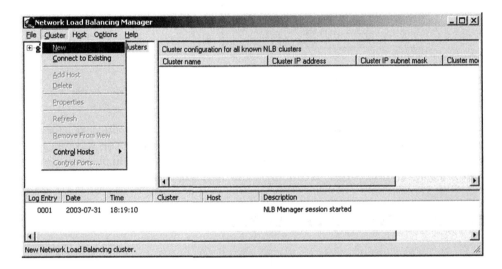

Figure 10-39. *The Network Load Balancing Manager*

We choose New from the Cluster menu to initiate the wizard that will help us create a new cluster. A window like the one in Figure 10-40 opens. First we need to fill in some information about the cluster, like the cluster IP address, subnet mask, and full Internet name. This is also where we specify whether the cluster operates in unicast (default value) or multicast mode. We will stick with the default here. We also choose not to enable remote control because of the security risks that comes with allowing this feature. We click Next to continue.

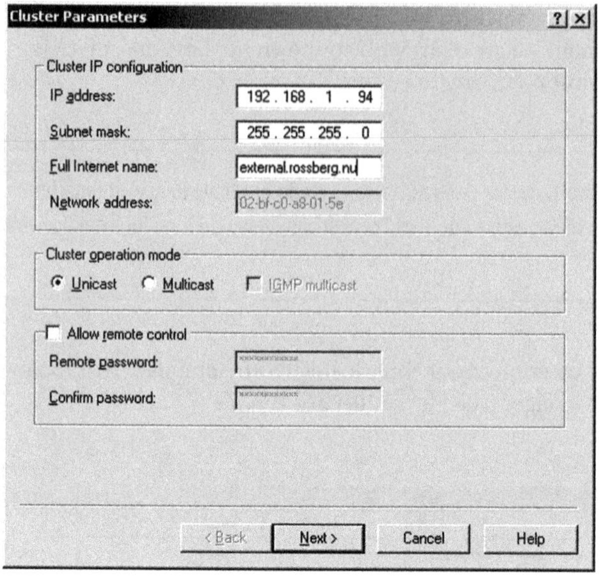

Figure 10-40. *The Cluster Parameters dialog box*

If we wanted to add more IP addresses to our cluster, we would do so in the next screen. We only do this if we are going to maintain several clusters on our machine. This way we can create an environment that can handle several load-balanced applications. In our case, we will only expose one, so we click Next to continue to the next screen (see Figure 10-41).

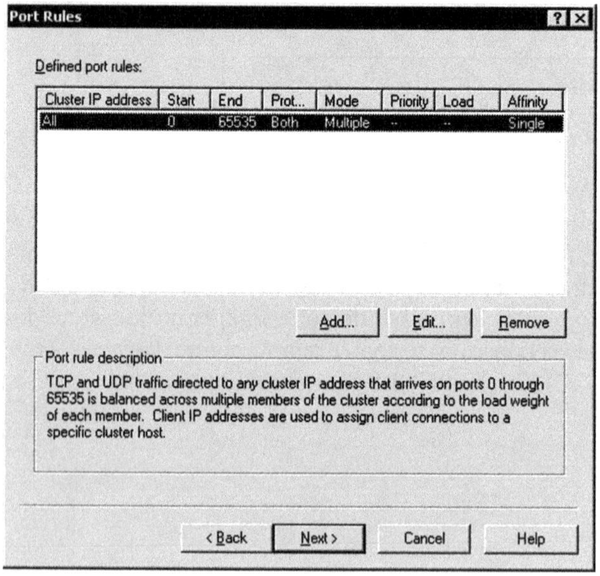

Figure 10-41. *Adding or editing the port rules*

This screen lets us add port rules to our configuration. By clicking Add or Edit we can add new port rules or edit our existing ones. If we highlight the default rule and click Edit, we can change rules regarding ports, protocols, filtering, and so on (see Figure 10-42). We can do this for all cluster IP addresses we added previously. We usually do not set port rules for other ports than those our applications use.

Note Remember that all port rules must be the same on each cluster member. Otherwise a new cluster member won't be accepted if it tries to join a cluster with port rules as different from the ones it has itself.

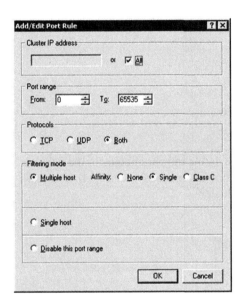

Figure 10-42. *Defining the port rules*

We click OK or Cancel to close the window and click Next to continue the wizard. Now it is time to select which of our network cards will expose the cluster. Or more correctly, we choose which network connection will expose it. We do this by typing the IP address of the server in the host text box and clicking Connect. This will show the available network connections we can use (see Figure 10-43). We are going to use Local Area Connection 2 for our cluster, so we highlight it and click Next.

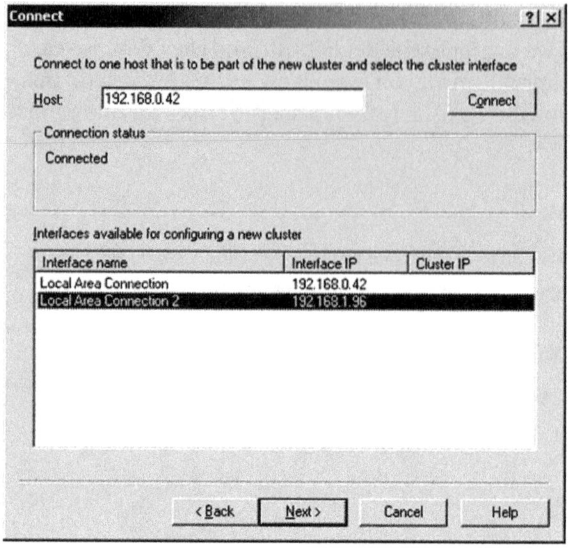

Figure 10-43. *Choosing which network connection to use*

The next screen shows the host parameters, which define the parameters for the network interface card we are using for the specified network connection (see Figure 10-44). If we are satisfied with them, we can click Finish to create the cluster.

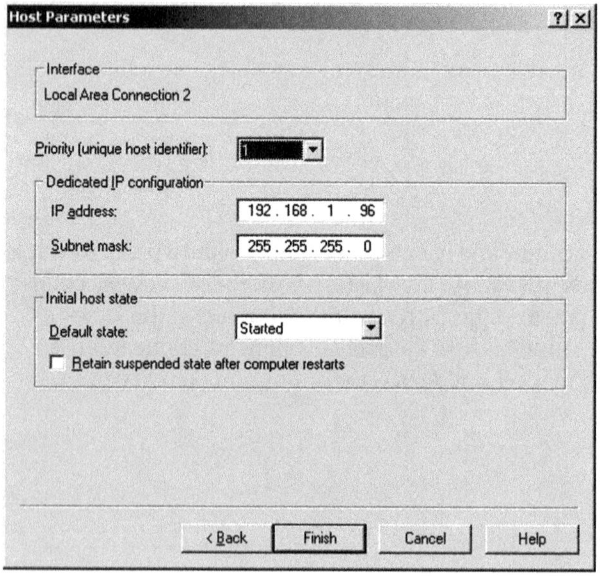

Figure 10-44. *Finishing the wizard*

Now Network Load Balancing Manager starts configuring the cluster. When it is finished, the new cluster member is listed in the Network Load Balancing Manager, as shown in Figure 10-45, and the icon beside it should appear green.

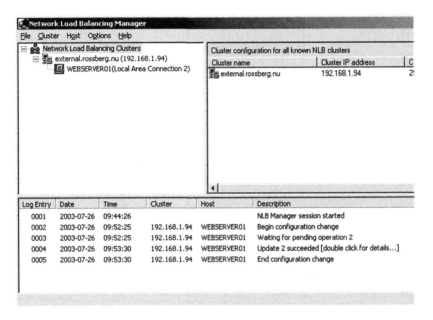

Figure 10-45. *The first member is configured.*

Now we can start adding our new members. To do so, we simply right-click the cluster and choose Add host to cluster. This will start a new wizard similar to the Create New Cluster Wizard discussed previously, but it will start with the dialog box shown in Figure 10-43 and continue from there. We can then add up to 32 servers to our cluster.

So what else do we need to do besides creating our cluster? Well, we decide to enable NLB logging so we would get a record of all cluster events in case we need to troubleshoot the cluster. We also restrict access to the directory where we save the log files so no one can manipulate them.

Now that we have set up our Web cluster, we can just purchase a new server, configure it with all application data and the same settings as the one we just configured, and add it to the cluster with the help of Network Load Balancing Manager. This is good way to increase performance quickly. Figure 10-46 shows the solution so far.

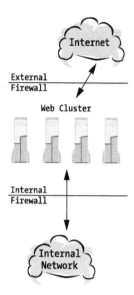

Figure 10-46. *The time reporting solution so far*

Next we move on to configuring the application cluster.

Application Layer

Our application layer will expose all functionality as Web services. Since they are hosted on an IIS server, we can follow the same procedures as we did with the Web cluster. We use Windows Server 2003 Standard Edition for this layer, and VMware to develop the solution. NLB will be used for load balancing.

By using Web services, we only need to have port 80 open in our internal firewall. Because we use SSL, we also need to open port 443; otherwise there is no need for extra configuration here. If we had chosen .NET Remoting, we would have to open up more ports with the help of our network administrators.

That is basically what we decided to do with the application cluster. In Figure 10-47 you can see what the solution looks like at this point.

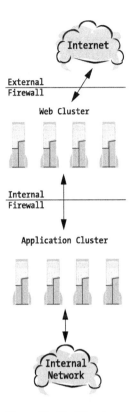

Figure 10-47. *The time reporting solution with the application layer*

Database

We covered how we were going to implement the physical design of our database earlier in the chapter in the section "Designing the Database." The server we use for this is Windows Server 2003 Enterprise Edition. This server has two NICs connected to two different networks. One is the network our clients (via the application layer) use to access the database. We call this the external network and configure it with the setting All Communications in Cluster Service. The other is a private network that only internal cluster communications occur on. The private network has no other computers on it beside our cluster members. This is configured with the setting Internal Cluster Communications Only. This network also has the highest priority for internal cluster communications.

All our NICs are configured with static IP addresses. We use no DHCP at all. They all also have the same communications settings, which we set manually.

Furthermore, we ensure the networks share no hardware, like switches, hubs, cables, and other communication devices. This way we try to eliminate the chance that both networks could fail at the same time.

We make sure both nodes were part of the same domain. This is one of the reasons we use two domain controllers in our lab environment.

We strongly recommend collaborating closely with experienced database administrators and network administrators when setting up an MSCS cluster. There are always a lot of specific settings that apply only to your networks. MSCS is a bit more complex to install than setting up NLB, and these people know the best settings for the hardware and networks you are using.

Figure 10-48 shows the final application layering of our solution.

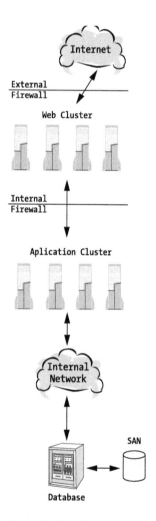

Figure 10-48. *The time reporting solution with the final layering*

The Implementation

OK, it is time to begin implementing our time reporting application. We have a couple of tasks to complete to implement the required solution. The different steps we will take are as follows:

- Check that all requirements have been covered.

- Create the enterprise template for our application.

- Set the references and the dependencies between the different layers.

- Add code to support Enterprise Services.

- Implement our data factory class.

- Implement specific data classes for use with SQL Server, which is our data store.

- Implement the MSMQ functionality.

- Enable facades for Web services access.

- Implement security.

- Test the application.

- Deploy the application.

In the following sections, we will look at each step in more detail.

Checking That All Requirements Are Covered

Before we start coding, we need to verify that all requirements have been caught in our UML diagram, and that all class diagrams support the functionality that the customer requires. As you have seen previously, the work to create use cases, sequence diagrams, and then class diagrams is an iterative process that may be run through many times before all cases have been written down and all requirements have been covered in UML, sequence, and class diagrams.

Looking back at the UML diagram and the classes we created earlier, we realize that some functionality is missing. Since the enterprise architecture we described in Chapter 5 is service oriented, the classes need to have be able to serve the caller with information. We will focus on adding such functionality to three different classes here: the WeekReport class, the User class, and the Projects class.

Note In this example, we will implement one of the classes and some of the functions to show the different steps that are needed to complete the tasks. The other classes and functions are then created in the same way.

The previously created UMLs are the ones that will form our facade classes in the enterprise architecture. The key is to let the user interface deal with as few objects as possible; therefore, we encapsulate all related actions (for example, a use case) into one object, so only one object from our enterprise application needs to be created in the user interface. We will now create a facade object to handle all functions the actor needs to be able to carry out to register the time report. We will call the facade object UserReportFacade, and we need functions for the following actions:

- Retrieve a complete time report.

- Save a time report.

- Submit a time report.

- Add projects to the time report.

- Remove projects from the time report.

- Update already-added lines in the time report.

The sequence diagrams show the Time Sheet object, which has the required functions for saving a time report and adding and removing projects from the time sheet.

The UserReportFacade object also needs to work with the Project object to retrieve all possible projects users can have in their time reports. Figure 10-49 shows how UserReportFacade works with different business objects in our enterprise application. The UserReport.aspx page (the user interface) uses only one facade object—UserReportFacade.

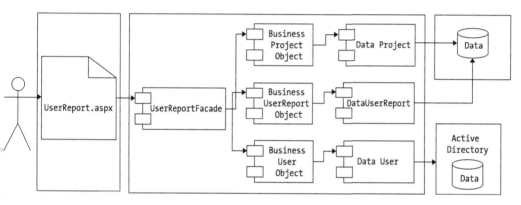

Figure 10-49. *Overview of the implementation and the facade class UserReportFacade*

Creating the Enterprise Template for Our Application

Now that all requirements have been checked, we need to create the enterprise templates that we will customize. Visual Studio 2003 contains a template that can be used for getting us on track quite fast. We open Visual Studio 2003 and under Templates select Visual Basic Distributed Application as shown in Figure 10-50. This template has the structure we need to create our application.

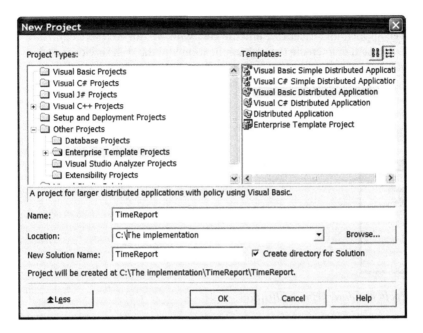

Figure 10-50. *Creating the enterprise template*

■Tip The enterprise template found in Visual Studio 2003 speeds up the development of an enterprise application. If you do not have Visual Studio Enterprise version, you can still develop the architecture by simply adding the different layers as separate projects to the solution file. However, you need to keep in mind the relationships between the different layers, which the policy files in the enterprise template keep track of for you automatically.

The IDE will ask for the URL for the site where the Web user interface should be created. We specify a URL to indicate where the Web application will reside as you can see in Figure 10-51.

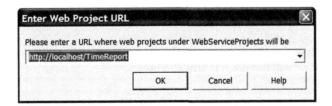

Figure 10-51. *Visual Studio will ask for a URL for the location where the Web Application will be created.*

Visual Studio will also ask where the Web services project should be hosted. We select the same URL as for the Web application, except we end the URL with WS (for Web service).

It will take a while for the IDE to create the Web application and the Web services application on the selected Web server. When the IDE has finished, the Solution Explorer will appear as shown in Figure 10-52.

Figure 10-52. *All projects in our enterprise application*

The solution contains the following seven different enterprise groups:

- The first one, BusinessFacadeProjects, contains our facade projects. In this application, we will have only one facade project called BusinessFacade. As mentioned in Chapter 5, the facade classes are used for grouping relative functionality together; normally a use case is placed in one facade class.

- The second project group is BusinessRulesProjects. Here our business rules project will reside, which in this case is named BusinessRules.

- Next project group is DataAccessProjects. It contains our data access project, named DataAccess.

- The SystemFrameworksProjects is where global projects should be placed—for instance, interface projects that need to be accessible from different projects.

- The WebServiceProjects group contains our Web service project. The project should be named WebService.

- The WebUIProjects group contains our Web application. The project should be named WebUI.

- The last group, WinUIProjects, contains the Windows application (in our case, an administration application), but we will not use it in this example.

Setting References and Dependencies Between Different Layers

Before we continue, we need to set up dependencies and references between the projects. This way we make sure they can communicate with each other. The time reporting application and all its layers will initially be run on a single box to allow easy scale out when the need arises.

First we set up how the projects depend on each other. This is the first step because Visual Studio builds the current projects based on how the other projects depend on each other. We start by right-clicking the solution icon in the Solution Explorer window and selecting Project Dependencies. The Project Dependencies dialog box appears (see Figure 10-53).

Figure 10-53. *The Project Dependencies dialog box*

As you can see, two tabs exist on this dialog box. The first tab shows the dependencies between the projects in the solution, while the second tab shows the build order. The build order is determined by the dependency between the projects. On the Dependencies tab you will find a combo box and a list box. The combo box contains all projects in a solution. Of the projects that appear in the list box, those that the specified project in the combo box depends on are indicated with a check mark in the list.

The dependencies between the different projects for our application are shown in Figure 10-54.

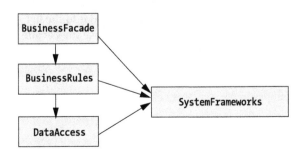

Figure 10-54. *The dependencies between the different projects*

To achieve the result in Figure 10-54 we need to check the DataAccess and SystemFrameworks as dependencies for the BusinessRules project. We also need to check the Businessrules and the SystemFrameworks as dependencies for the BusinessFacade project. The DataAccess project is only depending of the SystemFrameworks project.

After we fill in all dependencies, the build order is shown on the second tab (see Figure 10-55).

Figure 10-55. *The build order for all projects in our solution*

Now that we have specified the dependencies between the different projects, the compiler knows in which order the projects should be compiled. However, we also need to specify the references between the projects so we can create, for instance, a business object from a facade class. The process of adding references between the projects are the same as the dependencies. To add references between the BusinessFacade project and the BusinessRules project, we right-click the Reference folder in the BusinessFacade project and select Add Reference.

The Add Reference dialog box, shown in Figure 10-56, contains three different tabs: The .NET tab lists managed DLLs that we can use, the COM tab lists unmanaged DLLs that we can reference, and the Projects tab lists all projects in the current solution that we can refer to.

We click the Projects tab and double-click the BusinessRules project to add it to the list box at the bottom of the form. We also double-click SystemFrameworks, because the Facade needs a reference to that project as well. After we click the OK button, the references are added to the BusinessFacade project.

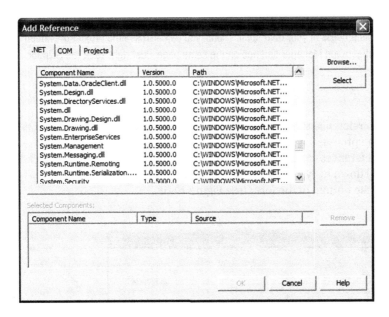

Figure 10-56. *The different kind of references we can use from a managed project*

Since we are not going to develop a Windows-based application in this example, we will therefore remove it from the build process. To do this, we right-click the Solution file, and select the Configuration Manager from the pop-up menu.

We deselect the checkbox for the WinUI project and specify that the shown configuration is for the debug configuration. After we select the release configuration in the combo box, we deselect the WinUI project in this configuration too (see Figure 10-57).

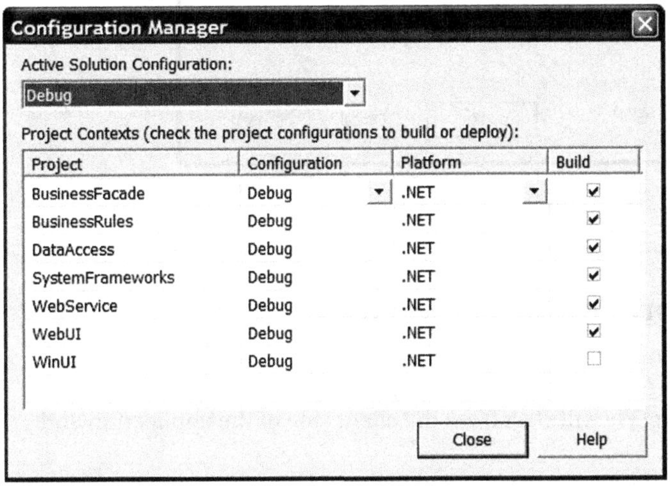

Figure 10-57. *Making changes in the Configuration Manager*

Tip When you are following this process in your own applications, you can also see the project dependencies, the build order, and the Configuration Manager settings on the same page. Just right-click the Solution file and select Properties.

Finally, we need to add a reference to System.EnterpriseServices to our BusinessFacade, BusinessRules, and DataAccess projects, because we want them all to take advantage of Enterprise Services. We right-click the references catalog under each of the mentioned projects and click Add reference. We then scroll down to System.EnterpriseServices on the first tab and double-click it to add it to the list at the bottom of the form (see Figure 10-58).

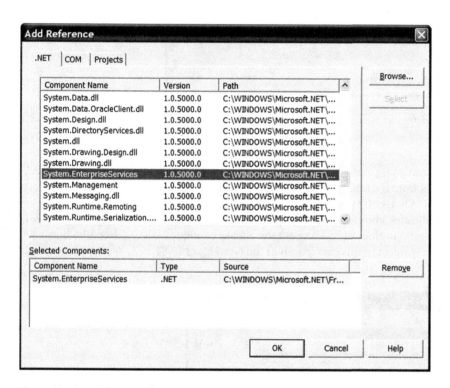

Figure 10-58. *Adding a reference to System.EnterpriseServices*

Adding Code to Support Enterprise Services

When we have added the System.EnterpriseServices reference to the BusinessFacade, BusinessRules, and DataAccess projects, we have configured most of the stuff we need to before being able to start coding. We will start from the client side of the application and work down toward the database.

First we need to implement the classes we found in our use cases and sequence diagrams. The first class from the client side is the BusinessFacade class UserReport. This class will contain all the functions and methods the actor needs to be able to complete his or her tasks. To implement the class, we open the BusinessFacade project in the Solution Explorer, right-click the project, and select Add | Add Class.

After we name the class UserReport and click OK, an empty class will be added to the BusinessFacade project. The first thing we need to do with this class is have it inherit from the EnterpriseServicedComponent:

```
Imports System.EnterpriseServices
Public Class UserReport
Inherits System.EnterpriseServices.ServicedComponent
```

To take advantage of COM+, we must add some custom attributes to the class to tell System.EnterpriseServices how the class should be registered in the COM+ application. From Chapter 5, you know that we need to add a strong name to the assembly. To achieve this, we use the sn.exe tool, which generates a key pair that is used for generating a strong name for our assembly. We generate one key pair for the application by opening the Visual Studio 2003 command prompt and executing sn –k c:\TimeReport.snk, this pair will be used in each layer. We then add an assembly attribute that references the key pair file by adding the following line to AssemblyInfo.vb in the BusinessFacade project:

```
<Assembly: AssemblyKeyFile("c:\TimeReport.snk")>
```

Now the key pair will be used to generate a strong name for the BusinessFacade project (which is the assembly).

■**Note** Remember to store the key pair file in a secure place since you will need them if you want to recompile the project in the future. We suggest that you store the key pair file on a server that is backed up regularly—finding out that the key pair file that you so urgently need in your project today was on the laptop you formatted last week isn't the kind of experience you want.

■**Tip** We can also use a relative path here. The path is from the bin catalog in the current project. If we put the strong name key file in the root of the project, the attribute will look as follows:
<Assembly: AssemblyKeyFile("..\..\TimeReport.snk")>.

To summarize what we have done so far: We first created the enterprise template for our time reporting application. This was done by using the enterprise template found in Visual Studio .NET 2003 Enterprise version. Then we created a facade class that should be used for the UserReport class. We also added a reference to the System.EnterpriseServices DLL and specified some attributes to the class for object pooling. All assembly-related attributes are collected in AssemblyInfo.vb. When we added attributes to this file for using the key pair file, we made it possible for the compiler to give a strong name to the assembly.

Note Before we will be able to compile the Enterprise solution we need to add the strong name to each project in the solution. That means that we need to add the assembly key file to the BusinessRules, the DataAccess and the SystemFrameworks project before we successfully can compile the solution—why? Because all strong named assemblies can only reference assemblies that have a strong name itself.

Next, we will add the first function we need in our UserReportFacade object. The function GetUserReport needs to be added to the class, and it should take two parameters—the user ID for the user and the week number for the report that should be retrieved. (We can later add another GetUserReport function that takes a date interval and returns all time reports between the specified intervals if we need to, but for now we want to keep it simple.) The code for the UserReportFacade class appears in Listing 10-1.

Listing 10-1. *The UserReportFacade Class*

```
Imports System.EnterpriseServices
<ObjectPooling(Enabled:=True, MinPoolSize:=1, MaxPoolSize:=8,
CreationTimeOut:=25000)>
Public Class UserReport
    Inherits ServicedComponent
    'Function that returns the requested time report.
    Public Function GetUserReport(ByVal UserID As String, _
                                  ByVal WeekNo As Integer) As DataSet
        'Our code goes here...
    End Function
End Class
```

The function GetUserReport will return a dataset with the complete time report inside. As we mentioned elsewhere in this book, it is best to try to catch input errors as soon as possible. Here we can already catch invalid week numbers and empty user IDs to ease the burden on the server. If any of the incoming parameters are wrong, we do not need to create a business object to verify the input. We also must create a business object and call the appropriate function to retrieve the time report. The business object will be named UserReport in the Business project and the function will be named GetUserReport with the same parameters as the equivalent Facade function.

The business logic in the function will check whether the requested time report is submitted or not. If it is submitted, the time report is returned as read-only. Well, we know this does not amount to much business logic, but there will be more when we attempt to update time reports. We try, however, to be proactive and set the time report as read-only to prevent the client from changing it if the time report has already been submitted. The complete code for the facade class calling the business class for the time report will look as shown in Listing 10-2.

Listing 10-2. *The Complete Facade Class*

```
Imports System.EnterpriseServices
<ObjectPooling(Enabled:=True, MinPoolSize:=1, MaxPoolSize:=8,
```

```
CreationTimeOut:=25000)>
Public Class UserReport
    Inherits ServicedComponent
    'Function that returns the requested time report.
    Public Function GetUserReport(ByVal UserID As String, _
                                  ByVal WeekNo As Integer) As DataSet
        Dim objUserReport As BusinessRules.UserReport
        Try
            If UserID.Length > 0 And WeekNo > 0 And WeekNo < 53 Then
                objUserReport = New BusinessRules.UserReport
                Return objUserReport.GetUserReport(UserID, WeekNo)
            Else
                'Not valid input parameters.
                Throw New Exception("Input parameters are invalid. " & _
                "UserId cannot be empty and/or WeekNumber not between 1 and 52)")
            End If

        Finally
            objUserReport.Dispose()
            objUserReport = Nothing
        End Try
    End Function
End Class
```

The facade class checks if the input parameters are valid. If they are not valid, the function raises an exception to the caller. If the parameters are valid, the function creates a business object and retrieves the dataset via the business function GetUserReport. To make the previous listing compile we need to create the corresponding business class. The business class for the time report is quite similar to the facade class and calls the data layer class to retrieve the dataset. The business code is shown in Listing 10-3 is located in the BusinessRules project.

Listing 10-3. *The Business Code for the UserReport Class in the BusinessRules Project*

```
Imports System.EnterpriseServices
Imports SystemFrameworks
<InterfaceQueuing(Interface:="IUserReportAsync"), _
ObjectPooling(Enabled:=True, MinPoolSize:=1, MaxPoolSize:=10, _
CreationTimeOut:=25000), JustInTimeActivation(True)> _
    Public Class UserReport
    Inherits ServicedComponent
    Implements IUserReportAsync
    Public Function GetUserReport(ByVal UserID As String, _
    ByVal WeekNo As Integer) As SystemFrameworks.dsUserReport
        'Our code goes here...
        Dim objUserReport As DataAccess.UserReport
```

```
        Try
            objUserReport = New DataAccess.UserReport
            Return objUserReport.GetUserReport(UserID, WeekNo)

        Finally
            objUserReport.Dispose()
            objUserReport = Nothing
        End Try
    End Function
End Class
```

As you can see, the code for the facade class and the business class is identical. We will later add some business functionality to the business layer. The architecture in an application can be follow strictly or loosely. By strictly, we mean that all calls go from the facade object to the business object and from the business object to the data object. In this case, we do not have any business rules at the moment, so we could have called the data object directly from the facade object to avoid instantiating the business object—this is the loose way to follow the architecture.

We recommend following the architecture strictly, since any business logic that may be needed (which we may have missed or omitted in this first release) should be put into the business layer. If we were calling the data object directly from the facade, a recode and recompile of the facade object would be necessarily if we suddenly realized that we needed business rules for the particular function. With the business object in place, we only need to change the code internally without changing anything else.

Implementing the Data Factory Class and the Typed Datasets

You saw in the previous examples that we return a dataset from the function GetUserReport. Datasets can either be nontyped or typed. In a normal dataset, the fields in tables are specified by the data that fills the dataset. If you have a database query that retrieves the first name and last name values from an employee table, the fields in the dataset will be named firstname, lastname. In a typed dataset, you specify the different fields that will occur in the dataset. For our example, we specify that the database field firstname should be named First Name in the dataset and the database field lastname should be named Last Name in the dataset.

The typed dataset is first derived from the dataset and the schema information (tables, columns, and so on) is generated and compiled into this new dataset class as a set of first-class objects and properties used to create a class. This is of great importance, since by specifying the field's names you isolate the database structure from the data carriers (the datasets) in the application. A change in any database fields will not be reflected in the data carriers and affect your code—it will only affect where you retrieve the data and put it into the dataset. Another benefit with the typed dataset is that you can retrieve the data fields by name instead of index position. If you have an employee table with employee data, the code to retrieve the field firstname from an untyped dataset is the following:

```
Dim s As String
s = CType(dsEmployee.Tables("Employees").Rows(0).Item("firstname"), String)
```

With a typed dataset, you can use the following code instead:

```
Dim s As String
s = dsEmployee.Employees(0).firstname
```

As you can see, this code is neater and there is less risk that you will retrieve the wrong column since you are using the name of the column for direct access. The design of the typed datasets that will serve as data carriers between the different layers in our application can be done in different way, but here we will show how to do it by creating a dataset from scratch. The typed datasets will be stored in the SystemFrameworks project, which contains all the definitions that need to be accessible from different projects.

Step One

The first step we need to do is right-click the project file for the SystemFrameworks project and select Add | Add New Item. In the Add New Item dialog box, we select Dataset, rename the dataset to dsUserReport, and then click Open. Visual Studio now adds a blank schema to the SystemFrameworks project. The name we give the dataset, dsUserReport, will also be used for the class that is generated.

Double-click dsUserReport to open it in design view. The Toolbox will now contain an XML Schema group that contains elements we can use in our dataset. We know from the analysis phase in the beginning of this chapter that dsUserReport should contain a UserReport table that has the following items:

- An ID

- Start date for the week

- End date for the week

- Week number for the week

- Expected hours for the week

- Status for the complete report (whether it is submitted to administration staff or not)

The dsUserReport dataset should also have a ReportLine table that contains all report lines for the selected week. The ReportLine table will include the following:

- An ID to the UserReport

- An ID for the report line

- A project number

- Number of hours

- Type of time

- A comment

By dragging elements from the toolbox onto the form, we build up the structure for our typed dataset.

We start by dragging an element from the toolbox onto the form to create our table definition. We will have two of them—one for the time report header and one for the time report lines. We name the table by overwriting element1 in the box at the top of the element.

When two elements have been added and renamed, our form looks like the one in Figure 10-59.

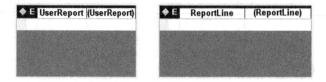

Figure 10-59. *The tables in the dataset*

Step Two

The next step is to add the individual properties for each table. We start with the UserReport table.

Clicking in the empty line below the UserReport header, we enter **Id** in the first column. The second column is the data type that should be used for the field, so we select data type ID. We easily add the previously mentioned properties to the UserReport and the ReportLine to arrive at the complete structure shown in Figure 10-60.

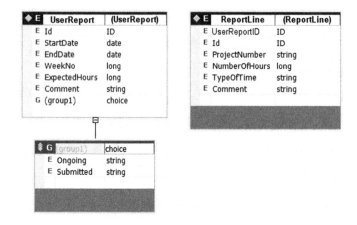

Figure 10-60. *The tables in the dataset and all its properties*

Step Three

The final step in implementing the dataset is to create a relationship between the two tables. First we need to define what fields in the UserReport and the ReportLine tables are key fields. This is done by simply dragging a key item from the toolbox onto the UserReport and the ReportLine tables. The Edit Key dialog box that appears will ask us for a key name and which field in the table should be used as the key (see Figure 10-61).

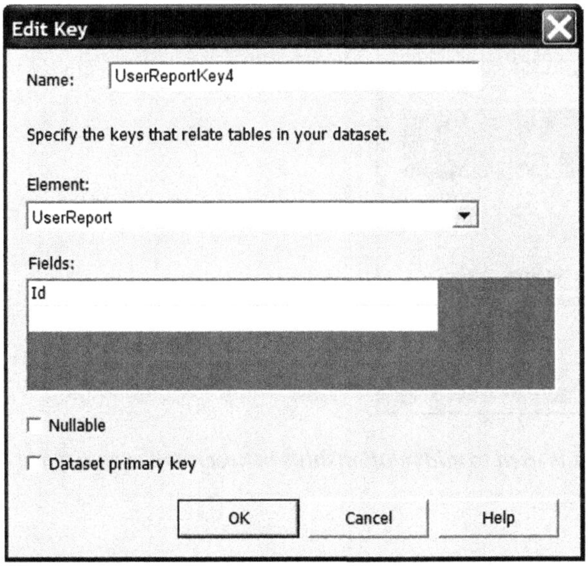

Figure 10-61. *The Edit Key dialog box*

We are using the UserReport key as part of the ReportLine key so that the application allows many time reports to be sent in the same dsUserReport dataset.

Next we drag a relation item from the toolbox onto the UserReport table, and the Edit Relation dialog box shown in Figure 10-62 appears.

Edit Relation ☒

Name: UserReportReportLine

To define a relationship (keyref), select the parent element and key, select the child element, and then select the child field corresponding to each parent field.

Parent element: Child element:
UserReport   ▾   ReportLines   ▾

Key:
dsTimeReportKey1   ▾   New...

Fields:

Key Fields	Foreign Key Fields
UserReportsID	ReportID

Dataset Properties
☐ Create foreign key constraint only

Update rule: Delete rule: Accept/Reject rule:
(Default)   ▾   (Default)   ▾   (Default)   ▾

OK   Cancel   Help

Figure 10-62. *The Edit Relation dialog box is used to add relationships between tables in a typed dataset.*

We simply select the parent element and the child element and then select the key that should be used for the relationship. If no key exists, we can create one by clicking the New button. The dataset properties are left as they are.

The final dataset is shown in Figure 10-63.

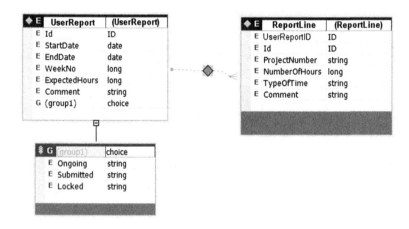

Figure 10-63. *The complete dataset with the relationship between the UserReport and the ReportLine tables*

To ensure that dsUserReport is returned from the GetUserReport function rather than and a general dataset, we change the return value from dataset to our dsUserReport.

Retrieving the Data

Now we have a typed dataset that will be used for transporting data between the layers and out to the client application that will be created in ASP.NET—but how do we retrieve the data that should be put into the dataset? The data class that should do the real work may be implemented to use ADO.NET directly, but doing so will decrease the possibilities for changing the data source in the future, since we would have code toward one data provider, such as SQL Server or OLEDB. Instead of using the specific data provider directly, we create something called a factory class. A factory class is a class that handles the creation of the object and passes back an object to the caller. The caller does not create the object itself. Therefore we make the creation and handling of the specific data provider abstract for the caller—our real data access class. The enterprise application we create here will live for a long time. If the company later decides to switch from SQL Server to Oracle, or to some other data storage system, the use of a data factory class to abstract data access is a wise approach to reduce the costs of making a change in the data provider.

We are using the data access application block found in the Enterprise Library released from Microsoft to get an easy framework to use for all our data access The data factory classes encapsulates the creation of connections, datasets, and calls to stored procedures that will be used from our data access component. The complete documentation of the data factory classes can be found at http://www.microsoft.com but we will here show the steps we need to take to configure the data access application block to work correctly in our TimeReport application.

Tip Instead of typing all lines in, we encourage you to visit http://www.apress.com, where you will find the complete project for download.

The Enterprise Library, and its application blocks, are described roughly in Chapter 5. The specific application we are using here is the Data Access Application Block (DAAB) and the Configuration Application Block (CAB).

Note For installation and setup procedures please download the Enterprise Library from
http://www.microsoft.com/downloads/details.
aspx?FamilyID=0325b97a-9534-4349-8038-d56b38ec394c&displaylang=en.

The first step we need to take is to create a configuration file that will be used by our project. To do this we'll use a tool that is shipped with the Enterprise Library called the Enterprise Library Configuration tool. This application will help us in the create process of the configuration file (See Figure 10-64).

First, right-click the Application icon and select New Application from the pop-up menu.

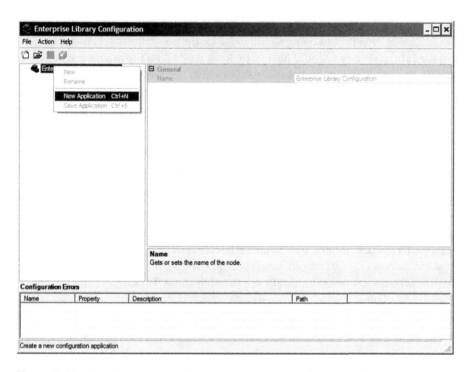

Figure 10-64. *Creating a new application in Enterprise Library Configuration tool.*

Name it TimeReport, right-click on it and select New Data Access application Block from the pop-up menu. The configuration will now look like Figure 10-65.

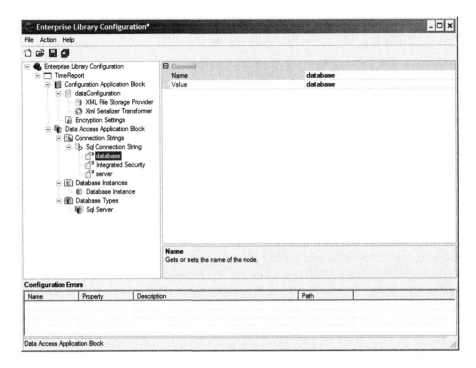

Figure 10-65. *Configuration file with data access block*

Next we'll need to configure the data connection parameters such as database name and server name. Fill in the appropriate information in the database and server properties highlighted in Figure 10-65.

The final step is to save the configuration file. Press the Save button and save it in the Data Access project folder.

The DAAB classes contain functions and methods for common tasks we do with data. Here we have functions like ExecuteDataSet, which executes a query and returns a dataset. This function is overloaded with different versions for executing a stored procedure, etc. We also have functions to create data parameters that can be used in the ExecuteDataSet function.

Implementing Specific Data Classes for SQL Server

Now we should use the DAAB class in our real data class. We start by creating a class in the DataAccess project. The class should be named UserReport and inherit ServicedComponent to take advantage of Enterprise Services, import Microsoft.Practices.EnterpriseLibrary.Data, Microsoft.Practices.EnterpriseLibrary.Data.Sql and SystemFrameworks.

One benefit by using the Enterprise Library is that we have support for keeping all our database connection strings in an xml file rather than in code This makes the solution more flexible, because we can change database connection without recompiling the code.

The function that should be used for retrieving time reports will be called GetUserReport as mentioned earlier.

The first thing we need to do is to create a DataBase Factory object. In the function GetUserReport we are doing so by adding the following line of code:

```
Dim db As Database = New DatabaseFactory.CreateDatabase()
```

Since we have encapsulated the creation of the dataset and the filling of it in the db object created previously, not much code is needed in the real data class.

GetUserReport simply uses the LoadDataSet function on the data helper object, and passes in the command object, the dataset to be filled and optional table names in the dataset that should be used.

The complete code for the GetUserReport is shown as follows:

```
Dim db as Database = New DatabaseFactory.CreateDatabase()
Dim sqlCommand As string = "get_TimeReport"
Dim dbCommandWrapper As DBCommandWrapper = _
 db.GetStoredProcCommandWrapper(sqlCommand)
'DataSet that will hold the returned results
Dim ds As SystemFrameworks.dsUserReport  = new SystemFrameworks. dsUserReport  ()
ds.Locale=System.Threading.Thread.CurrentThread.CurrentCulture
db.LoadDataSet(dbCommandWrapper,ds,
new string[3]{"UserReport","ReportLines","ReportStatus"})
return ds
```

The complete code for our DataAccess class is shown in Listing 10-4.

Listing 10-4. *The DataAccess Class*

```
Imports Microsoft.Practices.EnterpriseLibrary.Data
Imports Microsoft.Practices.EnterpriseLibrary.Data.Sql
Imports System.Data
 Imports SystemFrameworks
Imports System.EnterpriseServices
<EnterpriseServices.ConstructionEnabled(True), _
ObjectPooling(Enabled:=True, MinPoolSize:=1, MaxPoolSize:=5, _
CreationTimeOut:=25000)> _
Public Class UserReport
    Inherits ServicedComponent
#Region " Component Designer generated code "

    Public Sub New(ByVal Container As System.ComponentModel.IContainer)
        MyClass.New()

        'Required for Windows.Forms Class Composition Designer support
        Container.Add(Me)
    End Sub

    Public Sub New()
        MyBase.New()
        'This call is required by the Component Designer.
        InitializeComponent()
```

```
        'Add any initialization after the InitializeComponent() call.
    End Sub


    'Component overrides Dispose to clean up the component list.
    Protected Overloads Overrides Sub Dispose(ByVal disposing As Boolean)
        If disposing Then
            If Not (components Is Nothing) Then
                components.Dispose()
            End If
        End If
        MyBase.Dispose(disposing)
    End Sub
    'Required by the Component Designer
    Private components As System.ComponentModel.IContainer


    'NOTE: The following procedure is required by the Component Designer.
    'It can be modified using the Component Designer.
    'Do not modify it using the code editor.
    <System.Diagnostics.DebuggerStepThrough()> Private Sub InitializeComponent()
        components = New System.ComponentModel.Container
    End Sub


#End Region
#Region "Public functions"
    Public Function GetUserReport(ByVal UserID As String, _
                                  ByVal WeekNo As Integer) As dsUserReport
Dim db as Database = New DatabaseFactory.CreateDatabase()
Dim sqlCommand As string = "get_UserReport"
Dim dbCommandWrapper As DBCommandWrapper = _
db.GetStoredProcCommandWrapper(sqlCommand)
dbCommandWrapper.AddInParameter("@UserID ", DbType.Int32, UserID);
dbCommandWrapper.AddInParameter("@WeekNo ", DbType.Int32, WeekNo);
 'DataSet that will hold the returned results
Dim ds As SystemFrameworks.dsUserReport  = new SystemFrameworks. dsUserReport  ()
ds.Locale=System.Threading.Thread.CurrentThread.CurrentCulture
db.LoadDataSet(dbCommandWrapper,ds,
new string[3]{"UserReport","ReportLines","ReportStatus"})
return ds
    End Function
Public Function SaveUserReport(ByVal ds As dsUserReport)


'Update command
DBCommandWrapper dbCommandWrapperUpdate = _
db.GetStoredProcCommandWrapper("UpdateUserReport ")
dbCommandWrapperUpdate.AddInParameter _
 ("ID",DbType.Int32,"ID",DataRowVersion.Current)
dbCommandWrapperUpdate.AddInParameter _
 ("StartDate",DbType.Date,"StartDate",DataRowVersion.Current)
```

```
dbCommandWrapperUpdate.AddInParameter _
  ("EndDate",DbType.Date,"EndDate",DataRowVersion.Current)
dbCommandWrapperUpdate.AddInParameter _
("WeekNo",DbType.Int32,"WeekNo",DataRowVersion.Current)
dbCommandWrapperUpdate.AddInParameter _
  ("ExpectedHours",DbType.Int32,"ExpectedHours",DataRowVersion.Current)
dbCommandWrapperUpdate.AddInParameter _
("Comment",DbType.String,"Comment",DataRowVersion.Current)
dbCommandWrapperUpdate.AddInParameter _
  ("Status",DbType.Int32,"Status",DataRowVersion.Current)

'Insert Command
DBCommandWrapper dbCommandWrapperInsert = _
  db.GetStoredProcCommandWrapper("InsertUserReport ")
dbCommandWrapperInsert.AddInParameter ("ID",DbType.Int32,"ID", _
DataRowVersion.Current)
dbCommandWrapperInsert.AddInParameter _
  ("StartDate",DbType.Date,"StartDate",DataRowVersion.Current)
dbCommandWrapperInsert.AddInParameter _
  ("EndDate",DbType.Date,"EndDate",DataRowVersion.Current)
dbCommandWrapperInsert.AddInParameter _
  ("WeekNo",DbType.Int32,"WeekNo",DataRowVersion.Current)
dbCommandWrapperInsert.AddInParameter _
  ("ExpectedHours",DbType.Int32,"ExpectedHours",DataRowVersion.Current)
dbCommandWrapperInsert.AddInParameter _
  ("Comment",DbType.String,"Comment",DataRowVersion.Current)
dbCommandWrapperInsert.AddInParameter _
  ("Status",DbType.Int32,"Status",DataRowVersion.Current)

'Delete Command
DBCommandWrapper dbCommandWrapperDelete= _
  db.GetStoredProcCommandWrapper("DeleteUserReport ")
dbCommandWrapperDelete.AddInParameter ("ID",DbType.Int32,"ID", _
DataRowVersion.Current)
dbCommandWrapperDelete.AddInParameter _
  ("StartDate",DbType.Date,"StartDate",DataRowVersion.Current)
dbCommandWrapperDelete.AddInParameter _
  ("EndDate",DbType.Date,"EndDate",DataRowVersion.Current)
dbCommandWrapperDelete.AddInParameter _
  ("WeekNo",DbType.Int32,"WeekNo",DataRowVersion.Current)
dbCommandWrapperDelete.AddInParameter _
  ("ExpectedHours",DbType.Int32,"ExpectedHours",DataRowVersion.Current)
dbCommandWrapperDelete.AddInParameter _
  ("Comment",DbType.String,"Comment",DataRowVersion.Current)
dbCommandWrapperDelete.AddInParameter _
  ("Status",DbType.Int32,"Status",DataRowVersion.Current)
```

```
db.UpdateDataSet(ds,"Nomineringsgrupp", _
 dbCommandWrapperInsert,dbCommandWrapperUpdate, _
dbCommandWrapperDelete,trans)
    End Function
#End Region

End Class
```

As you can see, we use a DataFactory class that has functions to handle most of the actions we want performed on the data. The DataHelper class, in turn, inherits the provider factory and uses the interfaces for connections, commands, and so on, which makes it possible to switch between different providers quite easily.

Implementing the MSMQ Functionality

You saw from our requirements that a submission of a time report should be instantaneous—regardless of the number of concurrent users. This can be achieved by using serviced components that take advantage of MSMQ, or using MSMQ directly via the System.Messaging namespace. In Chapter 5 you saw the basic message flow for two components using a message queue. Here we will show you how to use the classes .NET provides.

Remember from Chapter 5 that you need to do the following to take advantage of MSMQ from your components:

- Create a queue that should be used for your messages.

- Add code to the component to write to the queue and to read from it.

The System.Messaging namespace contains classes that you use when working with queues. Here we will look at two different classes: the Message class and the MessageQueue class. The MessageQueue class contains all the necessarily functionality to work with MSMQ queues. The Message class contains everything necessary to define and use an MSMQ message.

Queues can be created either programmatically or manually. Programmatically this is done by using the shared Create method of the MessageQueue Object:

```
Try
  Dim queueAsMessageQueue
  queue = MessageQueue.Create(".\Private$\SavedUserReports",true)
  ' If there is an error creating a queue you get a MessageQueueException exception
  Catch ex As MessageQueueException
End Try
```

The path to the queue is specified as a parameter to the Create function. The dot serves as shorthand for this node, and to make this queue private, we put it in the Private$ folder by including Private$ in the path name. The Boolean tells MSMQ that the queue should have transactional support.

A public queue can be created or accessed by specifying the machine name\queue name. The other way to create a queue is to do it manually by using the Computer Management tool. We do this by opening the Computer Management tool, browsing down to the private queues, right-clicking and selecting New | Private Queue.

The wizard will ask us for a name of the queue. We name it SavedUserReports and also select the checkbox Transactional and click OK (see Figure 10-66). The queue is created and listed under the private Queues folder.

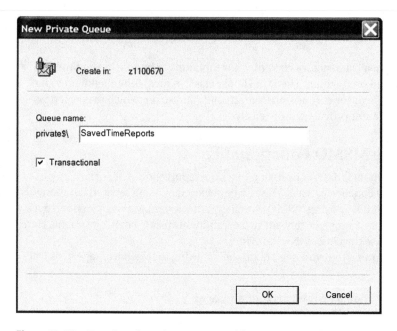

Figure 10-66. *Creating the private queue with transactional support*

Enabling the checkbox option Transactional ensures that all messages sent to the queue arrive in correct order and are not lost between the sender and the receiver. Since our application must be reliable, we select this checkbox—we can't afford to lose a time report. However, we will keep in mind that using transactional support costs us performance. If it does not matter in what order the messages arrive, or if a message is lost between the sender and the receiver, we can clear the checkbox and get a faster application.

■**Note** To be able to send a message to a transactional queue, you have to be in a transaction (internal or external), or else an error will be thrown.

To send information to the queue, we use the Send method on the MessageQueue class:

```
MyQueue.Send("<<Message>>", "<<Message Label>>")
```

Message can be a Message object or any other managed object—just like our dataset. If the object is not a Message object, the object is serialized and stored in the message body. Message Label is just a label on the message that can be used in message queue rules. We will not use it here.

There are two different functions to use when reading messages from a queue: *Peeking* and *Receiving*. The Receiving function simply receives messages and removes messages from the queue, whereas the Peek method reads messages but does not remove them from the queue.

OK, we won't dive into MSMQ too deeply here because we will use Queued Components instead of MSMQ directly, but we use the technique described previously behind the scenes of our queued components.

Queued components (QC) are a service provided by COM+ that let you call components asynchronously. The architecture of queued components is based on transactional messaging provided by MSMQ. When a queued component is created by the caller, the queued component is not created directly. Instead, a component called QC recorder is created. When the caller executes methods on the object, these method calls are packed into an MSMQ message by the QC recorder and posted on a transactional queue. A listening component picks up the message from the queue and replays the method calls on the real object in the order they where recorded. By using Queued Components, you ensure that all calls are definitely called and that no duplicate calls are executed.

To be able to use QC in our example application, we need to run our assembly as a server application. This will cost us performance, because the assembly will now run in its own process. This is how the listener is able to run asynchronously in the background. Since here we only have one method that is taking advantage of QC, we leave it in the same component as the other functions. If we have many functions, we can move these to a separate assembly that is run as a server application while the rest of the layer is running as a library application to avoid cross-process calls as much as possible.

The next step is to tell the component that it should act as a queued component. This is made by adding a custom attribute to the AssemblyInfo file for the BusinessRules project:

```
<Assembly: ApplicationQueuing(Enabled:=True, MaxListenerThreads:=3, _
  QueueListenerEnabled:=True)>
```

The MaxListenerThreads parameter allows us to control the number of threads that exist to process messages in the queue. Under Windows 2000, we can't directly control this value, but under COM+ 1.5 or higher (in Windows XP or higher), this value provides us with a powerful tool for adjusting the load that these components place on our server.

Then we need to add an interface that should be used for accessing our queued method SaveUserReport. We create a new interface in the BusinessRules project and name it IUserReportAsync. The interface will only have one function, named SaveUserReport, which takes dsUserReport as the only parameter.

We then implement this interface into the business layer (all transactions and message queues are started from the business layer) and add the code to call our data component:

```
Public Function SaveUserReport(ByVal ds As SystemFrameworks.dsUserReport) _
As Object ImplementsIUserReportAsync.SaveUserReport
      Dim objUserReport As DataAccess.UserReport
      Try
          objUserReport = New DataAccess.UserReport
          objUserReport.SaveUserReport(ds)

      Finally
          objUserReport.Dispose()
          objUserReport = Nothing
```

```
        End Try
    End Function
```

The final step is to tell Enterprise Services that the interface IUserReportAsync is to be used as a queued access point to our object:

```
InterfaceQueuing(Interface:="ISaveUserReport")>
```

The complete code for the business class will now appear as shown in Listing 10-5.

Listing 10-5. *The Complete Code for the Business Class*

```
Imports System.EnterpriseServices
Imports SystemFrameworks
<ObjectPooling(Enabled:=True, MinPoolSize:=1, _
MaxPoolSize:=8, CreationTimeOut:=25000), _
InterfaceQueuing(Interface:="ISaveUserReport")> _
    Public Class UserReport
    Inherits ServicedComponent
    Implements IUserReportAsync

    Public Function GetUserReport _
(ByVal UserID As String, ByVal WeekNo As Integer) _
As SystemFrameworks.dsUserReport
        'Our code goes here...
        Dim objUserReport As DataAccess.UserReport
        Try
            objUserReport = New DataAccess.UserReport
            Return objUserReport.GetUserReport(UserID, WeekNo)

        Finally
            objUserReport.Dispose()
            objUserReport = Nothing
        End Try
    End Function
    Private Function isUserReportSubmitted(ByVal dts As DataSet) As Boolean
        'Returns true if the time report in the dataset is submitted.
    End Function

    Public Function SaveUserReport(ByVal ds As SystemFrameworks.dsUserReport) _
As Object Implements IUserReportAsync.SaveUserReport
        Dim objUserReport As DataAccess.UserReport
        Try
            objUserReport = New DataAccess.UserReport
            objUserReport.SaveUserReport(ds)
        Finally
            objUserReport.Dispose()
            objUserReport = Nothing
        End Try
```

```
    End Function
End Class
```

To use the SaveUserReport from our facade class, we simply declare an object as
IUserReportAsync and call the SaveUserReport method on the interface as shown in Listing 10-6.

Listing 10-6. *The SaveUserReport Method in Our Facade Layer*

```
Public Function SaveUserReportAsync(ByVal ds As dsUserReport)
    Dim objUserReport As BusinessRules. IUserReportAsync          Try
    objUserReport= new BusinessRules.UserReport      objUserReport.SaveUserReport(ds)
    Finally
        objUserReport = Nothing
    End Try
 End Function
```

Enabling Our Facades for Web Service Access

At this point we have implemented functions to retrieve a time report and return it to the
database. This is fine if we are going to access our application layers from the same machine,
or if we can run Remoting between the different objects. However, sometimes we won't want
to install all layers on the same machine. In these cases, we can expose the facade layers, or
selected parts of the facade methods, as Web methods.

We can expose our facade methods in two different ways. We either add the Webmethod
attribute to the methods we would like to expose as Web services or implement a Web service
method in a dedicated Web service project that in turn calls our facade method.

The latter technique gives us more flexibility, since we can add specific validations that
should only occur when the call arrives via the Web service. The drawback with a separate Web
service project is that there will be more code to maintain. In this example, we will use the Web
service project.

To expose our two facade methods as Web methods, we first create a class in our Web service
project and name it UserReportServices.

The class should have two public methods, similar to the ones found in the facade class.
Each method is given the Webmethod attribute and a short description of what the method
does. The code will appear as shown in Listing 10-7.

Listing 10-7. *A Webmethod Attribute*

```
Imports System.Web.Services
Imports SystemFrameworks

<System.Web.Services.WebService(Namespace:= _
"http://msdotnet.nu/WebService/UserReport/UserReportService")> _
Public Class UserReportService
    Inherits System.Web.Services.WebService
 #Region "Web Services Designer Generated Code "
    ... code removed to conserve space..
 #End Region
<WebMethod(Description:="Saves a UserReport", EnableSession:=False)> _
```

```
Public Function SaveUserReport(ByVal ds As dsUserReport)
    Dim objUserReport As BusinessRules.IUserReportAsync = _
    New BusinessRules.UserReport
    Try
        objUserReport.SaveUserReport(ds)

    Finally
        objUserReport = Nothing
    End Try
End Function

<WebMethod(Description:="Gets a UserReport", EnableSession:=False)> _
    Public Function GetUserReport(ByVal WeekNo As Integer) As dsUserReport
        Dim objUserReport As New BusinessRules.UserReport
        Try
            Return objUserReport.GetUserReport( _
            HttpContext.Current.User.Identity.Name, WeekNo)
            End If

    Finally
        objUserReport = Nothing
    End Try
    End Function
End Class
```

The interesting part is SaveUserReport. Remember that we implemented it as a Queued Component. Here we declare objUserReport as a type of the interface IUserReportAsync. We then create an object that uses the mentioned interface.

Now we have a complete flow from the Web service, or the facade, down to the data layer.

The last thing to do is to create our fancy user interface. We open the WebUI project and add a Web form by right-clicking the project and selecting Add | Add Web Form.

We then rename the Web form to UserReport. This form will contain our time report.

Data binding support is one of many new features exist in .NET. Actually, this functionality exists in Visual Basic 6, but in .NET it has been developed further, and is much better than its predecessor. *Data binding* involves tying a visual control to data, and the control itself takes care of rendering the data. We are going to use this feature to bind a data grid to our dataset dsUserReport. This way we reduce the code in the UI, thereby decreasing development time.

In the toolbar there is a tab called Web Form that contains controls designed for use in a Web form. From these controls, we drag a data grid onto our form and change its name to datagridUserReport. We also drag a button from the toolbar onto the form and rename the button btnGetUserReport.

OK, now that we have a data grid on the Web form, the next step is to fill it with a particular time report. (Sure, we need some more stuff around the data grid, but we will hold off on the decorations until we have seen that this works.)

The Web form consists of two different pages: the Web form we recently added the data grid to, and the code-behind page. The code-behind page is just a normal managed class, and can be written in any of the languages that are supported under .NET. The code-behind page is where we will put the code to call our Web services method GetUserReport to retrieve the data that we should bind to the data grid.

There are many ways to open the code-behind window. One is to click the code-behind icon in the Solution Explorer toolbar when the Web form has focus. Another way is to press F7 when the Web form has focus.

One function already exists in the code-behind page: Page_Load. Since the code-behind class will contain all code for our Web form, the code-behind class can receive events from the Web form. One of them is the Page_Load event that is fired when the Web form is loaded. We will add some code to this event to fill our data grid with data.

The first step is to get in touch with our Web service (remember that all application logic layers, including the exposed Web services, are installed on a different server, as you saw in Figure 10-60).

We right-click the Reference folder in the WebUI project and select Add Web Reference.

Now we should browse for our Web service named UserReport. We click the link Web Services on the local machine (because during development we have all projects on the same machine) as shown in Figure 10-67.

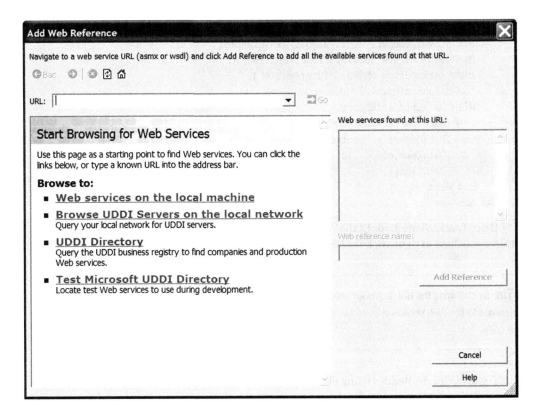

Figure 10-67. *The Web reference form*

All local Web services will show up in the lower window after a while. We locate the User-Report Web service and click it. (If you cannot find your service when you try this yourself, you probably have forgotten to compile the solution.)

We select our UserReport service and click the Add Reference button.

The next step is to add some code in the code-behind class to handle the click event on the button. When the user clicks the submit button, a time report for week 42 should be retrieved. Double-clicking the button results in the event handler in the code behind class opening. Listing 10-8 shows the complete code to retrieve our time report.

Listing 10-8. *The Complete Code for the Web Form Userreport.aspx*

```
Private Sub Page_Load(ByVal sender As System.Object, _
                    ByVal e As System.EventArgs) Handles MyBase.Load
        'Put user code to initialize the page here
        If Not MyBase.IsPostBack Then
            'This is the first time the page is loaded. fill the datagrid.
            'dim obj as new
        End If
    End Sub
Private Sub btnGetUserReport_Click(ByVal sender As System.Object, _
                            ByVal e As System.EventArgs) Handles _
                            btnGetUserReport.Click
        Dim dsMyUserReport As localhost.dsUserReport
        Dim objWS As New localhost.UserReportWS
        dsMyUserReport = objWS.GetUserReport(42)
        'Do databinding.
        With DataGridUserReport
            .DataSource = dsMyUserReport
            .DataMember = "UserReportHeader"
            .DataKeyField = "Id"
            .DataBind()
        End With
    End Sub
```

If newly added methods in the Web services do not show up in IntelliSense in the Web project, we need to right-click the Web reference and select Update Web Reference.

Tip By changing the URL behavior property on the Web reference for the Web service to dynamic, the reference to the Web service is stored in the web.config file and can later be changed without recompiling the code.

That's it! Or is it? Besides fixing the design of the page, we have one more important aspect to cover before we can say that we have a complete flow from the user interface down to the data source—security.

Enabling Security in Our Application

The security techniques we need to implement an authentication and authorization are important for the success of our enterprise application. Our application needs to be able to authenticate users to give them the right level of permissions and also access to the right projects.

Authentication and authorization can be done in several ways. In .NET there exists at least three different ways we can authenticate the user. Depending on the server and the clients involved, some of the authentication methods are more suitable than others. We need to take into account some or all of the following areas to be able to choose the best authentication type for our enterprise application:

- *The server and client operating systems.* If we are using only Microsoft Windows, we can use Windows authentication to make the authentication of our clients smooth.

- *The client browser type.* If the application is web-based, the client Web browser can impact the chosen authentication method. Some browsers don't support SSL, whereby a form authentication approach with SSL is impossible. Some browsers do not support basic authentication, so that may also be unavailable to us.

- *The number of users, and the location and type of username and password database.* The number of authentications that should be done and the type of storage for the data we should authenticate against may make some authentication methods more suitable than others. Using SSL to protect the traffic can sometimes be unwise, since SSL takes up a lot of resources on the server.

When using form-based authentication together with SSL in a Web application that has users, we suggest putting all SSL traffic to the login page on a separate Web server, and collecting all unencrypted traffic (HTTP) on the other Web servers. By separating the different transport protocols, you can achieve better performance. In this example application, we will not put the SSL traffic on a separate machine, because the number of concurrent users is not so big.

Deployment considerations, such as whether your application is Internet or intranet based and whether it is located behind a firewall, also come into play. If the application is Internet based, the use of Windows authentication is bad. Instead, we generally will use form authentication or some other authentication method for Internet-based application, such as Microsoft Passport.

If we want the application we have developed to run on our local intranet or on a LAN, we can use Windows authentication for maximum security and to ease the login behavior for the clients. When using Windows authentication, we can do a pass-through authentication that will result in the user being automatically authenticated when he or she browses a protected page.

The application type is a parameter we need to take into account. For example, is it an interactive Web site or a noninteractive Web service?

Performance and scalability factors in balance with sensitivity of the data we are protecting are also of importance for choosing the right security solution for our application.

Application authorization requirements must also be considered. For example, we may want to restrict our application to certain groups of registered users and other areas to administrators.

Our application will be used on an intranet. There will be known users in an environment that is separated from Internet. We are going to use form-based authentication and verify the user credentials with an Active Directory. The access to the Active Directory is implemented as a data service and located in our data layer. Roughly, the flow will be as follows:

1. The user tries to access a restricted page—our UserReport.aspx page. ASP.NET recognizes that the user has not been authenticated and redirects the user to our login.aspx page. This page employs HTTPS and SSL to secure the communication between the user and the server.

2. The user enters the username and the password and submits the page to the server. The server-side code (the code in the code-behind page) creates a facade object and sends the credentials down through the layers to our data service component.

3. The data service component in turn asks the Active Directory for the requested user, and returns an answer if the user has entered the right password or not.

If the user has entered the right password, a form authentication ticket is created and stored in the HTTP context.

Each time the user comes back during this session, the user will be authenticated by ASP.NET (until the authentication times out or the user disconnects from the session).

To add this to our Web application, we need to do the following:

First we need to tell our application what kind of authentication method we want to use. This is done by opening the web.config file and browsing down to the authentication element. The element has an attribute named mode, and this mode should be set to Forms. We also need to add a login URL that ASP.NET will use to redirect the user to if the user is not authenticated. This is done by adding a new element inside the authentication and naming it forms. The forms element should have three attributes. The first one is the login URL that has a value login.aspx (our login page). The second attribute is the name of the cookie that will be used during the session. The third attribute is the timeout in minutes for the authentication. When this time has elapsed, the user is redirected to the login page again.

After this, we need to restrict the access to our time report page. This is done by opening the web.config file in the Web application and browsing down to the section authorization mode.

This section contains one element called deny and one called allow—which are not too tricky to figure out. The first one tells ASP.NET which users should be denied access the application. In our case, all unauthenticated users should be denied. This is acquired by setting the users attribute to "?".

■**Tip** Access to parts of the site can also be restricted. This is done by adding a web.config file in the folder that should be restricted and setting the elements and attributes as previously described. The root web.config would be configured to allow unauthenticated access, whereas the restricted area (which will be a folder in the Web application) will have a web.config file that does not allow unauthenticated access.

The allow element tells ASP.NET which users are allowed. In our case, all authenticated users will be allowed. This is done by adding a "*" to the users attribute of the allow element.

The web.config file part that we change is shown in Listing 10-9.

Listing 10-9. *The Configuration File*

```
<authentication mode="Forms">
    <forms loginUrl="login.aspx" name="adAuthCookie" timeout="30" path="/">
    </forms>
```

```
</authentication>
<authorization>
    <deny users="?"/>
    <allow users="*"/>
</authorization>
```

When we have saved the web.config file, we are ready for the next step. We will create a data service component (this time we will work from the data layer out to the facade class when adding functions). The data service component will have code to access Active Directory via Lightweight Directory Access Protocol (LDAP).

Creating the VB Class

We start by creating a new VB class in our data project and naming the class LdapAuthentication. To be able to access Active Directory via LDAP, we need to add a reference to System.DirectoryServices.dll. Then we import the System.directoryServices into our class.

The class should have one public function named IsAuthenticated. It will have three parameters—the domain, the username, and the password. The function returns true if the user credentials are found; otherwise the return value will be false. Listing 10-10 shows the complete code for the function.

Listing 10-10. *The Complete Data Service Class*

```
Public Function IsAuthenticated(ByVal Domain As String, _
                                ByVal UserName As String, _
                                ByVal password As String) As Boolean
    Dim domainAndUserName As String = Domain & "\" & UserName
    Dim objEntry As DirectoryEntry
    Dim objSearcher As DirectorySearcher
    Dim obj As Object
    Dim objSearchResult As SearchResult
    Try
        If activeDirectoryPath.Length = 0 Then
            Throw New Exception("Not a valid Active Directory Path. " & _
            "Add a path to the constructor of this class in Component Services.")
        End If
        objEntry = New DirectoryEntry(activeDirectoryPath, UserName, password)
        'Bind to the AdsObject to force authentication of the user.
        obj = objEntry.NativeObject
        'No exception so far - go ahead and create a directory searcher object to
         'search for the user.
        objSearcher = New DirectorySearcher(objEntry)
        With objSearcher
            .Filter = "(SAMAccountName=" & UserName & ")"
            .PropertiesToLoad.Add("cn")
            objSearchResult = .FindOne
            If objSearchResult Is Nothing Then
                Return False
```

```
            Else
                    Return True
            End If
        End With
        ObjSearcher.Dispose()        ObjSearcher=nothing
        ObjEntry.Dispose()
        ObjEntry=nothing
        ObjSearchResult.Dispose()
        ObjSearchResult=nothing
    Finally
    End Try
End Function
```

The function IsAuthenticated retrieves a directory entry to the specified domain.

Binding to Active Directory

Next we try to bind to the Active Directory object to force an authentication of the supplied
user information. If the binding is successful, we create a DirectorySearcher object and search
for the username. We return true if the user is found in the directory.

We will also add another function to the class that will retrieve the different groups the
user belongs to. This can be used later to verify that the user belongs to a specific group that is
allowed to access the requested resource.

The function should be named GetUserGroups and has the same number of parameters
as the authentication function: domain, username, and password. The function will return
a collection of all the groups the requested user belongs to.

First GetUserGroups will use the LdapAuthentication function to authenticate the user.
Then we retrieve the groups the user belongs to (see Listing 10-11).

Listing 10-11. *The Complete LDAP Service Class*

```
Public Function GetUserGroups(ByVal domain As String, _
                            ByVal username As String, _
                            ByVal password As String) As String
        'returns the groups the user belongs to.
        'all functions are working separately -eg. a
                'call to a function should not depend on that other calls
        'Have already been made to other functions to initalize private variables.
        Dim objSearcher As DirectorySearcher
        Dim objSearchResult As SearchResult
        Dim intCounter, propertyCount, equalIndex, commaIndex As Integer
        Dim group As String
        Dim groupNames As System.Text.StringBuilder
        Dim enumerator As IEnumerator
        Const DELIMITER As String = "|"
        Try
            If IsAuthenticated(domain, username, password) Then
                'valid user credentials. retrieve the groups for the user.
                objSearcher = New DirectorySearcher(path)
```

```
        With objSearcher
            .Filter = "(cn=" & filterAttribute & ")"
            .PropertiesToLoad.Add("memberOf")
            objSearchResult = .FindOne()
        End With
      enumerator = objSearchResult.Properties("memberOf").GetEnumerator
            While enumerator.MoveNext
                group = enumerator.Current
                groupNames.Append(group.Substring((equalIndex + 1), _
                                  (commaIndex - equalIndex) - 1))
                groupNames.Append(DELIMITER)
            End While
            Return groupNames.ToString


      End If
    Catch exp As Exception
        Throw New Exception("Error in retrieving groups for user:" & _
        username & "error message:" & exp.Message)
    End Try
End Function
```

Changing the Layers

The last thing we need to do to pass the calls down to the data layer is to add functions in the
business layer, the facade layer, and the Web service project. The functions will have the same
parameters as the functions we have created in the data layer earlier.

To the Web service project we add a new web service named authenticateuser.asmx. This
web service will contain a function called GetUserGroups. The function should contain the
code in Listing 10-12.

Listing 10-12. *Web Service for Exposing Authentication Toward LDAP*

```
<WebMethod(Description:="Get a users's groups", EnableSession:=False)> _
    Public Function GetUserGroups(ByVal domain As String, _
                                  ByVal userName As String, _
                                  ByVal password As String) As String
      Dim objUser As BusinessRules.User = New BusinessRules.User
      Try
          If Not HttpContext.Current.User.Identity.IsAuthenticated Then
              Throw New Exception("User is not authenticated.")
          Else
              Return objUser.GetUserGroups(domain, userName, password)
          End If


      Finally
          objUser = Nothing
      End Try
End Function
```

We recompile the solution and refresh the web service reference in our WebUI project to ensure that the new function is visible to us.

We need to add a new web page to the WebUI project. To do so, we right-click the project, select Add web Form, name the page login.aspx, and click OK. We then add the controls listed in Table 10-4.

Table 10-4. *The Controls That Should Be Added to the Login Page*

Control Type	ID	Text
Label	LabelDomain	Domain Name:
Label	LabelUserName	User Name:
Label	LabelPassword	Password:
Text Box	txtDomain	
Text Box	txtUserName	
Text Box	txtPassword	
Button	btnLogin	Login
RequiredFieldValidator	reqDomain	•ErrorMessage: You must specify your domain.
RequiredFieldValidator	reqUserName	•ErrorMessage: Please type your username.
RequiredFieldValidator	reqPassword	•ErrorMessage: Password cannot be empty.
ValidationSummary	valSummary	

We lay out the controls as shown in Figure 10-68.

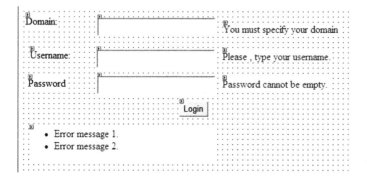

Figure 10-68. *The login page for our application*

To open the login button handler, we double-click the login button. At the top of the code-behind class, we import the System.Web.Security assembly to access the FormsAuthentication methods easily.

In the event for the button, we need to add code to create a web service request for our function GetUsersGroups. We could also have called the IsAuthenticated, but we know that GetUsersGroups also authenticates the call. Since we also need to retrieve the groups the user belongs to, we decide to call the GetUsersGroups to minimize the number of calls we need to make.

The code for the login button appears in Listing 10-13.

Listing 10-13. *The Login Button Code*

```
Private Sub btnLogin_Click(ByVal sender As System.Object, -
                    ByVal e As System.EventArgs) Handles btnLogin.Click
        Dim objUser As AuthenticateUserWebService.AuthenticateUser = _
        New AuthenticateUserWebService.AuthenticateUser
        Dim groups As String

        Try
            'Try to retrieve the user groups.
            groups = objUser.GetUserGroups _
            (txtDomain.Text, txtUserName.Text, txtPassword.Text)
            Dim authenticationTicket As FormsAuthenticationTicket = _
      New FormsAuthenticationTicket(1, txtUserName.Text, _
      DateTime.Now, DateTime.Now.AddMinutes(30), False, groups)
            'Encrypt ticket
            Dim encryptedTicket As String = _
  FormsAuthentication.Encrypt(authenticationTicket)
            Dim cookie As HttpCookie = _
New HttpCookie(FormsAuthentication.FormsCookieName, encryptedTicket)

            Response.Cookies.Add(cookie)
            Response.Redirect(FormsAuthentication.GetRedirectUrl _
(txtUserName.Text, False))

        Catch ex As Exception
            Dim lblMessage As New Label
            lblMessage.Text = "Invalid domain,username or password."
            valSummary.Controls.Add(lblMessage)
        Finally
            objUser.Dispose()
            objUser = Nothing
        End Try
    End Sub
```

OK, now we have code in the login button that authenticates the user and sends him or her to the requested page. To be able to use the roles in a role-based scenario, we need to retrieve the cookie from the client and create a GenericPrincipal object and a FormsIdentity object.

The GenericPrincipal object contains the different roles and groups the user belongs to. (These are the groups we retrieved with the getUsersGroups recently.)

To take care of this, we need to add some code to the global.asax file.

This file contains several events that will be useful for us, particularly AuthenticateRequest. This is called when the incoming request should be authenticated. In this method, we will look for the cookie we created recently and create an identity and a principal object that will follow this HTTP context. The complete code for the method is shown in Listing 10-14.

Listing 10-14. *The Authentication Request*

```
Sub Application_AuthenticateRequest(ByVal sender As Object, ByVal e As EventArgs)
        ' Fires upon attempting to authenticate the user
        Dim cookieName As String = FormsAuthentication.FormsCookieName
        Dim DELIMITER As Char = "|"
        If cookieName.Empty Then
            'There is no authentication cookie, proceed to the login.
        Else
            'There is an authentication cookie.
            Dim authTicket As FormsAuthenticationTicket
            Try
                authTicket = FormsAuthentication.Decrypt(cookieName)
                If Not authTicket Is Nothing Then
                    Dim roles() As String = authTicket.UserData.Split(DELIMITER)
                    Dim id As FormsIdentity = New FormsIdentity(authTicket)
                    Dim principal As GenericPrincipal = _
                    New GenericPrincipal(id,roles)
                    Context.User = principal
                End If
            Catch ex As Exception
                'Log the error
            End Try
        End If
    End Sub
```

Now our users will be redirected to the login page the first time they enter our application. When the user has entered a valid username and password, we create a cookie that we put on the user's computer. The next time the user enters the application, the cookie is used to create a principal object that is put in the current context.

Later on in our application this information can be used to verify that the user belongs to certain groups. For instance, in the project page, there might be an add button. This button should only be visible to users that belong to the admin group. In the load event of the projects page, we will include the following code snippet that retrieves the roles the current user belongs to and decides if the button should be visible or not:

```
btnAdd.visible= context.User.IsInRole("Admin")
```

Testing the Application

Testing the application should be conducted from the first line of code. Tests are done on at least three different levels as follows:

- Unit tests

- Code reviews

- Integration tests

- Acceptance tests

Unit tests can be done by using the freeware tool NUnit, which we discussed in Chapter 5. These tests should cover 100 percent of the code and should be done by the developer during the developing phase.

Note Using automatic unit tests takes time to implement, requiring you to write test classes that will validate the code. Automatic testing is no silver bullet that will solve all problems. By using automatic unit tests, you cannot slice the test time down to three hours; you still need test time to implement and run the tests. The benefit of automatic unit tests will mainly be visible when you have several develop iterations and you want to ensure that no code fixes or new functionality have changed already delivered functionality.

We want to mention *code reviews* here, even if they are not considered "real" tests of the application. We would like to emphasize that code reviews should be done on a regular basis to create an application that is following the decided architecture—to test that the architecture and the design guidelines are being followed. Code reviews are omitted far too often due to pressing deadlines. This will often result in an application containing an unclean architecture, with many different layouts that make it more difficult to maintain and debug the application. When doing a code review, we put up a list with the different coding conventions we should check. We then walk through the code and check that the coding conventions for the project are being followed. Code review and unit tests are more beneficial the sooner they are conducted. In the beginning of a project, most developers involved have not learned all the coding conventions yet. Putting some extra effort into reinforcing these conventions at the beginning of projects will pay off later, since all developers will learn the coding conventions for this particular project much faster if they have someone who reviews their code.

Note Avoid letting the developers review their own code. Instead, create a list through which you delegate the review of each module to another developer.

Integration tests, sometimes called *system tests*, should be performed for a complete iteration of the development phase. These tests are based on test scripts that are already written during the design phase of the application and are based on the use cases. NUnit can also be used in integration tests, but the test classes for an integration test can sometimes be hard to code, so we seldom use this tool. By leveraging use cases to generate test cases, however, testing teams can get started much earlier in the life cycle, allowing them to identify and repair defects that would be very costly to fix later, ship on time, and ensure that the system will work reliably.

The final test is called an *acceptance test* and is performed by the customer. This test should verify that the delivered system has the requested functionality and performance. It is very important that the customer writes the acceptance scripts to be sure that his or her needs are reflected in the scripts.

Deploying the Application

The first step in deploying our application is to write a deployment document. This document should contain all the steps we need to take to deploy each component on the server. The most important items in this document are the manual steps that need to be done with the components.

Next we will create a deployment project that should help us with the installation of the application. This deployment project will take care of setting up the web application on the server and putting our pages in the right place. The deployment project could also register our components in Component Services, but we will do this manually.

To create a deployment project, we select Add project from the File menu in Visual Studio and click the Setup and Deployment Project option shown in Figure 10-69.

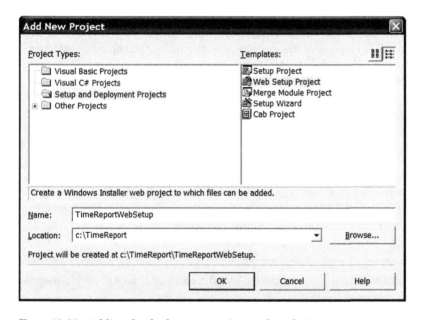

Figure 10-69. *Adding the deployment project to the solution*

Next, we select the Web Setup Project option and name it TimeReportWebSetup. Figure 10-70 shows the setup project.

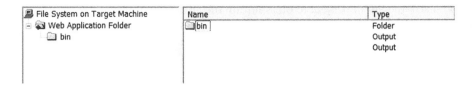

File System on Target Machine	Name	Type
Web Application Folder	bin	Folder
bin		Output
		Output

Figure 10-70. *The folders in the default view of the web setup project*

Now we add the output from our WebUI project to the deployment project. This is done by right-clicking the Web Application folder (which is our root for the web application) and selecting Add | Project Output.

After specifying the WebUI project in the combo box, we select Primary Output (which is our webui.dll—the code-behind classes) and Content Files (which are our web pages) as shown in Figure 10-71.

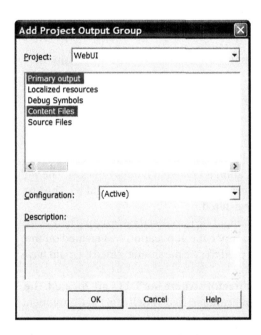

Figure 10-71. *The output from the WebUI project*

Done! Now when we build the deployment project, a setup program will be created that will install the output (our web pages and the code-behind DLL) from the WebUI onto the machine where the setup program is executed.

Tip By clearing the Build checkbox in the Configuration Manager for the deployment project, you indicate you want the compiler to omit the deployment project in every build. When you want to build the deployment project you simply right-click the deployment project and select Build.

We add a new deployment project to our solution file and name it TimeReportWebServiceSetup. We perform the same steps as for the TimeReportWebSetup, but this time we select the primary output and the content output for our web service project. This setup will be run at the application server, since the web services will be hosted there to support the web server with our components.

The next step is to manually register our components on the application server. When we have copied the DLLs to the application server, we need to register them in Component Services. The traditional way to do this is to register the components via the MMC snap-in for Component Services. However, this will not work for managed serviced components!

Note To register the components in Component Services, you need to use the Regsvcs util. Trying to register the components via the MMC snap-in for Component Services will fail.

For our components, we need to use the Regsvcs utility. The tool can be found in the .NET Framework catalog.

We create a batch file and name it installcomponents.bat. The file should contain the following lines of code:

```
Regsvcs /fc /appname:TimeReport BusinessFacade.dll
Regsvcs /exapp /appname: TimeReport BusinessRules.dll
Regsvcs /exapp /appname: TimeReport DataAccess.dll
```

The parameter /fc in the first command line tells Regsvcs that it should first try to find an existing application named TimeReport. The application is created if it does not exist. The second parameter, /appname, tells Regsvcs what the name of the application should be. The last parameter is the name of our DLL that should be registered.

The second command is a bit different. The command /fc is replaced by /exapp. This means that Regsvcs should look for an existing application (since the application was created on the previous command line). We could, of course, have used the /fc parameter, since it would have found the application we created in the first step.

When we execute this batch file in the same directory where our DLLs are located, the components in the DLLs will be installed into an application called TimeReport in Component Services.

All the enterprise attributes we have set in the classes will be used by Regsvcs to configure the components.

However, we need to configure the data connection string that should be located in the constructor string for the data access component. We also need to configure the path to the LDAP that should be used by the data Service component LdapAuthentication.

To do so, we start by opening the Component Services Administration tool and expanding My Computer as shown in Figure 10-72.

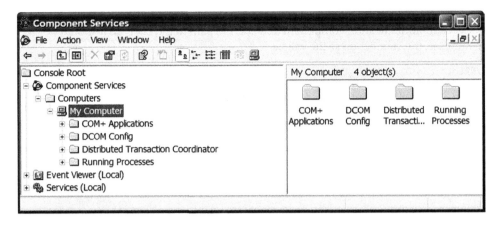

Figure 10-72. *The Component Services Admin tool*

Our time reporting application will be located in the COM+ Applications folder.

We browse down to the DataAccess.UserReport component, right-click it, and select Properties. We then click the Activation tab and add the connection string to the database in the Constructor String Field (see Figure 10-73).

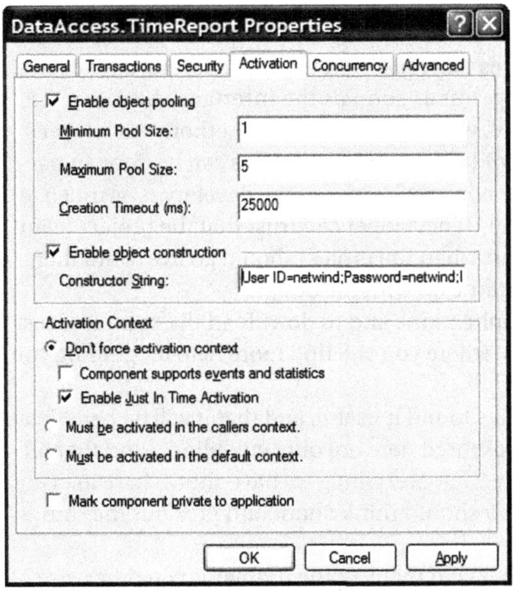

Figure 10-73. *Adding the data connection string to the UserReport data access component*

The connection string can be stored in several places in our application. We have the connection string accessed via the constructor to make changing the database that should be used more dynamic. Other ways are to add it to the application config file or to code it as a constant in the data access class. The last approach is often not suitable. If the database server changes, we would need to recompile the data class to change the connection string.

Adding the connection string to the LDAP is done in the same way. We browse to the DataAccess.LdapAuthentication component and add the path to the LDAP that should be used. In our case, the connection string will be

```
LDAP://RRCorp.com/DC= RRCorp,DC=com
```

That's it. To install our application, we simply need to follow these steps:

1. Run the TimeReportWebSetup on the web server to install our web application.

2. Copy our components to the application server and run our installcomponents.bat file to install them into Component Services.

3. Run the TimeReportWebServiceSetup to install the web services for the application layers.

Finally, we are ready to test the application. When entering the UserReport.aspx page, ASP.NET realizes that we are not authenticated and redirects us to the login.aspx page. When we have filled in user credentials, the code-behind file verifies with LDAP that we have entered the correct information. If we have, we are redirected back to the UserReport.aspx page.

Back on the UserReport.aspx page, we click the GetUserReport button and receive the time report for week 42.

Summary

As you have seen, there are many steps to conduct in developing an enterprise application, and still we have not shown you all the different classes that make up our time reporting application. The burden can sometimes feel overwhelming, but as soon as the interfaces between the different layers have been decided (for example, which functions and methods each layer's class should expose), the building of the different layers and components can be done in parallel. The exposed functions and methods are a "contract" between the developers as much as between the components in the application. The UI developer can trust that the project team will provide components to retrieve a time report when the project should go live. Until then, he or she should just add dummy calls and continue on with the design.

For more information about enterprise applications and to download the complete test application, please visit http://www.apress.com, where you will find more help for guiding you through your enterprise application project.

This also finishes our book. We trust you have found it useful, and that it will be beneficial in your work. Remember that what we have presented here are only guidelines, and that all projects are different. This makes it hard to implement everything we have shown here in every project, but use this book as a guide to what you should think about and pick out the things that apply to your specific situation.

Remember that with a good design, you can avoid many of the problems you otherwise would run into. It is an essential part of every serious project.

Also make sure to test every aspect of the application before deployment. Far too many errors are passing through some applications that could have been found with a good test methodology.

APPENDIX A

∎∎∎

Test Equipment At Dell

Here is a list of the equipment we were privileged to use at Dell (see Figure A-1).

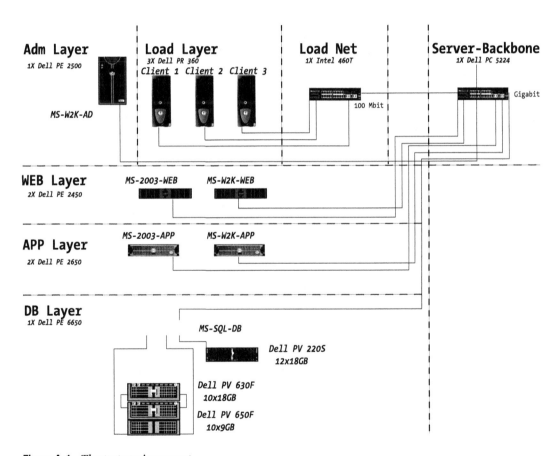

Figure A-1. *The test environment*

MS-W2K-AD: Dell PE 2500. 1 PIII 1.0 GHz (512 Kb cache), 512 Mb RAM.

Client 1: Dell PR 360. P4 2.8 GHz, 1 Gb RAM

Client 2: Dell PR 360. P4 2.2 GHz, 256 Mb RAM

Client 3: Dell PR 360. P4 2.8 GHz, 1 Gb RAM

MS-2003-WEB: Dell PE 2450. 2xPIII 866 MHz (512 Kb cache), 512 Mb RAM

MS-W2K-WEB: Dell PE 2450. 2xPIII 866 MHz (512 Kb cache), 512 Mb RAM

MS-2003-APP: Dell PE 2650. 2xXEON DP 2 GHz (512 Kb cache), 2 Gb RAM

MS-W2K-APP: Dell PE 2650. 2xXEON DP 2 GHz (512 Kb cache), 2 Gb RAM

MS-SQL-DB : Dell PE 6650. 4xXEON MP 1.6 GHz (1 Mb cache), 6 Gb RAM

SCSI disk : Dell PV 220S. 3xRAID 10

Fiber channel: Dell PV 630F. 10x18 Gb disk, 2 RAID 10, 1 RAID 1

Fiber channel: Dell PV 650F. 10x9 Gb disk, 1 RAID 5

Server-Backbone: Dell PC 5224, Gigabit network

Load-Net: Intel 460T. 100 Mbit network

PE = PowerEdge

PR = Precision

PV = PowerVault

PC = PowerConnect

APPENDIX B

■■■

Coding Conventions

This appendix contains coding conventions that can be used as guidelines in your development. We can't say that you should use all the conventions in this appendix, since we all know that a normal project often has a limited number of hours/monies. Unfortunately, the conventions will often suffer when you don't have enough time, but we encourage you to at least follow the same standard through the whole project (not changing course in the middle of it, or allowing different developers to have their own conventions), and secondly, comment the code so that you can come back to your own code later and understand what you did and why.

Comments

Commenting the code is very important for spreading the knowledge of what your code does for other developers, and for maintenance of the code in future releases. Many programmers have problems reading their own code after a couple of months, so what if someone other than the original programmer is going to read code after the same amount of time has passed? It's better to spend ten minutes extra in a class commenting on it than to spend ten hours six months later figuring out what the class does. Or, even worse, you might not be able to figure out what the class does and have to write a new one.

If developing in C#, use the XML Documentation feature. There are a couple of ways you can document your code. The first one, traditionally used, is through standard templates. If you are using C#, you can use the built-in standard documenter—similar to Java's Javadoc, which gives you the ability to extract comments automatically. Unfortunately, this feature is only implemented in C#. Other languages such as VB .NET do not have this nice function. In VB .NET, you need to document the traditional way or introduce user-defined attributes on methods and functions. By using attribute-based documenting, you can extract the documentations of a class via the reflection API. Because the attributes are stored together with the code, the documentation always follows the code. This makes it possible to retrieve the documentation without having the source code, which is a great benefit compared to the C# solution or traditional boilerplates.

When modifying code, always keep the commenting around it up to date. Whatever kind of approach you use to document your code, you need to update the documentation when modifying the code. It is worse to dive into old code that has comments mismatching the logic than to watch a *Police Academy* sequel!

Put a comment at the beginning of every routine and class. It's helpful to provide standard comments indicating the routine's purpose, assumptions, and limitations. A comment should be a brief introduction that explains why the routine exists and what it can do. If you are not using C# you can use the following boilerplate:

```
'Purpose:       Traps the click event of the first group's combo box
'Assumptions:   None
'Effects:       The click event fires when the selection changes.
'Inputs:
'None
'Returns:
'None
```

A slightly modified version of the template should also be used for the class itself. The class-level comment header may look like this:

```
'Project:
'Name:          myclass
'Description: Client component of the myapp Tool
'               Provides functionality to manage very large groups
'Module
'Name           frmMain
'Description    Presentation tier of the component
'History
'30JAN2003      Mr Bond       Created from template
```

If you are using C#, use the built-in functionality for commenting the code. An example of a header for a function may look like this:

```
/// <summary>
/// Class-level summary documentation goes here.</summary>
/// <remarks>
/// Longer comments can be associated with a type or member
/// through the remarks tag</remarks>
public class SomeClass
{
    /// <summary>
    /// Store for the name property</summary>
    private string myName = null;
    /// <summary>
    /// The class constructor. </summary>
    public SomeClass()
    {       // TODO: Add Constructor Logic here
    }
```

Note All comments begin with /// and contain simple XML tags for telling the compiler what kind of data it is. By using this kind of documentation in C#, you are able to auto-generate the documentation (for example, extracting the comment tags from the code).

Avoid adding comments at the end of a line of code. Even if it is easy to create a lot of comments, and quite fun when you can auto-generate the documentation, we recommend you avoid adding comments at the end of a line of code. We advise this because end-line comments make code more difficult to read. However, end-line comments are appropriate when annotating variable declarations, in which case you should align all end-line comments at a common tab stop.

Avoid comments that clutter the source code, such as an entire line of asterisks. Instead, use white space to separate comments from code. Do not surround a block comment with a typographical frame. It may look attractive, but it is difficult to maintain.

Clean up comments before check-in. Before checking in a modified class to SourceSafe (or whatever kind of version handling system you are using), always remove all temporary or extraneous comments to avoid confusion during future maintenance work. This is especially important before delivering to production.

Avoid using long comments to explain complex parts of code—rewrite instead. If you realize that you need several sentences to describe a complex part of your code, your code is probably too difficult and you should try to rewrite the code to something more easily understood. Even if you understand the comments you have added today, you probably won't have an idea of what the code does four months from now. Although performance should not typically be sacrificed to make the code simpler for human consumption, a balance must be achieved between performance and maintainability.

Comments should clarify, not confuse. Use complete sentences when writing comments. Comments should clarify the code, not add ambiguity. Comment at the same time as you code, because you will not likely have time to do this later. Also, should you get a chance to revisit code you have written, what is obvious today probably will not be obvious six weeks from now.

Avoid superfluous or inappropriate comments, such as humorous asides. It might be fun at the time, but it is unprofessional and will be there long after you have released the code. It also might distract the reader from the importance of what you are trying to say.

Comment anything that is not readily obvious in the code. Use comments to explain the intent of the code. They should not serve as inline translations of the code.

Use comment techniques that can be auto-extracted. Use comments based on the C# comment specification to be able to auto-generate documents for classes. If working with code written in VB .NET, you can use custom attributes for documenting and thereby be able to extract the documentation programmatically.

Comment bug fixes. To prevent recurring problems, always use comments on bug fixes and workaround code, especially in a team environment. These should be applied in the class comment header and also in the version of the file that is checked into Clear Case or Visual SourceSafe.

Use comments on code that consists of loops and logic branches. These are key areas that will assist source code readers.

Separate comments from comment delimiters with white space. Doing so will make comments obvious and easy to locate when viewed without color clues.

Note Despite the availability of external documentation, source code listings should be able to stand on their own, because hard-copy documentation can be misplaced. External documentation should consist of specifications, design documents, change requests, bug history, and the coding standard that was used.

Naming

The naming conventions you should follow in general are those outlined by the .NET Framework Developer Specifications (see Microsoft's design guidelines for class library developers at http://msdn.microsoft.com/library/en-us/cpgenref/html/cpconnetframeworkdesignguidelines.asp and http://msdn.microsoft.com/library/default.asp?url=/library/en-us/vsent7/html/vxconcodingtechniques.asp), but here we will mention some of the rules that we think can boost the development speed and maintenance speed of an enterprise application.

Class Naming Guidelines

When creating a class, name it with nouns or noun phrases. Also use Pascal casing (for example, CalculateInvoiceTotal) and try to use abbreviations in class names sparingly. Do not use any class prefix (such as C), since that will not add any information for the programmer—the interfaces have a prefix of I, which is enough. Do not use an underscore in the name because it takes space and seldom gives any extra information to the programmer (it doesn't make it easier to read, either).

An example of a class following these naming guidelines is shown here:

```
public class Account {
}
public class Salary {
}
public class Company {
}
```

Interface Naming Guidelines

When creating interfaces, we recommend that you follow some common rules that give your interfaces a common look and feel, which will make it easier for others to use and maintain them.

The name of the interface should be created with nouns or noun phrases, or adjectives describing behavior—for example, IComponent (descriptive noun), ICustomAttributeProvider (noun phrase), and IPersistable (adjective). In our examples, we use Pascal casing and try to write out the complete name—abbreviations mostly make it unclear what an interface is for.

Try to avoid using underscores in the interface name, since they only take up space and seldom mean anything to the observer.

Prefix the interface names with the letter I to indicate that the type is an interface and can easily be separated from the classes in your project. However, do not prefix class names with C, which has no meaning in this case because you have a prefix for the interfaces.

When you are designing class/interface pairs, try to keep the names similar. For example, the difference should be that the interface has an I in front of the interface name, as follows:

```
public interface IComponent {
}
public class Component : IComponent {
}
public interface IServiceProvider{
}
public interface IFormatable {
}
```

Enumeration Naming Guidelines

Use Pascal casing for enumerations and for their enumeration value names. Try to avoid using abbreviations in enumeration names and enumeration values and do not use a prefix/suffix on enumeration names (for example, adXXX for ADO enumerations, rtfXXX for rich text enumerations, and so on). When you construct enums, try to use singular names except for bit fields that have plural names. Try to use enums for parameters where the parameter has a defined range of possible values, as shown in the following example. This allows the development environment to know the possible values for a property or parameter:

```
public enum FileMode{
    Create,
    CreateNew,
    Open,
    OpenOrCreate,
    Truncate
}
```

If you are going to use an enum in bitwise operations, add the Flags custom attribute to the enum to enable this as follows:

```
[Flags]
public enum Bindings {
    CreateInstance,
    GetField,
    GetProperty,
    Static
}
```

An exception to this rule is when you're encapsulating a Win32 API—it is common in this case to have internal definitions that come from a Win32 header. It is okay to leave these with Win32 casing, which are usually all uppercase.

Try to use Int32 as the underlying type of enum. An exception to this rule is if the enum represents flags and there are many of them (over 32), or you anticipate the enum might grow too many flags in the future, or the type needs to be different from the integer type for backward compatibility. Only use enums if the value can be completely expressed as a set of bit flags. Never use them for open sets (such as operating system version and so on).

Read-Only and Const Field Names

When you are defining constants, try to name static fields with nouns, noun phrases, or abbreviations for nouns. Use the Pascal casing, as for most other types, but don't use the Hungarian type notation.

Parameter Names

Parameter names should be descriptive enough so that in most scenarios the name of the parameter and its type can be used to determine its meaning. We recommend using camel casing (for example, typeName, as shown in the following code snippet) for parameter names. Aim to name a parameter based on a parameter's meaning rather than based on the parameter's type.

Programmers expect development tools to provide information about type in a handy manner, so the parameter name can be put to better use describing semantics instead of type. We therefore suggest abandoning the Hungarian type notation, which takes up some space and is difficult for everyone to strive for. (We all get tired at the end of a project and start missing the notation, don't we?) Do not use reserved parameters. If more data is needed in the next version, a new overload can be added:

```
Type GetType (string typeName)
string Format (string format, object [] args)
```

Method Naming Guidelines

Method names should be named with verbs or verb phrases using Pascal casing, as demonstrated in these examples:

```
RemoveAll(), GetCharArray(), Invoke()
```

Property Naming Guidelines

Property names should be constructed from nouns or noun phrases, again with Pascal casing. We don't recommend using properties and types with the same name.

Defining a property with the same name as a type can cause some ambiguity. It is best to avoid this ambiguity, unless there is a clear justification for not doing so. For example, System.WinForms has an Icon property, and even though there is an Icon class, Form.Icon is so much easier to understand than Form.FormIcon or Form.DisplayIcon, and so on.

However, System.WinForms.UI.Control has a color property. But because there is a Color class, the Color property is named BackgroundColor, as it is a more meaningful name that does not conflict.

Following are a few examples of property names:

```
Text, LastIndex, Value[5]
```

Event Naming Guidelines

When creating event handlers, name them with the EventHandler suffix as follows:

```
Public delegate void MouseEventHandler (object sender, MouseEvent e);
```

The event handler should have two parameters: sender and e. The sender parameter represents the object that raised the event. The sender parameter is always of type object, even if it is possible to employ a more specific type. The state associated with the event is encapsulated in an instance of an event class named e. Use an appropriate and specific event class for its type.

```
public delegate void MouseEventHandler(object sender, MouseEvent e);
```

Classes that handle events should be named with the EventArgs suffix as follows:

```
public class MouseEventArgs : EventArgs {
    int x, y;
    public MouseEventArgs(int x, int y)
```

```
        { this.x = x; this.y = y; }
    public int X { get { return x; } }
    public int Y { get { return y; } }
}
```

Event names that have a concept of pre- and post-operation should be prefixed using the present and past tense (do not use the BeforeXxx\AfterXxx pattern). For example, a Close event of a file that could be canceled would have events named Closing and Closed:

```
public event ControlEventHandler Closing {
    //..
}
```

Always try to name events with a verb.

Variables Naming Guidelines

Naming of variables in an enterprise application is important. It is much easier to maintain an application with variable names that describe the use of those variables than with an application that has single-character variables that do not give any clues to the programmer how those variables are used.

The following variable naming guidelines are an extract of the complete guidelines that can be found at http://msdn.microsoft.com/library/default.asp?url=/library/en-us/vsent7/html/vxconcodingtechniques.asp:

- Since most names are constructed by concatenating several words, use mixed-case formatting to simplify reading them. In addition, to help distinguish between variables and routines, use Pascal casing (CalculateInvoiceTotal), in which the first letter of each word is capitalized, for routine names. For variable names, use camel casing (documentFormatType), in which the first letter of each word except the first is capitalized.

- Boolean variable names should contain Is, which implies yes/no or true/false values, such as fileIsFound.

- Avoid using terms such as Flag when naming status variables, which differ from Boolean variables in that they may have more than two possible values. Instead of documentFlag, use a more descriptive name such as documentFormatType.

- Even for a short-lived variable that may appear in only a few lines of code, you should still use a meaningful name. Use single-letter variable names, such as i, or j, for short-loop indexes only.

- The Hungarian naming convention prefix all variables with their scope and their data type. An example is: dim g_blnIsDeleted as Boolean where the g stands for global scope of the variable, the bln for Boolean.

> **■ Note** If using Charles Simonyi's Hungarian naming convention, or some derivative thereof, develop a list of standard prefixes for the project to help developers consistently name variables; however, with IntelliSense support, there is no need to use the Hungarian type convention except for some some cases where it can be convenient to use the Hungarian naming convention—namely for screen development. By using the Hungarian type convention we "collect" all our textboxes, listboxes, and comboboxes together in the IntelliSense pop-up menu.

Database Conventions

Designing the database is as important as designing the rest of the enterprise application. Without naming conventions for the database and its structure, the database will soon end up in such a messy state that no database administrator will be able to fix it without major changes. The following conventions are what we recommend to streamline the layout of the database to ease future maintenance.

First of all, limit the length of names and fields to 30 characters maximum. Some databases can't handle more than 30 characters for some types, and a field name like thisIsMyFieldThatIamUsingForCalculatingTheAccountStatus is quite messy.

The name of the object should start with an alphabetic character. The remaining characters should be letters or numbers. Try to avoid the _, @, #, and $ characters, since they also may confuse the user or database administrator. One thing you should avoid for certain is having blanks in the name. Also, avoid using reserved words for Transact-SQL or PL/SQL, as they can give you trouble.

Because enterprise applications are often used in companies whose employees speak different languages (and you therefore can assume that the administration of the application is multilanguage), use only English-language characters in the design of the database—no local characters—to avoid code-page-related problems, and also to ease the maintenance of the application. Write out all names with whole words so that they are easy to comprehend. Names containing more than one word should be written as one word with leading capitals for every word except for the first word it contains—for example, "customer number" should be written as "customerNumber".

Table 5-1 summarizes the naming conventions for databases.

Table 5-1. *Database Naming Conventions*

Object	Naming Convention	Example
Database	<database name>	Customer
Data device	<database name>Data	customerData
Log device	<database name>Log	customerLog
Table	t_<table name>	t_customer
Column	<column name>	Name
View	v_<view name>	v_Mycustomer
Stored procedure	p_<procedure name>	p_Getcustomer
Trigger	t_<i/u/d>_<table name>	t_i_customer

Object	Naming Convention	Example
User-defined type	tp_<type name>	tp_Address
Primary key	pk_< table name>_<key name>	pk_customer_Id
Foreign key	fk_< table name >_	fk_customer_Order_Id_ <table name 2>_<keyname>
Unique constraint	u_< table name >_<column name>	u_customer_Name
Check constraint	c_< table name >_<column name>	c_customer_Status
Default constraint	df_< table name >_<column name>	df_Address_City
Index	i_<c/n/u>_<table name>_	i_n_customer_Name_ <column name>

The following should help clarify the conventions presented in Table 5-1:

- A database name can be the same as the name of the application it serves.

- Table names should always be singular.

- Stored procedures should not be confused with system stored procedures, and therefore sport the prefix p_, not sp_.

- Triggers should have a name depending on the type: i = insert, u = update, d = delete.

- Indexes should be named based on the type: c = clustered, n=nonclustered, u = unique. For example, a unique clustered index for customer number in a table named customer might appear as follows:

```
i_cu_customer_ Customernumber
```

Note Try to use stored procedures and functions (which are faster to execute than a standard SQL query), as much as possible to achieve good performance on the system. By using stored procedures, we also encapsulate the logic to retrieve the data to a single point, which makes its easier to correct bugs or extend in the future. Because an enterprise application seldom will be moved between different platforms and databases, it is possible to use stored procedures. For a standard application that may exist on a different platform, use of stored procedures may require different database access layers for the different types of databases and environments.

Error Handling and Exceptions

The following conventions for error raising are extracted from the complete guidelines that can be found at http://msdn.microsoft.com/library/default.asp?url=/library/en-us/cpgenref/html/cpconerrorraisinghandlingguidelines.asp.

A multilayered application can detect errors at any level and pass them back through its various layers. For example, an error in the data access layer that occurs in response to a SQL query error may eventually be displayed to a user via an ASP.NET page on the web layer.

To display error messages in an ASP.NET application, you use a custom error-handling ASP.NET page named errorpage.aspx. The errorpage.aspx file is specified in the <customErrors> section of the Web.Config file:

```
<customErrors defaultRedirect="errorpage.aspx" mode="On" />
```

Error handling in layered architectures is more complex than in nonlayered counterparts. Adding to this complexity is the necessity of the application to display helpful, nontechnical error messages to users. Following are a few recommended error-handling practices:

- *Return codes*. Use return codes to report status conditions.

- *Preconditions*. The system should test for preconditions in public methods.

- *Post conditions*. The system should check on the exit from a function as appropriate.

Structured Exception Handling

Use the try-catch-finally statement in C# to do the following:

- Handle situations involving a function that cannot fulfill its contract.

- Catch expected error conditions—but do not rely on exceptions. What we mean is that you should validate the data with code, not validate it by catching an error that occurs because of invalid data.

- Ensure cleanup after unexpected exception conditions.

If we omit a try catch the generated error will escalate up through the caller tree.

Error Raising and Handling

There are some useful conventions for error raising and handling. For example, Do end Exception class names with Exception to separate them from normal classes:

```
public class FileNotFoundException : Exception {
}
```

You should also use at least these common constructors for your own exception classes:

```
public class XxxException : Exception {
    XxxException() { }
    XxxException(string message) { }
    XxxException(string message, Exception inner) { }
}
```

We recommend using the predefined exception types. Only define new exception types for programmatic scenarios. Introduce a new exception class so that a programmer can take a different action in code, based on the exception class. Do not define a new exception class unless it is possible that a developer might need the exception class.

For example, it makes sense to define FileNotFoundException because the programmer might decide to create the missing file, whereas FileIOException is not something that would typically be handled in code.

In exceptions that do not have an explicit message, make sure the message property traverses down the tree to the next real text.

Do not derive new exceptions from the base class Exception. The base class will have multiple subclasses according to the individual namespace.

Remember that under the system exception will be another container exception called Core, which will contain the handful of EE exceptions that bring the system down completely. Users cannot throw these exceptions.

Group new exceptions of the base class Exception by their namespace. For example, subclasses will exist for XML, IO, Collections, and so on; each of these areas subclass their own exceptions as appropriate. Any exceptions that other library or application writers wish to add will extend the Exception base class directly. A single name for all related exceptions should be made, and all exceptions related to that application or library should extend from that bucket.

Use a localized description string. An error message displayed to the user will be derived from the description string of the exception that was thrown, and never from the exception class. Include a description string in every exception to clarify for the end user what happened.

Use grammatically correct error messages, including ending punctuation. Each sentence in a description string of an exception ends in a period. Code that generically displays an exception message to the user handles the case when a developer forgets the final period.

Provide Exception properties for programmatic access. Include extra information in an exception (besides the description string) only when there is a programmatic scenario in which that additional information would be useful. It is rare to need to include additional information in an exception.

Throw exceptions only in exceptional cases:

Do not use exceptions for normal or expected errors.

Do not use exceptions for normal flow of control, as there is an overhead for generating exceptions instead of checking that you have valid values.

Return null for extremely common error cases. For example, File.Open returns a null if the file is not found, but throws an exception if the file is locked.

Design classes so that in the normal course of use there will never be an exception thrown. For example, a FileStream class exposes another way of determining if the end of file has been reached to avoid the exception that will be thrown if the developer reads past the end of the file. For example:

```
class Foo {
    void Bar() {
        FileStream stream = File.Open("mytextfile.txt");
        byte b;

        // ReadByte returns -1 at EOF
        while ((b = stream.ReadByte())  > = 0) {
            // Do something
        }
    }
}
```

Throw an InvalidOperationException if in an inappropriate state. The System.InvalidOperationException exception is supposed to be thrown if the property set or method call is not appropriate given the object's current state.

Throw an ArgumentException or subclass thereof if bad parameters are passed. When bad parameters are detected, throw a System.ArgumentException or a subclass thereof.

Do realize that the stack trace starts at the throw. The stack trace's origin is located where the exception is thrown, not where it is reviewed. Be aware of this fact when deciding where to throw an exception.

Use exception builder methods. It is common for a class to throw the same exception from different places in its implementation. To avoid code bloat, use a helper method that creates a new exception and return it. For example:

```
class File {
    string fileName;

    public byte[] Read(int bytes) {
        if (!ReadFile(handle, bytes))
            throw NewFileIOException();
    }
      FileException NewFileIOException() {
       string description = // Build localized string,
//including fileName
        return new FileException(description);
      }
}
```

Another alternative is to use the constructor of the exception to build the exception. This is more appropriate for global exception classes like ArgumentException.

Throw exceptions in favor of returning an error code (or HResult).

Throw the most specific exception possible.

Use existing exceptions where possible instead of creating new ones.

Set all the fields on the exception you use.

Use inner exceptions (chained exceptions).

Create meaningful message text targeted at the developer in the exception.

Do not include methods that throw NullReferenceException or IndexOutOfRangeException.

Do argument checking on protected (family) members. Write clearly in the documentation if the protected method does not do argument checking. Unless otherwise stated, assume argument checking is done. You may get some performance gains in not doing argument checking.

Clean up intermediate results when throwing an exception. Callers should be able to assume that there are no side effects when an exception is thrown from a function.

For example, if Hashtable.Insert throws an exception, then the caller can assume that the item was not added to the hash table (the hash table implementation breaks this rule, but that's another issue).

Miscellaneous

Try to minimize the use of abbreviations, but use those that you have created consistently. An abbreviation should have only one meaning; likewise, each abbreviated word should have only one abbreviation. For example, if you use min to abbreviate minimum, do so everywhere, and do not use min to also abbreviate minute. When naming functions, include a description of the value being returned, such as GetCurrentWindowName().

File and folder names, like procedure names, should accurately describe their purpose.

Avoid reusing names for different elements, such as a routine called ProcessSales() and a variable called iProcessSales.

Avoid homophones, such as write and right, when naming elements to prevent confusion during code reviews.

When naming elements, avoid commonly misspelled words. Also, be aware of differences that exist between American and British English, such as color/colour and check/cheque.

Index

forums.apress.com

JOIN THE APRESS FORUMS AND BE PART OF OUR COMMUNITY. You'll find discussions that cover topics of interest to IT professionals, programmers, and enthusiasts just like you. If you post a query to one of our forums, you can expect that some of the best minds in the business—especially Apress authors, who all write with *The Expert's Voice™*—will chime in to help you. Why not aim to become one of our most valuable participants (MVPs) and win cool stuff? Here's a sampling of what you'll find:

DATABASES
Data drives everything.

Share information, exchange ideas, and discuss any database programming or administration issues.

PROGRAMMING/BUSINESS
Unfortunately, it is.

Talk about the Apress line of books that cover software methodology, best practices, and how programmers interact with the "suits."

INTERNET TECHNOLOGIES AND NETWORKING
Try living without plumbing (and eventually IPv6).

Talk about networking topics including protocols, design, administration, wireless, wired, storage, backup, certifications, trends, and new technologies.

WEB DEVELOPMENT/DESIGN
Ugly doesn't cut it anymore, and CGI is absurd.

Help is in sight for your site. Find design solutions for your projects and get ideas for building an interactive Web site.

JAVA
We've come a long way from the old Oak tree.

Hang out and discuss Java in whatever flavor you choose: J2SE, J2EE, J2ME, Jakarta, and so on.

SECURITY
Lots of bad guys out there—the good guys need help.

Discuss computer and network security issues here. Just don't let anyone else know the answers!

MAC OS X
All about the Zen of OS X.

OS X is both the present and the future for Mac apps. Make suggestions, offer up ideas, or boast about your new hardware.

TECHNOLOGY IN ACTION
Cool things. Fun things.

It's after hours. It's time to play. Whether you're into LEGO® MINDSTORMS™ or turning an old PC into a DVR, this is where technology turns into fun.

OPEN SOURCE
Source code is good; understanding (open) source is better.

Discuss open source technologies and related topics such as PHP, MySQL, Linux, Perl, Apache, Python, and more.

WINDOWS
No defenestration here.

Ask questions about all aspects of Windows programming, get help on Microsoft technologies covered in Apress books, or provide feedback on any Apress Windows book.

HOW TO PARTICIPATE:
Go to the Apress Forums site at **http://forums.apress.com/**.
Click the New User link.